International Law and Civil Wars

This book examines the international law of forcible intervention in civil wars, in particular the role of party-consent in affecting the legality of such intervention.

In modern international law, it is a near consensus that no state can use force against another – the main exceptions being self-defense and actions mandated by a UN Security Council resolution. However, one more potential exception exists: forcible intervention undertaken upon the invitation or consent of a government, seeking assistance in confronting armed opposition groups within its territory. Although the latter exception is of increasing importance, the numerous questions it raises have received scant attention in the current body of literature.

This volume fills this gap by analyzing the consent-exception in a wide context, and attempting to delineate its limits, including cases in which government consent power is not only negated, but might be transferred to opposition groups. The book also discusses the concept of consensual intervention in contemporary international law, in juxtaposition to traditional legal doctrines. It traces the development of law in this context by drawing from historical examples such as the Spanish Civil War, as well as recent cases such as those of the Democratic Republic of the Congo, Somalia, Libya and Syria.

This book will be of much interest to students of international law, civil wars, the Responsibility to Protect, war and conflict studies and IR in general.

Eliav Lieblich is Lecturer (US Assistant Professor) at the Radzyner School of Law, the Interdisciplinary Center (IDC) Herzliya, Israel. He holds a doctorate from Columbia Law School.

Law, Conflict and International Relations
Series Editors: Chandra Lekha Sriram, *SOAS*, Julie Mertus
American University
Karin Aggestam
University of Lund
and
Lorraine Elliott
Australian National University

This series will bring together cutting-edge, interdisciplinary scholarship on law, conflict, and international politics, encompassing the fields of international criminal law, international human rights law, and international humanitarian law, and law relating to the use of force, and conflict prevention, resolution, peacemaking, and peacebuilding, and resort to the use of force.

International Law, Politics and Inhumane Weapons
The effectiveness of global landmine regimes
Alan Bryden

Transitional Justice and Peacebuilding on the Ground
Victims and ex-combatants
Edited by Chandra Lekha Sriram, Jemima Garcia-Godos, Johanna Herman and Olga Martin-Ortega

International Law and Civil Wars
Intervention and consent
Eliav Lieblich

International Law and Civil Wars

Intervention and consent

Eliav Lieblich

Routledge
Taylor & Francis Group
LONDON AND NEW YORK

First published 2013
by Routledge
2 Park Square, Milton Park, Abingdon, Oxon OX14 4RN

Simultaneously published in the USA and Canada
by Routledge
711 Third Avenue, New York, NY 10017

Routledge is an imprint of the Taylor & Francis Group, an informa business

British Library Cataloguing in Publication Data
A catalogue record for this book is available from the British Library

Library of Congress Cataloging-in-Publication Data
Lieblich, Eliav, 1979–
International law and civil wars: intervention and consent/Eliav Lieblich.
p. cm. – (Law, Conflict and International Relations)
Includes bibliographical references and index.
1. Intervention (International law) 2. Civil war. I. Title.
KZ6368.L54 2013
341.6′8–dc23

2012033882

ISBN: 978-0-415-50790-5 (hbk)
ISBN: 978-0-203-58891-8 (ebk)

Typeset in Baskerville
by Wearset Ltd, Boldon, Tyne and Wear

Printed and bound in the United States of America by Publishers Graphics, LLC on sustainably sourced paper.

Contents

Selected case law

Permanent Court of International Justice

Settlers of German Origin in Poland, Advisory Opinion, 1923 P.C.I.J. 22 (ser. B) No. 6 (September 10)

S.S. Lotus (Fr. v. Turk) 1927 P.C.I.J. Ser. A-No. 10 (September 7)

International Court of Justice

The Corfu Channel Case (U.K. v. Albania), 1949 I.C.J. 4 (April 9)

Case Concerning The Barcelona Traction (Belgium v. Spain), 1970 I.C.J. 3 (February 5)

Legal Consequences for States of the Continued Presence of South African in Namibia (South West Africa) Notwithstanding U.N. Security Council Resolution 276 (1970), Advisory Opinion, 1971 I.C.J. 16 (June 21)

Military Aid and Paramilitary Activities in and against Nicaragua (Nicar. v. U.S.), 1986 I.C.J. 14 (June 27)

Legality of the Threat of Use of Nuclear Weapons, Advisory Opinion, 1996 I.C.J. 226 (July 8)

Case Concerning Oil Platforms (Iran v. U.S.), 2003 I.C.J. 161 (November 6)

Legal Consequence of the Construction of a Wall in the Occupied Palestinian Territory, Advisory Opinion, 2004 I.C.J. 136 (July 9)

Armed Activities on the Territory of the Congo (DRC v. Uganda), 2005 I.C.J. 168 (December 19)

Case Concerning the Application of the Convention on the Prevention and Punishment of the Crime of Genocide (Bosnia and Herzegovina v. Serbia and Montenegro), 2007 I.C.J. (February 26)

Accordance with International Law of the Unilateral Declaration of Independence in Respect of Kosovo, Advisory Opinion, 2010 I.C.J. 141 (July 22)

International Criminal Tribunal for the Former Yugoslavia

Prosecutor v. Tadic, Case No. IT-94–1-I, Decision on Defence Motion for Interlocutory Appeal on Jurisdiction (International Criminal Tribunal for the Former Yugoslavia October 2, 1995)

Prosecutor v. Tadic, Case No. IT-94–1-A, Appeals Chambers Judgment (International Criminal Tribunal for the Former Yugoslavia, July 15, 1999)

Prosecutor v. Haradinaj, Case No. IT-04–84-T, Judgment (International Criminal Tribunal for the Former Yugoslavia April 3, 2008)

Special Court for Sierra Leone

Prosecutor v. Taylor, Case No. SCSL-03–1-T, Trial Chamber Judgment (Special Court for Sierra Leone, April 26, 2012)

European Court of Human Rights

Al-Skeini v. U.K., European Court of Human Rights (2011)

Inter-American Commission on Human Rights

Abella v. Argentina, Case 11.137, Inter-American Commission on Human Rights, Report No 55/97, IACHR OEA/Ser.L/V/II.95 Doc. 7 rev. at 221

Arbitration

The Tinoco Case (Great Britain v. Costa Rica), 1 R.I.A.A. 375, 377 (1923)

The Oriental Navigation Company v. The United Mexican States (Docket No. 411, October 3, 1928), Claims Commission – U.S. & Mex., 23 American Journal of International Law 434 (1929)

Opinion 1, Arbitration Commission of the Peace Conference on the Former Yugoslavia (Badinter Commission) (November 29, 1991)

Canada

Reference re Secession of Quebec, [1998] 2. S.C.R. 217 (Can.)

Israel

H.C.J. 769/02 The Public Committee Against Torture in Israel v. The Government of Israel [2006] IsrSC 57(6) 285

US

The Santissima Trinidad, 20 U.S. 283 (1822)

The Gran Para, 20 U.S. 471 (1822)

The Prize Cases, 67 U.S. 635 (1862)

U.S. v. The Lilla, 26 F. Cas. 938 (1863)

The Three Friends, 17 S. Ct. 495 (1897)

The Paquete Habana, 175 U.S. 677 (1900)

O'Neill v. Central Leather Co., 87 N.J.L. 552 (1915)

Hamdan v. Rumsfeld, 548 U.S. 557 (2006)

UK

The Helen, (1865–67) L.R. 1 (1865)

Ex Parte Chavasse, 46 E.R. 1072 (1865)

Selected UN resolutions and treaty body documents

Selected Security Council resolutions

S.C. Res. 2, U.N. Doc. S/RES/2 (January 30, 1946) (Iran–Kurdistan)
S.C. Res. 128, U.N. Doc. S/4023 (June 11, 1958) (Lebanon Intervention)
S.C. Res. 203, U.N Doc. S/RES/203 (May 14, 1965) (Dominican Republic Intervention)
S.C. Res. 205, U.N. Doc. S/RES/205 (May 22, 1965) (Dominican Republic Intervention)
S.C. Res. 387, U.N. Doc. S/RES/387 (March 31, 1976) (Angola-Preference of Government)
S.C. Res. 733, U.N. Doc. S/RES/733 (January 20, 1992) (Somalia-Arms Embargo)
S.C. Res. 940, U.N. Doc. S/RES/940 (July 31, 1994) (Haiti Intervention)
S.C. Res. 1244, U.N. Doc. S/RES/1244 (June 10, 1999) (Kosovo – UNMIK and KFOR)
S.C. Res. 1246, U.N. Doc. S/RES/1246 (September 15, 1999) (East-Timor Intervention)
S.C. Res. 1279, U.N. Doc. S/RES/1279 (November 30, 1999) (DRC-MONUC)
S.C. Res. 1296, U.N. Doc. S/RES/1296 (April 19, 2000) (Protection of Civilians)
S.C. Res. 1368, U.N. Doc. S/RES/1368 (September 12, 2001) (September 11th Attacks)
S.C. Res. 1373, U.N. Doc. D/Res/1373 (September 28, 2001) (September 11th Attacks)
S.C. Res. 1464, U.N. Doc. S/RES/1464 (February 4, 2003) (Côte d'Ivoire–French Forces)
S.C. Res. 1483, U.N. Doc. S/RES/1483 (May 22, 2003) (Iraq War)
S.C. Res. 1484, U.N. Doc. S/RES/1484 (May 30, 2003) (DRC-MONUC)
S.C. Res. 1511, U.N. Doc. S/RES/1511 (October 16, 2003) (Iraq War)
S.C. Res. 1546, U.N. Doc. S/RES/1546 (June 5, 2004) (Iraq War)
S.C. Res. 1559, U.N. Doc. S/RES/1559 (September 2, 2004) (Syria–Lebanon)
S.C. Res. 1587, U.N. Doc. S/RES/1587 (March 15, 2005) (Somalia-TFG)
S.C. Res. 1674, U.N. Doc, S/RES/1674 (April 28, 2006) (RtoP)
S.C. Res. 1706, U.N. Doc. S/RES/1706 (August 31, 2006) (Darfur-RtoP)
S.C. Res. 1725, U.N. Doc. S/RES/1725 (December 6, 2006) (Somalia-Arms Embargo)
S.C. Res. 1744, U.N. Doc. S/RES/1744 (February 21, 2007) (Somalia-AMISOM)
S.C. Res. 1843, U.N. Doc. S/RES/1843 (November 20, 2008) (DRC-MONUC)
S.C. Res. 1851, U.N. Doc. S/RES/1851 (December 16, 2008) (Somalia-Piracy)
S.C. Res. 1856, U.N. Doc. S/RES/1856 (December 22, 2008) (DRC-MONUC)
S.C. Res. 1859, U.N. Doc. S/RES/1859 (December 22, 2008) (Iraq War)
S.C. Res. 1894, U.N. Doc. S/RES/1894 (November 11, 2009) (RtoP)

S.C. Res. 1907, U.N. Doc. S/RES/1907 (December 23, 2009) (Eritrea-Sanctions)
S.C. Res. 1925, U.N. Doc. SC/RES/1925 (May 28, 2010) (DRC)
S.C. Res. 1962, U.N. Doc. S/RES/1962 (December 20, 2010) (Côte d'Ivoire-Gbagbo)
S.C. Res. 1970, U.N. Doc. S/RES/1970 (February 26, 2011) (Libya-Sanctions)
S.C. Res. 1973, U.N. Doc. S/RES/1973 (March 17, 2011) (Libya-RtoP)
S.C. Res. 1975, U.N. Doc. S/RES/1975 (March 30, 2011) (Côte d'Ivoire-RtoP)
S.C. Res. 1991, U.N. Doc. S/RES/1991 (June 28, 2011) (LRA)
S.C. Res. 2009, U.N. Doc. S/RES/2009 (September 16, 2011) (Libya-Democracy)
S.C. Res. 2014, U.N. Doc. S/RES/2014 (October 21, 2011) (Yemen-Transition)
S.C. Res. 2042, U.N. Doc. S/RES/2042 (April 14, 2012) (Syria-Observers)
S.C. Res. 2043, U.N. Doc. S/RES/2043 (April 21, 2012) (Syria-Observers)

Selected General Assembly resolutions

Uniting for Peace, G.A. Res. 377(V), U.N. Doc. A/377 (November 30, 1950)
Declaration on the Granting of Independence to Colonial Countries and Peoples, G.A. Res. 1514, U.N. Doc. A/1514 (December 14, 1960)
Declaration on the Inadmissibility of Intervention in the Domestic Affairs of States and Protection of their Independence and Sovereignty, G.A. Res. 2131 (XX), U.N. Doc. A/RES/20/2131 (December 21, 1965)
Declaration on Principles of International Law concerning Friendly Relations and Co-operation among States, G.A. Res. 2625 (XXV), U.N. Doc. A/8082 (October 24, 1970)
Definition of Aggression, G.A. Res. 3314 (XXIX), U.N. Doc. A/9631 (December 14, 1974)
Declaration on the Inadmissibility of Intervention in the Domestic Affairs of States, G.A. Res. 36/103, U.N. Doc. A/36/51 (December 9, 1981)
G.A. Res. 38/7, U.N. Doc. A/RES/38/7 (November 2, 1983) (Grenada)
Declaration on the Enhancement of the Effectiveness of the Principle of Refraining from the Threat or Use of Force in International Relations, G.A. Res. 42/22, U.N. Doc. A/Res/42/22 (November 18, 1987)
2005 World Summit Outcome, G.A. Res. 60/1, U.N. Doc. A/60/L.1 (September 15 2005) (RtoP)
G.A. Res. 61/89, U.N. Doc. A/RES/61/89 (December 18, 2006) (arms transfers)
G.A. Res. 63/240, U.N. Doc. A/Res/63/240 (January 8, 2009) (arms transfers)
G.A. Res. 63/308, U.N. Doc. A/RES/63/308 (October 7, 2009) (RtoP)
G.A. Res. 64/48, U.N. Doc. A/RES/64/48 (December 2, 2009) (arms transfers)
G.A. Res. 66/1A, U.N. Doc. A/RES/66/1A (September 16, 2011) (Libya-Credentials)

Selected treaty body documents

Commission on Economic, Social and Rights, General Comment No. 8, The Relationship between Economic Sanctions and Respect for Economic, Social and Cultural Rights, U.N. Doc. CESCR/E/C.12/1997/8 (December 12, 1997)
Human Rights Commission, General Comment No. 31, Nature of the Legal Obligation Imposed on States Parties to the Covenant, U.N. Doc. CCPR/C/21.Rev.1/Add.13 (2004)
The Crime of Aggression, art. 8bis(g), Resolution RC/Res.6, RC/11 (June 11, 2010)

Selected treaties

Treaty of Westphalia (1648)
Hague Convention II: Laws and Customs of War on Land, October 18, 1907 (1910) U.K.T.S. 9
Hague Convention V: Respecting the Rights and Duties of Neutral Powers and Persons in Case of War on Land, October 18, 1907, 36 Stat. 2319, U.S.T. 540
Hague Convention XIII: Concerning the Rights and Duties of Neutral Powers in Naval War, October 18, 1907, U.S.T.S. 545
Covenant of the League of Nations, June 28, 1919, 4 U.K.T.S. 153
Convention on Supervision of International Trade in Arms and Ammunition and in Implements of War (June 17, 1925), League of Nations Doc. A.16.1925.IX (1925)
Convention on Duties and Rights of States in the Event of Civil Strife, February 20, 1928, 134 L.N.T.S. 45
General Treaty for Renunciation of War as an Instrument of National Policy (Kellogg–Briand Pact), August 27, 1928, 94 L.N.T.S. 57
Convention on the Rights and Duties of States (Montevideo Convention), December 26, 1933, 165 L.N.T.S. 19
Charter of the United Nations, 24 October 1945, 1 U.N.T.S. XVI
Pact of the Arab League of States, March 22, 1945, 70 U.N.T.S. 237
Charter of the Organization of American States, April 30, 1948, 119 U.N.T.S. 48
Convention on the Prevention and Punishment of the Crime of Genocide, December 9, 1948, 78 U.N.T.S. 277
North Atlantic Treaty, April 4, 1949, 34 U.N.T.S. 243
Treaty of Guarantee, 1960, 382 U.N.T.S. 3
International Covenant on Civil and Political Rights, December 16, 1966, 999 U.N.T.S. 171
International Covenant on Economic, Social and Cultural Rights, December 16, 1966, 993 U.N.T.S. 3
Vienna Convention on the Law of Treaties, May 23, 1969, 1155 U.N.T.S. 331
Protocol Additional to the Geneva Conventions of 12 August 1949, and Relating to the Protection of Victims of International Armed Conflicts (Protocol I), June 8, 1977, 1125 U.N.T.S. 3
Protocol Additional to the Geneva Conventions of 12 August 1949, and Relating to the Protection of Victims of Non-International Armed Conflicts (Protocol II), June 8, 1977, 1125 U.N.T.S. 609
Vienna Convention on Succession of States in Respect of Treaties, August 23, 1978, 1946 U.N.T.S. 3

Protocol of Amendment to the Charter of the Organization of American States "Protocol of Washington" (December 14, 1992)

Status of Forces Agreement Between the Government of the Federal Republic of Nigeria and the Government of the Republic of Sierra Leone Concerning the Provision of Military and Security Assistance to the Republic of Sierra Leone, 1997

Rome Statute of the International Criminal Court, July 17, 1998, U.N. Doc. A/CONF.183/0

ECOWAS Protocol Relating to the Mechanism for Conflict Prevention, Management, Resolution, Peace-Keeping and Security, December 10, 1999

Constitutive Act of the African Union, July 11, 2000, 2158 U.N.T.S. 3

Protocol Relating to the Establishment of the Peace and Security of the African Union, July 9, 2002

Agreement on the Withdrawal of the United States Forces from Iraq and the Organization of their Activities during their Temporary Presence in Iraq, U.S.–Iraq, November 17, 2008, S. EXEC. DOC. 09–6 (2009)

Acknowledgments

This book is based on a revised edition of my J.S.D. dissertation written, between the years 2009–2012, at Columbia Law School. First and foremost, I would like to thank my supervisor, Professor Michael W. Doyle, for encouraging me to convert the dissertation into a book, and for granting me sufficient independence – coupled with ever-present backing – to find my own voice when approaching this complex subject. I am also grateful to the members of my J.S.D. committee: Professor Lori Fisler Damrosch, for her extremely helpful comments, which have helped me to take this work to the next level; and Professor Sarah H. Cleveland, for initially encouraging me to embark on this project and agreeing to serve on my committee, despite her many other commitments. In addition, I am thankful to Professor Matthew Waxman, my external reader. I owe special thanks to Professor Eyal Benvenisti, for his support in general, as well as for his immense contribution to my perception of international law at large.

This book is a product of work conducted during my stay in several institutions. I am indebted, of course, to Columbia Law School, and specifically to the staff at Graduate Legal Studies – Dean Sylvia T. Polo and Director Jill Marden Casal – who have patiently addressed my logistical concerns. My stay at Columbia was made possible by the generous funding of the Norman E. Alexander Scholarship, along with the support of the Faculty of Law at Hebrew University. I have also enjoyed, during 2010–2011, the gracious hospitality of the Cegla Center for Interdisciplinary Research of the Law at Tel Aviv University's Buchmann Faculty of Law, and wish to thank its then-director Professor Daphne Barak-Erez and the rest of the staff. In addition, thanks are due to the Institute for National Security Studies at Tel Aviv University, and in particular to the Joseph and Jeannette Neubauer Foundation. I am further indebted to my colleagues at IDC's Radzyner Law School, as well as the staff, for their material and logistical support.

During my academic and professional path until now, I have been fortunate to come across a few individuals without whom I could have never reached my achievements so far. I am grateful to Adv. Yuval

Elbashan and Adv. Sharon Sionov, with whom I have worked, between 2003–2006, at the Clinical Legal Education Center at Hebrew University; and The Honorable Judge David Cheshin, for whom I have clerked during his term as an Acting Justice at the Supreme Court of Israel, in 2006–2007. Furthermore, this project would not have been possible without the general support of a wide network of peers, colleagues, and friends who are too numerous to name here. Since the risk of forgetting someone is too high, I'll resort to the easy way out by presuming that you know who you are (or, alternatively, I will thank you in person!).

I am especially thankful to Andrew Humphrys at Routledge for his initial interest in the topic and his prompt treatment of my book proposal, and to Annabelle Harris, who swiftly responded to every need or question arising during my never-ending work on the manuscript. I am likewise grateful to the anonymous reviewers for their in depth and detailed reports.

In the past years, I had the opportunity to present talks based on chapters of this work in several conferences and colloquia. These discussions contributed greatly to the development of this work. I would especially like to thank the participants in the European Science Foundation's conference on "The Responsibility to Protect: From Principle to Practice" held in Linköping in June 2010, chaired by Prof. Andre Nollkaemper; the 2012 research group on the Migration of Criminal Law Principles from National to International Law at the Institute for Advanced Studies at Hebrew University, organized by Professor Miriam Gur-Arye; and the faculty seminars of the Faculty of Law at Haifa University and Radzyner Law School, IDC, Herzliya.

Chapters 1, 3 and 8 include some revised elements of material published, in earlier versions, in Eliav Lieblich, *Intervention and Consent: Consensual Forcible Interventions in Internal Armed Conflicts as International Agreements*, 29 Boston University International Law Journal 338 (2011); and Eliav Lieblich, *Consensual Intervention and the Responsibility to Protect*, *in* The Responsibility to Protect: From Theory to Practice 141 (Andre Nollkaemper and Julia Hoffman eds., 2012).

Last, special thanks are due to my family. My mother, Professor Amia Lieblich, who has demonstrated to me that academia is possible, and has always supported and encouraged me to dare – first to pursue doctoral studies, and later to take on this project. To my brother and sister, Yuval and Maty, thank you for being there for me. To Stav, thank you for the never ending support. You have all been my home-base during my travels and long years of work on this project.

Abbreviations

ADFL	Alliance of Democratic Forces for the Liberation of Zaire
AFRC	Armed Forces Revolutionary Council (Sierra Leone)
AMISOM	African Union Mission to Somalia
ARPCT	Alliance for Restoration of Peace and Counter-Terrorism (Somalia)
AU	African Union
AUPSC	African Union Peace and Security Council
CNDP	National Congress for the Defense of the People (DRC)
COIN	Counterinsurgency
DARIO	Draft Articles on Responsibility of International Organizations
DASR	Draft Articles on State Responsibility
DRC	Democratic Republic of the Congo
EC	European Communities
ECOMOG	ECOWAS Monitoring Group
ECOWAS	Economic Community of West African States
EU	European Union
EU NAVFOR	European Union Naval Force (Somalia)
FDLR	Democratic Forces for the Liberation of Rwanda
FN	Forces Nouvelles (Côte d'Ivoire)
GAL	Gobal Administrative Law
GCC	Gulf Cooperation Council
ICC	International Criminal Court
ICCPR	International Covenant on Civil and Political Rights
ICESCR	International Covenant on Economic, Social and Cultural Rights
ICISS	International Commission on Intervention and State Sovereignty
ICJ	International Court of Justice
ICTR	International Criminal Tribunal for Rwanda
ICTY	International Criminal Tribunal for the Former Yugoslavia
ICU	Islamic Courts Union (Somalia)
IGAD	Intergovernmental Authority on Development

IGASOM	IGAD Peace Support Mission in Somalia
IHL	International Humanitarian Law
IHRL	International Human Rights Law
ILC	International Law Commission
ISAF	International Security Assistance Force (Afghanistan)
KFOR	Kosovo Force (NATO)
LONS	League of Nations
LRA	Lord's Resistance Army (Uganda)
MLC	Movement for the Liberation of Congo
MONUC	United Nations Organization Mission in the Democratic Republic of the Congo
MONUSCO	United Nations Organization Stabilization Mission in the Democratic Republic of the Congo
MPLA	People's Movement for the Liberation of Angola
NATO	North Atlantic Treaty Organization
NIA	Non-Intervention Agreement (Spanish Civil War)
NTC	National Transitional Council (Libya)
OAS	Organization of American States
OESC	Organization of Eastern Caribbean States
PKK	Kurdistan Workers' Party
PLA	Palestine Liberation Army
PLO	Palestine Liberation Organization
RCD	Rally for Congolese Democracy
ROC	Republic of China
RPA	Rwandan Patriotic Army
RPF	Rwandan Patriotic Front
RtoP	Responsibility to Protect
RUF	Revolutionary United Front (Sierra Leone)
SOFA	Status of Forces Agreement
SPCSL	Special Court for Sierra Leone
TFG	Transitional Federal Government of Somalia
UK	United Kingdom
UN	United Nations
UNCLOS	UN Convention on the Law of the Sea
UNGA	United Nations General Assembly
UNITA	União Nacional para a Independência Total de Angola
UNMIK	UN Interim Administration in Kosovo
UNOCI	United Nations Operation in Côte d'Ivoire
UNSC	United Nations Security Council
UNSG	United Nations Secretary General
US	United States
USSR	Union of Soviet Socialist Republics
VCLT	Vienna Conventions on the Law of Treaties
WSOD	World Summit Outcome Document (2005)

Introduction

In the decades since the coming into being of the UN Charter, a near legal consensus has been solidified that no state may use force against another. The two primary exceptions to this rule – that a state may use force in self-defense, or when authorized to do so by the UN Security Council (UNSC) – have been robustly debated in the literature.[1] Regarding the latter exception, vast scholarship has been devoted to the competence of the UNSC to act in relation to "internal" conflicts, and whether, if the UNSC fails to do so, states could intervene unilaterally in such conflicts. This discussion represents the dilemma of *humanitarian intervention*.[2] The question of humanitarian intervention arises in the nexus between the general principle of non-intervention in internal affairs of states, the prohibition on the use of force, the law of international human rights and the corpus of laws on the protection of civilians. However, at the same nexus, another much less explored, but equally important, question surfaces: what if during an internal armed conflict, one of the parties invites an external force to intervene, or consents to such an intervention?

Intervention of the latter type is usually referred to as *intervention upon invitation*.[3] However, the potential legalizing element of such an intervention, if at all, is the substantive element of *consent*: a proactive invitation being only one possible form for its expression. Therefore, this book suggests a more inclusive term – *consensual intervention* – to describe this phenomenon. Importantly, the term "consensual," in our context, does not connote the agreement of *all* parties to the conflict – quite the opposite.

1 *See, e.g.*, Tom Ruys, "Armed Attack" and Article 51 of the U.N. Charter: Evolutions in Customary Law and Practice (2010); Christine Gray, International Law and the Use of Force Ch. 7 (2008).

2 *See, e.g.*, Humanitarian Intervention: Ethical, Legal and Political Dilemmas (J.L. Holzgrefe and Robert O. Keohane eds., 2003).

3 *See, e.g.*, Gray, *supra* note 1, Ch. 3; Louise Doswald-Beck, *The Legal Validity of Military Intervention by Invitation of the Government*, 56 Brit. Y'Book International L. 189 (1985); Georg Nolte, Eingreifen auf Einladung (1999).

The intervention must be against the will of *at least* one party; otherwise it would be a peacekeeping operation, rather than a forcible intervention.

International law has been traditionally unclear on the question of consensual intervention. Some went so far as to label practice, in this context, as "chaotic."[4] This confusion derives from the widely diverging views and inconsistencies found (mainly) in the literature. According to one view, forcible intervention upon the invitation or consent of a beleaguered government constitutes a potential exception to the prohibition on the use of force, as enshrined in Article 2(4) of the UN Charter, since the intervention is conducted in accordance with the will of the host-state. Thus, the argument goes, as long as the government can exercise sovereign power, or is deemed to represent the general will of the internal communities, its consent precludes any violation of the norm of non-intervention.

However, this approach has been constantly contested, at least by some international thinkers. The values traditionally protected by the principle of non-intervention – namely sovereignty, and later on also self-determination – are perceived, by the most orthodox of these thinkers, as being fulfilled only if internal parties are left alone to resolve their differences, even if by brute force. As they claim, a party unable to take or maintain power on its own, without external support, could not be considered as possessing sovereign power, nor as representing the internal community. The less orthodox of these thinkers concede that a government possesses *some* consent power – so long as the conflict remains below a certain threshold, usually fixed in relation to loss of territorial effective control.

Nevertheless, in recent years, the consent-exception, in some form, has come to be almost taken for granted, at least in state practice. Indeed, "state" consent forms a part of the legal basis for counterinsurgency operations in Afghanistan, Iraq and elsewhere, as well as for other transnational forcible acts, ranging from drone attacks to full-scale invasions. The solidifying acceptance of consent-power is a result of several geopolitical, conceptual – and ultimately legal – processes. Namely, it is a corollary of the end of the eras of colonization and the Cold War – in which interventions by ex-colonial powers or bloc-rivals carried a special potential of abuse – and the advent of a new era, in which interventions were no longer necessarily assessed in light of zero-sum dynamics. In parallel, the increasing centrality of the protection of individuals in international law, manifested mainly in international human rights law, has led to a transformation in the understanding of the principle of non-intervention – steering it away from its Westphalian origins towards a perception more sensitive to the protection of basic rights. This transformation, in turn, challenges notions according to which external parties were to treat internal strife impartially, found in some traditional literature.

4 *See Independent International Fact-Finding Mission on the Conflict in Georgia*, Report (Vol. 2), at 276 (September 30, 2009).

Moreover, the advent of transnational terrorism, the increasing number of internal conflicts and their accompanying atrocities, as well as the rise of armed non-state actors pursuing transnational agendas from territories of weak states, all spawn a strong international interest in the regulation of internal strife. This need often results in a convergence of interests between powerful and weaker states. The former might seek the latter's consent to legitimize forcible action against non-state actors in their territories or, perhaps, to halt atrocities; and the latter might be willing to grant such consent, in order to solidify their control. Accordingly, it seems that nowadays, less in the international community – whether sovereigns, international organizations or commentators – have a substantial interest in challenging the consent-exception per se. On the contrary: it seems that the contemporary international system even *pressurizes* states, at times, to grant consent to such interventions.

The question of intervention and consent is especially important – but as we shall see, not only – when the UNSC fails to act. This importance derives from the fact that when the consenting party is a government, and while the UNSC does not decide otherwise, the intervention can be viewed as removed from the realm of international *jus ad bellum* – the law on the use of force – since the government consented to the intervention by exercising its own sovereign power as the representative of the state.[5] However, this cannot mean that consent-power is unlimited. Indeed, it is implausible that contemporary international law will be constructed to accept that a government, engaged in mass atrocities, will be able to crush its opposition with the support of external parties – while all that is left to the international community is to observe the UNSC deadlock. This danger has been demonstrated in the events of the Arab Spring, and most significantly, perhaps, in the international reactions to the Syrian crisis.[6] Conversely, it seems equally unreasonable that a government – even when seeking assistance in confronting atrocities committed by the *opposition* – would lose its consent-power, merely because of "technical" loss of effective control over territory, as suggested in some traditional writing.

When addressing the various problems of intervention and consent, this book discusses a broad spectrum of related issues, hopefully contributing to the general understanding of the concept of intervention. Doing so, our discussion inevitably encounters ever-present, seemingly intractable dilemmas of international law: effective control versus legitimacy; state

5 This notion has roots in the traditional understandings of the principle non-intervention. *See, e.g.*, Lassa Oppenheim, 1 International Law §134 (2nd ed., 1912) (labeling consensual intervention, such as Russia's 1849 intervention in Hungary by request of Austria, as "co-operation" rather than intervention).

6 At least as of December 2012. *See* Chris McGreal, *U.S. Says Russian-Made Weapons are Killing Syrians on "an Hourly Basis,"* Guardian, June 13, 2012, *available at* www.guardian.co.uk/world/2012/jun/13/us-claim-syria-russian-civilians.

consent versus universal values; sovereignty and non-intervention versus individual rights; and self-determination versus territorial integrity, to name just a few. In absence of universally binding interpretation mechanisms available to resolve them, these dilemmas, sometimes, require choices that international lawyers are often reluctant to make.

When making such choices is inevitable, we must look for guidance in the objectives that we believe international law ought to promote.[7] We proceed from the assumption that these objectives correspond to an increasing – and justified – preoccupation with the protection of basic rights, and specifically those of civilians caught in armed conflict. We thus seek to demonstrate that in contemporary international law, internal strife is assessed from a *substantive* standpoint, rather than from a technical, seemingly impartial point of view. International law, as it presents itself, is concerned mainly about the protection of civilians; much less so about the traditional rights of sovereigns, notions of impartiality, the economic interests of third-party states, or even ideas of procedural democracy – when the latter are viewed in detachment from other substantive considerations.

Nowadays, the question of consensual intervention is governed, first and foremost, by *jus ad bellum*. However, the question has deeper roots, reaching down to an era in which limitations on the war-right of sovereigns were still inconceivable. In contrast, perhaps, to the common notion that traditional international law did not concern itself with internal strife, the status of conflicting internal parties has disturbed diplomats and lawyers for centuries. Considerations of non-intervention, neutrality and – significantly – the interest to secure maritime trade, have prompted states to develop intricate norms in order to regulate their relations to conflicting parties.

Like all areas of international law, questions regarding the rights, powers and obligations of parties to internal strife have been subject to changes in the philosophy, jurisprudence, power-structure and institutions of the international system, throughout the centuries. However, the specific issue of consensual intervention has gained substantial legal significance only with the prohibition on the use of force, which can be traced back to the 1928 Kellogg Briand Pact, and to previous, weaker attempts to regulate war, such as the 1907 Hague Convention on the Pacific Settlement of Disputes and the 1919 Covenant of the League of Nations.[8] It can be said that the question, in its proper legal sense, was only a product of this era, since the existence of a prohibition on the use of force is a logical precondition for any discussion of its potential exceptions. Indeed, in

7 *See* Martti Koskenniemi, The Politics of International Law 38–40 (2011).

8 Convention for the Pacific Settlement of International Disputes (Hague I), October 18, 1907; General Treaty for Renunciation of War as an Instrument of National Policy (Kellogg–Briand Pact), August 27, 1928, 94 L.N.T.S. 57; Covenant of the League of Nations, June 28, 1919, 4 U.K.T.S. 153.

earlier times, when states could go to war at will, it made little sense to ask whether the consent of the government, or of its rivals, had any implications on the *legality* of external intervention – that is, beyond transferring the bilateral relations between the parties from the realm of peace to the realm of war, if the intervention was undertaken against the government.

This realization does not imply that the norm of non-intervention, in some form, did not exist prior to the prohibition on the use force. It could have been, however, effectively extinguished by the war-right of states, if they were willing to pay the price that war entailed. Nonetheless, as mentioned above, the rights of parties to internal armed conflicts did, in fact, concern states even before the prohibition on the use of force, for various reasons. Discovering the underlying rationale of their concerns – as we shall attempt to do – can assist in shedding light on the development of international jurisprudence on internal armed conflicts, and allows us to place the question of intervention and consent in a wider doctrinal and historical context.

Besides the coming into being of the prohibition on the use of force, there are other major, intertwining processes that should be considered when analyzing the development of the law on consensual intervention. Notable among these processes is the decline of strict legal positivism, which dominated international law in the nineteenth century; the movement from a multi-polar, international balance of power system to a system that increasingly relies on collective institutions; and, significantly, the aforementioned change in the perception of the norm of non-intervention. As part of these processes, the question of intervention and consent is intrinsically woven in the centuries-long battle between effective control over territory and legitimacy (in the strict sense) as competing sources of sovereign power. In this context, it is a sub-question of the wider field of recognition of entities in international law, and in particular, the branch of recognition dealing with the determination of the rights of parties to internal conflicts.

Indeed, the recognition of such rights was long determined by strict territorial effective control (and related) standards, reflected in the *belligerency* and *insurgency* doctrines. Territorial effectiveness as the chief determinant of sovereign, or sovereign-like power, was viewed as a necessary corollary of the norm of non-intervention, which was perceived at the time as protecting the "internal affairs" of effective regimes, regardless of their merits. Leaders, diplomats, scholars, lawyers and judges of the time took pride in the seemingly amoral nature of these doctrines, as manifestations of the progress of international law. It was especially viewed in stark contrast to the legitimism doctrine, espoused by the conservative Holy Alliance, which was a priori adverse to any revolutionary movement challenging the "divine right" of the ruler.

However, throughout the decades of the twentieth century and beyond, the concept of territorial effective control as the sole source of power was challenged by a set of other competing, substantive principles – recently, the understanding of sovereignty as the fulfillment of the responsibility to protect civilians. In accordance with these challenges, the approach of international law to internal conflicts has moved from being almost exclusively concerned with the commerce rights of external parties – asking "how does the conflict affect *us*" – to asking also "how does the conflict affect the political and humanitarian rights of *internal* parties."[9]

Yet, this process raises, in turn, complex questions. In the context of intervention and consent, these emanate from the difficulty to delineate accepted criteria for the substantive assessment of the consent-power of parties to internal strife. To argue that the prohibition on the use of force, as embodied in the UN Charter, provides an answer to these questions by enshrining a complete preference of governments, does not take us too far. In essence, the root of the problem lies in the fact that Article 2(4) of the UN Charter prohibits the threat or use of force against *states*, but nowhere is it clarified who is entitled to speak for the state in extreme situations. The usual reply, according to which the "government" is entitled to do so, raises, in turn, a plethora of perplexing questions regarding the determination of the identity of the government; and even if this is clear – the question still arises regarding the limits of the government's power to receive forcible support in a given instance. Another possible solution to these questions could be that it is only for the UNSC to determine the scope of consent-power, in light of the circumstances of the specific case. While such an approach could be prudent from the perspective of international policy, and can indeed solve the problem in certain situations, it by no means provides a comprehensive solution. This is because the UNSC, because of the veto power enjoyed by its permanent members, has not been historically quick to react to catastrophes that occur in contemporary internal conflicts.

This book seeks to clarify the processes and questions mentioned above. It inquires into the existence, nature and limitations of government-consent as an exception to the prohibition on the use of force, and attempts to place the question in a wider legal, theoretical and, sometimes, historical context. However, once we concede that the understanding of the principle of non-intervention has transformed to encompass also the protection of basic rights of individuals – rather than strictly the rights of sovereigns – we cannot avoid addressing, in a careful manner, the parallel and controversial question: regarding the implications, if at all, of consent expressed by opposition groups, in particular where these basic rights are not protected.

The first chapters seek to define and clarify the main concepts addressed in this book. Chapter 1 clarifies the use of the term "consensual

9 For a similar observation *see* Prosecutor v. Tadic, Case No. IT-94-1-I, Decision on Defence Motion for Interlocutory Appeal on Jurisdiction, ¶¶96–97 (International Criminal Tribunal for the Former Yugoslavia October 2, 1995).

intervention," by exemplifying the modalities and dynamics of such interventions. Namely, it explores the wide spectrum of the term, the nature of the relationship between the intervener and the consenting party, and the interaction between consent and UNSC authorized interventions.

The next two chapters present, rather briefly, general issues relating to intervention in internal armed conflicts, in order to frame our discussion. Chapter 2 addresses the concepts of intervention and internal armed conflicts, both in terms of definition and in substance. It discusses various issues that arise when embarking on a legal discourse of the elusive term of "intervention," and clarifies several distinctions necessary for the term's understanding. Importantly, it discusses the shifting meaning of the norm of non-intervention in contemporary thought, and offers a basic typology of interventions. Thereafter, the chapter discusses the legal concept of internal armed conflict, and attempts to present a typology that demonstrates the complexity of such conflicts. The legal definition of internal armed conflict is of significance, as we shall see, since it potentially affects the legality of external forcible intervention.

Chapter 3 discusses the concept of *forcible* intervention. It lays down the "normative duality" of such interventions; and attempts to delineate the actions that fall within the scope of forcible interventions and their attributions to states. It discusses the categorization of intervention by UN mandated forces, and briefly addresses – mainly to set this issue aside – some unique aspects of arms transfers as a form of intervention.

Thereafter, we turn to discuss the law regarding the rights and powers of parties to internal armed conflicts in the pre-UN Charter era. This serves three purposes. First, to clarify, to the extent possible, an area in traditional international law that has been notoriously vague. Second, we demonstrate that prior to the prohibition on the use of force, the question of consent was largely irrelevant, since sovereigns enjoyed an unlimited war-prerogative. Third, we exemplify the generally amoral, territorial effectiveness-based doctrines that dominated the era. These can be juxtaposed with substantive doctrines of later decades, allowing us to better understand them.

Accordingly, Chapter 4 addresses internal armed conflicts and consent in the era of the "prerogative of war." It starts by setting forth the perception of the use of force in that era, and moves to survey the effectiveness-based doctrines of belligerency and insurgency. It demonstrates that the latter doctrines – in contrast to some modern understandings of them – had no effect over the question of consensual intervention. The chapter closes by exemplifying the amoral application of international law in the context of the American Civil War, where the gleaming immorality of slavery did not play a part in the determination of the rights of the parties.

Chapter 5 discusses the question of consensual intervention in the inter-war period, where nascent limitations on the use of force were already in place, and the international system started to shift towards collective decision making, as exemplified in the Spanish Civil War. The latter conflict can also be seen as the point where the old doctrines regarding internal armed conflict were, to a certain extent, abandoned, and calls for the substantive analysis of parties were advanced.

Afterwards, we turn to the law of consensual intervention in the era of the UN Charter. Indeed, since the prohibition on the use of force was firmly set in place, questions regarding the *exception* to the prohibition – based on consent – have gained distinct importance. Chapter 6, thus, addresses the doctrines of intervention as these developed in the first decades of the UN, and identifies a presumption in favor of governments in the context of consensual intervention. This approach contradicts the traditional notion of "strict-abstentionism" – asserting that when internal conflict or "civil war" erupts, external actors should abstain from any intervention. We argue and demonstrate that the former view is obsolete. However, like all presumptions, the presumption in favor of governments is rebuttable. In subsequent chapters, the book analyzes its limitations.

Chapter 7 inquires into the contemporary relevancy of the question of consensual intervention, namely with regards to the struggle against transnational terrorism and the need to protect civilians from mass atrocities. Thereafter, it analyzes the scope of government consent power, by setting forth several thresholds. Notably, the chapter proposes a reformulation of some traditional approaches that limit consent power precisely when significant internal conflicts take place, by suggesting that nowadays, the existence of an armed conflict is a *precondition* for the capacity to consent to forcible support – since otherwise the matter has to be dealt with through law enforcement mechanisms. The chapter further attempts to place the traditional doctrine of counter-intervention in the contemporary context.

Chapter 8 sets forth the concept of protection of civilians as an emerging fundamental principle of international law, which in turn spawns the doctrine of *effective protection* – manifested in the Responsibility to Protect concept – as a chief source of sovereign power. Mainly, the chapter argues that the notion of effective protection is (and should be) the dominant factor in the assessment of the question of consensual intervention in contemporary international law – both when analyzing the power to express consent and the power to withdraw it, in particular in the context of forward-looking intervention treaties.

Recognizing this conclusion, Chapter 9 discusses other substantive considerations for the assessment of consent power. It discusses the question of consent given by non-democratic regimes, as well as consent in the context of the right to self-determination. The chapter attempts to place these key concepts within a modern framework, in which effective protection is the immediate concern of the law of intervention. We claim that, essentially, our understanding of democracy and self-determination "collapses," during internal armed conflict, into the concept of protection of civilians – and that this understanding affects, in turn, the consent-exception.

Up to this point, the book, in general, addresses the *limits* of government consent-power (a negative result), rather than the difficult question of whether such power can be transferred to opposition groups (a positive result). Chapter 10 ventures into this controversial question, and explores the potential role of opposition consent in the face of government atrocities. In essence, the chapter analyzes the relations between external parties and opposition groups, as these can be placed on the spectrum between recognition and humanitarian intervention. The chapter demonstrates that opposition consent cannot legalize intervention against recognized governments, but carefully suggests that it can nevertheless play a part in traditional just-war considerations, which are widely accepted as ethical thresholds for unilateral humanitarian intervention.

Finally, a methodological disclaimer is in place: this book draws extensively from many internal conflicts, in a manner that can by no means reflect their factual complexity and the diverging narratives regarding them. To the extent that these representations oversimplify, I ask the reader to bear with me and focus on the overarching principles we might deduce from them nonetheless.

1 The dynamics of consensual intervention

1 The wide spectrum of consensual intervention

1.1 The insufficiency of the intervention upon invitation paradigm

The attempt to define the phenomenon of "consensual" interventions, as opposed to other types of interventions, presents a significant challenge. Indeed, one can envision the pure "intervention upon invitation" scenario – in which a government explicitly, ad hoc and in a written treaty – invites a previously uninvolved state to assist it in confronting opposition groups seeking to overthrow it. In this "pure" scenario, the intervener has no independent interests in the intervention itself, beyond the fact that it was requested to assist the inviting government. Furthermore, the intervener will have no interaction with other international actors, nor will it seek any authorization from the UNSC. This altruistic – perhaps "Kantian"[1] – intervener will therefore present no other justification for its actions other than its "good-will" and the invitation itself.

However, the concept of "intervention by invitation," while seemingly providing a clearly definable and identifiable categorization, does not reflect the reality of the contemporary international system, or the complexity of the question of intervention and consent in international law. Practically – needless to say – states will rarely display the Kantian virtues as reflected in the pure "intervention by invitation" paradigm. Legally, moreover, the term "invitation" is imprecise, since it focuses on the technical element of the question rather than on the substantive one: it merely refers to the *instrument* of the expression of *consent*. Since the potential "active" legalizing agent regarding a consensual intervention is the consent itself, it makes little sense to ask whether an invitation, in the narrow sense, has been extended. Instead, when focusing on the substantive element of consent, the term consensual intervention encompasses a much wider scope of instances. Accordingly, an abundance of complex scenarios become possible, each presenting significant legal challenges.

1 Immanuel Kant, Fundamental Principles of the Metaphysic of Morals sec. 1 (1875).

For instance, consent will not always be – in practice – in the form of an invitation in advance. It might be expressed, on the time continuum, not only proactively but also retroactively (when external forces are already present on the state's territory, for one reason or another), and can theoretically be conveyed, in both cases, explicitly or implicitly. Its legality, in all these cases, depends on its firm and unequivocal establishment in the relations between the consenting entity and the intervener, and cannot, as such, be simply presumed by the latter.[2] Moreover, consent can be ad hoc and specific, expressed in real-time in relation to a concrete instance of intervention; or, conversely, be granted in the form of a general, forward-looking intervention treaty. The latter treaties, in most cases, give rise to significant legal challenges.[3] For instance, a perplexing problem can occur when a government, party to a forward-looking intervention treaty, seeks to withdraw its consent in real-time in the face of an impending intervention.[4] In practice – setting aside, for now, the issue of legality of such situations – consent can be expressed by governments or opposition groups; the latter situation challenges, of course, the prohibition on the use of force and the norm of non-intervention as classically understood.

Furthermore, consent can be addressed to various types of external actors. It can be granted to states and to groups of states acting within a regional organization; but also to other entities such as non-state actors or multinational forces established by a UNSC resolution. When a state agrees that a non-state actor "intervene" on its behalf, the intervening group may or may not be considered as having been integrated into the consenting state's armed forces. Such a determination will be made in light of the application, in the specific circumstances, the relevant rules of international humanitarian law (IHL) and state responsibility.[5] In cases where consent is expressed in the context of a UNSC authorized

2 Roberto Ago, *Eighth Report on State Responsibility*, 2 Yearbook of the International Law Commission, 3, 35–36 (1979), *cited in* David Wippman, *Military Intervention, Regional Organizations, and Host-State Consent*, 7 Duke Journal of Comparative and International Law 209, 209 n.1 (1996); *see also* International Law commission, The International Law Commission's Draft Articles on State Responsibility, pt. 1, arts. 1–3, 316–317 (Shabtai Rosenne ed., 1991) (referring to the distinction between *implied* consent and *presumed* consent, which is actually tantamount to no consent at all); *compare* Tristan Ferraro, International Committee of the Red Cross, Expert Meeting: Occupation and Other Forms of Administration of Foreign Territory 22 (2012) (positing that for consent to relieve an intervener from its duties under occupation law, it has to be explicit).

3 These led the Institute of International Law to opine that ad hoc consent must be given even when a general intervention treaty exists between the parties. *See* Institut de Droit International, Military Assistance on Request, art. 4(3), (September 8, 2011).

4 On such treaties *see* Chapter 8, sec. 3.

5 On the integration of organized armed groups into a state's armed forces *see* Nils Melzer, International Committee of the Red Cross, Interpretive Guidance on the Notion of Direct Participation in Hostilities under International Humanitarian Law 21–26 (2009). Regarding state attribution *see* Chapter 3, sec. 2.3.

intervention, the consent, as we shall see, interacts with a Chapter VII-based mandate and supplements it.

Naturally, instances in which the consent is both proactive and explicit, and is extended ad hoc by a state to another state, are relatively simple cases – *at least* with regards to the relations between the consenting state and the intervener – that correspond with the classic "intervention upon invitation" paradigm. Any other combination raises difficult questions – in particular regarding the free nature of the consent,[6] but also concerning a plethora of other issues. Indeed, the diverse modalities of consensual intervention result in a wide variety of complex cases. For instance, such a case occurs when consent is given to a foreign force which is already present in the state's territory, with many independent interests of its own, perhaps operating in conjunction with international forces.[7] Another complex case can be when consent is granted implicitly, in parallel with a transnational armed conflict between the intervening party and a non-state actor operating from within the consenting territorial state. This is arguably the case in some instances of the so-called "war on terror." In such situations, as we shall exemplify shortly through the Kenyan intervention in Somalia – and as invoked by the US in the context of targeted killing operations – claims of self-defense can intertwine with the territorial state's consent.[8] Furthermore, the lawfulness of such consensual interventions can be conditioned on the question whether the consenting state *itself* is involved in an internal armed conflict with the non-state actor.[9]

Since the term "consent" alludes to a wide variety of instances, this work adopts an admittedly flexible view of the situations that constitute consensual interventions. The latter term, thus, refers to every forcible intervention – unilateral or multilateral – in an internal armed conflict, undertaken

6 *See, e.g.*, John Lawrence Hargrove, *Intervention by Invitation and the Politics of the New World Order*, *in* Law and Force in the New International Order 113, 117–118 (Lori Fisler Damrosch and David. J. Scheffer eds., 1991) (outlining briefly a framework of principles for the genuineness of consent and evidentiary factors that should be taken into account).

7 Such was the case regarding operation Enduring Freedom in Afghanistan. *See infra* sec. 1.2.

8 *See, e.g.*, Harold Hongju Koh, Keynote Address at the Annual Meeting of the American Society of International Law: The Obama Administration and International Law (March 25, 2010), *available at* www.state.gov/s/l/releases/remarks/139119.html; Eric Holder, Speech at Northwestern University School of Law (March 5, 2012), *available at* http://opiniojuris.org/2012/03/05/ag-holders-national-security-speech-text. This is arguably the situation involving at least some of the US drone attacks in Pakistan, although the existence of consent, in this context, is debatable. *See generally* Laurie R. Blank and Benjamin R. Farley, *Characterizing U.S. Operations in Pakistan: Is the United States Engaged in an Armed Conflict?* 34 Ford. International L. J. 151 (2010); *compare* Michael N. Schmitt, *Drone Attacks under the Jus ad Bellum and Jus in Bello: Clearing the "Fog of Law"* 13 Yearbook of International Humanitarian Law 311, 315 (2010). This paradigm could account for some US attacks also in Yemen and Somalia. *See id.*

9 *See* Chapter 7, sec. 2.1.

in practice, in part or in whole, for the benefit of one of the parties, regarding which genuine consent can be inferred, whether explicitly or implicitly. In essence, then, a substantial element of the *prima facie* qualification of an intervention as consensual is the *partiality* of the intervention. Indeed, every non-impartial intervention is likely to further – even if only tactically – the interests of one party to the conflict over the other. Here lies the *nexus between partiality and consent*: it is reasonable to presume – albeit in a rebuttable fashion – that a party which benefits from an intervention has consented, in some way or the other, to the operation. Therefore, we assume, for the sake of our analysis, that every de facto non-impartial intervention can be viewed as consensual, in relation to a certain party, unless the intervention is publicly and credibly rebuffed by all relevant parties. For instance, every intervention in an internal armed conflict, in which opposition forces are attacked by the intervener, and is not denounced by the territorial government as unlawful, is presumably conducted with the latter's consent. Likewise, when an intervention receives the support and cooperation of opposition groups, it is quite possible to deduce that the latter have consented to it. This realization, of course, does not prejudge the *legality* of the action – it merely allows us to establish that the intervention might be consensual, and that methodologically, the actual or potential legal implications of the consent can be analyzed. However – our wide definition of consensual intervention notwithstanding – when the intervention is not authorized by the UNSC the question is at its most acute, since it is precisely in these cases where consent might have a powerful legalizing role.

1.2 Consensual intervention and multiple justifications

Bearing in mind their complexity, in most scenarios of consensual interventions the consent justification will frequently be explicitly or implicitly advanced in conjunction with other, substantive justifications for the intervention. In these instances, the relation between the different justifications should be analyzed.

Forcible interventions, in general, have been historically justified from two distinct points of view. The first strictly reflects the interests of the intervening state. Such justifications may include interventions for the protection of nationals abroad; interventions as self-defense; or counter-interventions aimed to restore a perceived balance of power. As we shall see in later chapters, this point of view was prevalent in the decentralized, multi-polar system of the nineteenth and early twentieth centuries, although not entirely absent from contemporary discourse. A second set of justifications, more prevalent nowadays, concerns mainly the rights of the people within the target state, sometimes linking them also to the interests of the international community at large. Such justifications, for instance, are discussed in terms such as self-determination, humanitarian intervention, and the Responsibility to Protect (RtoP).

At this stage, the legal validity of both sets of justifications is not of our concern. What is important, however, is that each of them can be supplemented by consent. The question whether consent is a legal precondition, in any combination of justifications, is a complex question – some aspects of it will be explored later on in this work. However, the mere fact that consent constitutes but one of several justifications invoked in relation to one instant of intervention does not necessarily mean that it is devoid of legal value of its own.[10]

Indeed, these justifications often overlap and are many times raised simultaneously. The examples, throughout the decades, are numerous. For instance, Britain has justified its 1957 intervention in Muscat and Oman on three grounds. First, it claimed, the intervention was conducted by "request of a friendly ruler" (consent); second, it claimed, "the dissidents have clearly received assistance from outside territories" (counter-intervention); and, third, it mentioned "direct British interests."[11] France, intervening in Rwanda in 1990 in favor of the Rwandan Hutu regime – facing at the time an imminent defeat by the Tutsi RPF – had justified its intervention both on counts of explicit invitation by Hutu Rwandan president Habyarimana, as well as on its duty to intervene for the protection of French nationals.[12]

Russia, when intervening in the Georgian conflict of 2008 between the central government and the breakaway territories of South Ossetia and Abkhazia, justified its actions both on humanitarian grounds, and upon consent by the breakaway authorities – in addition to its immediate reliance on the fact that Russian peacekeepers were allegedly attacked by Georgian armed forces. Furthermore, Russia subsequently recognized the independence of these territories, and invoked the doctrine of *international* collective-self-defense as another justification for its intervention.[13]

In other instances, consent by one party coincides with a self-defense claim by the intervening party. This is a common characteristic of modern transnational armed conflicts. For instance, Rwanda's involvement in the 1996–1997 internal conflict in Zaire/Congo was portrayed as a self-defense action against cross-border incursions by Hutu militias supported by Zaire; but was also a consensual intervention in favor of

10 *See* Terry D. Gill, *Military Intervention at the Invitation of a Government, in* The Handbook of the International Law of Military Operations 229, 229 (Terry D. Gill and Dieter Fleck eds., 2010).

11 Statement by British Foreign Secretary Lloyd (July 22, 1957), *quoted in* Antonio Tanca, Foreign Armed Intervention in Internal Conflict 150–151 (1993).

12 *See* Mel McNulty, *From Intervened to Intervener: Rwanda and Military Intervention in Zaire/DRC, in* African Interventionist States 173, 176–177 (Oliver Furley and Roy May eds., 2001).

13 *See* discussion in Chapter 10, sec. 3.

the Congolese president to be Laurent-Desiré Kabila.[14] Angola, intervening in support of the government of the Democratic Republic of the Congo (DRC) in 1998, justified its intervention on counts of an "explicit request" by President Joseph Kabila; "legitimate" national interests; and in order to "pre-empt" actions by the Angolan rebel movement UNITA.[15] Likewise, the 2006 Ethiopian intervention in Somalia was justified by Ethiopia *inter alia* as self-defense against Islamist militias; however, their can be no doubt that Ethiopia operated with full consent and cooperation of the Somali Transitional Federal Government (TFG).[16]

An informative example for the interaction between consent and self-defense could be found in the Kenyan operation in Somalia, which commenced in late-2011. This case clearly reflects the tendency of states, when engaged in transnational armed conflicts against non-state actors, to rely on state-consent as an augmentation of other claims. On October 16, 2011 Kenyan forces invaded Somalia aiming to "inflict trauma and damage" on the Al-Shabaab militia, which controlled much of south-west Somalia, including the border area with Kenya.[17] Besides being locked in an ongoing armed conflict with the internationally supported Somali authorities,[18] Al-Shabaab's presence on its borders was also harming the interests of the relatively stable Kenyan state.

The main motivation for the Kenyan operation seems to have been the instability on its borders. However – and perhaps since self-defense claims against decentralized acts by non-state actors can raise legal and political difficulties – Kenya has also justified its actions on counts of the consent of the Somali government. This claim was based on an October 18 joint communiqué between the countries, signed two days after the beginning of the Kenyan operation, which called for joint "decisive action" against Al-Shabaab. The countries pledged "to cooperate in undertaking security and military operations, and to undertake coordinated pre-emptive action, and pursuit of any armed elements that continue to threaten and attack

14 *See generally* William G. Thom, *Congo-Zaire's 1996–1997 Civil War in the Context of Evolving Patterns of Military Conflict in Africa in the Era of Independence*, 19 Journal of Conflict Studies (1999).

15 Norrie McQueen, *Angola*, *in* African Interventionist States, *supra* note 12, at 93, 108–109.

16 *See* Chapter 7, sec. 2.4. In September 2012, the TFG was replaced by new authorities, formally ending Somalia's transitional period. See, e.g., S.C. Res. 2067, U.N. Doc. S/RES/2067 (September 18, 2012).

17 *See Kenya Invades Somalia: a Big Gamble*, The Economist, October 29, 2011, www.economist.com/node/21534828l; *Kenyan Troops Push into Somalia*, Wall Street Journal, October 17, 2011, http://online.wsj.com/article/SB10001424052970204479504576635301627490590.html. Shortly thereafter, Ethiopia too invaded Somalia. *See* Jeffery Gettleman, *Ethiopian Troops Said to Enter Somalia, Opening New Front against Militants*, New York Times, November 20, 2011, www.nytimes.com/2011/11/21/world/africa/ethiopian-troops-enter-somalia-witnesses-say.html.

18 On the situation in Somalia, *see* Chapter 7, sec. 2.4.

both countries."[19] Simultaneously, and in reference to the communiqué, Kenya has notified the UNSC that:

> with the concurrence of the Transitional Federal Government of Somalia, [Kenya] has been compelled to take robust, targeted measures to protect and preserve the integrity of Kenya and the efficacy of the national economy and to secure peace and security in the face of the Al-Shabaab terrorist militia attacks emanating from Somalia.[20]

Somalia's public reaction to the invasion was somewhat muffled and ambiguous – a fact that highlights the blurry line between "partial" and "consensual" interventions – ranging from laconically acknowledging the presence of Kenyan troops; to welcoming Kenyan support to the extent that it was only "logistical"; and later to distancing itself from the intervention.[21] In the course of these reactions, there have also been conflicting public statements issued by the Prime Minister of Somalia, initially supporting the action, and the President, later expressing objection to it. Thus, there is general confusion concerning the government's genuine stance regarding the invasion.[22] Nevertheless, the existence of the joint communiqué, the ambiguous initial reaction by Somalia, the potential benefit the TFG could reap from the invasion, and its failure to pursue action against Kenya in the UNSC establishes the reasonable assumption that the Kenyan operation received the consent of Somalia – although the latter attempted to maintain public ambiguity regarding the operation, perhaps for internal political purposes. The Kenyan intervention has accordingly been met by international acquiescence.[23]

Indeed, multiple justifications can understandably lead to political and ethical skepticism, as they can imply that consent was used as a pretext for

19 Joint Communiqué Issued at the Conclusion of a Meeting between the Government of Kenya and the Transitional Federal Government of Somalia, October 18, 2011, *available at* http://graphics8.nytimes.com/packages/pdf/world/joint-communique-kenya-somalia.pdf.

20 Letter Dated October 17, 2011 from the Permanent Representative of Kenya to the United Nations addressed to the President of the Security Council, U.N. Doc. S/2011/646 (October 18, 2011).

21 *See Kenyan Troops Push into Somalia, supra* note 17; *Kenya Invades Somalia, supra* note 17; Josh Kron, *Kenyan Offensive is not Welcome, Somalia's President Says*, New York Times, October 24, 2011, www.nytimes.com/2011/10/25/world/africa/grenade-attack-on-kenyan-bar-raises-fear-of-widening-conflict.html.

22 Mohamed Shiil, *Kenya's Invasion of Somalia Raises Controversy*, All Headline News, November 8, 2011, www.allheadlinenews.com/articles/90063851?Kenya's%20invasion%20of%20Somali%20raises%20controversy.

23 A Security Council resolution concerning Somalia, adopted only two weeks after the Kenyan invasion, extended the mandate of the African Union in Somalia (AMISOM) without any reference to the Kenyan operation. *See* S.C. Res. 2010, U.N. Doc. S/RES/2010 (September 30, 2011).

intervention.[24] However, in the legal sphere, the mere fact that an action was justified on a number of different grounds does not necessarily implicate each claim's separate legality. For instance, different justifications can sometimes be mutually complementing, such as in the case of a counter-intervention conducted in favor of a beleaguered government facing a foreign-supported armed insurrection.[25] In other cases, consent and other justifications can be raised as alternative claims, still retaining their power – as "fallback" justifications – in case others are found baseless or otherwise exhausted. Such can be the case, as with regards to Kenya's 2011–2012 intervention in Somalia, when a state obtains consent to act forcibly against an armed group operating from another state's territory. Consent in such cases supplements the self-defense claim in at least two different aspects.

First, "pure" self-defense arguments in actions against non-state actors can be controversial or at least hard to prove.[26] Second, if the intervention is significantly wider than the attack by the non-state actor, obtaining the consent of the territorial state can counter claims that the intervener's self-defense actions are in violation of the *jus ad bellum* concept of proportionality in self-defense, as well as, perhaps, relieve the intervener from the status of an occupying power.[27] For instance, it is one thing to recognize the immediate right of self-defense of the US to act against Afghanistan in light of the attacks of September 11th;[28] it is arguably a different thing to justify the decade-long presence of American forces there on such counts. This could partly explain why the international community opted for the establishment of an international security force (ISAF), mandated by the UNSC pursuant to the Bonn Agreement, which was concluded between various Afghan delegations.[29] Granted, the Bonn Agreement was supplemented by a UNSC resolution; however, as was the case with the US–Iraq Status of Forces Agreement (SOFA) of 2008,[30] it is reasonable that the

24 Walzer calls this phenomenon "mixed motives." *See* Michael Walzer, Just and Unjust Wars 101–102 (4th ed. 2006); *see also* Military Aid and Paramilitary Activities in and Against Nicaragua (Nicar. v. U.S.), 1986 I.C.J. 14, ¶127 (June 27) (on mixed motives in the conduct of the US in the context of intervention in Nicaragua).

25 *See* Chapter 7, sec. 3.

26 For a detailed discussion *see* Noam Lubell, Extraterritorial Use of Force against Non-State Actors 25–69 (2010); *see also* Blank and Farley, *supra* note 8; Carsten Stahn, *Terrorist Acts as "Armed Attack": The Right to Self-Defense, Article 51(1/2) of the U.N. Charter, and International Terrorism*, 27 Fletcher Forum of World Affairs 35, 47–51 (2003).

27 On proportionality in self-defense *see, e.g.,* Yoram Dinstein, War, Aggression and Self-Defense 235–244 (4th ed., 2005). On host-state consent as negating occupation *see* discussion in Expert Meeting on Occupation, *supra* note 2, at 20–23, 29–30.

28 S.C. Res 1368, U.N. Doc. S/RES/1368 (September 12, 2001); S.C. Res 1373, U.N. Doc. S/RES/1373 (September 28, 2001).

29 *See* Chapter 9, sec. 1.

30 Agreement on the Withdrawal of the United States Forces from Iraq and the Organization of their Activities during their Temporary Presence in Iraq, U.S.-Iraq, November 17, 2008, S. EXEC. DOC. 09–6 (2009).

agreement could have, potentially, legitimized the presence of Coalition forces in Afghanistan even *absent* such a resolution.[31]

Thus, the mere assertion that consensual interventions are usually justified also by other claims, does not, in itself, have effect over the legal status of such consent; the relation between the different justifications varies according to their combination in specific circumstances.

2 Consent: the distinction between external validity and internal consent power

2.1 Valid and genuine consent as conferring revocable agency upon the external intervener

The concept of consent, in the context of consensual intervention, is commonly addressed as one, organic term. However, in actuality it encompasses two different meanings. The first concerns the genuineness of the consent in relation to the *external* element. It is not concerned with the *internal* legitimacy of the consent, which is addressed by the second meaning of the term. The former meaning of consent thus encompasses questions such as whether, in specific circumstances, genuine consent was granted; or rather, it was merely a product of coercion or other consent-vitiating circumstances. For instance, such would be the question whether the presence of US forces in Iraq since June 2004, or, at least, from November 2008, received the free-willed consent of the Iraqi government (the latter officially, and repeatedly, invited the US to assist it in stabilizing the country)[32] or, conversely, it was a product of coercion.

Another interesting case, relating to the genuineness of consent, can be found in the massive Syrian involvement in Lebanon between 1976 and 2005. Although Syria claimed that its June 1976 intervention in Lebanon's bloody

31 ISAF, which is commanded by NATO, operates in parallel – and generally independent from – the US-led Coalition of Operation Enduring Freedom, which too operates, albeit with different rules of engagement, in support of the Afghan government. *See* Rebecca J. Barber, *The Proportionality Equation: Balancing Military Objectives with Civilian Lives in the Armed Conflict in Afghanistan* 15 J. Conflict & Security L. 467, 469–474 (2010) (outlining the distinction between ISAF and Operation Enduring Freedom); *see also* Michael N. Schmitt, *Targeting and International Humanitarian Law in Afghanistan,* 85 International Legal Studies Series U.S. Naval War College 307, 308 (2009).

32 *See* S.C. Res. 1546, annex, U.N. Doc. S/RES/1546 (June 5, 2004). Further Iraqi requests for the extension of the multinational forces' mandate were authorized in S.C. Res. 1637, U.N. DOC. S/RES/1637 (November 8, 2005); S.C. Res. 1723, U.N. Doc. S/RES/1723 (November 28, 2006); and S.C. Res. 1790, U.N. Doc. S/RES/1790 (December 18, 2007); this consent supplemented the recognition by the Security Council of the Coalition forces as a Multinational Force operating under Chapter VII; thereafter, US presence was authorized through the SOFA. *See supra* note 30; *see also* Letter Dated December 7, 2008 From the Prime Minister of Iraq addressed to the President of the Security Council, S.C. Res 1859, annex, U.N. Doc. S/RES/1859 (December 22, 2008).

Civil War was requested by the Lebanese government – a claim reaffirmed over the years in various treaties[33] and Lebanese statements[34] – the UNSC, eventually, and following attempts by Syria to force constitutional changes in Lebanon, ceased to view Lebanon's consent as genuine. This approach was reflected in the arguments[35] in support of Security Council Resolution 1559, which called for the withdrawal of all forces from Lebanon, despite the interesting fact that both Syria and Lebanon itself objected to the resolution.[36]

Since the latter questions concern the relationship between a consenting party and an external actor, they do not invoke the complex substantive problems relating to the determination of rights and powers of parties during internal armed conflicts. Indeed, despite the difficulties in its application in specific cases, the issue of consent-genuineness is addressed in widely accepted principles of international law – as these are found in the law of treaties and state responsibility – governing the question of agreement, coercion and state representation.[37] Namely, intervention agreements are controlled by fundamental norms such as *pacta sunt servanda*[38] and the invalidity of coerced acts.[39]

Assuming that genuine consent exists, the law of consensual intervention is further complicated by the virtually unlimited capacity of the host-state – stemming from the prohibition on the use of force, the notion of state-sovereignty and Article 3(e) of the Definition of Aggression[40] – to withdraw its consent. The almost ever-present right of withdrawal – limited only in situations in which internal consent power, as defined in the next section, is lacking – positions consensual interventions as hybrids between rights-creating agreements and instruments that confer *authority* to act within a host-state territory. As such, consent to forcible intervention can

33 *See, e.g.*, Treaty of Brotherhood, Cooperation and Coordination, Syria–Leb., May 22, 1991, 1675 U.N.T.S. I-28932, 154.

34 Some as late as 2004. *See* U.N. SCOR, 59th Sess., 5028th mtg. at 2–3, U.N. Doc. S/PV.5028 (September 2, 2004) (statement of Lebanon).

35 *See id.* at 3–4 (statements of the US and France.)

36 S.C. Res. 1559, U.N. Doc. S/RES/1559 (September 2, 2004). For the Lebanese and Syrian positions *see*, respectively, U.N. Doc. S/2004/699 (August 31, 2004); U.N. Doc. S/2004/706 (September 1, 2004).

37 *See Military Intervention, Regional Organizations, and Host-State Consent, supra* note 2, at 209.

38 *Pacta sund Servanda* is viewed by some as the "categorical imperative" of international law. *See* Josef L. Kunz, *The Meaning and the Range of the Norm Pacta sunt Servanda* 39 American Journal of International Law 180, 180–181 (1945).

39 *See* Anthony Aust, Modern Treaty Law and Practice 12 (2007); Vienna Convention on the Law of Treaties arts. 51–52, May 23, 1969, 1155 U.N.T.S. 331; *see also* Dinstein, *supra* note 27, at 40; on coerced consent *see* Expert Meeting on Occupation, *supra* note 2, at 21–23.

40 *See*, Eliav Lieblich, *Intervention and Consent: Consensual Forcible Interventions in Internal Armed Conflicts as International Agreements*, 29 Boston University International Law Journal 338, 357–366 (2011); *see also* Chapter 8, sec. 3.1; on Article 3(e) of the Definition of Aggression *see* Chapter 8, sec. 1; *see also* Institut de Droit International, Military Assistance on Request, art. 5 (September 8, 2011).

be understood, perhaps, as creating a revocable principal-agent relationship between the consenting party and the intervener.[41]

This distinction is of substantive importance. It clarifies that while the legality of forcible intervention is sometimes discussed in terms of whether a "right" of intervention exists or not,[42] the prohibition on the use of force and state-sovereignty actually allude to the fact that such relationships, essentially, are closer to fiduciary relationships – in which the intervener acts as the trustee of the consenting party. This notion coincides with the emerging perception of the international community as bearing "responsibilities," rather than rights, concerning the protection of civilians in other states.[43] Indeed, a "right" of forcible intervention can only be asserted if one adopts the controversial view that certain situations, if considered *erga omnes* violations of international law, can give rise to such a right.[44]

As an agent, the intervener cannot pursue interests contrary to those of the consenting party; although it is unrealistic to expect – in contrast to expectations from domestic administrative bodies – that in the international system, the intervener will have absolutely no interests of its own. Thus, the limits of the intervener's authority to act are circumscribed by the scope of the consent, and can be extended only when other justifications, such as self-defense, are lawfully invoked. It is only within the confines of such justifications where the interests of the intervener can be translated into action. Furthermore, the intervening agent is bound by the treaty obligations of the consenting party: powers that the consenting party itself does not possess cannot be conferred to it.[45]

2.2 Internal consent power: between effective control and legitimism

The second meaning of the concept of consent alludes to the substantive question of *internal consent power* – meaning, the material consent-capacity of the *internal* actors.[46] Here, we assume that consent is genuine, and turn

41 For a brief explanation of principal-agent relationships *see* Arnold J. Goldman and William D. Sigismond, Business Law: Principles and Practices 401–402 (2010); *see also* Restatement (Second) of Agency §1 (1958).

42 *See, e.g.*, Jane Stromseth, *Rethinking Humanitarian Intervention: The Case for Incremental Change, in* Humanitarian Intervention: Ethical, Legal and Political Dilemmas 232, 245 (J.L. Holzgrefe and Robert O. Keohane eds., 2003).

43 *See* Chapter 8, sec. 2.2.

44 On *erga omnes* violations *see* Case Concerning The Barcelona Traction (Belgium v. Spain), 1970 I.C.J. 3, ¶¶33–34 (February 5); Legal Consequence of the Construction of a Wall in the Occupied Palestinian Territory (Advisory Opinion) 2004 I.C.J. 136, ¶155 (July 9).

45 *See* Hargrove, *supra* note 6, at 116–117; *Military Intervention, Regional Organizations, and Host-State Consent, supra* note 2, at 215.

46 Elsewhere, I have referred to the distinction between external genuineness and internal legitimacy as "procedural" versus "substantive" questions of consent. *See* Lieblich, *supra* note 40, at 344–346.

to analyze the legal implications of the consenting entity's characteristics. Namely, we consider whether it represents the state, or whether it gained, in any other way, status – or performs a function – that allows it to speak for a certain community. Essentially, questions of internal consent power are questions of recognition and legitimacy. As such, they give rise to many difficult dilemmas.

Logically, for legally valid consent to materialize – meaning, consent that can potentially serve to legitimize a forcible intervention – both elements of consent must exist. For instance, in a specific case, consent must not only be freely given, but also be expressed by an actor possessing internal consent power. In the latter context, international law's centuries-old "pendulum swing" between considerations of de facto effectiveness and *de jure* legitimacy as generators of rights has decisive legal importance.

The struggle between effective control and substantive legitimacy as determinants of rights – chief among them of sovereignty – has deep roots within the philosophy of international law. Prior to the French Revolution of 1789, the prevalent theory of sovereignty was based on legitimism, according to which sovereignty was a corollary of a divine or historic right of the ruler, and not of de facto reality.[47] Legitimism was closely linked to the universal jurisdiction of the Pope and the Holy Roman Emperor, thought to extend well beyond the territories that were actually under their physical control.[48]

However, already in the seventeenth and eighteenth centuries, the pioneers of international law had begun to explore a rival doctrine – in which sovereign power, as recognized on the international level, was attached to de facto control over territory. The emergence of this doctrine was a direct challenge to the ostensible universal jurisdiction of the Pope and Emperor, and correlated with the rise of states in Europe.[49] It stemmed from the understanding that the "subjectivity of value" prevails over natural, religious or monarchic sources of authority.[50] The most immediate result of the challenge to legitimism was the realization that revolutionary removal of monarchs can be legally justified under certain situations.[51] As noted by Lauterpacht, international jurists such as Grotius, Pufendorf, Bynkershoek and Vattel were thus willing to recognize the effective sovereignty of revolutionaries, even if temporarily. They saw, at large, the principle of effective control as a practical necessity to maintain

47 Thomas D. Grant, The Recognition of States: Law and Practice in Debate and Evolution 8 (1999).

48 Anne Orford, International Authority and the Responsibility to Protect 143–150 (2011).

49 *Id.* at 150.

50 *See* Martti Koskenniemi, The Politics of International Law 36 (2011).

51 *See, e.g.*, Emmerich De Vatell The Law of Nations ¶51 (1797), *available at* http://books.google.com; 1 Hugo Grotius, The Rights of War and Peace, Book 2, Ch. 25, §8 (William Whewell trans., 1853), *available at* http://books.google.com.

stability and an important aspect of the principle of non-intervention.[52] This link between effectiveness and non-intervention – connected, in later times, also to the principle of self-determination[53] – has been a recurring feature of the debate regarding questions of recognition and intervention throughout the centuries.[54]

Legitimism witnessed a doctrinal comeback in the beginning of the nineteenth century. The challenge posed by the French Revolution – in which an ancient monarchy was overthrown – and the subsequent Napoleonic Wars motivated the conservative powers of Europe to rejuvenate the concept.[55] The Holy Alliance – a conservative coalition of monarchies, which lasted roughly from 1815 until 1848 – sought to curtail revolutionary movements, at times by intervening in support of beleaguered rulers. This approach was in stark contrast to the general British policy of non-intervention, and thus declined with the increase of Britain's dominance.[56] Accordingly, legitimism eroded through the decades of the nineteenth century, as the effective control doctrine gained ground. Therefore, revolutionary governments, throughout the nineteenth century and the first half of the twentieth century – and especially after the fall of the great monarchies in 1918[57] – were not categorically denied recognition merely on counts of their revolutionary nature, nor due to their violent ascent to power.[58]

Thus, the effectiveness doctrine – a seemingly "amoral" perception of the rights of entities in international law – was adopted by prominent legal philosophers of the first half of the twentieth century, such as Hans Kelsen.[59] Indeed, this process corresponded with the character of the modern international system: as realistically commented by Lauterpacht, traditional legitimist tests for sovereignty have become "clearly illogical" in the new world, "in which all governments owe[d] their origin to a revolutionary event in a more or less distant past."[60]

52 *See* Hersch Lauterpacht, Recognition in International Law 99–102 (1948) (providing a summary of the approaches of the mentioned pioneers of international law); *see also* Brad R. Roth, Governmental Illegitimacy in International Law 136–137 (2001).

53 *See, e.g.*, Alex J. Bellamy, Responsibility to Protect 16 (2009) (regarding self-determination and non-intervention in the context of decolonization).

54 *See, e.g.*, Montague Bernard, On the Principle of Non-Intervention (1860).

55 *See* Roth, *supra* note 52, at 136, 142–144.

56 *See* Guglielmo Ferrero, Problems of Peace: From the Holy Alliance to the League of Nations 34–35 (1919); *see also* Grant, *supra* note 47, at 8–9; 1 Lassa Oppenheim, International Law, a Treatise: Peace §139 (2nd ed., 1912), *available at* http://books.google.com; Augustus Granville Stapleton, Intervention and Non-Intervention; or, The Foreign Policy of Great Britain from 1790 to 1865 27–37 (1866) (contrasting between the Holy Alliance and British policies).

57 Grant, *supra* note 47, at 9.

58 *See* Lauterpacht, *supra* note 52, at 103–108.

59 Hans Kelsen, General Theory of Law and State 220–221 (1961); *cited in* Roth, *supra* note 52, at 137.

60 Lauterpacht, *supra* note 52, at 105.

The principle of territorial effective control has thus trickled to virtually every field of international law that addressed the question of recognition rights and powers of entities, in internal armed conflicts or otherwise. It can be found, for instance, in the Montevideo Convention of 1933, which laid down the most authoritative pronunciation of the effective control approach towards the definition and recognition of states.[61] The belligerency and insurgency doctrines, which served as the main tools for the determination of the status of entities during internal armed conflict, were too based mainly on effectiveness criteria.[62]

However, as pendulum-swings go, triumphs of effectiveness have constantly led to legitimist reactions and vice versa. These reactions and counter-reactions were by no means limited to the old debate regarding monarchic legitimism. Roth identified four historical challenges to effectiveness in the last two centuries:[63] divine right legitimism (the Holy Alliance);[64] constitutional legitimism (the Tobar Doctrine);[65] Cold War ideological legitimism (Brezhnev and Reagan Doctrines);[66] and the concept of democratic legitimism, relating to the perception of democratic governance as a right.[67] It is also possible to identify trends of non-recognition of governments set up by external aggression;[68] as well as a growing "procedural" tendency towards regionalism and multilateralism when assessing parties to internal armed conflicts.[69] A major claim of this work is that in our context, a potential hybrid has emerged: one that recognizes the importance of effectiveness on the one hand, but binds this concept with substantive considerations of civilian protection. For now, however, it suffices to keep in mind that the rivalry between

61 Convention on the Rights and Duties of States (Montevideo Convention), December 26, 1933, 165 L.N.T.S. 19.

62 *See* Chapters 5–6.

63 Roth *supra* note 52, at 136–152.

64 *See also* Sean D. Murphy, *Democratic Legitimacy and Recognition, in* Democratic Governance and International Law 123, 140 (Gregory H. Fox and Brad R. Roth eds., 2000).

65 The Tobar Doctrine of 1907, accepted by many American states (including the US), denied recognition from governments seizing power unconstitutionally. *See* Roth, *supra* note 52, at 144–145; Murphy, *supra* note 64, at 141.

66 *See also,* Chapter 8, sec. 2.

67 Thomas M. Franck, *The Emerging Right to Democratic Governance,* 86 American Journal of International Law 46 (1992).

68 *See* Murphy, *supra* note 64, at 151.

69 Regionalism means, in this context, the deference to decisions by regional or sub-regional bodies. See, for instance, the universal non-recognition of Somaliland, which follows the policy of the African Union. Benjamin Farley, *Calling a State a State: Somaliland and International Recognition,* 24 Emory International Law Review 777, 809–815 (2011). Multilateralism refers to the general aversion from unilateral solutions to internal armed conflicts, exemplified, for instance, in the arguments of states rejecting Kosovo's 2008 unilateral declaration of independence. *See* the positions expressed in U.N. SCOR, 63rd Sess., 5839th mtg., U.N. Doc. S/PV.5839 (February 18, 2008).

effectiveness and legitimacy has been, for centuries, a key driving force behind international law's development. As such, this ever-present interaction affects our contemporary perception of the modalities of internal consent power.

3 Exemplifying the dynamics of intervention and consent: Congo 1996–2010

3.1 The first Congolese conflict, 1996–1997: the ousting of Mobutu

The tragic series of armed conflicts in the DRC demonstrates the different dynamics of intervention and consent in a complex contemporary setting. We shall not, for now, analyze the legality of the actions of the various parties; we shall only use this conflict – in a simplified manner and without addressing its root causes – as a factual exemplification for the dynamics of consensual interventions, thus facilitating the understanding of their different characteristics.[70]

Mobutu Sésé Seko ruled Zaire (today, the DRC) from 1965. In 1994, following the genocide committed by Hutu elements against the Tutsis in neighboring Rwanda, and the subsequent overthrow of the Hutu regime by Rwandan Tutsi warlord Paul Kagame, Hutu refugees fled to Zaire fearing retaliation by the new Tutsi government. Intermingled with the refugees were members of the extreme Hutu militias – the *interahamwe* – that have played a pivotal role in the Rwandan Genocide. The presence of genocidal elements in Eastern Zaire spawned a series of tragic conflicts which are yet to be resolved. These Hutu militias gained effective control over the refugee camps in east Zaire, and used them as bases to launch attacks against Tutsis in east Zaire and across the border into Rwanda. Doing so, they were supported to varying extents by Mobutu's army.

In late 1996, some of Mobutu's rivals formed the Alliance of Democratic Forces for the Liberation of Zaire (ADFL) – with encouragement and support from Rwanda, which became increasingly frustrated by the cross-border attacks launch against it from East Zaire.[71] Laurent-Desiré Kabila, a long-time foe of Mobutu, emerged as the ADFL's leader. Thereafter, the ADFL, supplemented by Rwandan (RPA)[72] and Ugandan forces, moved to weaken the *interahamwe* in East Zaire's refugee camps.[73]

70 For a more detailed presentation of these conflicts *see* Lieblich, *supra* note 40, at 350–357.

71 *See* International Crisis Group, *How Kabila Lost His Way: The Performance of Laurent Désiré Kabila's Government* 4, ICG Congo Report No. 3 (May 21, 1999); *see also* McNulty, *supra* note 12, at 174–179.

72 An organ of Rwandan president Kagame's political party, the Rwandan Patriotic Front. *See id.* at 177–179.

73 *See id.* at 180–181.

Capitalizing on their early successes in East Zaire, the opposition forces staged an assault westward toward Kinshasa – Zaire's capital – defeating Mobutu's government forces and the Rwandan Hutu militias supporting him. In subsequent months, Angolan troops also joined to aid the rebels, while Angolan dissidents (UNITA) joined to support Mobutu, since they enjoyed Mobutu's acquiescence to their use of Zaire's territory to stage attacks against Angola.[74] By mid-1997 Kabila's forces were on the outskirts of Kinshasa.[75] Mobutu fled the country and, on May 17, 1997, Kabila declared himself president and established an authoritarian regime, renaming the state the Democratic Republic of the Congo.

The first Congolese conflict exemplifies some of the complex dynamics of consensual intervention. For instance, most of the interventions in this conflict involve retroactive consent – instances in which a party's consent was granted *ex post*, after the intervening power has already made forcible moves in the target state's territory. Such cases, naturally, raise grave concerns of coercion or pretext. The retroactivity of the opposition's consent, at this stage of the Congolese conflict, is manifested in the fact that the intervening powers (except Angola) were actively involved in the formation of the ADFL – the same opposition body that they came later to support militarily. Obviously, this raises serious questions regarding the independent capacity of the ADFL to express consent (setting aside the issue of legality). Retroactive consent can be found also in the relations between the government and the *Interahamwe* and UNITA, since these elements were already present in Zaire when the conflict started. These relations are complicated by the fact that these parties are non-state actors. As aforementioned, consent can come in many forms and expressed proactively or retroactively, provided that it is genuine. Instances of retroactive consent will obviously require a high threshold of proof that the consent was not coerced, perhaps giving rise to a strong presumption against the intervening party.

3.2 The second Congolese conflict, 1998–2003: withdrawal of consent and invitation of other powers

The end of the first conflict saw Laurent Kabila installed as president of the DRC, while many foreign forces were still present on its soil. On July 27, 1998, Kabila ordered all foreign forces – and Rwandan forces in particular – to leave the country:

> The Supreme Commander of the Congolese National Armed Forces, the Head of State of the Republic of the Congo and the Minister of

74 *See* McQueen, *supra* note 15, at 104–105.

75 *See* Thom, *supra* note 14.

> National Defence, advises the Congolese people that he has just terminated, with effect from this Monday 27 July 1998, the Rwandan military presence which has assisted us during the period of the country's liberation … he would like to thank all of the Rwandan people for the solidarity they have demonstrated to date. … This marks the end of the presence of all foreign military forces in the Congo.[76]

However, Rwanda and Uganda were unwilling to withdraw their forces.[77] Uganda claimed that the Kabila did not actually withdraw the consent to its presence, namely because Uganda was not mentioned explicitly in his statement.[78] The withdrawal of consent by Kabila was perceived by the Tutsis of East Congo as a threat, since they relied on support from Rwanda. This prompted them to form the Rally for Congolese Democracy (RCD) and a renewed armed conflict erupted on August 1998.[79] With the active participation of Rwanda and Uganda, the rebel forces – mainly the RCD, the newly formed and Uganda-supported Movement for the Liberation of Congo (MLC) and anti-Kabila elements from within the former ADFL – swiftly took over resource-rich areas in Eastern Congo. The DRC, in retaliation, sought the support of Hutu militias (known as the Democratic Forces for the Liberation of Rwanda (FDLR) since 2000) – the same elements that supported, in the first conflict, President Kabila's arch-enemy Mobutu – and urged them to retaliate against Tutsis.

Thus, this stage of the Congo conflict involved a withdrawal of consent by the DRC, which was ignored by the intervening powers; and, once again, retroactive consent to Ugandan and Rwandan intervention – granted by the new rebel groups. When Kabila's government started to lose ground, it turned to invite Namibia, Zimbabwe, Angola and Chad to assist it.[80] These circumstances led to the eruption of a multi-party war by September 1998.[81]

The Zimbabwean and Namibian intervention in favor of Kabila was based on proactive consent, as neither of these state's forces were forcibly on DRC territory beforehand;[82] the same can be said of the intervention of

76 Armed Activities on the Territory of the Congo (DRC v. Uganda), 2005 I.C.J. 168, ¶49 (December 19).

77 *See* McNulty, *supra* note 12, at 182–183.

78 Another claim by Uganda was that the DRC's consent to its intervention was renewed in the Lusaka Agreement of 1999. *See* DRC v. Uganda, *supra* note 76, ¶¶92–105.

79 McNulty, *supra* note 12, at 183–184.

80 For a detailed survey of the various players in the second Congolese conflict and their interests, *see* Gary Cleaver and Simon Massey, *D.R.C.: Africa's Scramble for Africa, in* African Interventionist States, *supra* note 12, at 193.

81 *See*, International Crisis Group, *Congo At War: A Briefing of the Internal and External Players in the Central African Conflict* 6, ICG Congo Report No. 2 1–3, 14–25 (November 17, 1998).

82 *See id.* at 20–22.

Chad.[83] Conversely, Angola's intervention was arguably based on retroactive consent, as Angolan forces assisted Kabila previously in the overthrow of Mobutu's regime.[84] All of these forces were invited to intervene explicitly.[85]

Uganda and Rwanda justified their actions on counts other than mere consent, exemplifying the dynamics of multiple justifications as discussed above. The intervening powers (mainly Rwanda) also raised concerns of genocide against the Tutsis in DRC – essentially invoking the humanitarian intervention doctrine, even if not by name;[86] and self-defense against continuing cross-border actions by various militias.[87] Uganda has also invoked a counter-intervention claim, alleging that the DRC has invited Sudan – Uganda's rival – to support it in various conspiracies with opposition groups against Uganda.[88]

The Lusaka Agreement, concluded in 1999 in an attempt to end the conflict, did not hold. However, it called for the establishment of a UN peacekeeping mission (United Nations Organization Mission in the Democratic Republic of the Congo – MONUC), which, upon its establishment, was not mandated to use force.[89] In January 2001 Laurent Kabila was assassinated, to be replaced by his son Joseph.[90] Throughout 2002 Joseph Kabila managed to solidify his rule over the DRC, much with the help of his foreign allies.[91] In July and September 2002 Rwanda and Uganda respectively signed a peace treaty with the DRC. Subsequently, Rwanda withdrew its troops. On December 17, 2002 the various Congolese parties signed an agreement to form a transitional government, thus, *de jure*, bringing an end to this stage of the Congolese conflict.[92] Uganda withdrew its troops on June 2, 2003. A transitional government was formed in the DRC in July 2003. However, as we shall see, parts of the state still remain in conflict, in varying intensities.

83 *See id.* at 25.

84 *See id.* at 22.

85 *See id.* at 20; *see also* McQueen, *supra* note 15, at 108.

86 *See Congo at War, supra* note 81, at 6. This example highlights the relation between humanitarian intervention and consent. We discuss this in Chapter 10, sec. 4.

87 *See Congo at War, supra* note 81, at 14, 16; DRC v. Uganda, *supra* note 76, ¶¶106–109.

88 *See Congo at War, supra* note 81, at 17–19; DRC v. Uganda, *supra* note 76, ¶¶120–127.

89 MONUC was established in S.C. Res. 1279, U.N. Doc. S/RES/1279 (November 30, 1999), pursuant to Article 11(a) of the Lusaka Agreement. Although the agreement asked for a Chapter VII resolution, peacekeeping forces are usually operating under Chapter VI, and this is indeed the chapter according to which MONUC was initially founded.

90 International Crisis Group, *From Kabila to Kabila, Prospects for Peace in the Congo* 1, ICG Africa Report No. 27 (March 16, 2001).

91 *See* McQueen, *supra* note 15, at 107.

92 International Crisis Group, *The Kivus: The Forgotten Crucible of the Congo Conflict* i–ii, Africa Report No. 56 (January 24, 2003).

3.3 The conflict in the Kivus, 2004–2010: pro-government intervention by Rwanda and forcible MONUC operations

The conflict in the Kivus was a direct continuation of the second Congolese conflict, the end of which did not see a solution to the ethnic tensions between FDLR forces in East Congo and Tutsi groups supported by Rwanda, supplemented by economic interests.[93]

Laurent Nkunda was a commander in the Rwandan-backed RCD during the second Congolese conflict. After that conflict ended *de jure* in 2003, and following a brief stint with the new transitional government's forces, Nkunda formed a new force in the Eastern Congo provinces of the Kivus – the National Congress for the Defence of the People (CNDP).[94] Nkunda's newly formed organization, much like the RCD before it, received aid from Rwanda – albeit covertly.[95] In 2004, after claiming that genocide against the Tutsis in East Congo was taking place (an allegation dismissed by the UN), the CNDP took control of the city of Bukavu in South Kivu, to withdraw under international pressure.[96] In subsequent years, Nkunda continued to build his forces, while occasionally clashing with the government forces and calling for the overthrow of Kabila and the removal of FDLR forces from the DRC.

In 2007 the conflict intensified, as MONUC forces occasionally assisted the DRC against the CNDP. In 2008, clashes between the CNDP and the FDLR worsened. In the end of that year, when Nkunda's forces took over a strategic area in North Kivu, MONUC forces attacked the CNDP with heavy weaponry, with little success. Nonetheless, MONUC's operations were conducted, at this stage, under a Chapter VII mandate for the protection of civilians, requiring it to work in "close cooperation" with the DRC.[97] The DRC, accordingly, has viewed MONUC's forcible actions favorably, and wholeheartedly consented to them. In the discussion leading to the adoption of UNSC Resolution 1856, in which MONUC's mandate was significantly expanded, the representative of the DRC expressed his government's consent to this move:

> [T]he Government of the Democratic Republic of the Congo welcomes this new resolution. We are especially pleased that MONUC

93 *See* International Crisis Group, *The Congo's Transition Is Failing: Crisis in the Kivus* 8, Africa Report No. 91 (March 30, 2005).

94 *See id.* at 4–6.

95 *See* International Crisis Group, *Congo: A Comprehensive Strategy to Disarm the FDLR* 3–4, Africa Report No. 151 (July 9, 2009).

96 *The Congo's Transition Is Failing*, *supra* note 93, at 6, 11–12, 19–20.

97 MONUC's mandate, as expanded in Security Council Resolutions 1843 and 1856 (December 22, 2008), required it to protect civilian population. *See* S.C. Res. 1843, U.N. Doc. S/RES/1843 (November 20, 2008); S.C. Res. 1856, U.N. Doc. S/RES/1856 (December 22, 2008); *see also U.N. Joins Battle with Congo Rebels*, B.B.C. News, October 27, 2008, http://news.bbc.co.uk/2/hi/africa/7692932.stm.

> missions, in close cooperation with the Government, are being strengthened and consolidated in the protection of the civilian population.... The Congolese Government and people therefore expect these new United Nations forces to be deployed rapidly.[98]

Thus, MONUC's forcible intervention was a Chapter VII-based intervention, supplemented by explicit consent on part of the DRC. As we shall elaborate shortly, while the UNSC has power to order such interventions even without such consent, it would have been far more difficult politically, and to some extent, also legally.

In parallel with the strengthening of MONUC, the DRC invited Rwanda on December 5, 2008 to intervene on in its behalf. The premise of the surprising deal was that Rwanda would be allowed to act against the FDLR in the DRC's territory, and in return, it would cease supporting Nkunda, and assist in removing him from influence. From that point on, the CNDP was effectively neutralized, Nkunda was replaced, and CNDP troops began integrating into the DRC's armed forces.[99] On January 20, 2009, joint military operations by Rwanda and the DRC commenced, and two days later Nkunda was arrested in Rwanda.[100] On February 25 the joint operations officially ended, and Rwandan troops subsequently withdrew.[101] These joint operations by the DRC and Rwanda represent a relatively clear cut proactive and explicit consensual forcible intervention by a state, on behalf of a government.

On March 23 of that year, the CNDP signed a peace treaty with the government.[102] However, the FDLR was only partially weakened by the joint operations.[103] In May 2009 the FDLR launched deadly attacks against civilians,[104] spawning military operations by the DRC and MONUC, which ended in December 2009.[105] Joint military action by the DRC and MONUC continued in 2010.

However, in April 2010, Kabila called for the termination of MONUC's mandate, and demanded the complete withdrawal of all foreign forces by mid-2011. Nonetheless, MONUC's mandate (renamed United Nations Organization Stabilization Mission in the Democratic Republic of the

98 U.N. SCOR, 63rd Sess., 6055th mtg. at 9, U.N. Doc. S/PV.6055 (December 22, 2008).

99 *See A Comprehensive Strategy to Disarm the FDLR, supra* note 95, at 2, 3–6.

100 *Id.* at 6.

101 *Id.* at 9.

102 Peace Agreement between the Government and Le Congrès National Pour La Defense Du Peuple (CNDP), March 23, 2009, *available at* www.iccwomen.org/publications/Peace_Agreement_between_the_Government_and_the_CNDP.pdf.

103 *See A Comprehensive Strategy to Disarm the FDLR, supra* note 95, at 9–13.

104 *Id.* at 12.

105 *See U.N. Ends Criticized Congo Campaign*, B.B.C. News, December 16, 2009, http://news.bbc.co.uk/2/hi/africa/8417450.stm.

Congo – MONUSCO)[106] has been extended until June 2012.[107] The interaction between the DRC and the UNSC mandated forces on its territory exemplify the relation between consent and Chapter VII interventions, which we will now turn to address.

4 Consent and Security Council authorized interventions: a complex interaction

4.1 Chapter VII resolutions and consent

Arguably, forcible interventions authorized by the UNSC, adopted under Chapter VII of the UN Charter, should not fall with the scope of this work – since these are legally based on the existence of a threat to international peace and security, and are thus oblivious to consent. However – and although the question of consent is far more acute when UNSC authorization is absent – closer analysis demonstrates that Chapter VII interventions are not entirely irrelevant to the analysis of the question of consensual intervention.

As we have seen, during the Kivus conflict, the DRC has explicitly consented to the expansion of MONUC's mandate.[108] Had the DRC expressed objection to these resolutions would the legal situation be different? The *prima facie* answer is negative. As aforementioned, Chapter VII, unsurprisingly, does not require consent as a *legal* precondition for enforcement measures, once a threat to peace, breach of peace or aggression has occurred.[109] Indeed, the UNSC, in its relevant resolutions, did not refer explicitly to the DRC's consent as a legal basis for MONUC's forcible intervention.[110]

106 MONUC was renamed MONUSCO on May 28, 2010, with the adoption of S.C. Res. 1925, U.N. Doc. SC/RES/1925 (May 28, 2010).

107 S.C. Res. 1991, U.N. Doc. S/RES/1991 (June 28, 2011).

108 *See* U.N. SCOR, 63rd Sess., 6055th mtg. at 9–10, U.N. Doc. S/PV.6055 (December 22, 2008).

109 *See* UN Charter art. 39. In general, Chapter VII enforcement measures override state consent, whether the relevant government is a potential beneficiary of the intervention or a target of it. *See* Oscar Schachter, *The Right of States to Use Armed Force*, 82 Michigan Law Review 1620, 1621 (1984). However, UNSC "recommendations" under Chapter VI, naturally, require consent in order to materialize. *See* D.W. Bowett, United Nations Forces: A Legal Study 412–413 (1964). Some posit that the sending of neutral peacekeeping forces – whether through Chapter VI or VII – always requires consent by all relevant parties, since these forces, inherently, cannot enter a state's territory forcibly. *See, e.g.*, Jeremy Levitt, *African Interventionist States and International Law*, *in* African Interventionist States, *supra* note 12, at 15, 21. What is clear, however, is that the UNGA, even when acting under the Uniting for Peace procedure, cannot send peacekeeping forces without consent of the relevant state. *See* Bowett, at 415–417; Orford, *supra* note 48, at 66; Nicholas Tsagourias, *Consent, Neutrality/Impartiality and the Use of Force in Peacekeeping: Their Constitutional Dimension*, 11 Journal of Conflict and Security Law 465 (2009).

110 *See* S.C. Res. 1843 and 1856, *supra* note 97.

Nevertheless, in practice, the UNSC virtually always seeks the consent of the territorial state when authorizing forcible enforcement measures in the context of an internal conflict.[111] This tendency was evident in the debate on possible intervention in Darfur, where lack of government consent on part of Sudan seems to have played a significant part in UNSC decision making.[112] Indeed, even the 1999 Australian-led operation in East Timor, effectively leading to the territory's removal from Indonesian occupation, was conducted with Indonesia's consent (although this conflict was not internal per se).[113] In fact, the UNSC has not explicitly authorized a partial, forcible intervention in an internal armed conflict *against* the will of an incumbent, functioning and recognized government, until the 2011 intervention in the Libyan conflict.[114] Even in that exceptional case, the UNSC was careful, in practice, to tailor its resolution around the demand of the Libyan opposition and the Arab League that any forcible action will be conducted "with no boots on the ground," meaning, with no use of ground forces.[115] Accordingly, Resolution 1973 authorized all necessary measures to protect civilians, "while excluding a foreign occupation force of any form on any part of Libyan territory."[116]

With the impending defeat of the forces loyal to Libyan ruler Al-Qadhafi, and the widespread recognition of the opposing NTC as the lawful authority of Libya, the UNSC was quick to link the continuing mandate granted in Resolution 1973 to the consent of the new authorities. It stressed, in Resolution 2009, that the termination of the mandate would be possible, "as appropriate and when circumstances permit," "in *consultation* with the Libyan authorities."[117] The mandate for forcible measures was finally terminated in October 2011, after the "Declaration of Liberation" by the NTC.[118]

The tendency of the UNSC to seek consent, even when authorizing a Chapter VII-based forcible intervention, is hardly surprising. Consent

111 *See* Alex J. Bellamy, *Libya and the Responsibility to Protect: The Exception and the Norm*, Ethics and International Affairs 1, 1–2 (2011).

112 Bellamy, *supra* note 53, at 149–153.

113 S.C. Res. 1246, prmbl, U.N. Doc. S/RES/1246 (September 15, 1999); *see* Tom J. Farer, *Humanitarian Intervention Before and After 9/11*, *in* Humanitarian Intervention: Ethical, Legal and Political Dilemmas, *supra* note 42, at 53, 57 n. 15, 57–58.

114 *See Libya and the Responsibility to Protect: The Exception and the Norm, supra* note 111, at 1–2.

115 Kareem Fahim and David D. Kirkpatrick, *Libyan Rebels Said to Debate Seeking U.N. Airstrikes*, New York Times, March 1, 2011, www.nytimes.com/2011/03/02/world/africa/02libya.html; Ethan Bronner and David E. Sanger, *Arab League Endorses No-Flight Zone Over Libya*, New York Times, March 12, 2011, www.nytimes.com/2011/03/13/world/middleeast/13libya.html?_r=1&hp.

116 S.C. Res 1973. ¶4, U.N. Doc. S/RES/1973 (March 17, 2011) (authorizing forcible intervention in Libya).

117 S.C. Res 2009, ¶20, U.N. Doc. S/RES/2009 (September 16, 2011) (emphasis added).

118 S.C. Res 2011, U.N. Doc. S/RES/2011 (October 27, 2011).

naturally facilitates the operation; it can moreover bolster the political legitimacy of the authorizing resolution. Indeed, Bowett, while acknowledging this tendency, explained it in terms of "political wisdom" rather than "legal necessity."[119] However, upon a closer look, consent can also fortify the *legal* merits of the action, on five levels.

First, it can mitigate challenges arising from the obligations the UNSC owes to the principle of non-intervention, as entrenched in Article 2(7) of the UN Charter.[120] Indeed, if the Council can link its enforcement actions to the consent of an element within the target state that enjoys substantial *legitimacy* – setting aside, for now, the nature of such legitimacy – it would be harder to claim that the action violates the principle of non-intervention in its substantive sense, as the latter is discussed in Chapter 2.[121] Conversely, if a legitimate entity within the target-state explicitly *objects* to a Chapter VII intervention – although it would supposedly benefit it – it is hard to envision that the Council will proceed, or indeed be justified in doing so,[122] with its enforcement measures, unless an utter humanitarian catastrophe is taking place.

For instance, imagine that during the discussions regarding the 2011 Chapter VII intervention in Côte d'Ivoire,[123] Alassane Ouattara – recognized internationally as the country's lawful president – had unequivocally proclaimed that his standoff with lingering ruler Laurent Gbagbo should be resolved strictly by Ivorians, without any international involvement. In such a case, and in the circumstances of the Ivorian crisis, it seems implausible that the Council would have authorized an action meant ultimately to reinstate Ouattara, since it would be not only viewed as a blunt

119 Bowett, *supra* note 109, at 412.

120 Article 2(7) provides that the principle of non-intervention "shall not prejudice" enforcement actions taken pursuant to a Chapter VII resolution. However, this does not mean that that the principle ceases to apply altogether in such cases. This notion is reflected in UNSC practice: many Chapter VII resolutions affirm the "sovereignty" and "independence" of target states, *notwithstanding* the interventions they authorize. *See, e.g.*, S.C. Res 1511, ¶13, U.N. Doc. S/RES/1511 (October 16, 2003) ("authorizing" a multinational force in Iraq, while reaffirming "the sovereignty and territorial integrity of Iraq"); S,C. Res. 1843, *supra* note 97 (expanding the mandate of MONUC and reaffirming "its commitment to respect the sovereignty, territorial integrity and political independence of the Democratic Republic of the Congo"). For a similar argument, *see* Djura Ninčić, The Problem of Sovereignty in the Charter and in the Practice of the United Nations 175–176 (1970); *see also* Bowett, *supra* note 109, at 423–424.

121 Sec. 2.

122 *Compare* Jeff McMahan, *Humanitarian Intervention, Consent and Proportionality, in* Ethics and Humanity: Themes from the Philosophy of Jonathan Glover 44, 54 (N. Ann Davis *et al.* eds., 2010) ("whenever an external agent undertakes a humanitarian intervention in the absence of compelling evidence that it is welcomed by the intended beneficiaries, it takes a significant moral risk.").

123 S.C. Res. 1975, U.N. Doc. S/RES/1975 (March 30, 2011). For the details of the Ivorian situation *see* Chapter 9, sec. 1.3.

intervention in the internal affairs of Côte d'Ivoire, but would also be entirely counterproductive. Relying on a formally "impartial" mandate for the forcible protection of civilians, as was in fact done,[124] would not have sufficed in our hypothetical: since Gbagbo was the obvious culprit, the intervention would have still been perceived as conducted in the benefit of Ouattara.

In the same vein, one can analyze the 1994 UNSC authorized intervention in Haiti in light of the dynamics of consent, or its absence. After the democratically elected president Jean Bertrand Aristide was ousted by a military junta in 1991, he was reluctant to receive any forcible external assistance.[125] This disinclination might have accounted for the fact that the intervention in Haiti was prescribed by the UNSC only three years later[126] – and two days after Aristide expressed his despair regarding the prospects of a political solution, and requested that the international community take "prompt and decisive action" against the junta.[127] Thus, it is hard to argue that Aristide's consent was irrelevant to the UNSC's decision to authorize forcible intervention.[128] This seems true for political reasons, but also, as aforementioned, when assessing enforcement measures in light of Article 2(7) of the UN Charter.

Second, the role of consent in the legitimization of UNSC-mandated interventions is somewhat contingent upon our understanding of the nature of that body. Indeed, the traditional perception views the UNSC as enjoying almost unfettered discretion on two levels: in determining that a threat to international peace exists, as well as in prescribing measures in response.[129] Should this be our understanding of the role of the Council, consent indeed seems to play a minor normative part, if at all, in its considerations.

124 *See* Chapter 9, sec. 1.3.

125 David Wippman, *Pro-democratic Intervention by Invitation, in* Democratic Governance and International Law, *supra* note 64, at 293, 301.

126 S.C. Res. 940, U.N. Doc. S/RES/940 (July 31, 1994).

127 Letter Dated 29 July 1994 from the President of the Republic of Haiti addressed to the Secretary-General, U.N. Doc. S/1994/905 (July 29, 1994).

128 *See* Michael Byers and Simon Chesterman, "*You, the People*": *Pro-Democratic Intervention in International Law, in* Democratic Governance and International Law, *supra* note 64, at 259, 287.

129 See discussion in Antōnios Tzanakópoulos, Disobeying the Security Council: Countermeasures against Wrongful Sanctions 60–64 (2011); on the reluctance of the ICJ to exercise judicial review of Security Council Chapter VII measures *see* Eyal Benvenisti, *The Interplay Between Actors as a Determinant of the Evolution of Administrative Law in International Institutions* 68 Law and Contemporary Problems 319, 336 (2005); *see also* Jose E. Alvarez, *Judging the Security Council*, 90 American Journal of International Law 1 (1996); Dapo Akande, *The International Court of Justice and the Security Council: Is there Room for Judicial Control of Decisions of the Political Organs of the United Nations?* 46 International and Comparative Law Quarterly 309 (1997).

However, it can also be argued that the Council's discretion is limited by proportionality and necessity requirements. These can be deduced from the text of the UN Charter;[130] from the emerging idea of global administrative law, which attributes to the Council executive characteristics, spawning, in turn, administrative-legal limitations on its discretion;[131] or, at least as a residual claim, traced to well established notions of just-war theory that arguably ought to guide the Council's discretion.[132] If we accept such approaches, deliberation with internal entities – *a fortiori* their consent – reflects a "proper" process of administrative discretion, essential for a "reasonable" or "rational" decision;[133] it furthermore contributes to the action's legitimacy from a just-war perspective. For instance, US President Obama has highlighted several justifications for the 2011 military action in Libya – that could correspond with classic just-war conditions[134] – among them: (a) the imminent danger of violence on a horrific scale (just cause and last resort); (b) the unique ability to stop the atrocities (reasonable prospects of success); (c) the existence of an international mandate (a version of right authority); and (d) the plea for help from the Libyan people (consent as augmentation for other just-war justifications).[135] We shall elaborate on consent and just-war, in a related context, in Chapter 10.

Third, in situations where the initial forcible action was *not* mandated by the UNSC, consent by the target state can, perhaps, immune the Council from claims that by authorizing the deployment of international forces in a later resolution, it has *ex post* legalized the initial unlawful action. Thus, noting the existence of state consent, in such cases, can allow the Council to distance itself from the ostensibly unlawful justification previously given. We can think this way with regards to UNSC Resolution 1546, adopted in the context of the Iraq invasion, which can be understood as conditioning the presence of a multinational force (effectively, the Coalition forces) in Iraq, on the consent of the Iraqi Interim Government:

130 Tzanakópoulos, *supra* note 129, at 64–67 (identifying such requirements in the relations between Articles 39 and 41 of the UN Charter).

131 *See* Benedict Kingsbury *et al.*, *The Emergence of Global Administrative Law*, 68 L. & Cont. Prob. 15 (2005) (introducing the concept of global administrative law, *inter alia* in the context of the UNSC).

132 *See generally* Michael W. Brough *et al.*, *Introduction*, *in* Rethinking the Just War Tradition 1, 1–3 (Michael W. Brough *et al.* eds., 2007).

133 *See* M. Elizabeth Magill and Daniel R. Ortiz, *Comparative Positive Political Theory*, *in* Comparative Administrative Law 134, 139–145 (Susan Rose-Ackerman and Peter L. Lindseth eds., 2010).

134 *See* Chapter 10, sec. 4.3.

135 Barack Obama, Remarks at National Defense University, Washington, D.C. (March 28, 2011) *available at* www.whitehouse.gov/the-press-office/2011/03/28/remarks-president-address-nation-libya; *see also* James Pattison, *The Ethics of Humanitarian Intervention in Libya*, Ethics and International Affairs 1, 3 (2011).

> [The Security Council] [*n*] *otes* that the presence of the multinational force in Iraq is *at the request* of the incoming Interim Government of Iraq and *therefore reaffirms* the authorization for the multinational force under unified command established under resolution 1511 (2003), having regard to the letters annexed to this resolution.[136]

Fourth, receiving state consent can reconcile, to a certain extent, the need to forcibly intervene in internal armed conflicts with the principle of "sovereign equality," as enshrined in Article 2(1) of the UN Charter, which applies also to the UNSC.[137]

Fifth, lack of consent (or its withdrawal) might arguably result in the subjection of intervening UN Forces to occupation law under IHL, unless, perhaps, stipulated otherwise by the UNSC.[138] While the obtainment of such status has no direct bearing on *jus ad bellum* legality, it can significantly narrow the forces' transformative powers within the target state, and also diminish their perceived legitimacy – due to the negative connotations of occupation.[139]

In light of the above, while lack of consent – *in itself* – is not sufficient to annul the Council's authority to take such actions,[140] consent might add to the political and legal legitimacy of Chapter VII interventions. Once we realize that consent plays (and should play) a part in UNSC considerations, we can consider whose consent makes a difference and under what circumstances.

4.2 Chapter VII resolutions and withdrawal of consent

As discussed in section 2.1, withdrawal of consent to a forcible intervention is virtually an absolute right. Does the same rule apply when the intervening force is mandated by the UNSC? Returning to the Kivus conflict, in April 2010 the DRC called for the termination of MONUC, and demanded the withdrawal of all foreign forces by mid-2011.[141] Can such actions alter the legal position of operations like MONUC? Recall that the establishment of MONUC was requested explicitly by the parties in the Lusaka Agreement of 1999.[142] Accordingly, UNSC Resolution 1279 has noted this request, and established MONUC, mainly mandating it to conduct

136 S.C. Res. 1546, *supra* note 32, ¶9 (emphasis added).

137 Jennifer Welsh, *Civilian Protection in Libya: Putting Coercion and Controversy Back into RtoP*, Ethics and International Affairs 1, 4 (2011).

138 *See* Expert Meeting on Occupation, *supra* note 2, at 79–82.

139 *Id.* at 84.

140 Bowett, *supra* note 109, at 414–415.

141 *See The United Nations and Congo: Unloved for Trying to Keep the Peace*, The Economist, April 17, 2010, www.economist.com/node/15912838.

142 *See supra*, note 89.

missions of liaison, observation and information gathering.[143] Resolution 1279 was based on Chapter VI of the Charter, which authorizes the Council to make recommendations. Therefore, in this initial stage, since MONUC was established as a *neutral* peacekeeping force, the DRC's consent – and in practice, the opposition's consent as well – was indeed constitutive with regards to its mandate.[144]

However, since 2003, MONUC has been operating under a Chapter VII mandate,[145] which was expanded in 2008 to include forcible actions.[146] From this point on, and since a threat to international peace and security was established, the DRC's consent, as aforementioned, was not legally necessary, in the strict sense, to authorize the forcible operations by MONUC. Therefore, it must follow that a withdrawal of such consent could not pre-empt the authority of the UNSC, although the initial establishment of MONUC was done pursuant to the request of the parties to the Lusaka agreement. On the other hand, UNSC Resolution 1856 provided that MONUC's expanded mandate will be exercised in "close cooperation" with the DRC[147] – meaning, the operation was bound, in practice, to the DRC's consent. The UNSC's general tendency to seek consent has been discussed above. When a UNSC resolution goes further and explicitly refers to the consent or "cooperation" of a party in relation to specific operations – a withdrawal of consent can indeed implicate the operation's mandate.

In Resolution 1925 (and subsequently in Resolution 1991) the UNSC extended the mandate of MONUC, now renamed MONUSCO.[148] The name change was explained on counts of the "new phase" in the DRC.[149] While not altering MONUSCO's mandate to use force, the Council called for "enhanced dialogue and partnership" with the DRC; authorized the withdrawal of up to 2000 UN troops; and decided to continuously review MONUSCO's mandate in accordance with future assessments by the United Nations Secretary General (UNSG) and the DRC.[150] Therefore, while Kabila's initial demand to terminate MONUC was not fulfilled, his position still affected – to some extent – the mandate of UN forces in the DRC.

143 S.C. Res. 1279, *supra* note 89, prmbl., ¶¶ 4–5.

144 Chapter VI recommendations, by nature, require the consent of those to whom the recommendation is addressed. *See supra* note 109.

145 MONUC's mandate was revised to a Chapter VII one in S.C. Res. 1484, U.N. Doc. S/RES/1484 (May 30, 2003).

146 S.C. Res. 1843, *supra* note 97.

147 S.C. Res. 1856, *supra* note 97.

148 S.C. Res. 1925, *supra* note 106; S.C. Res. 1991, *supra* note 107.

149 S.C. Res. 1925, *supra* note 106, ¶¶1–3.

150 *Id.* ¶7, ¶12.

In sum, and unlike the legal situation regarding intervention by states, withdrawal of consent, in itself, does not negate the UNSC's authority when conducting a forcible intervention under Chapter VII, although it might result in the triggering of occupation law under IHL.[151] However, in cases where the Council itself binds the mandate of the UN forces with a requirement of cooperation or consent by the target state, a withdrawal of consent might require a new Security Council resolution. Having clarified, hopefully, the modalities and dynamics of consensual forcible intervention, we shall now proceed to enquire further into the concept's foundations, by exploring the notions of internal armed conflict and forcible intervention.

151 *See supra*, note 138.

2 The concepts of intervention and internal armed conflict

1 A legal discourse of intervention

Due to the illusive nature of the term "intervention," a few distinctions should be made prior to its discussion. The first requires the understanding that intervention can mean different things across different disciplines. It can be addressed, namely – but not only – on the ethical, strategic or legal levels.[1] The first level asks when it is morally right to intervene,[2] while the second analyzes when and why do interventions occur, and what are the conditions for their success.[3] The analysis of these questions is mainly conducted by philosophers and political scientists, respectively. The legal discourse on intervention, however, is concerned with the attempt to outline the circumstances, if at all, where states or organizations have the *legal* power, responsibility, right or duty to intervene.[4] It analyzes the sources of international law, in attempt to circumscribe a set of normative rules and principles. This aspect is the main focus of this work.

While the above disciplines might seem far apart, they often intertwine.[5] The legal dimension of intervention interacts with the other dimensions – which interact also with each other.[6] For instance, to the extent that we

1 *Compare* James N. Rosenau, *Intervention as a Scientific Concept*, 13 Journal of Conflict Resolution 149 (1969).

2 For such questions, *see, e.g.*, John Stuart Mill, *A Few Words on Non-Intervention* (1859), *in* Dissertations and Discussions 238 (1882), *available at* http://google.books.com; Michael Walzer, Just and Unjust Wars: A Moral Argument with Historical Illustrations 86–109 (4th ed., 2006).

3 *See, e.g.*, The International Dimensions on Internal Conflict (Michael E. Brown, ed., 2001); Peacemaking and Peacekeeping for the New Century (Olara A. Otunu and Michael W. Doyle eds., 1998).

4 *See, generally*, Simon Chesterman, Just War or Just Peace? Humanitarian Intervention in International Law (2001).

5 *Compare* Rosenau, *supra* note 1, at 151.

6 For instance, when adopting a *utilitarian* standpoint, an intervention would only be *moral* where it is *strategically* effective. Thus, Mill, true to his utilitarian approach, outlines a *moral* framework to intervention which requires that it would be likely to achieve the desired consequences. *See* Mill, *supra* note 2; *see also* Michael W. Doyle, Ways of War and Peace 395 (1997) (addressing Mill's view in the wider context of the liberal approach towards intervention and non-intervention).

accept that ethics can play a part in the interpretation of open-textured legal norms,[7] the interpretation of international rules concerning intervention can interact with the ethical approach to intervention. Furthermore, concepts such as necessity and proportionality, which reflect, to some extent, strategic questions – constitute also an integral part of classic just-war criteria, which inform the traditional ethical assessment of intervention; and, moreover, they are also considerations that must be taken into account in the exercise of executive discretion by international functions.[8]

The legal discussion of intervention must first make a preliminary distinction, essential for its clarity. When we use the term intervention, we may refer to two different meanings. The first refers to the *physical*, or descriptive sense. Thus, whenever a state engages parties in an internal armed conflict – whether or not by invitation or consent of a certain party; by forcible or non-forcible measures; lawfully or unlawfully – it *intervenes physically* in the conflict. A physical intervention can be defined as a "finite and temporary" phenomenon; beginning in the moment when "conventional modes of conduct are abandoned"; and ending when "the conventional modes are restored or the convention-breaking mode becomes conventional through persistent use."[9] Indeed, in the descriptive sense, short of the adoption of a pure neutral stance – which in itself could be sometimes construed as a type of intervention[10] – any action (or omission) by a state regarding events that take place within another state, ranging from utterances of officials to military invasions, can be theoretically considered as acts of intervention.

The second aspect of the term intervention is in the *normative*-prescriptive sense: meaning, the unlawful interference or encroachment upon the territorial integrity or internal political affairs of another state.[11] This meaning refers to the centuries-old principle of non-intervention – usually traced to the 1648 Treaty of Westphalia – which is entrenched in

7 *See* Walzer, *supra* note 2, at xx–xxii. On the distinction between legality and ethics in the context of intervention *see*, e.g., Michael W. Doyle, *The Folly of Protection*, Foreign Affairs (March 20, 2011), *available at* www.foreignaffairs.com/articles/67666/michael-w-doyle/the-folly-of-protection?page=show.

8 *See, e.g.*, International Commission on Intervention and State Sovereignty, The Responsibility to Protect 29 (2001).

9 Rosenau, *supra* note 1, at 161.

10 *See*, in this context, the discussion of the non-intervention agreement in the Spanish Civil War in Chapter 5, sec. 4.

11 Lori Fisler Damrosch, *Introduction*, *in* Enforcing Restraint: Collective Intervention in Internal Conflicts 1, 3 (Lori Fisler Damrosch, ed., 1989).

numerous sources of international law,[12] and is classically understood as protecting the sovereignty of states from "dictatorial" external intervention.[13] Thus, while every involvement, of any kind, of an external party in an internal armed conflict is per se a physical intervention, only engagements which violate the norm of non-intervention amount to interventions in the normative sense.

Of course, coupling any notion of normativity with the term "intervention" – and especially when admitting that strategic questions can influence legal analysis – immediately sparks the longstanding debate between the realist approach to international relations (and law) and the liberal, idealist or constructivist approaches. This debate, naturally, extends also to the question of consent. Realists – and specifically neorealists from the school of Kenneth Waltz – stress the structural anarchy of the international system, which spawns inter-state interactions that are determined strictly by *power* relations. Accordingly, legal or moral norms, or the internal political structure of the state, are virtually irrelevant as determinants of state action on the international level.[14] Since they regard all states "as caught in a state of war in which the only source of security is self-help," their analysis of forcible interventions will be mainly based on the "relative capabilities" of states.[15] It therefore only makes sense that realists see forcible intervention – or non-intervention – merely as a tool utilized by states to achieve security, perhaps through an intended or resulting international balance of power.[16]

International liberals, on the other hand, agree that at least some forcible interventions are based on principles independent from pure power

12 *See, e.g.*, Article LXIV of the Treaty of Westphalia (1648); Covenant of the League of Nations art. 10; Convention on the Rights and Duties of States, art. 8, December 23, 1933, 165 L.N.T.S 19; U.N. Charter art. 2(7) (note, however, that this article is addressed to the UN rather than to its member states); Pact of the Arab League of States, art. 8, March 22, 1945, 70 U.N.T.S. 237; Charter of the Organization of American States art. 2, April 30, 1948, 119 U.N.T.S. 48; Vienna Convention on Diplomatic Relations, art. 41(1), April 18, 1961, 500 U.N.T.S. 95; Declaration on Principles of International Law concerning Friendly Relations and Co-operation among States, G.A. Res. 2625 (XXV), U.N. Doc. A/8082 (October 24, 1970); Military Aid and Paramilitary Activities in and against Nicaragua (Nicar. v. U.S.), 1986 I.C.J. 14 (June 27), ¶¶202–209; The Corfu Channel Case (U.K. v. Albania), 1949 I.C.J. 4, 35 (April 9). *See also* Antonio Cassese, International Law 53–58 (2005); Lori Fisler Damrosch, *Politics across Borders: Nonintervention and Nonforcible Influence over Domestic Affairs*, 83 Am. J, International L. 1, 6–9 (1989) and the sources cited therein. For an historical overview of the development of the norm, *see* J.H. Leurdijk, Armed Intervention in International Politics: A Historical and Comparative Analysis 5–26 (2006).

13 Lassa Oppenheim, 1 International Law §134 (2nd ed., 1912).

14 *See* Kenneth Waltz, Theory of International Politics 102–129 (1979); *See* Robert O. Keohane, *Realism, Neoralism and the Study of World Politics*, *in* Neorealism and its Critics 1–27 (Robert O. Keohane ed., 1986); Jack L. Goldsmith and Eric A. Posner, The Limits of International Law (2005).

15 Doyle, *supra* note 6, at 390; Waltz, *supra* note 14, at 117–120.

16 Doyle, *supra* note 6, at 392.

calculations.[17] They argue that international institutions and economic interactions create interdependence that reduces conflicts and enhances cooperation.[18] They identify the development of inter-governmental networks which modify state actions through socialization processes,[19] and emphasize the role of fairness and legitimacy in the international system.[20] They reject the neorealist separation between domestic politics and inter-state relations, and advance *liberal peace* arguments, drawing on Kantian principles to demonstrate that the internal structure of liberal states maintains peace between them.[21] Still others argue for a concept of international morality which is independent from the realist view of inter-state relations as a Hobbesian anarchy.[22]

In our context, it is plain to see that realists will not attribute major importance to the existence or absence of consent when a state contemplates intervention, at least as long as the consent does not affect its power calculations. Liberals, on the other hand, might view consent as a legitimizing factor – whether morally or legally – independent from the question of power relations. This work does not purport to solve this debate. The international lawyer is indeed in a bind; if she must always, a priori, prove the mere possibility of international law before embarking on any study of it, she will inevitably find herself – in the terms of Koskenniemi – trapped in an endless cycle between apologetics and utopianism. We must avoid these dynamics by bearing in mind international law's weaknesses, but also the moral and practical imperatives to continuously develop it.[23]

2 The shifting meaning of the principle of non-intervention

The principle (or norm) of non-intervention forms the main normative basis for any legal discussion of intervention.[24] However, it is notoriously

17 What these principles exactly are (or should be), and when they amount to a justification of intervention differs among different schools of liberals. *See* Doyle, *supra* note 6, at 396–402.

18 *See* Robert O. Keohane and Joseph S. Nye, Power and Interdependence: World Politics in Transition (1977); Helen V. Milner, *Power, Interdependence and Nonstate Actors in World Politics: Research Frontiers, in* Power, Interdependence and Nonstate Actors in World Politics 3–30 (Helen V. Milner and Andrew Moravcsik eds., 2009).

19 *See* Anne-Marie Slaughter, A New World Order (2004).

20 Thomas M. Franck, Fairness in International Law and Institutions (1998); Allen Buchanan, Justice, Legitimacy, and Self-Determination: Moral Foundations for International Law (2004); *see also* Oona Hathaway and Scott J. Shapiro, *Outcasting: Enforcement in Domestic and International Law,* 121 Yale L. J. 252 (2011).

21 *See, e.g.,* Michael W. Doyle, *Kant, Liberal Legacies and Foreign Affairs* 12 Philosophy and Public Affairs 205, 206 (1983); *see* Immanuel Kant, Perpetual Peace: A Philosophical Essay (1759) (Mary Campbell Smith trans., 1903) (Fifth Preliminary Article of Perpetual Peace), *available at* http://books.google.com.

22 *See* Charles R. Beitz, Political Theory and International Relations (1979).

23 *Compare* Martti Koskenniemi, The Politics of International Law 33–63 (2011).

24 *See supra,* note 12.

vague – both regarding actions that constitute unlawful intervention and concerning the values it sets out to protect. The traditional reference to unlawful interventions as those that are "dictatorial"[25] is hardly helpful, since the latter term is itself open-textured. This is especially true in the context of economic relations, where the line between "legitimate" pressure and "unlawful" coercion is often thin. Accordingly, while the validity of the principle of non-intervention is rarely challenged per se, it was never viewed as rigid or absolute by the mainstream of international lawyers.[26]

Much of the contemporary understanding of the scope of the principle is traced to the 1986 International Court of Justice (ICJ) landmark ruling in the *Nicaragua* case.[27] However, and as detailed later,[28] the doctrine it set forth – and specifically regarding intervention and consent – is too thin to be considered exhaustive. The ruling was a product of the last years of the Cold War. The world has changed dramatically since, reflecting substantial shifts in the perception of sovereignty and non-intervention.[29] The human rights discourse has become a dominant voice in international law, supplemented by arguments urging the recognition of an international "democratic entitlement."[30] The Responsibility to Protect (RtoP) concept has emerged, suggesting that the understanding of sovereignty – the very intrinsic value non-intervention traditionally sought to solidify – has transformed from encapsulating a set of rights emanating from an entity's exclusive effective control over territory,[31] to a concept bound to the fulfillment of a *responsibility to protect* populations.[32] Arguably, thus, the norm

25 *See supra*, note 13.

26 *See, e.g.*, 1 Oppenheim, *supra* note 13, §134.

27 Nicaragua, *supra* note 12; *see also* Armed Activities on the Territory of the Congo (DRC v. Uganda), 2005 I.C.J. 168, ¶164 (December 19).

28 Chapter 6, sec. 4.3.

29 *See* Tom J. Farer, *Humanitarian Intervention Before and After 9/11, in* Humanitarian Intervention: Ethical, Legal and Political Dilemmas 53, 72 (J.L. Holzgrefe and Robert O. Keohane eds., 2003); The Independent International Commission on Kosovo, The Kosovo Report 168–169 (2000).

30 Thomas M. Franck, *The Emerging Right to Democratic Governance*, 86 American Journal of International Law 46 (1992).

31 *See, e.g.*, 1 Oppenheim, *supra* note 13, §§123–124 (defining sovereignty as comprising from independence and territorial and personal supremacy); *see* Hersch Lauterpacht, Recognition in International Law 103 (1947).

32 *See* Francis M. Deng *et al.*, Sovereignty as Responsibility 1–34 (1996); ICISS Report, *supra* note 8, at 8–34 (discussing this process). The most dramatic of these challenges may be the interventionist attitude that is reflected in new security treaties of African regional organizations. These will be addressed *infra*, Chapter 8, sec. 3; *see also* Oliver Furley and Roy May, *Introduction, in* African Interventionist States 1, 4 (Oliver Furley and Roy May eds., 2001); Jeremy Levitt, *African Interventionist States and International Law, in* African Interventionist States, *id.* at 15. In general, the official attitude of African regional organizations regarding the norm of non-intervention has been described as having shifted to "non-indifference." *See* Paul D. Williams, *From Non-Intervention to Non-Indifference: The Origins and Development of the African Union's Security Culture*, 106 African Affairs 253 (2007).

of non-intervention has been refocused from strictly ensuring non-intervention in *sovereign* will, to the protection of other interests.

In this context, two main levels of challenge to the traditional understanding of non-intervention can be identified. The first – relatively narrow challenge – considers non-intervention as contingent upon the sovereign's physical protection of its population or civilians under its control. This is very much the approach of RtoP. A wider challenge posits that non-intervention is set to entrench the substantive democratic will of peoples, meaning, not only their physical protection but also broader political values. The term "substantive" alludes to conditions that go beyond the principle of majority rule, and extend also to the protection of basic rights that are a prerequisite for any true democratic process.[33] This challenge corresponds with, but is more robust than, the notion of "internal" self-determination as political participation, or the perception of electoral democracy as a human right in itself – as put famously by Franck, democracy as an "entitlement" that has "trumped the principle of non-interference."[34]

Challenges on both levels – and in the spectrum between them – reflect the dilemmas that the principle of non-intervention presents, especially to liberal thinkers.[35] This "liberal dilemma" emanates from the principle's seemingly contradicting meanings in liberal discourse. On one hand, liberal thought condones the principle of non-intervention, since it solidifies peoples' right to freely determine their path, as part of the right to self-determination. On the other hand, the same principles can be invoked to justify intervention when the people of the target state are denied this choice.[36] Attempts to reconcile the liberal dilemma argue along the lines that "[s]ometimes the national self-determination that non-intervention is designed to protect is so clearly undermined by the domestic oppression and suffering that the principle should simply be disregarded."[37]

Another way to express the relations between non-intervention and its substantive challenges would not posit that the latter have "trumped" the former, or that it should be "disregarded," but rather that the former should be interpreted in light of the latter. In such situations, the intervener's actions will not be considered as violating or "disregarding" the principle to begin with, but rather as being in line with its substantive

33 On "substantive" democracy *see* Aharon Barak, Proportionality: Constitutional Rights and Their Limitations 218 (2012).

34 Thomas M. Franck, *Legitimacy and Democratic Entitlement, in* Democratic Governance and International Law 25, 46 (Gregory H. Fox and Brad R. Roth, eds. 2000); *see also Politics across Borders, supra* note 12, at 6, 18.

35 The norm has also challenged socialist thinkers. In the context of the Brezhnev doctrine, *see* Chapter 6, sec. 2.

36 *See* Michael W. Doyle, *A Few Words on Mill, Walzer, and Non-intervention* 23 Ethics and International Affairs 349 (2009); *see also* Doyle, *supra* note 6, at 394–402.

37 *See id.*, at 361.

meaning. Be it as it may, the practical meaning of the above approaches would be that states would not be able to invoke the principle of non-intervention when they – themselves – are failing to protect populations under their control, or are otherwise denying basic political rights of their citizens.[38]

However, it should be stressed that the redefinition of the norm of non-intervention does not always affect the question of *forcible* intervention. As we shall see later on, when the challenges to the norm are based on a government's failure to *protect* civilians, they might affect its sovereign power, and thus result in implications on the issue forcible intervention. Conversely, while the norm of non-intervention might also be considerably weakened when *democratic* principles are violated, it is doubtful, in general, whether this in itself always has bearing over the laws on the use of force. This is because non-intervention and the laws on the use of force are two intertwining – but nevertheless distinct – normative frameworks.[39]

3 Typology of intervention

Intervention can occur in many forms, encompassing a virtually infinite variety of actions.[40] The primary distinction is between *non-forcible* and *forcible* ones. Actions of the latter kind are controlled, generally, by the principle of non-intervention, as well as by international humanitarian rights law (IHRL).[41] Forcible intervention, the main concern of this work, is controlled too by the norm of non-intervention, but also, first and foremost, by the international law regarding the use of force.

A related distinction is between *negative* and *positive* forms of intervention.[42] The boundaries of these distinctions are admittedly vague. Negative interventions are naturally non-forcible; they involve the complete withdrawal or partial reduction of existing interactions with a target

38 *See* Sarah H. Cleveland, *Norm Internalization and U.S. Economic Sanctions*, 26 Yale Journal of International Law 1, 53–55 (2001).

39 *See* Chapter 3, sec. 1.

40 *See, e.g.*, Patrick M. Regan, Civil Wars and Foreign Powers: Outside Intervention in Intrastate Conflict 25 (2002); Enforcing Restraint, *supra* note 11, at 4.

41 *See* Commission on Economic, Social and Cultural Rights, General Comment No. 8, The Relationship between Economic Sanctions and Respect for Economic, Social and Cultural Rights, U.N. Doc. CESCR/E/C.12/1997/8 (December 12, 1997). Of course, this position assumes that IHRL instruments apply extra-territorially: *see* Fons Coomans, *Some Remarks on the Extraterritorial Application of the International Covenant on Economic, Social and Cultural Rights*, *in* Extraterritorial Application of Human Rights Treaties 183 (Fons Coomans and Menno T. Kamminga eds., 2004); Human Rights Commission, General Comment No. 31, Nature of the Legal Obligation Imposed on States Parties to the Covenant, U.N. Doc. CCPR/C/21.Rev.1/Add.13 (2004); Legal Consequences of the Construction of a Wall in the Occupied Palestinian Territory, Advisory Opinion, 2004 I.C.J. 136 ¶¶ 108–111 (July 9).

42 *Compare Politics Across Borders*, *supra* note 12, at 6, 31 (1989).

state, or forward-looking bans or limitations on such interactions. They include economic sanctions as well as political and cultural sanctions. Such methods of interventions are regulated by a rather flexible legal framework. For instance, in *Nicaragua*, the ICJ held that withdrawal of aid previously given, or imposing trade sanctions, do not constitute unlawful forms of intervention.[43] Indeed, economic sanctions – the most common form of negative non-forcible intervention – are not considered, in general, as unlawful interventions unless they amount to extreme economic coercion, or otherwise violate the human rights of the population in the target state.[44] This notion is based on the traditional idea that states are sovereign to conduct their economic policies, whether internal or external,[45] and that as long as state action is not limited by treaties or customary international law, it is generally not prohibited.[46]

Positive interventions are actions involving changes which go *beyond* withdrawals or bans. These can be non-forcible (e.g., the granting of economic aid or officially recognizing the opposition) or forcible (the use of military force, arms transfers). As opposed to negative intervention, positive non-forcible intervention, at least in favor of opposition groups, is severely limited in international law.[47]

The regulation of consensual intervention has positive as well as negative aspects. Should we claim that international law negates, in some circumstances, the power of consent, we are essentially arguing for a norm of negative non-forcible intervention. Similarly, if we claim that law recognizes, in some circumstances, the power of consent – we are arguing for a norm of positive forcible intervention. Therefore, the normative frameworks that are relevant to both types of interventions (negative or positive) might also affect the question of consent; this means, in turn, that negation of consent power is subject to a rather flexible normative regime.

43 Nicaragua, *supra* note 12, ¶245 (Singh, J.). *See also Politics Across Borders, supra* note 12, at 34.

44 Declaration on Friendly Relations, *supra* note 12. The claim that economic sanctions could be unlawful was usually invoked by developing countries, but rejected by developed countries. *See Politics across Borders, supra* note 12, at 32–33. In any case, even "extreme economic coercion" was not defined as "aggression" by the UNGA in the Definition of Aggression, G.A. Res. 3314 (XXIX), U.N. Doc. A/9631 (December 14, 1974); *See* Tom J. Farer, *Political and Economic Coercion in Contemporary International Law*, 79 American Journal of International Law 405, 413 (1985). Regarding human rights and sanctions, *see supra* note 41.

45 *See, e.g.*, Lassa Oppenheim, International Law §129 (1992); *see also* Laura Picchio Forlati, *The Present Sate of Research Carried out by the English Speaking Section of the Centre for Studies and Research, in* Economic Sanctions in International Law 129, 131 (2000); Cleveland, *supra* note 38, at 53.

46 This is the famous "Lotus" principle. *See* S.S. Lotus (Fr. v. Turk.) 1927 P.C.I.J. Ser. A-No. 10 (September 7).

47 Declaration on Friendly Relations, *supra* note 12; Nicaragua, *supra* note 12, ¶228; Declaration on the Inadmissibility of Intervention in the Domestic Affairs of States and Protection of their Independence and Sovereignty, G.A. Res. 2131 (XX), U.N. Doc. A/RES/20/2131 (December 21, 1965).

The last important distinction, applicable to all types of interventions, is between *unilateral* and *multilateral* interventions. The term unilateral intervention, when we use it, refers to any intervention, forcible or non-forcible, conducted by a state or a group of states (through an international organization or otherwise), absent a Chapter VII UNSC resolution. Multilateral intervention, conversely, is undertaken in accordance with such a resolution. In general, since forcible intervention is governed by the UN Charter's law on the use of force – the normative status of unilateral and multilateral forcible interventions is effectively separated. The law regarding non-forcible interventions, conversely, places both unilateral and multilateral interventions roughly under the same normative system. The main difference between them is that multilateral non-forcible interventions are universally binding,[48] while unilateral ones are not.

4 Internal armed conflicts: a working definition and basic typology

Determining whether an internal armed conflict exists has long been an important question in the ethics of intervention. Kant, for instance, argued that substantial internal strife represents, in a visible and distinctive manner, situations where "anarchy prevails" within a state, in which the idea of non-intervention loses much of its theoretical appeal.[49] Mill, conversely, stressed the importance of the local population's *independent* participation in "arduous struggle" for freedom, for the development of "the feelings and virtues" required for maintaining freedom.[50]

The existence of internal armed conflicts could also matter from the point of view of democratic ethics. A democratic standpoint will always prefer to settle internal differences through deliberation. The existence of armed internal strife constitutes an indication that a democratic process in the state is completely absent; or that democratic options have been exhausted. In any case, deliberation or other non-violent measures have been effectively *abandoned.* When deliberation is abandoned, it is easier for one to justify an intervention as an action of "last resort," in the classic just-war sense.[51]

Setting ethics aside, the attempts to define non-international armed conflicts, including *internal* conflicts, has been of increasing importance in contemporary international law. This is mainly because of the definition's

48 *See* U.N. Charter, art. 25. Some use the terms "unilateral," "multilateral" or "collective" differently. *See, e.g.*, Regan, *supra* note 40, at 105; Enforcing Restraint, *supra* note 11, at 2.

49 *See* Kant, *supra* note 21 (Fifth Preliminary Article of Perpetual Peace). Kant, however, distinguished between different levels of conflicts: only when a state "has become split up through internal corruption into two parts, each of them representing by itself an individual state which lays claims to the whole" a state of anarchy "prevails," in which foreign intervention does not constitute "interference."

50 Mill, *supra* note 2, at 259–260; *See also* Walzer, *supra* note 2, at 87–88; Doyle, *supra* note 6, at 395.

51 *See, e.g.*, ICISS Report, *supra* note 8, at 36–37.

effect over the determination, in specific instances, of the applicable normative framework. As we shall see, owing to the interaction between IHRL and *jus in bello*, determining whether an internal armed conflict exists can affect also the legality of a forcible intervention – since only during an internal armed conflict, a state can resort to armed force, under IHL, against armed opposition. This fact has thus bearing both on the legality of the resort to force by the beleaguered government, and, consequently, on its power to consent to external support.[52]

In any case, using the term *civil war* is largely unhelpful in this context. Although we occasionally use it in a generic manner, it is rather imprecise. As commonly understood, a civil war is "a war between opposing groups of citizens of the same country."[53] This definition does not encompass the complexity of modern internal strife. For instance, while many internal conflicts involve state actors and institutions, others include parties which are not necessarily comprised of citizens of the relevant state.[54] In the legal sphere, the term suffers from further limitations. Using the term *war*, when describing internal strife, presupposes the existence of conditions which traditionally had implications on the rights of the parties involved. As such, its use can prejudge the situation and be therefore misleading.[55] In addition – and conversely – the use of the term *war* to describe hostilities has given way, in the era of the UN Charter and the 1949 Geneva Conventions, to the factual terms *use of force* and *armed conflict*.[56] This is why we prefer the more precise term *internal armed conflict*.[57]

52 *See* Chapter 7, sec. 2.1.

53 *Available at* www.merriam-webster.com/dictionary/civil%20war.

54 For instance, in the Lebanese Civil War of 1975–1990, Palestinian refugees and P.L.O. militants (who were never granted Lebanese citizenship) played a central role. *See* Edgar O'Ballance, Civil War in Lebanon, 1975–1992 1–20 (1998). Another example could be the involvement of foreign fighters in the internal strife in Iraq following the invasion of 2003. *See, e.g.*, Zaki Chehab, Iraq Ablaze, 33–69 (2006); or the involvement of the FDLR in the conflict in Congo. *See* Chapter 1, sec. 3.

55 This is because the term "war" might imply that belligerency was recognized. *See* Chapter 5, sec. 1.

56 *See, e.g.*, Laurie R. Blank and Benjamin R. Farley, *Characterizing U.S. Operations in Pakistan: Is the United States Engaged in an Armed Conflict?* 34 Fordham International Law Journal 151, 160 (2010).

57 The term *non-international armed conflict* is not used, since it refers, in the context of IHL, also to instances which are not necessarily internal: it encompasses also the complex phenomenon of *transnational* armed conflict. *See* Hamdan v. Rumsfeld, 548 U.S. 557, 630 (2006) (holding that the term non-international armed conflict, as it appears in Common Article 3 of the Geneva Conventions does not apply only to internal armed conflicts.) Another example is the ongoing conflict between Israel and Hamas in Gaza. It is not a clear international armed conflict, since Hamas is not a "High Contracting Party" to the Geneva Conventions; however, since Gaza is not a territory of Israel, it cannot be labeled as an internal armed conflict. *Compare* H.C.J. 769/02 The Public Committee Against Torture in Israel v. The Government of Israel [2006] IsrSC 57(6) 285, ¶21; *but see* Eyal Benvenisti, *The Legal Battle to Define the Law on Transnational Asymmetric Warfare*, 20 Duke Journal of Comparative and International Law 339, 341–344, 350 (2010).

Essentially, then, an internal armed conflict is a violent dispute, where armed violence takes place primarily within the boundaries of a single entity recognized as a state on the international level.[58] The accepted contemporary legal definition of the term can be found in the ICTY's famous *Tadic* case:

> an armed conflict exists whenever there is a resort to armed force between States or *protracted* armed violence between governmental authorities and *organized* armed groups or between such groups within a state.[59]

The term *protracted* implies – as opposed to international conflicts, which do not require such a condition[60] – that internal armed conflicts have to be both *sustained* (along the time continuum) and *large-scale* (in terms of the intensity of the friction between the parties).[61] Importantly, for an internal armed conflict to materialize there must be at least one armed group of sufficient *organization* challenging the government.[62] Accordingly, as defined in Article 1(2) of Additional Protocol II, the term excludes "situations of internal disturbances and tensions, such as riots, isolated and sporadic acts of violence and other acts of similar nature."[63]

The existence of an internal armed conflict is a factual question,[64] meaning, it should be entirely separated from our perception regarding the merits of the conflict. In general, it is possible to ascertain whether such conflict exists by analyzing the actions undertaken by the involved parties. For instance, it is helpful to ask whether the state has deployed its regular armed forces, or rather it is confronting the upheaval through law enforcement measures employed by its police force and justice system.[65] However, even if a state *does* deploy its armed forces, this is not in itself sufficient for

58 *See, e.g.*, Michael E. Brown, *Introduction*, *in* The International Dimensions of Internal Conflict, *supra* note 3, at 1, 1.

59 *See* Prosecutor v. Tadic, Case No. IT-94-1-I, Decision on Defence Motion for Interlocutory Appeal on Jurisdiction, ¶70 (International Criminal Tribunal for the Former Yugoslavia October 2, 1995) (emphasis added).

60 *See* Noam Lubell, Extraterritorial Use of Force against Non-State Actors 86–88 (2010).

61 *Compare* Richard A. Falk, *Toward a New International Law for Civil War*, *in* The International Law of Civil Wars 16, 18 (Richard A. Falk ed., 1972); *see also* Lori Fisler Damrosch, *Introduction*, *in* Enforcing Restraint, *supra* note 11, at 1, 4.

62 Blank and Farley, *supra* note 56, at 163–164; *see also* Special Rapporteur on Extrajudicial, Summary or Arbitrary Executions, *Study on Targeted Killings*, Human Rights Council, ¶¶46–56, U.N. Doc. A/HRC/14/24/Add.6 (May 28, 2010) (by Philip Alston); Lubell, *supra* note 60, at 109–110.

63 Protocol Additional to the Geneva Conventions of 12 August 1949, and Relating to the Protection of Victims of Non-International Armed Conflicts (Protocol II), June 8, 1977, 1125 U.N.T.S. 609 art. 1(2).

64 Blank and Farley, *supra* note 56, at 160–162; Tadic, *supra* note 59, ¶70; *cited in* Blank and Farley, at 162.

65 *Id.* at 163 and the many sources cited therein; Lubell, *supra* note 60, at 107.

the materialization of an armed conflict, since there must also be an organized armed group that confronts the government. If there are no such groups, then the violence between the state apparatus and civilians can generally be dealt with sufficiently through domestic criminal law, and the situation is controlled, in turn, by the law enforcement paradigm of IHRL.

In this context, it is worthwhile to note that in contrast to Additional Protocol II, the *Tadic* ruling does not refer to control over territory by opposition groups as a condition for the existence of an internal armed conflict.[66] However, control over territory can still serve as an indication for the existence of such conflict, since loss of control might imply that the government is unable to curtail the opposition's activities through law enforcement mechanisms, as provided for in IHRL, and must therefore resort to military force to assert control over the state's territory. Thus, for instance, de facto occupation of a part of state's territory by an armed organization (or an unrecognized junta, in certain cases) might be considered a component of an internal armed conflict, for the sake of the application of IHL, even when outright hostilities cease.[67]

Notwithstanding the requirement that internal armed conflicts be both sustained and large-scale, it is reasonable that for such conflict to materialize there can be some inverse ratio between duration and intensity. For instance, a very short but extremely intense period of violence may be looked upon as an armed conflict;[68] and conversely, a long and relatively low-intensity conflict may also qualify as one.[69] It seems that both duration and scale serve as indicators for the conflict's effect over the ability of the state to extinguish it through its justice system and by law enforcement measures. In this sense, prolonged low-intensity conflicts, as well as short high-intensity ones, can both be indications that such ability is hindered.

Thus, in contemporary international law, the main corollary of the determination whether an internal armed conflict exists concerns the

66 Additional Protocol II, *supra* note 63, art. 1(1).

67 However, it is important to note that "revolutions" are not always accompanied by internal armed conflicts. *See* Jack A. Goldstone, *Toward a Fourth Generation of Revolutionary Theory*, 4 Annual Review of Political Science 139, 142 (2001). The distinction between revolutions and internal armed conflicts is an ancient one. Aristotle also distinguished between the "revolution" itself and "use of force," noting that "[f]orce may be applied either at the time of making the revolution or afterwards." He also contended that revolutions can come to be either by "force" or by "fraud." *See* Aristotle, The Politics 111 (Benjamin Jowett trans., 2009).

68 *See* the decision by the Inter-American Commission on Human Rights in the Abella Case, Abella v. Argentina, Case 11.137, Inter-American Commission on Human Rights, Report No 55/97, IACHR OEA/Ser.L/V/II.95 Doc. 7 rev. at 221, *cited in* Lubell, *supra* note 60, at 105.

69 *Compare* Prosecutor v. Haradinaj, Case No. IT-04-84-T, Judgment, ¶49 (International Criminal Tribunal for the Former Yugoslavia April 3, 2008) (holding that the term "protracted," in the context of internal armed conflicts, refers more to the intensity of the violence than to its duration), *cited in* Lubell, *supra* note 60, at 105–106.

question whether the application of IHL is triggered, or rather, that the situation is controlled strictly by the more restrictive law enforcement paradigm as entrenched in IHRL.[70] For instance, the gist of the requirement that the opposition be an *organized* armed group is that there must be, in fact, at least two real parties to the conflict, as opposed to a situation where the state is simply using armed violence against largely unarmed and unorganized civilians. Absent this requirement, states would be capable of diluting their obligations under IHRL by claiming, as a pretext, that a fabricated internal armed conflict exists.

Indeed, the development of IHRL has generally shifted the discourse on the existence of armed conflicts, internal as well as transnational. In the past, states were reluctant to acknowledge the existence of a "civil war" within their territories, both since such recognition entailed international status for the opposition,[71] and because domestic law enforcement was beyond the reach of international law, and was therefore less restricted – if at all – than the laws of war. Nowadays, in contrast, the restrictions imposed by IHRL actually make the law of armed conflict more permissive – especially in the context of the use of lethal force – possibly incentivizing states to claim that they are involved in armed conflict. For instance, in the initial stages of the ongoing crisis in Syria, the Al-Assad regime was quick to assert that it was facing an armed insurgency, as a principled justification for its use of lethal force – a claim that has had some factual merits.[72] In addition, an especially robust debate has taken place, in a different but related context, regarding the methods employed by the US in its global "war on terror," in which it was keen to describe its struggle with Al-Qa'ida as an armed conflict, while various commentators maintained that the effort against transnational terrorism should be treated by methods of law enforcement.[73]

Once it is established that an internal armed conflict exists, it is important to look at the objectives the parties wish to achieve – as far as these can

70 *See* Study on Targeted Killings, *supra* note 62, ¶¶31–33; *see also* Nils Melzer, International Committee of the Red Cross, Interpretive Guidance on the Notion of Direct Participation in Hostilities under International Humanitarian Law 24 (2009).

71 *See* Chapter 4, sec. 3.

72 *See* U.N. SCOR, 66th Sess., 6627th mtg., at 12–14, U.N. Doc. S/PV.6627 (October 4, 2011) (statement by the Syrian representative in front of the UNSC); *Syria Defectors "Attack Military Base in Harasta,"* B.B.C. News, November 16, 2011, *available at* www.bbc.co.uk/news/world-middle-east-15752058. The general situation in Syria was recognized by the ICRC as an internal armed conflict in July 2012. *See* Stephanie Nebehay, *Exclusive: Red Cross Ruling Raises Questions of Syrian War Crimes*, Reuters, July 14, 2012, *available at* www.reuters.com/article/2012/07/14/us-syria-crisis-icrc-idUSBRE86D09H20120714.

73 *See, e.g.*, Rosa Ehrenreich Brooks, *War Everywhere: Human Rights, National Security and the Law of Armed Conflict in the Age of Terrorism*, 153 University of Pennsylvania Law Review 675 (2004); Mary Ellen O'Connell, *When is War Not a War? The Myth of the Global War on Terror*, 12 ILSA Journal of International and Comparative Law 5 (2006); Study on Targeted Killings, *supra* note 62, ¶¶46–56; Lubell, *supra* note 60, at 112–121; *compare* Philip Bobbitt, Terror and Consent 128–134 (2008).

be credibly ascertained.[74] While commonly treated as a unitary phenomenon in international-legal literature, such a perception of all internal armed conflicts can result in the overlooking of relevant legal differences. Indeed, there is a wide variety of internal conflicts, which can be categorized by numerous methods, as found in political science literature.[75] These typologies may have legal implications in IHRL, considering the growing focus on the "root causes" of human rights violations.[76] In our context, however, an important distinction is between conflicts that challenge the principle of *territorial integrity*, such as struggles for secession, and conflicts that do not do so, such as struggles for control over the state apparatus.[77]

In the latter cases, the parties aim to take control over the state apparatus, or to bring significant change to its structure.[78] The conflict may involve the government, as a unit, deploying its armed forces to curtail counter-governmental activities; it may involve an intra-governmental rift in which various institutions of the state confront each other; it may also be the case that the government becomes irrelevant and neutral, or ceases to exist in its entirety, while different groups fight to replace the government or wield more power over it. The conflict strictly takes place within the boundaries of the state, and foreign powers may become involved in the conflict through the support of one party or the other.[79] Naturally, the position – or mere existence – of the government in such conflicts can affect the question of consensual intervention, assuming that government consent can, in principle, legalize forcible intervention.

74 The causes of such conflict are addressed in a vast political science literature. *See, e.g.*, Ted Robert Gurr, Why Men Rebel 317 (1970); Brown, *supra* note 58, at 13–23; Barry R. Posen, *The Security Dilemma and Ethnic Conflict*, 35 Survival (1993) 27; David A. Lake and Donald Rotschild, *Containing Fear: The Origins and Management of Ethnic Conflict*, *in* Nationalism and Ethnic Conflict 126, 137 (Michael E. Brown *et al.* eds., 2001).

75 For instance, it is possible to classify conflicts by the nature of their participants, by their success or by their intensity. *See, e.g.,* D.E.H. Russel, Rebellion, Revolution and Armed Force 60–62 (1974).

76 *See* Susan Marks, *Human Rights and Root Causes*, 57 Modern Law Review 57 (2011).

77 *Compare* Falk, *supra* note 61, at 18–19.

78 Such change can range from minor constitutional corrections to altering the entire "basic norm" of the state. On the "Basic Norm" (Grundnorm) *see* Hans Kelsen, Pure Theory of Law 7–8, 201 (5th ed. 2008); *compare* Aristotle, The Politics 295 (T.A. Sinclair trans., 1992). A challenge to the basic norm occurs, for instance, when an authoritarian government is challenged by a liberal or Marxist opposition or vice-versa. Such was the case of the Spanish Civil War. *See* Chapter 5, sec. 4. Often it is difficult to distinguish whether the conflict erupts over the validity of the basic norm, or rather regarding its specific application. For instance, the Lebanese crisis of 1958, can be looked upon either as a "regular" constitutional crisis or as an attempt, by Pan-Arab elements, to change the state's structure entirely. For a detailed account of the 1958 Lebanese crisis *see* Malcolm Kerr, *The Lebanese Civil War, in* International Regulation of Civil Wars 65 (Evan Luard ed., 1972).

79 The Spanish Civil War is a classic case. *See* Chapter 5, sec. 4.

Since such struggles usually do not aim to alter the state's borders, they do not risk the basic external order and the corresponding principle of *territorial integrity*. Strictly in this sense, they represent less of a challenge to the existing international system than secession struggles. However, in the context of intervention, they raise the classic dilemmas, explored later in this work, regarding the substance and application of the principles of non-intervention and self-determination.

Struggles for secession, conversely, are situations in which an ethnic, religious, ideological or social-economical segment of a state's population demands to separate itself from the state and establish a new state. The challenging group does not contest the legitimacy of the government or the existence of the state per se, but only to the extent that it exercises its authority over a territory associated with the group.[80] Such conflicts, as opposed to struggles for control, present additional dilemmas to the international system. First, they have the potential to become "international" once the seceding party receives widespread recognition. In addition, they challenge the basic principle of territorial integrity of states. These complexities, addressed later on, should be taken into consideration when assessing interventions in secession conflicts.

In general, secession demands can be based on two classes of claims. The first involves claims according to which a central government oppresses or neglects a certain group, thereby prompting it to demand secession, which would in turn spawn an alleged right to be recognized as an independent state vis-à-vis the international community. A historic example for such a demand can be found in the narrative of the Confederacy during the American Civil War. Nowadays, this claim relates to the controversial doctrine of *remedial secession*.[81] A second type of struggle for secession occurs when the challenging party denies that the rump state has ever had any legitimacy to rule over it. An example for such a situation can be found in the conflict in Chechnya.[82]

Secession struggles are distinct from colonial struggles. As we shall see later on, "colonial" struggles were generally considered, in the age of empires, as "regular" internal conflicts. However, this rule was a product

80 It is important to distinguish, in this context, between secession and *dissolution*. When several groups struggle for separation simultaneously, the state itself can dissolve and then the question of *succession* arises. An example is the dissolution of Yugoslavia; *see* Opinion 1, Arbitration Commission of the Peace Conference on the Former Yugoslavia (Badinter Commission) (November 29, 1991).

81 *See* Jefferson Davis, The Rise and Fall of the Confederate Government preface (1881). On remedial secession *see* the discussion in Chapters 9–10.

82 Chechens claim that with the collapse of the Soviet Union, Chechnya was entitled to be independent, rather than to remain under Russian Rule. *See* Mathew Evangelista, *Historical Legacies and the Politics of Intervention in the Former Soviet Union, in* The International Dimensions of Internal Conflict, *supra* note 3, at 108, 112; Anatol Lieven, Chechnya: Tombstone of Russian Power 58 (1998).

of an era in which colonialism was – at least in the eyes of the major powers – an accepted international phenomenon. It is clear that the latter approach has become outdated in the era of decolonization, and that conflicts in the colonial contexts were categorized, in contemporary law, as closer to *international* ones.[83]

Another category of conflicts occurs when a group, within a state, attempts to achieve political unification or reunification of a territory with the territory of a (usually) neighboring state. Such conflicts are based on *irredentism* – meaning, claims for expansion or unification based on shared ethnic, national or historical narratives.[84] These conflicts naturally challenge the principle of territorial integrity, and may involve active support by the government of the neighboring state.[85] In such cases the latter might admit that it, itself, seeks to acquire the disputed territory; conversely, it may only tacitly admit such aspirations while maintaining – on the formal level – that it supports a certain party for a different reason. These dynamics can be found in the struggle in Northern Ireland,[86] as well as in the conflict between Georgia, Russia and local elements in South Ossetia and Abkhazia, culminating in the Georgian–Russian war of 2008.[87] The latter conflict can be viewed as a borderline case between a struggle for secession and a struggle for unification; or as a situation in which secession is championed with the encouragement of a neighboring power, as a pretext for annexation; or as a continuous process in which secession is meant to precede consensual unification.[88]

Another complex type of an irredentist struggle occurs when a group is dispersed throughout a few states, none of which are under that group's domination; and, accordingly, elements of this group – within these states – struggle for unification in the form of a new state which, as they aspire, will be comprised of territories seceded from the several states and united together. This may be the case of the struggle of the Kurdish PKK – which

83 *See* Chapter 9, sec. 2.1.

84 *See* Thomas Ambrosio, Irredentism 2 (2001).

85 Falk, *supra* note 61, at 19.

86 In general, Irish Nationalists believe that Northern Ireland should be removed from British rule, and incorporated to Ireland; *see* John McGarry and Brendan O'Leary, Explaining Northern Ireland, 17–49 (1995). However, the Irish Republic itself does not explicitly claim to support, in practice, such unification. *See* Department of Foreign Affairs, Anglo-Irish Relations/The Peace Process, http://foreignaffairs.gov.ie/home/index.aspx?id=334.

87 For an in-depth investigation of the 2008 Georgia-Russia conflict *see Report of the Independent International Fact-Finding Mission on the Conflict in Georgia* (September 30, 2009), *available at* www.ceiig.ch/Report.html. In short, the Mission found that the conflict was sparked by Georgia; however, it also found that South Ossetia has no right to secede under international law, and that the Russian counterattack on Georgia was disproportionate.

88 There is an ethnic linkage between the people of South Ossetia and the population of Russia's North Ossetia. Moreover, since 1992 and 1994, Russian troops have been deployed (as "peacekeepers") in South Ossetia and Abkhazia respectively. *See id.* at 13–14; in addition, since 2002, Russia carried out a policy of "passportization," in which Russian passports are conferred *en masse* to residents of Abkhazia and South Ossetia. *See id.* at 18.

sought, at least in the past, to form a state in Kurdish populated areas across Syria, Turkey, Iran and Iraq.[89]

The last category of conflicts involves struggles for the dismantlement of the state as part of a decentralized transnational movement. Here an armed conflict is taking place within the boundaries of one state, when the opposition forces are linked to a decentralized – yet interconnected – transnational movement, which is not effectively controlled by any government, and aims to dismantle the state and to ultimately bring about a fundamental change to the global international structure. Such struggles include both intra-state and transnational elements. Their intra-state elements involve confrontations between the state and forces which operate from within it, whether comprised entirely of the states' citizens or supplemented by foreigners. Their transnational elements are reflected in the opposition's state-transcending aspirations and its cooperation with similar actors outside of the state. Such may be the conflicts taking place between governments and transnational jihadist movements, as might be the case in Iraq – to the extent that these movements indeed aim to establish a "global caliphate."[90] However, as in other contexts, it is not always easy to determine if this is indeed the sought objective of such groups.[91]

Struggles of the latter type raise numerous questions regarding the responses of international law to terrorism, and their relations to traditional approaches towards internal strife. Arguably, regarding the question of consensual intervention, struggles for dismantlement represent "easy cases," at least with regards to the principle of non-intervention. Indeed, when the opposition does not accept the state-structure to begin with, arguments of self-determination and non-intervention – which are inherent to the discussion of intervention in the international system of *states* – are effectively quashed.

89 Michael M. Gunter, The Kurds Ascending: The Evolving Solution to the Kurdish Problem in Iraq and Turkey 1 (2006); *see also* David L. Phillips, National Committee on American Foreign Policy, Disarming, Demobilizing and Reintegrating the Kurdistan Workers Party 11 (October 15 2007) www.ncafp.org/.

90 Bobbitt, *supra* note 73, at 62 (2008).

91 For instance, it is unclear whether Abu Mus'ab Al-Zarqawi, former leader of Al Qa'ida in Iraq, was genuinely aiming to establish an Islamic Caliphate, or whether he was acting upon sectarian interests. *See* Hind Haider, U.S. Institute of Peace. What Makes Zarqawi Tick? (2006), *available at* www.usip.org/resources/what-makes-zarqawi-tick.

3 The modalities of forcible intervention

1 The "normative duality" of forcible intervention

It has been claimed that the occurrence of intervention, in the technical-physical sense, can be identified by its "convention-breaking" nature – meaning, by its clear departure from the *status quo ante.* Since military interventions usually reflect the most clear-cut of such departures, they are supposedly easier to identify than non-forcible interventions.[1] However, when attempting to define exactly when an intervention is considered "forcible" – in the *legal* sense – the task is more complicated than intuitively expected.

The question of distinction between non-forcible and forcible interventions is crucial from the legal perspective, since these two categories are controlled by different sets of legal norms. Indeed, both types are subject to the ambiguous principle of non-intervention; however, only the latter is regulated also by the more restrictive law on the use of force. Although these two normative frameworks sometimes protect the same interests, they are not entirely similar. While the objectives of *jus ad bellum* include the protection of elements protected by the norm of non-intervention – such as sovereignty and self-determination – they also set out to achieve different purposes. This divergence is related to the fact that the principle of non-intervention has preceded the prohibition on the use of force by three centuries, although the existence of the former without the latter raised a host of doctrinal problems.[2]

Nonetheless, the principle of non-intervention generally rejects the use of force because it almost always represents a form of *coercion* inflicted upon the sovereignty of the target state. Thus, as held by the ICJ, a breach of the norm of non-intervention is "particularly obvious" where force is being used.[3] This is because, in contradistinction to most cases of

1 James N. Rosenau, *Intervention as a Scientific Concept,* 13 Journal of Conflict Resolution 149, 163 (1969).

2 This problem is discussed in Chapter 4, sec. 1.

3 *See* Military Aid and Paramilitary Activities in and against Nicaragua (Nicar. v. U.S.), 1986 I.C.J. 14 (June 27), ¶205; *see also* Dino Kritsiotis, *Topographies of Force, in* International Law and Armed Conflict: Exploring the Faultlines. Essays in Honour of Yoram Dinstein 29, 67 (Michael N. Schmitt and Jelena Pejic eds., 2007).

non-forcible intervention, forcible intervention "directly interferes with the capacity of a domestic authority to operate on its own territory. It effectively displaces the domestic authority."[4] The law on the use of force also serves to curtail such coercion. However, the latter has further objectives – first and foremost, it is concerned with the prevention of the "scourge" of war in inter-state relations.[5] Importantly, while the norm of non-intervention, because of its ambiguous nature, represents a flexible "standard," the prohibition on the use of force is closer to an absolute "rule," less amenable, in general, to teleological interpretation.[6] Therefore, since the interests protected by the principle of non-intervention and *jus ad bellum* are not entirely similar, it seems that rather than being controlled by a "pure" *lex generalis/lex specialis* relationship, the two sets of norms apply in parallel – in a complementary manner – in every instance of forcible intervention.[7]

One effect of this normative-duality is that even when an instance of use of force is legal (for instance, in self-defense), it must also conform to the norm of non-intervention.[8] A manifestation of this idea can be found in the Hague law of occupation. Assuming an occupation itself is lawful (by standards of *jus ad bellum*), the occupying party is still obliged – "unless absolutely prevented" – to respect the laws "in force" in the occupied territory (and setting aside the question regarding the effects of IHRL on the occupier's legislative powers, or the controversial concept of "transformative occupation").[9] The mirror image of this reasoning is more intuitive: even where the norm of non-intervention does not in theory prohibit an action (such as an intervention for the protection of nationals abroad), the limitations imposed by the law on use of force are not necessarily negated.

4 Report to the International Commission on Intervention and State Sovereignty, The Responsibility to Protect 29 (2001); *see also* Oscar Schachter, *The Right of States to Use Armed Force*, 82 Michigan Law Review 1620, 1625 (1984).

5 U.N. Charter, prmbl.

6 *Compare* Gabriella Blum, *On a Differential Law of War*, 52 Harvard International Law Journal 164, 187 (2011) (discussing rules and standards in the context of international humanitarian law).

7 As ruled by the ICJ, supply of arms to opposition forces is a violation of the law of use of force (but does not constitute an armed attack) *and* a violation of the norm of non-intervention. *See* Nicaragua, *supra* note 3, ¶247; *see also* Armed Activities on the Territory of the Congo (DRC v. Uganda), 2005 I.C.J. 168 (December 19) ¶164; Kritsiotis, *supra* note 3, at 64.

8 For similar reasoning *see* Michael Walzer, Just and Unjust Wars: A Moral Argument with Historical Illustrations xi (4th ed., 2006) ("[e]ven when a humanitarian crisis has rightly triggered intervention, we can still hope to minimize the coercive imposition of foreign ideas and ideologies").

9 Hague Convention II: Laws and Customs of War on Land (1899), 32 Stat. 1803, art. 43; *compare* Tristan Ferraro, International Committee of the Red Cross, Expert Meeting: Occupation and Other Forms of Administration of Foreign Territory 56–59,67–72 (2012).

The question of consensual intervention, thus, must be viewed according to this normative-duality. Party-consent should be analyzed in light of *jus ad bellum*, but also on counts of its interaction with the norm of non-intervention. For instance, unilateral intervention upon the consent of a non-recognized opposition group, facing a government that commits mass atrocities, might not violate the norm of non-intervention per se – considering the contemporary understanding of the norm as discussed earlier – however, it might still violate the prohibition on the use of force.[10] Conversely, consent by a recognized, long-established non-democratic regime might – in a hypothetical situation – legalize a forcible intervention in terms of *jus ad bellum*;[11] but it can be argued – if we accept that the norm is affected by notions of democratic entitlement – that the action will still be deemed a violation of the norm of non-intervention.

2 Defining unilateral forcible intervention: scope, means and state attribution

2.1 Scope, means and methods of forcible intervention

Since our analysis is concerned with consensual *forcible* interventions, understanding the terms *use of force* and *armed attack* as these appear in the UN Charter is a good place to start. Once we establish which actions fall into these categories, we can deduce that when they occur in the context of an internal armed conflict, with the consent of a party, they will be considered as consensual forcible interventions.

Article 2(4) of the UN Charter famously prohibits the threat or use of force by states.[12] It is complemented by Article 51, recognizing the right of self-defense when "an armed attack occurs." Two immediate questions must be answered, before we can "translate" the definition of these terms into the context of forcible intervention. First, what actions, in terms of means, are considered forcible, and actions of what scope amount to a "use of force" or an "armed "attack"? Second, when is a forcible act of intervention attributable to a state?

10 However, as discussed in Chapter 10, the opposition might be granted recognition on counts of considerations of protection of civilians, which might result also in consent power.

11 This theoretical scenario should be read in a qualified manner. As we shall *see* in Chapters 8 and 9, non-democratic regimes, when confronted by a pro-democratic opposition, will almost always commit atrocities, in which case their consent will be nullified, and thus cannot justify intervention whether in the realm of *jus ad bellum* or otherwise.

12 I will not address separately the issue of "threats" of forcible intervention. It suffices that when an intervention would be considered illegal, a threat of intervention would also be illegal. *See* Legality of the Threat of Use of Nuclear Weapons, Advisory Opinion, 1996 I.C.J. 226, ¶47 (July 8). For various interpretations on the prohibition on the threat of force *see* Nicholas Stürchler, The Threat of Force in International Law 37–61 (2009).

The interpretation of the term *use of force* sets forth several questions, in which the issues of scope (how "comprehensive," in duration and intensity, does an action have to be?) and means (what measures are considered forcible ones?) intertwine. For an action to be sufficient in scope to constitute a "use of force" – and thereby considered as a "forcible intervention" – it does not need to amount to a full-scale war in the classic, technical meaning of the term.[13] Accordingly, forcible acts which are "short-of-war" may also be considered as "uses of force."[14] This conclusion coincides with the general process, since the coming into being of the UN Charter, in which the term *war*, in the legal sense, has been marginalized; this is mainly because the prohibition on *force* was never made contingent, in Charter law, upon the existence of a formal state of war.[15]

Hence, according to *Higgins* – and relying on the *Corfu Channel* case – for an act to fall within Article 2(4) of the Charter, it does not make a difference "how brief, limited or transitory" it is; even a "simple aerial incursion" can forcefully violate the territorial integrity of a state.[16] Thus, it suffices that the scope of forcible actions be brief; and that the means employed include actions that do not necessarily involve the active use of kinetic weapons. Accordingly, actual hostilities between the intervener and parties within the conflicting state do not have to occur: for instance, the US Marines encountered no resistance during their landing on Beirut beach in 1958.[17] This mere fact does not negate the forcible nature of the American intervention. In the same vein, unilateral imposition of "humanitarian corridors" by external states within the territory of a conflict-ridden state – such as those considered by some states during the ongoing crisis in Syria[18] – are also forcible acts even if not actively resisted by the territorial state.

The twenty-first century brings about a plethora of questions regarding the definition of forcible acts. One concerns acts of international terrorism. Indeed, forcible acts potentially encompass grave instances of

13 For the traditional definition of the term "war," requiring large-scale use of force *see* Lassa Oppenheim, International Law 202 (1952). *Compare* Yoram Dinstein, War, Aggression and Self-Defense 3–15 (5th ed. 2011).

14 *See* Anthony C. Arend and Robert J. Beck, International Law and the Use of Force: Beyond the U.N. Charter Paradigm 30–31 (1993).

15 *See* Kritsiotis, *supra* note 3, at 34–37.

16 Rosalyn Higgins, Problems and Process: International Law and How We Use It 240 (1995). The ICJ in the *Corfu Channel Case* held that British minesweeping activities in Albanian territorial waters constituted a use of force. The Corfu Channel Case (U.K. v. Albania), 1949 I.C.J. 4 (April 9).

17 *See* Malcolm Kerr, *The Lebanese Civil War*, *in* International Regulation of Civil Wars 65, 81–83 (Evan Luard ed., 1972).

18 As of December 2012. *See Turkey Urges "Immediate" Opening of Syria Aid Corridor after Bombing of Refugee Bridge*, Al-Arabiya News, March 6, 2012, *available at* http://english.alarabiya.net/articles/2012/03/06/198936.html.

unorthodox use of deadly force – even if not "military" in the traditional sense – such as the methods used in the September 11th attacks in New York. The UNSC, in Resolutions 1368 and 1373, as well as states and international organizations, found no difficulty to view such acts as giving rise to the right to self-defense.[19] Therefore – and without exhausting the debate on this issue – in certain grave situations, such attacks can amount to uses of force rather then mere "criminal" actions.[20] The same wide standard should be used when defining forcible intervention in internal armed conflict.

Another especially perplexing question is the distinction of acts of information warfare ("cyber attacks") and, in our case, whether such acts – carried independently from other forceful acts – constitute forcible interventions. The resolution of this complex question is beyond this work; however, to the extent that acts of information warfare could be considered uses of force, our conclusions will naturally apply to them also.[21]

2.2 "Grave" and "less-grave" forcible interventions

By now we have a reasonably good idea of the scope and means of actions that amount to forcible interventions. However, for the sake of clarity, it is helpful also to consider the term in light of the relations between the terms *use of force* and *armed attack* as these appear in the UN Charter (Articles 2(4) and 51 respectively). Do forcible interventions, per se, fall under one term or the other? Indeed, the former term has been interpreted by the ICJ as one which is wider than the latter. The majority opinion in the *Nicaragua* ruling has distinguished between "grave" forms of the use of force – meaning, those that involve an armed attack – and "less grave" forms, which usually do not constitute such an attack.[22] The practical implication of the distinction between "armed attacks" and "less grave" uses of force, according to the ICJ, was that while every use of force is

19 S.C. Res. 1368, U.N. Doc. S/RES/1368 (September 12, 2001); S.C. Res. 1373, U.N. Doc. D/Res/1373 (September 28, 2001); Carsten Stahn, *Terrorist Acts as "Armed Attack": The Right to Self-Defense, Article 51(1/2) of the U.N. Charter, and International Terrorism*, 27 Fletcher Forum of World Affairs 35, 37–38 (2003).

20 *See id.* at 41–46.

21 These questions are addressed in the draft Manual on International Law Applicable to Cyber Warfare, Rules 10–13 (The Tallinn Manual, 2012). *See* www.ccdcoe.org/249.html; on the question in general *see* Michael N. Schmitt, *Computer Network Attack and the Use of Force in International Law: Thoughts on a Normative Framework*, 37 Columbia Journal of Transnational Law 885 (1999); Mathew C. Waxman, *Cyber-Attacks and the Use of Force: Back to the Future of Article 2(4)*, 36 Yale Journal of International Law 421 (2011).

22 Nicaragua, *supra* note 3, ¶191. The same reasoning is found in Case Concerning Oil Platforms (Iran v. U.S.), 2003 I.C.J. 161, ¶51 (November 6); *see also* Christine Gray, International Law and the Use of Force 8 (2008).

prohibited by the Charter, only "grave" forms of use of force constitute an "armed attack" that spawns the right to self-defense.[23]

"Grave" forms of use of force, or "armed attacks," were defined in *Nicaragua* as including actions, beyond mere "frontier incidents" – whether taken by a state's regular armed forces, or by other forces sent by the state or on behalf of it – across an international border.[24] "Less grave" forms were defined by the Court as the actions considered prohibited in the Declaration on Friendly Relations.[25] These activities include, among others, a state's *acquiescence* to or *toleration* of acts committed by non-state actors operating from its territory, in the context of an internal armed conflict taking place in another state, as well as arming and training of opposition forces.[26] An example for such a situation may be found in Zaire's acquiescence to the operation of UNITA forces from its territory, against the government of Angola.[27]

It is important to note, however, the dissenting opinion of Judge Schwebel concerning this distinction, which corresponded to a significant rift in the understanding of international law between the dominant actors of the time. According to Judge Schwebel, arming, training and providing logistical support to groups in an internal armed conflict, as well as other forms of *substantial involvement* (as the term appears in Article 3(g) of the Definition of Aggression) in the activities of such groups, is tantamount to an armed attack and potentially to aggression.[28]

In our context – whether an action is an "armed attack" or not; constitutes a "grave" or "less grave" form of use of force – the key importance is in the fact that all of the said actions are considered *forcible*. Thus, forcible interventions can include "grave" uses of force: meaning, armed

23 However, such acts may give rise to "proportionate countermeasures." The Court did not elaborate regarding the nature of such countermeasures. *See* Nicaragua, *supra* note 3, ¶¶247–249. Judge Schwebel, in *obiter dictum*, rejected this approach, maintaining that Article 51 does not circumscribe the limits of self-defense, which is grounded in customary law. Nicaragua, ¶¶171–173 (Schwebel, J., dissenting.)

24 Nicaragua, *supra* note 3, ¶195. This definition leaves much to be desired nowadays, considering the emergence of means such as cyber warfare, as discussed *supra*, note 21.

25 Declaration on Principles of International Law concerning Friendly Relations and Cooperation among States, G.A. Res. 2625 (XXV), U.N. Doc. A/8082 (October 24, 1970); Nicaragua, *supra* note 3, ¶191. It seems reasonable that the Court included "mere frontier incidents" in the category of "less-grave" uses of force, since it exempted these actions from the definition of "armed attack."

26 These principles were reaffirmed in Article 6 of the Declaration on the Enhancement of the Effectiveness of the Principle of Refraining from the Threat or Use of Force in International Relations, G.A. Res. 42/22, U.N. Doc. A/Res/42/22 (November 18, 1987), and repeated in Armed Activities on the Territory of the Congo (DRC v. Uganda), 2005 I.C.J. 168 (December 19) ¶276–305; *see also* Gray, *supra* note 22, at 79–80.

27 *See* Chapter 1, sec. 3.1.

28 Judge Schwebel advanced this interpretation to vindicate the US intervention in Nicaragua, in collective self-defense of El-Salvador in response to the former's attack. *See* Nicaragua, *supra* note 3, ¶¶154–171, 176 (Schwebel, J., dissenting.).

interventions by a state's military forces, or by non-state actors operating under the state's control; and "less grave" uses of force, such as acquiescence and toleration of actions taken by non-state actors operating from the state's territory, and transfers of arms.

2.3 The question of state attribution: forcible intervention by irregular forces and non-state actors

When can a forcible intervention be attributable to a state?[29] Naturally, this question does not pose major difficulties when a state overtly deploys its regular armed forces. However, when irregular forces are involved, the issue of attribution becomes paramount. The question of state responsibility for acts of irregular forces – or state attribution – has been one of increasing importance since the end of World War II, as the use of irregular forces became a dominant feature of forcible interventions in internal conflicts. This has occurred in the Cold War's proxy conflicts;[30] in Africa's disastrous internal conflicts since the 1990s;[31] and in contemporary struggles involving religious extremists in the early twenty-first century.[32]

An informative example of these dynamics can be found in the first stage of the Syrian intervention in the Lebanese conflict of 1975, in which Syria sent the "Palestine Liberation Army" (PLA) – an officially Palestinian, but effectively Syrian force – to intervene in favor of the rebelling National Front. The PLA forces were directed from Damascus and operated Syrian military hardware hastily covered in PLA insignia.[33] Another instance of forcible intervention through irregular forces is the

29 Article 2(a) of the ILC Articles on State Responsibility conditions state responsibility for the act being attributable to the state; however, the articles relevant to the issue of attribution leave ample room for interpretation. *See* International Law Commission, Draft Articles on Responsibility of States for Internationally Wrongful Acts, with Commentaries, arts. 51, 53 in Report of the International Law Commission, U.N. GAOR, 53d Sess., Supp. No. 10, A/56/20 (2001), ¶¶1–5.

30 For instance, the relation between North Vietnam and the Pathet Lao insurgents in the Laotian internal conflict of the 1960s; the alleged connection between the Nasserite rebels and the United Arab Republic in the Lebanese conflict of 1958 (both prompted UN commissions to investigate these connections – both found no conclusive evidence). *See* John Main, *The Civil War in Laos, in* International Regulation of Civil Wars, *supra* note 17, at 91; Malcolm Kerr, *The Lebanese Civil War, in* International Regulation of Civil Wars, *id.*, at 65, 66–67.

31 For instance, in Rwanda, Burundi, Sierra Leone and Sudan. *See* William G. Thom, *Congo–Zaire's 1996–1997 Civil War in the Context of Evolving Patterns of Military Conflict in Africa in the Era of Independence*, 19 Journal of Conflict Studies (1999).

32 For instance, the perplexing status of Hizbullah within Lebanon's political structure. *See* International Crisis Group, *Drums of War: Israel and the "Axis of Resistance,"* Middle East Report No. 97, 4–6 (August 2, 2010) (analyzing the possible consequences of the "embedding" of Hizbullah in the Lebanese state).

33 *See* Naomi Joy Weinberger, Syrian Intervention in Lebanon: The 1975–1976 Civil War 142 (1986).

involvement of the Rwandan Patriotic Army (RPA) in the 1996–1997 Zaire/Congo conflict, in which RPA forces, loyal to Rwandan president Kagame, were instrumental in the removal of Zaire's dictator Mobuto Sésé Seko.[34] Recently, Iranian officials reportedly admitted that units of Hizbullah, crossing from Lebanon, have participated in the defense of army bases in Syria, after these have allegedly come under attack by the Syrian opposition.[35] The latter situation demonstrates the attribution problem in full force, namely, whether Hizbullah's intervention can be attributed to Lebanon, Iran, both or neither.

Regarding irregular forces, Article 3(g) of the Definition of Aggression – augmented by a similar provision in the 2010 Kampala definition of the crime of aggression[36] – provides that the term includes

> [t]he sending by or on behalf of a State of armed bands, groups, irregulars or mercenaries, which carry out acts of armed force against another State of such gravity as to amount to the acts listed above, or its substantial involvement therein.[37]

The ICJ, in *Nicaragua*, reaffirmed this article as reflecting customary international law, holding that it

> sees no reason to deny that, in customary law, the prohibition of armed attacks may apply to the sending by a State of armed bands to the territory of another State, if such an operation, because of its scale and effects, would have been classified as an armed attack rather than as a mere frontier incident had it been carried out by regular armed forces.[38]

Thus, the ICJ has recognized the attribution between a state and irregular forces *actively sent* by it. Regarding the level of state control required for such attribution, the Nicaragua court held that the state must exercise "effective control" over the specific operation.[39] The ICTY, conversely, in the famous *Tadic* case, required a more lax standard of "overall control."[40] Article 8 of the Articles on State Responsibility (DASR) requires, in this context, that "the person or group of persons is in fact acting on the

34 Thom, *supra* note 31.

35 *Source: Lebanese, Syrian Situation May Lead to Abductions*, Now Lebanon, January 22, 2012, *available at* www.nowlebanon.com/NewsArticleDetails.aspx?ID=355577.

36 The Crime of Aggression, art. 8bis(g), Resolution RC/Res.6, RC/11 (June 11, 2010).

37 Definition of Aggression, G.A. Res. 3314 (XXIX), ¶3(g), U.N. Doc. A/9631 (December 14, 1974).

38 Nicaragua, *supra* note 3, ¶195 (emphasis added).

39 *Id.* ¶¶115–116.

40 Prosecutor v. Tadic, Case No. IT-94-1-A, Appeals Chambers Judgment ¶¶115–145 (International Criminal Tribunal for the Former Yugoslavia, July 15, 1999).

instructions of, or under the direction or control" of the state.[41] The Commentary on Article 8 addressed the different standards established in *Nicaragua* and *Tadic*, and summarized that "it is a matter for appreciation in each case whether particular conduct was or was not carried out under the control of a State, to such an extent that the conduct controlled should be attributed to it."[42] In the 2007 *Bosnia Genocide* case, the ICJ once again advanced the "effective control" test as established in *Nicaragua*, critiquing the ruling in *Tadic* and holding that the effective-control standard is also compatible with the aforementioned Article 8 of DASR, which it saw as reflecting customary international law.[43]

The seeming recognition by the ICJ – based on the Declaration on Friendly Relations – that a state's *toleration* of or *acquiescence* to forcible acts by non-state actors operating from its territory can also amount to a forcible act *by* that state (albeit a "less grave" form),[44] also raises the question of attribution between the tolerated or acquiesced acts and the state. Since it is essentially an issue of forbearance, determining the *level* of toleration or acquiescence required to link between the state and the non-state actor is a complex endeavor, which must allude to a standard of reasonableness. We shall not elaborate on this question; suffice it to say that since the attacks of September 11, 2001, and the ensuing (and widely accepted) forcible response, some have argued that a positive duty of "due diligence" to prevent acts by non-state actors has solidified.[45] Such a positive duty to prevent actions can perhaps justify – at least in extreme situations, for instance, when a state endorses such acts ex post – viewing attacks launched from a state's territory, as forcible interventions attributable to the latter.

Indeed, some have read the "due diligence" concept into the "overall control" standard, as imposing "protective duties" on the territorial state vis-à-vis other states. However, it is unclear to what extent, if at all, they see this duty as creating an attribution sufficient to implicate the territorial state itself, beyond allowing the attack of the non-state actor in its territory.[46] In this context, it has been claimed – and this indeed seems reasonable – that the question whether a state is genuinely "unable" to reign in

41 DASR and Commentaries, *supra* note 29, at 31.

42 *Id.* at 48.

43 Case Concerning the Application of the Convention on the Prevention and Punishment of the Crime of Genocide (Bosnia and Herzegovina v. Serbia and Montenegro), 2007 I.C.J. ¶398, ¶¶405–406 (February 26); *see also* Antonio Cassese, *The Nicaragua and the Tadic Tests Revisited in Light of the I.C.J. Judgment on Genocide in Bosnia*, 18 European Journal of International Law 649 (2007).

44 *See* sec. 1.2.

45 *See, e.g.*, Robert P. Barnidge, Non-State Actors and Terrorism: Applying the Law of State Responsibility and the Due Diligence Principle 53–110 (2007); *see generally* Tal Becker, Terrorism and the State: Rethinking the Rules of State Responsibility (2006).

46 For a discussion *see, e.g.*, Stahn, *supra* note 19, at 47–48, 50–51; for an analytical treatment of the question, *see* Noam Lubell, Extraterritorial Use of Force against Non-State Actors 36–42 (2010).

the activities of non-state actors operating from its territory, or is rather merely "unwilling" to do so, can affect the scope of the right to self-defense of the attacked state.[47] Such a distinction can also be understood as affecting the attribution of actions of non-state actors to territorial states – and also in the context of intervention. However, the exact ramifications of the concept of "due diligence," and related notions, are beyond the scope of this work.

In sum, forcible intervention by states encompasses not only the direct use of regular armed forces, but also actions conducted through irregular forces sent or controlled by a state. The attributing link is determined according to the "effective" or "overall" control tests, in cases of active encouragement; or, in cases of toleration or acquiescence – meaning, of forbearance – by duties of "due diligence," however they are defined.

3 Multilateral forcible intervention by UN mandated forces

The aforementioned modalities of forcible intervention apply also to cases in which the intervening powers are mandated to use force by UNSC resolutions adopted under Chapter VII of the UN Charter ("enforcement measures") – notwithstanding the different legal status of such forces. Thus, when UN authorized forces forcefully engage a party to an internal conflict, these forces may be looked upon as forcible interveners. This is the case, for instance, of the UN Mission in the Democratic Republic of Congo's (MONUC) involvement in the government offensive against rebel forces in East Congo between 2008 and 2010;[48] or the 2011 international bombing campaign against forces loyal to the Libyan regime, in favor – even if tacitly – of rebel groups, as authorized by the UNSC.[49]

It is important to distinguish between the situations mentioned above, which represent robust UN operations characteristic of the post-Cold War era, and classic, formally impartial peacekeeping missions. The latter consist of the consensual deployment of neutral humanitarian or peace-keeping forces. As such, they are excluded from the definition of forcible intervention.[50] These operations will usually be conducted by UN or (regional organization) authorized peace-keeping forces, which (at least *de jure*) are not mandated to actively assist – whether directly or indirectly – either party to the conflict.

47 *See* Theresa Reinold, *State Weakness, Irregular Warfare, and the Right to Self-Defense Post-9/11*, 105 American Journal of International Law 244 (2011).

48 *See* Chapter 1, sec. 3.3.

49 S.C. Res. 1973, U.N. Doc. S/RES/1973 (March 17, 2011).

50 This is irrespective of whether these forces are deployed pursuant to Chapter VI or VII of the Charter. The intervention is "forcible" if the mandate of the UN force includes forcible engagement, and is "non-forcible" when the mandate does not include forcible actions beyond the use of unit self-defense. *See* Terry D. Gill and Dieter Fleck, *Concept and Sources of the International Law of Military Operations*, *in* The Handbook of the International Law of Military Operations 3, 4 (Terry D. Gill and Dieter Fleck eds., 2010).

The difference between non-forcible and forcible UNSC authorized operations can be exemplified by comparing two resolutions concerning MONUC's mandate. Resolution 1279 of 1999,[51] establishing MONUC, primarily designated the operation as an impartial ceasefire observation force, established pursuant to the Lusaka Agreement between the conflicting parties. As such, it had no mandate to use force. Resolution 1856 of 2008, conversely, mandated MONUC to use of force in "close cooperation" with the Congolese government.[52]

4 The question of arms transfers to parties in internal armed conflicts

4.1 Unique aspects of arms transfers

A common type of forcible intervention is undertaken through the transfer of arms to a party to an internal conflict, for the purpose of enhancing its military capabilities.[53] In the context of *jus ad bellum* – excluding, perhaps, the question of whether it gives rise to the right to self-defense – the issue of arms transfers to parties in internal strife can be regulated by the same normative framework that governs "grave" forcible intervention. However, the problem of arms transfers raises some unique questions, which call for some separate treatment.

The main difference between direct invasion and provision of arms – as methods of intervention – is that the latter is of dual-character: it is not only a form of use of force, but also a form of international trade. As such, arms transfers are more readily undertaken by private entities, a fact that historically allowed for more flexibility in the provision of arms, even during internal strife. This feature of arms trade accounted for great controversy, for instance, during the American Civil War, when private British shipyards supplied warships to the Confederacy – which ultimately spawned the famous Alabama Arbitration.[54] Moreover, arms transfers raise difficult problems of illicit trade, especially with regards to small arms. Considering these difficulties, it is clear that the "easy" case, in this context, arises when a state directly transfers arms to parties in an internal armed conflict. The more challenging legal situation, however, occurs when private entities do so. In a sense, this problem reflects dilemmas related to the question of attribution, as discussed in section 1.3 above.

51 S.C. Res. 1279, U.N. Doc. S/RES/1279 (November 30, 1999).

52 S.C. Res. 1856, U.N. Doc. S/RES/1856 (December 22, 2008) ¶3.

53 For a definition of arms transfers *see* Maya Brehm, *The Arms Trade and States' Duty to Ensure Respect for Humanitarian and Human Rights Law,* 12 Journal of Conflict and Security Law 21, 23 (2008).

54 *See generally* Adrian Cook, The Alabama Claims: American Politics and Anglo-American Relations, 1865–1872 (1975).

Without exhausting all aspects of this complex issue, we shall briefly delineate the main features of this confusing element of intervention, in order to clarify our later discussion.

In practice (and reserving for now the question of legality), transfers of arms to parties in internal armed conflicts – whether to governments or to opposition forces – has been a recurring phenomenon in the international system. During the Cold War, for instance, internal armed conflicts were frequently used as proxy-wars between the rival powers; accordingly, arms transfers, by multiple parties, were a common tactic. The USSR, for instance, transferred weapons to opposition forces in Namibia (1961), Angola (1964) and others.[55] In the secession struggle between Nigeria and the breakaway republic of Biafra, for example, interests were more complex than "east versus west," as France (indirectly) provided arms to Biafra; the USSR, Czechoslovakia, Britain (albeit in a limited manner) and some Arab states chose to transfer arms to Nigeria.[56] The practice of arms transfers has not ceased in the post-Cold War era. For instance, NATO provided arms to the Kosovo Liberation Army in its secession struggle against Serbia prior to 1999; and the US supplied arms to opposition forces in Iraq during the mid-1990s.[57] In the 2011–2012 crisis in Syria, western states and their allies contemplated providing arms to Syrian rebels, while Russia and Iran, allegedly, continued arming the regime even during the height of the conflict.[58]

Theoretically, arms transfers can also be part of a UNSC authorized forcible intervention, perhaps as an alternative for external land operations. For instance, UNSC Resolution 1973 authorized states to take "all necessary measures" to protect civilians in Libya, but excluded the deployment of an "occupation force."[59] When it became clear that aerial attacks were insufficient to bring a swift end to the actions by the Libyan regime, the option of transferring arms to the Libyan rebels surfaced. US Secretary of State Clinton emphasized that the term "all necessary measures" indeed encompasses also arms transfers to the Libyan opposition.[60]

55 Lucy Mathiak and Lora Lumpe, *Government Gun-Running to Guerillas*, *in* Running Guns, The Global Black Market in Small Arms 56–57 (Lora Lumpe ed., 2000).

56 *See* Gary Clyde Hufbauer *et al.*, Economic Sanctions Reconsidered, Supplemental Case Histories Case 67–1 (3rd ed. 2007); *see also* John De St. Jorre, The Nigerian Civil War (1972).

57 *See* Mathiak and Lumpe, *supra* note 55, at 66–70.

58 Daniel Dombey and Borzou Daragahi, *U.S. Signals Support for Arming Syria Rebels*, Financial Times, April 1, 2012, *available at* www.ft.com/cms/s/0/3a8057e8–7bf1–11e1–9100–00144feab49a.html#axzz1sqsEOpFy; Josh Rogin, *State Dept.: Russia and Iran Still Arming Bashar Al-Assad*, Foreign Policy, February 15, 2012, *available at* http://thecable.foreignpolicy.com/posts/2012/02/15/state_dept_russia_and_iran_still_arming_bashar_al_assad.

59 S.C. Res. 1973, *supra* note 49, ¶4.

60 Mark Landler *et al.*, *Washington in Fierce Debate on Arming Libyan Rebels*, New York Times, March 29, 2011, *available at* www.nytimes.com/2011/03/30/world/africa/30diplo.html?_r=3&hp.

4.2 Arms transfers by private entities

As we shall see later on, traditional international law has been clear that prior to recognition of the conflicting parties as *belligerents*, transfer of arms to opposition groups was an unfriendly act that could lead to war, while transfer of arms to governments was not. After belligerency recognition, the widely accepted view asserted that, should they wish to remain neutral, states were required to refrain from arming *either* party.[61]

However, even in cases where belligerency was recognized, states were not obliged to *prevent* arms sales by private entities; rather, they could choose whether to allow such sales or prohibit them, as long as the policy would be applied equally to the conflicting belligerents.[62] The only positive duty incurred by the neutral state was to prevent, within its jurisdiction, the fitting out or arming of warships (or aircraft) intended to engage in hostilities against a belligerent, even if the warships were built by a private entity.[63] Restrictions on arms transfers by private entities have been debated over the decades, and could indeed be found in the non-intervention agreement of the Spanish Civil War as well as in domestic neutrality acts, notably of the US and Britain.[64] However, although attempts to do so were made, such restrictions were never codified as comprehensive international norms.[65]

A 1925 convention to regulate arms transfers by private entities, in which states undertook "not to export or *permit* the export" of arms unless in "direct supply to the Government" never went into force.[66] This rule possibly applied also in internal strife, allowing private arms transfers only to governments. However, when the conflict amounted to "war" – meaning, when belligerency was recognized – the convention would be trumped by the laws of neutrality, and the problem of arms transfers by private entities would again arise.[67]

61 *See* Hague Convention XIII: Concerning the Rights and Duties of Neutral Powers in Naval War (1907), art. 6; interestingly, such a categorical prohibition is not found in *land* neutrality law. *See* Hague Convention V: Respecting the Rights and Duties of Neutral Powers and Persons in Case of War on Land (1907), U.S.T.S. 540. However, Dinstein holds that it is "incontestable" that the same rule also concerns neutrality on land. *See* Dinstein, *supra* note 13, at 28.

62 *See id.*

63 This exception is traced to the Alabama Claims arbitration. *See* Hague Convention XIII: Concerning the Rights and Duties of Neutral Powers in Naval War (1907), art. 8; The Hague Rules of Air Warfare (1923), art. 46; Dinstein, *supra* note 13, at 29.

64 *See* Chapter 5, sec. 4.

65 For a historic overview *see* David G. Anderson, *The International Arms Trade: Regulating Conventional Arms Transfers in the Aftermath of the Gulf War*, 7 American University International Law Review 749, 758–770 (1992).

66 Convention on Supervision of International Trade in Arms and Ammunition and in Implements of War (June 17, 1925), League of Nations Doc. A.16.1925.IX, art. 2(1) (1925) (emphasis added); Anderson, *supra* note 65, at 761–762.

67 Convention on Supervision of International Trade in Arms, *supra* note 66, art. 33.

This approach was repeated in the 1928 Convention on Duties and Rights of States in the Event of Civil Strife.[68] The signatory states pledged that in the event of "civil strife," they shall "*forbid* traffic in arms and war material, except when intended for the Government, while the belligerency of the rebels has not been recognized, in which the latter case the rules of neutrality shall be applied."[69] Essentially, the said provision meant that in internal strife, only transfer of arms to governments was permitted, unless *belligerency* of the parties was declared – and then states shall remain *neutral*. The latter obligation, again, entailed the abstention from transfer of arms by governments to *either* party, but did not, in general, address private arms trade.

Modern international law has not been clear on this issue. It seems intuitive that, at large, in the era of the UN Charter, transfers of arms to *governments* involved in internal armed conflicts are not contradictory to international law, subject to the limitations we shall address later on, while arms transfers to opposition groups – whether by governments of private entities – will in general be unlawful.[70]

This notion was reaffirmed in the *Nicaragua* ruling. There, the ICJ refused to recognize a customary international norm "whereby the level of armaments of a sovereign State can be limited";[71] while holding, conversely, that US arms transfers to the Contras violated the norm of non-intervention and of the prohibition on the use of force.[72] Since the Court relied extensively on the Declaration on Friendly Relations,[73] it is reasonable to extend this principle also to arms transfers by private entities: accordingly, a state that tolerates or acquiesces to arms transfers to opposition groups might conduct – in the language of the Nicaragua Court – a "less grave" violation of Article 2(4) of the Charter and also, perhaps, violate its "due diligence" requirements.[74]

4.3 Towards the substantive analysis of arms transfers?

Like our analysis of consensual forcible interventions at large, arms transfers to governments can also be controlled by substantive doctrines, as addressed in later chapters. However, because of their unique aspects, there are ongoing attempts to regulate arms transfers separately from general questions of the use of force.

68 Convention on Duties and Rights of States in the Event of Civil Strife, February 20, 1928, 134 L.N.T.S. 45.

69 *Id.* art. 1(3).

70 Chapters 6–10. *See* Emanuela Chiara-Gillard, *What's Legal? What's Illegal?*, *in* Running Guns, *supra* note 55, at 27, 30, 36.

71 Nicaragua, *supra* note 3, ¶269; *see also* Brehm, *supra* note 53, at 25.

72 Nicaragua, *supra* note 3, ¶ 238, 247.

73 *Supra*, note 15.

74 *See* sec. 1.2–1.3.

Indeed, arms transfers have been all but non-regulated throughout the twentieth century,[75] excluding a limited number of treaties prohibiting the transfer of specific kinds of weapons due to humanitarian concerns.[76] However, in recent years, the UN has begun to address this issue. Thus, United Nations General Assembly (UNGA) Resolution 61/89 of 2006 recognized that international standards on arms transfers are absent, and called for the establishment of a group of experts to examine the drafting of a binding legal instrument concerning this issue.[77] The Resolution also acknowledged "the right of all States to manufacture, import, export, transfer and retain conventional arms for self-defence and security needs" – while balancing this right with its reaffirmation of respect "for international law, including international human rights law and international humanitarian law, and the [UN] Charter."[78] Thus, the resolution alluded to concerns raised by arms transfer in the realms of IHRL, *jus in bello* and *jus ad bellum*. The resulting expert report noted that any treaty should consider the issue of "transfers to non-State actors," and should also "reflect respect for the sovereignty of every State, without interfering in the internal affairs of States." In addition, the report noted that IHRL and IHL may also have effect over the question of arms transfers.[79] In subsequent discussions, the UNGA decided to further address this issue, and to "elaborate a legally binding treaty" concerning arms transfers.[80]

Simultaneously, humanitarian concerns have given rise to various potential doctrines, discussed in different forums, suggesting that arms transfers – even by private individuals – can be substantively limited by existing due-diligence requirements enshrined in IHL or IHRL,[81] or by

75 Except, of course, mandatory arms embargos imposed by the UNSC. *See also* Brehm, *supra* note 53, at 27.

76 *See id.* at 28–30.

77 G.A. Res. 61/89, prmbl., ¶2, U.N. Doc. A/RES/61/89 (December 18, 2006).

78 *Id.* prmbl.

79 Report of the Group of Governmental Experts to Examine the Feasibility, Scope and Draft Parameters for a Comprehensive, Legally Binding Instrument Establishing Common International Standards for the Import, Export and Transfer of Conventional Arms, U.N. Doc. A/63/334 (August 26, 2008); endorsed by the UNGA in G.A. Res. 63/240, U.N. Doc. A/Res/63/240 (January 8, 2009) ¶¶17–18, 24.

80 G.A. Res. 64/48, U.N. Doc. A/RES/64/48 (December 2, 2009); for the updated situation regarding the treaty *see* UN Arms Trade Treaty Preparatory Committee, www.un.org/disarmament/convarms/ATTPrepCom (last visited March 11, 2012).

81 Based on Article 1 Common to the Geneva Conventions (requiring states to "respect and to ensure respect" for IHL) and states' general duty to exercise due diligence under Article 2(1) of the ICCPR (requiring states to "respect and to ensure" protection of rights), International Covenant on Civil and Political Rights, December 16, 1966, 999 U.N.T.S. 171; *see* Brehm, *supra* note 53, at 30, 44; *see also* Barbara Frey, *The Question of Trade, Carrying and the Use of Small Arms and Light Weapons in the Context of Human Rights and Humanitarian Norms*, Economic and Social Council, U.N. Doc. E/CN.4/Sub.2/2002/39 (May 30, 2002); Gillard, *supra* note 70, at 31–32, 38–40.

general principles such as the principle of protection of civilians.[82] Such doctrines, if codified within an upcoming arms trade treaty, may affect and further clarify the legality of arms transfers as a form of forcible intervention. It remains to be seen what balance will be reflected, in any future treaty, between the issues of non-intervention, sovereignty, *jus ad bellum*, IHL and IHRL, and how it will treat arms transfers in the context of internal armed conflicts. It is clear, however, that the approach of international law towards this question, like the issue of intervention at large, is moving towards a substantive approach. Nonetheless, until such a binding instrument comes into force, the issue of arms transfers to parties in internal armed conflicts should be assessed according to the general principles governing forcible intervention, as outlined in the following chapters.

82 *See* Chapter 8.

4 Internal armed conflicts and consent in the war-prerogative era and effectiveness as a source of rights

1 General

The following two chapters inquire into the sources, roots and implications of the main doctrines that governed internal armed conflicts in the pre-UN Charter era – the doctrines of belligerency and insurgency and their interaction with the nascent laws on the use of force which came into being in the era of the League of Nations (LONS). As we shall see, these doctrines did not directly concern the question of consensual intervention, since there was virtually no limitation on states' prerogative to use force prior to the UN Charter – or at least before the 1928 Kellogg–Briand Pact (hereinafter, this era is referred to as the *war-prerogative era*). The main effects of these doctrines concerned neutral maritime trade, rather than the question of forcible intervention. Indeed, they reflected an international system that was explicitly preoccupied with the interests of external parties, and *less* with the political rights of the parties to the conflict themselves.

However, this by no means implies that the understanding of these doctrines, as they developed prior to the prohibition on the use of force, is irrelevant to our context – for several reasons. For instance, some scholars have made connections between the belligerency doctrine and the law of consensual intervention, and these are worthy of exploration and clarification. As we shall demonstrate, the question of intervention and consent has had substantial legal validity only *after* the prohibition on the use of force has been set forth. Moreover, whether having implications on the law of consensual intervention or not, the belligerency and insurgency doctrines were the main tools in traditional international law utilized to assess the rights and duties of parties to internal armed conflicts – and as such they are of interest to us. Although they did not directly confer or negate any rights regarding external parties' legal capacity to *use force* (which was always a viable option), it did affect substantive rights in the narrower realm of *neutrality* – which, to an extent, can also be looked upon as passing judgment on the merits of the conflict.[1] A clearer understanding of these doctrines can therefore assist us in realizing the concerns of the international system in the war-prerogative era, allowing us to better perceive the differences between that era and today.

Furthermore, surveying the law of that time can demonstrate the seemingly amoral nature by which law operated in an era when territorial effective control was the main criteria for the assessment of the rights of parties in internal conflicts. Juxtaposing these approaches with the more substantive concerns of contemporary international law – as these will be addressed later on – can assist in contextualizing the development of international law regarding internal armed conflicts.

This, of course, does not imply that the question of consensual intervention was not debated *morally* by the great thinkers of the time. For instance, John Stuart Mill was much concerned with the 1849 Russian pro-government intervention upon the invitation of the Austrian Emperor, to assist it in quashing Hungary's struggle for secession. Mill was so much against the Russian intervention that he argued that a counter-intervention by Britain would be justified.[2] Conversely, as we shall see, Mill's vehement condemnation of the Confederate States of America, on ethical grounds, led him to completely reject the possibility of forcible intervention by Britain to assist the South.[3] However, such considerations remained on the ethical level, far removed from the legal realm.

Two important – perhaps intertwined – processes, which can allow us to better grasp the present state of international law, are revealed when assessing the traditional doctrines regarding the status of parties to internal armed conflicts. First, the movement from rigid frameworks such as the belligerency doctrine, most notably applied in the American Civil War, to more elastic norms as represented in the insurgency doctrine, as it was manifested in the Spanish Civil War. This approach is still echoed in the relatively flexible, ad hoc, nature of contemporary international law's approach to internal armed conflicts. It is reflected, for instance, in the diminishing importance of the technical-legal term "war," and the increasing predominance of the material concept "armed conflict." The second process is the movement from the largely amoral criterion of effective control – again, exemplified in the general obliviousness of states towards the issue of slavery in the American Civil War – into a more value-inclusive system of substantive considerations, which was advocated by certain states already during the Spanish Civil War, and is prevalent also today.

1 *See* Norman J. Padelford, *International Law and the Spanish Civil War*, 31 American Journal of International Law 226, 237 n. 59 (1937) (referring to Wilson and Westlake).

2 John Stuart Mill, *A Few Words on Non-Intervention* (1859), *in* Dissertations and Discussions 238, 261–262 (1882), *available at* http://google.books.com; *see also* Michael Walzer, Just and Unjust Wars: A Moral Argument with Historical Illustrations 91–95 (4th ed., 2006) (examining Mill's approach towards the Hungarian Revolution).

3 *See infra*, sec. 6.3.

2 The use of force in the era of the war-prerogative

Discussing intervention and consent in the era before the prohibition on the use of force requires understanding the general legal framework of the time. Doing so, we shall demonstrate two main points: that the laws on the use of force could not, at the time, substantially serve to limit consensual forcible interventions; and that the laws that *did* exist to regulate the rights of parties to internal conflicts, were heavily based on amoral notions of territorial effectiveness or similar concerns. Both of these realizations can assist us to contrast with – and therefore better understand – contemporary law, while placing it in historical context.

By the late eighteenth century, just-war theory had lost much of its appeal, and thus had a negligible influence over the emerging norms of the laws of war.[4] Rooted in the philosophy of ancient Rome and adopted by Catholic Christian theology – notably by Thomas Aquinas – the just-war doctrine purported to assess the "justness" of war according to various procedural and substantive criteria, namely, the "just cause" of the war and the "right intention" to promote it. The just-war doctrine found its way, in numerous variations, into the writings of the sixteenth and seveteenth centuries' naturalist pioneers of international law.[5]

However, the process of separation between church and state led to the doctrine's decline: when the Catholic Church could not anymore pronounce authoritatively whether a war is indeed "just" – and in absent of alternative binding organizations[6] – both parties would inevitably claim the justness of their cause, a claim no actor could substantially challenge.[7] This fact must have had implications over the question of intervention in internal conflicts, as particular forms of war. Indeed, Vattel, whose approach towards just-war was complex,[8] subjected the question of consensual intervention to states' *own* conceptions of "right." Thus, he argued that in cases of internal strife, states may "take the merits of the cause into consideration, and assist the party which they shall judge to have right on

4 In distinction from the *ethical* discussion of just-war which was always present, to some extent. For a detailed historical account *see* Stephen C. Neff, War and the Law of Nations: A General History 167–277 (2005).

5 On the "just-war" doctrine *see* Yoram Dinstein, War, Aggression and Self-Defense 65–69 (5th ed. 2011); *see also* Robert D. Sloane, *The Cost of Conflation: Preserving the Dualism of Jus ad Bellum and Jus in Bello in the Contemporary Law of War*, 34 Yale Journal of International Law 48, 57–63 (2009). For a classic source *see*, e.g., Hugo Grotius, 1 The Rights of War and Peace, Book 1, Ch. 2 (laying down the naturalist-era view that war has to be substantively just).

6 *See, e.g.*, John Bassett Moore, *International Law: Its Present and Future*, 1 American Journal of International Law 11 (1907) (arguing briefly that the main shortcoming of international law of the time was the absence of international organizations).

7 Dinstein, *supra* note 5, at 68–69.

8 *See* Simone Zurbuchen, *Vattel's Law of Nations and Just War Theory*, 35 History of European Ideas 408 (2009). It seems that while denouncing unjust wars, Vattel denied the practical applicability of such a rule absent an international judge. *See* Sloane, *supra* note 5, at 62.

its side, in case that a party requests their assistance or accepts the offer of it."[9]

In the nineteenth and early twentieth centuries the development of international law was influenced, among other things, by two factors – one philosophical and the other structural. The first was legal positivism, espoused by the likes of John Austin, which dominated contemporary jurisprudence.[10] In the realm of international law, positivism essentially meant that there could be no law beyond that established by explicit consent of sovereigns.[11] The second feature was the decentralized and multi-polar nature of the nineteenth century's international system, which led to the development of norms that were generally fitting for "pure" balance of power dynamics.[12]

Accordingly, the question of war was removed, at the time, from the realm of abstract "justice" to the realm of tangible "consequence." Justness of cause could be used as rhetoric – perhaps to appease internal public opinion – but was not a factor in the legal realm.[13] States would not ask whether their cause for war was just – or legal – but rather, if they were willing to pay the price that war entailed. Law was structured, then, for the purpose of ascertaining when "war" existed between two states, so as to enable third parties to take steps in order stay *neutral*, thereby avoiding the consequences of being dragged into the conflict. This was the background of the development of the intricate law of neutrality. A violation of neutrality could result – in grave circumstances – in the accruement of belligerent status.[14] As phrased by the US Supreme Court, the prevailing view of the time was that "war may be the consequence of failure in the performance of obligations [e.g. of neutrality] towards a friendly power."[15] It is imperative to

9 Emmerich De Vattel, *supra* note 45, Book III, §296. Note that Vattel's argumentation that intervention should be in support of the "right" party could be understood as a just-war condition to be implemented, absent a judge, by each party on its own. For a critique of Vattel in this context, *see* Montague Bernard, On the Principle of Non-Intervention 20–21 (1860).

10 John Austin, The Province of Jurisprudence Determined 117–118 (1832, Wilfred E. Rumble ed., 1995); *see also* Wilhelm G. Grewe, The Epochs of International Law 503 (Michael Byers trans., 2000).

11 *See* Neff, *supra* note 4, at 169–177.

12 On the administration of international law absent organized international institutions during the nineteenth century, *see* Quincy Wright, *The American Civil War*, *in* The International Law of Civil War 30, 94 (Richard A. Falk ed., 1972); *see also* Michael W. Doyle, Ways of War and Peace 161–194 (1997).

13 Dinstein, *supra* note 5, at 69; Lassa Oppenheim, 2 International Law §64 (2nd ed., 1912).

14 *See* Wolff Heintschel von Heinigg, "*Benevolent Third States in International Armed Conflicts: The Myth of the Irrelevance of the Law of Neutrality*, *in* International Law and Armed Conflict: Exploring the Faultlines 543, 544–545 (Michael N. Schmitt *et al.* eds., 2007). On the relations between the law of neutrality and the modern law on the use of force, *see, e.g.*, Andrea Gioia, *Neutrality and Non-Belligerency*, *in* International Economic Law and Armed Conflict Economic Warfare 51 (Harry H.G. Post ed., 1994).

15 The Three Friends, 17 S. Ct. 495, 502 (1897).

understand, however, that in absence of a special treaty,[16] a violation of neutrality, when amounting to an act of hostility in the eyes of the belligerent state, was not an unlawful act per se, but simply one that signified the *end of neutrality*, thus triggering the set of consequences a state of war entailed.[17]

In order to control their relations with belligerent parties, *inter alia* by enforcing the requirements of international neutrality law upon their citizens, states enacted domestic statutes such as the American Neutrality Act of 1794 and the British Foreign Enlistment Act of 1819. Domestic neutrality laws were aimed, in practice, to regulate the actions of private persons within the jurisdiction of the neutral state, and usually prohibited, for instance, organizing expeditions against beleaguered states with which the legislating state was at peace, as well as providing belligerent states with warships.[18] Although they were domestic, such laws have been of key significance to international law – and in particular when internal conflicts erupted – since, even if indirectly, they effectively conferred rights to foreign entities in an era in which "international legislation" was scarce.[19]

Moreover, in the war-prerogative era, for the purpose of ascertaining when *war* existed, a rigid distinction between "wars" and means "short-of-war" developed. For instance, reprisals – including forcible ones – undertaken in order to compel a state to cease unlawful action or make reparation, could be pursued without actually being considered acts of *war*, and thus without altering the otherwise peaceful relations, in the legal sense, between the involved states.[20] War, on the other hand, required actual "fighting" between armed forces, or, at least, a declaration of war or a declaration by a state that another state's actions are acts of war.[21] This distinction, too, led to the international preoccupation with the question whether war, in the technical-legal sense, existed in a given instance. It is in this context that the belligerency doctrine – discussed shortly – developed: chiefly, it was meant to ascertain whether an internal conflict amounted to a state of "war," entailing consequences on neutral states. In sum, from the end of the "just-war" era, through the nineteenth century, and prior to the prohibition on the use of force imposed by Article 2(4) of the UN Charter – and to a more limited extent, the founding of the LONS[22] – the question of intervention in internal armed conflicts was addressed, mainly, through the prism of neutrality law.

16 Dinstein, *supra* note 5, at 79–81.

17 2 Oppenheim, *supra* note 13, §§358–359.

18 *See, e.g.*, Neutrality act of 1794, §3, §5; *see also, e.g.*, N.A. Rogoff and E. Collins, *The Caroline Incident and the Development of International Law*, 16 Brooklyn Journal of International Law 493 (1990).

19 *See* Edward Dumbauld, *Neutrality Laws of the United States*, 31 American Journal of International Law 258, 258 (1937).

20 2 Oppenheim, *supra* note 13, §37, 42.

21 *Id.* §55, 93.

22 *See* L. Kopelmanas, *The Problem of Aggression and the Prevention of War*, 31 American Journal of International Law 244 (1937).

In addition, interventions were assessed, to some ambiguous extent, in light of the norm of non-intervention. However, the latter concept, although much revered in the discourse of the time, was especially vague in light of the dominant contemporaneous perception, viewing war as the quintessential sovereign prerogative. War could be declared as a remedy for an international wrong, as well as for strictly political reasons.[23] As famously noted, states could "resort to war for a good reason, a bad reason, or no reason at all"[24] – a right limited, sometimes, by a "lip-service" requirement of engaging in previous negotiations.[25] Indeed, as commonly phrased, international law in the war-prerogative era did not *prohibit* war, but merely attempted to regulate the way it was carried out through *jus in bello.*[26]

Therefore, and as noted by Dinstein, the war-prerogative resulted in a grave anomaly: on the one hand, international law sought to protect the sovereignty of states; however, on the other hand, any sovereign could subjugate the sovereignty of another by wantonly waging war. It is therefore fair to question the value of the norm of non-intervention – which originally set out to protect sovereignty – absent a complementary prohibition on the use of force. Nonetheless, most international lawyers of that era did not treat this inconsistency as detrimental to international law, or simply disregarded this problem.[27] A fascinating example can be found in Bernard's 1860 defense of the principle of non-intervention, in which he sets forth an almost absolute perception of the principle, with virtually no attempt to reconcile it with the dominance of the war-prerogative.[28] This anomaly will constantly hover over our discussion of the dominant doctrines of the time – which we will now turn to consider – including the (rather futile) attempts to apply them to the question of intervention and consent.

3 Effective control as a source of rights: the belligerency doctrine

3.1 The rationale and development of the belligerency status

The belligerency doctrine was the dominant traditional doctrine of international law regarding internal strife. The concept has developed gradually from the American Revolution, throughout a number of conflicts in the early mid-nineteenth century, until it was galvanized as a

23 2 Oppenheim, *supra* note 13, §54.

24 H.W. Briggs, The Law of Nations 976 (1952); *cited in* Dinstein, *supra* note 5, at 78.

25 2 Oppenheim, *supra* note 13, §93.

26 *See, e.g., id.* §53; Arnold D. Mcnair, *Collective Security*, 17 British Year Book of International Law 150, 150–152 (1936).

27 Dinstein, *supra* note 5, at 78–79, and the sources cited therein. *Compare* Augustus Granville Stapleton, Intervention and Non-Intervention; or, The Foreign Policy of Great Britain from 1790 to 1865 13–14 (1866) (claiming that forcible intervention must be justified with a *casus belli, i.e.*, "external injury" to the intervener).

28 Bernard, *supra* note 9.

cognizable doctrine in the American Civil War.[29] Its early appearances as a distinctly defined and coherent legal doctrine can be traced to Richard Dana's 1866 edition of Wheaton's Elements of International Law.[30]

As defined by Lauterpacht, the recognition of belligerency was a "declaration, express or implied, that hostilities waged between two communities ... are of such character and scope as to entitle the parties to be treated as belligerents engaged in a war in the sense ordinarily attached to that term by international law."[31] Accordingly, upon such recognition, the internal conflict – traditionally beyond the reach of international law – became a "war" in the international sense, generating international legal effects.[32]

The recognition of belligerency, in essence, was an "interim" status, frequently conferred through a proclamation of neutrality – or by acquiescence to belligerent measures imposed by the parties[33] – in which rebels would acquire warfare rights and obligations normally attributable to governments, *without* being recognized formally as governments or as separate states. As phrased by Bernard, such status merely constituted the recognition of the "precarious power which it [the belligerent] possesses in fact."[34] It was thus only an acknowledgment that the belligerent "claims to be a state [or government] and is de facto making war as such."[35] As emphasized by Oppenheim, there was "a broad and deep gulf" between such recognition and the recognition of a new state (or government).[36] Therefore, belligerency meant that the opposition possessed a limited or "apparent" international legal personality.[37]

An example of the intermediate status of belligerency could be found in the declaration of neutrality proclaimed by the French Emperor on June 10, 1861, in the context of the American Civil War:

> His Majesty the Emperor of the French, considering the state of peace between France and the United States of America, has resolved to maintained strict neutrality in the struggle between the union government and the states which *claim* to form a separate confederation.[38]

29 Roscoe R. Oglesby, Internal War and the Search for Normative Order VI–VIII, 18–32 (1971).

30 *Id.* at 33; Wheaton's Elements of International Law §23 n, 15 (Richard Henry Dana ed., 1866).

31 Hersch Lauterpacht, Recognition in International Law 175 (1948).

32 2 Oppenheim, *supra* note 13, §59; *see also* Padelford, *supra* note 1, at 228.

33 Lauterpacht, *supra* note 31, at 177–181.

34 Montague Bernard, A Historical Account of the Neutrality of Great Britain during the American Civil War 115 (1870).

35 Joseph H. Beale, Jr., *The Recognition of Cuban Belligerency*, 9 Harvard Law Review 406, 406 (1896).

36 Lassa Oppenheim, 1 International Law §74 (2rd ed., 1912).

37 *Id.* §63.

38 Reprinted in Bernard, *supra* note 34, at 144 (emphasis added).

Besides its intermediate nature, the status of belligerency was also temporary. For instance, if the recognized opposition group was defeated, its status as a belligerent elapsed, negating any belligerent rights it might have gained.[39]

The doctrine of belligerency relied heavily on the idea of effective control as a source of rights. As such, it developed in stark contrast to the Holy Alliance's doctrine of legitimism, which denied any status from revolutionary movements, regardless of the achievements they might have achieved on the ground.[40] By focusing on territorial effectiveness, the doctrine was seemingly devoid of value-based considerations, except – perhaps – for its precondition that belligerents act according to the laws of war. However, even this requirement was thin: the laws of war were themselves not immensely developed, and in practice requirement had mainly to do with the application of the laws of war as these related to treatment of maritime prize.

The belligerency doctrine developed out of practical necessity. International law, being a system of states, was viewed has having "no place in a struggle between a Sovereign Government and its rebellious subjects."[41] However, it was understood that in reality, rebels will not be concerned by this distinction, since they refuse to admit that they are "subjects" to begin with. Thus, they will inevitably employ the same military means that governments use. Denial of belligerent rights would therefore be useless, since it will be certainly disregarded by the rebels; ultimately, such denial could draw third parties into conflict with the rebels. Recognition of the belligerency of both sides was thus a "simple practical solution," entitling them, vis-à-vis neutral states, "to all those exceptional rights or powers with which Sovereign States at war with one another are clothed by International Law."[42]

The practical need for the doctrine – as well as its connection to the amoral principle of effective control – was summarized in the British explanation to the Ottoman Empire, as recorded later by Lord Russell, following Britain's recognition of Greek belligerency in the 1825 rebellion:

> the character of belligerency was *not so much a principle as a fact*; that a certain degree of force and consistency acquired by any mass of population engaged in war entitled that population to be treated as a belligerent, and *even if their title were questionable*, rendered it the interest

39 2 Oppenheim, *supra* note 13, §59. An application of this rule can be exemplified in the practice of Britain after the defeat of the Confederacy. In May 1865, Britain ceased to permit access of Confederate warships to British ports, and also withdrew other belligerent privileges that Confederate vessels enjoyed during the Civil War. *See* Bernard, *supra* note 34, at 143.

40 Oglesby, *supra* note 29, at 8, 13, 16–17; Stapleton, *supra* note 27, at 27–28.

41 Bernard, *supra* note 34, at 113–114.

42 *Id.* at 114.

> well understood of all civilized nations so to treat them; for what was the alternative? A power or a community (call it which you will) which was at war with another, and which covered the sea with its cruisers, must either be acknowledged as a belligerent or dealt with as a pirate.[43]

The same approach can be found in an 1870 statement by US President Grant, in the context of the Cuban conflict, asserting that "[t]he question of belligerency is one of fact, not to be decided by sympathies for or prejudices against either party."[44]

According to Bernard, the recognition of belligerency was to be granted "as soon as it exists," a situation that did not "admit of precise definition."[45] Bernard's American contemporary, Dana, suggested, conversely, a more nuanced view of the doctrine. He saw the recognition of belligerency as due when the internal hostilities amounted to *war*; when the opposition adhered to laws of war; and could, if allowed to govern, constitute a state reasonably capable of discharging its duties. Furthermore, a practical necessity on the part of third parties was required for such determination to be made. Such necessity, according to Dana, would be the strongest when maritime questions were involved.[46]

Over the decades – and certainly by the end of the nineteenth century – scholars consolidated this doctrine, drawing from state practice, to formulate several preconditions for belligerency recognition.[47] In the absence of these, such recognition was considered an infringement of the government's rights,[48] namely the norm of non-intervention, and could be construed as an unfriendly act.[49]

The customary conditions for the recognition of belligerency (a duty according to some,[50] and a discretionary freedom according to many)[51] were four, bearing in mind certain nuances between different authorities:

43 *Cited in* Beale, *supra* note 35, at 412 (emphasis added). As we shall see, this dichotomy between "belligerent" and "pirate" was challenged by the later "insurgency" doctrine.

44 Message to Congress on June 13, 1870, *cited in* Vernon A. O'Rourke, *Recognition of Belligerency and the Spanish War*, 31 American Journal of International Law 398, 400 (1937).

45 Bernard, *supra* note 34, at 116–117.

46 Wheaton's, *supra* note 30; W.E. Hall, A Treatise on International Law 39 (1924).

47 *See, e.g.*, Institut de Droit International, Annuaire 18, 229 (1900).

48 2 Oppenheim, *supra* note 13, §298.

49 Ann Van Wynen Thomas and A.J. Thomas, Jr., *International Legal Aspects of the Civil War in Spain, 1936–1939*, *in* The International Law of Civil War, *supra* note 12, at 111.

50 Lauterpacht, *supra* note 31, at 175–176, 240–243; O'Rourke, *supra* note 44, at 407–408.

51 *See* Institut de Droit International, *supra* note 47 (asserting that third parties can withdraw recognition of belligerency notwithstanding the situation on the ground); *see also* O'Rourke, *supra* note 44, at 401–402; H.A. Smith, *Some Problems of the Spanish Civil War*, 18 British Year Book of International Law 17, 22–23 (1937); for a concise summary of the debate regarding the obligation to recognize belligerency *see* Oglesby, *supra* note 29, at 62–69.

1 the existence of an armed conflict of a general character;
2 effective control by a government set by the opposition over a substantial (or certain) part of the territory;
3 adherence to the laws of war, through organized armed forces under a responsible authority;
4 the existence of circumstances that make it necessary for outside states to define their attitudes towards the conflict through the recognition of belligerency.[52]

3.2 The results of recognition of belligerency in traditional international law

In general, as we shall see, prior to the recognition of belligerency, governments enjoyed certain privileges over the opposition. Generally speaking, states at peace with the government were not to interfere in the latter's efforts to quell the uprising.[53] After recognition of belligerency, the government lost some of these privileges, as third states could assume a neutral disposition *without* violating their peaceful relations with the challenged government. However, as discussed later on, a major qualification was that before the prohibition on the use of force, these were only conditions required to maintain *peace*, in the legal sense; a third state could choose to exercise its war-prerogative and intervene forcefully *regardless* of belligerency recognition or its absence. It is thus clear that whether belligerency was recognized or not, *consent* could indeed be an important tactical asset for the intervener; or a precondition for maintaining peace with the government; however, it could not constitute a legal requirement for intervention.

As aforementioned, belligerency led to a complex system of rights and obligations. In the political sense, logic dictates that the existence of a war must also imply a limited recognition of an independent authority that conducts it. Therefore, recognition of belligerency must have meant also a limited recognition of rebelling government, for the purpose of warfare.[54] Accordingly, for instance, a belligerent power would not enjoy the consular and diplomatic rights – the right of "legation" – of a recognized

52 Lauterpacht, *supra* note 31, at 176; *see also* Beale, *supra* note 35 at 407; Annual Message of President Grant (December 7, 1875); Annual Message of President McKinley (December 6, 1897). Oppenheim did not include the fourth condition in his analysis; *see* 2 Oppenheim, *supra* note 13, §74; *see also* Wheaton's, *supra* note 30 (explaining at length the rationale of such a condition); *see also* Theodore S. Woolsey, *The Consequences of Cuban Belligerency*, 5 Yale Law Journal 182 (1896).

53 Lauterpacht, *supra* note 31, at 230 (citing the 1900 resolution by the Institute of International Law.)

54 Smith, *supra* note 51, at 18, 21.

government or state; however, its representatives – or political agents – could be party to "informal" negotiations, and enjoy certain immunities.[55]

In the era of the dominance of naval warfare, much of the preoccupation regarding the question of belligerency concerned the rights of belligerents to disturb international commerce on the high seas.[56] In this context, a belligerent power was entitled to issue letters of marque and to deploy privateers,[57] and to have its men-of-war enjoy the immunities guaranteed for warships under international law. It incurred the right to visit and search neutral merchant vessels, on the high seas, for contraband; to impose a third-party binding blockade, enforceable on the high seas;[58] and even to establish prize courts for condemnation of captured neutral vessels carrying contraband or running a blockade.[59] As such, the recognition of belligerency could significantly disturb neutral commerce.[60]

Moreover, transfers of arms to rebels were considered wrongful, prior to the recognition of belligerency, while such actions vis-à-vis recognized governments were not. After recognition of belligerency, if the third state wished to remain neutral, government transfer of arms to *both* parties was prohibited.[61] There was also a later view, surfacing in the context of the Spanish Civil War, that prior to such recognition it was illegal to impose an arms embargo, binding also private actors, on the recognized

55 1 Oppenheim, *supra* note 36, §362, 453; *see also* Woolsey. *supra* note 52, at 182; this question rose in the "Trent Affair" of 1861, in which a Union vessel intercepted a British vessel carrying Confederate agents en route to Britain and France. Britain, which recognized the Confederacy as a belligerent, claimed that these individuals enjoyed immunity. The affair almost sparked a dispute between Britain and the US. The latter eventually released the Confederate agents, apologized and paid reparations to Britain. *See* Charles Francis Adams, The Trent Affair: An Historical Retrospect (1912). *See also* 2 Oppenheim, *supra* note 13, §408 n.3; Wright, *supra* note 12, at 90–93, 97–98.

56 *See, e.g.*, Wheaton's *supra* note 30.

57 Privateers were private vessels authorized by letters of marque to carry naval hostilities, mainly the capture of enemy merchant ships as prize. *See* Natalino Ronzitti, The Law of Naval Warfare: A Collection of Agreements and Documents with Commentaries 66 (1988). Privateering declined over the centuries as the technological gap between private and military vessels increased. *See* Theodore D. Woolsey, Introduction to the Study of International Law 80–81 (1879); privateering was abolished, between signatory states, in the Declaration of Paris of 1856.

58 *See* Institut de Droit International, *supra* note 47; 1 Oppenheim, *supra* note 36, §273; 2 Oppenheim, *supra* note 13, §298; *see also* Padelford, *supra* note 1, at 231–232. For a relatively recent statement of customary international law regarding rights and obligations of belligerents in naval warfare *see* the San Remo Manual on International Law Applicable to Armed Conflicts at Sea (June 12, 1994).

59 *See* Edwin D. Dickinson, *The Closure of Ports in Control of Insurgents*, 24 American Journal of International Law 70, 70 (1930); Woolsey, *supra* note 52, at 183–184. For a succinct summary of the logic of traditional prize law and neutrality, *see* the opinion of the Lord Chancellor in Ex Parte Chavasse, 46 E.R. 1072 (1865) (Gr. Brit.).

60 *See, e.g.*, Annual Message by President Grant, *supra* note 52.

61 O'Rourke, *supra* note 44, at 409; Lauterpacht, *supra* note 31, at 231–233. *See* discussion in Chapter 3, sec. 4.

government.[62] Only after such recognition, this position argued, an embargo on both parties was considered legitimate, provided that it was impartial.[63] This view, however, did not gain hold.[64]

Furthermore, before recognition, if states chose to remain on friendly terms with a beleaguered government, they were required to prevent the organization, in their territories, of private armed expeditions against the government. This requirement can be compared, perhaps, to the contemporary notion of due diligence regarding activities of non-state actors operating from a state's territory. Upon recognition of belligerency, if states wished to maintain neutrality, they were required to prevent such actions undertaken on behalf of *both* parties. However, they were not held responsible for acts of unorganized individuals that crossed the borders to assist either belligerent.[65]

A belligerent would incur responsibility for wrongful acts committed in the territory under its control[66] – and thus, naturally, would release the government from liability for the same acts.[67] Although prevalent authorities, for centuries, opined that the laws of war apply to every party to internal strife,[68] even if the opposition was not recognized as a belligerent, the position of most jurists was that prior to recognition the laws of war do not bind parties, in the strict sense, but ought to be applied on counts of considerations of humanity.[69] However, after recognition of belligerency, it was understood that contending parties were *bound* to observe the laws of war regarding their enemies as well as concerning neutrals, on land and on sea.[70] Consequently, belligerents' troops were generally entitled to the status of prisoners of war.

4 Effective control as a source of rights: the insurgency doctrine

4.1 Insurgency: the status of rebels without belligerency recognition

The recognition of belligerency was not without costs to third parties. On the one hand, it disturbed their relations with the recognized government;

62 *See* Thomas and Thomas, *supra* note 49, at 143.
63 *Id.* at 144.
64 Lauterpacht, *supra* note 31, at 243 n. 1.
65 Thomas and Thomas, *supra* note 49, at 144–145; Hague Convention V: Respecting the Rights and Duties of Neutral Powers and Persons in Case of War on Land (1907), U.S.T.S. 540, arts. 4, 6.
66 Oppenheim 1, *supra* note 36, §167.
67 Woolsey, *supra* note 52, at 184; *see also* O'Rourke, *supra* note 44, at 399–401.
68 *See, e.g.*, Emmerich De Vatell, The Law of Nations §§294–295 (1797).
69 *See* Instructions for the Government of Armies of the United States in the Field (Lieber Code), art. 152 (April 24, 1863); Wright, *supra* note 12, at 55; *see also* Padelford, *supra* note 1, at 229.
70 Smith, *supra* note 51, at 22.

on the other hand, it exposed their merchant fleets to interruptions. However, absent any recognition the state of affairs was left unclear; and awkward situations could occur, in which rebel vessels would be treated as pirates.[71] Soon enough, states had to address the status of rebels, involved in a significant internal struggle, that for one reason or the other were not recognized as belligerents.[72] This was especially true when there were no maritime hostilities grave enough to force a third-party to pass a judgment regarding belligerent actions on the high seas.[73] When faced with such situations, states realized that in order to apply their domestic neutrality laws to persons within their jurisdictions, recognition of belligerency was not needed.[74] Thus, they could avoid the diplomatic and economic pitfalls that such recognition entailed,[75] by devising a doctrine that would in general limit the effects of a conflict to the territorial state, thereby minimizing its international consequences.[76]

This was the backdrop of the development of the "elastic device" of *insurgency* (or insurrection) recognition.[77] Developing throughout the nineteenth century – in parallel to the belligerency doctrine[78] – it was considered by the beginning of the twentieth century a distinct status accepted in state practice,[79] at least by Britain and the United States.[80] The flexible

71 Oglesby, *supra* note 29, at 22; *see also* Neff, *supra* note 4, at 269–270.

72 Beale, *supra* note 35, at 419:

> because there is no political organization on the part of the insurgents; or belligerency may in fact exist, but a state may not wish or need to recognize it. It may nevertheless be necessary to recognize the existence of hostilities, either to avoid dealing with an insurgent as a pirate, or to warn citizens against taking part in the contest. Such a recognition is of insurgency, not of belligerency.

See also Annual Message of December 7, 1875, *cited in* George Grafton Wilson, *Insurgency and International Maritime Law,* 1 American Journal of International Law 46, 47 (1907) (statement by President Grant explaining the denial of belligerent status from Cuban rebels).

73 For instance, in the Cuban context, Beale thought that recognition of belligerency was not warranted since there was no factual ability to determine that the conditions of belligerency existed in Cuba, and since maritime hostilities did not exist. *See* Beale, *supra* note 35, at 417–418.

74 *Id.*

75 Oglesby, *supra* note 29, at 103–104.

76 *See* Neff, *supra* note 4, at 269–270.

77 Lauterpacht, *supra* note 31, at 236, 270–271.

78 For early nineteenth-century manifestations of the notion of insurgency *see* Oglesby, *supra* note 29, at 18–32; Notably, insurgency seems to have been recognized in the Hungarian war of independence of 1848, in which the US did not recognize the belligerency of Hungary, although it was otherwise merited, since the former was not directly affected by the land-locked conflict. Wheaton's, *supra* note 30, at 45–47 n.16. Eventually Russia intervened in favor of its Holy Alliance partner, the Austrian Empire, in 1849, leading to the defeat of Hungary.

79 Wilson, *supra* note 72, at 46, 59.

80 Dickinson, *supra* note 59, at 72.

approach of the insurgency doctrine is reflected, to some extent, in contemporary international practice, as we shall see later on.

Owing to its flexibility, the insurgency doctrine was better suited to address the unpredictable nature of internal conflicts than the rigid belligerency doctrine. Nevertheless, it was also largely devoid of substantive, value-based, considerations. For instance, in his annual message of 1897, US President McKinley vehemently criticized Spain's repression of Cuban rebels, exclaiming that "[i]t was not civilized warfare. It was extermination." Nonetheless, the rebels were not recognized as belligerents,[81] but rather as insurgents,[82] subjected to the prohibitions entrenched in US neutrality law.[83] In this context, the US Supreme Court stressed the effectiveness-based nature of the law, stressing that it applied equally to "all possible forms of government, monarchical, aristocratical, and democratic."[84] Such statements highlighted the amoral application of both the belligerency and insurgency doctrines. Indeed, like the belligerency doctrine, insurgency was based on the concept of effective control, or related de facto considerations, as sources of legal rights or status. It was premised on the logic that a "contest of armed forces" or "war in the material sense," can take place de facto even without recognition of belligerency.[85]

4.2 Insurgency as liability: unequal application of domestic neutrality acts

The insurgency doctrine is elusive in two substantial aspects. First, it is often difficult, absent an explicit statement, to draw the line between recognition of insurgency and belligerency, since both were made, to some degree, by declarations of neutrality;[86] this is true although recognition of insurgency was usually affected in an expression by the executive that warns its citizens to obey *domestic,* rather than strictly international neutrality laws. These executive declarations would

81 Annual Message of President McKinley, *supra* note 52. For the analysis of American interests concerning the recognition of Cuban belligerency, *see* Woolsey, *supra* note 52, at 184; on President McKinley's approach *see also* Smith, *supra* note 51, at 20.

82 *Id.*

83 The Three Friends, *supra* note 15, at 502–503; *see also* Annual Message of December 2, 1895 (President Cleveland) *cited in* Wilson, *supra* note 72, at 48.

84 The Three Friends, *supra* note 15, at 501.

85 O'Rourke, *supra* note 44, at 403.

86 *See, e.g.,* the proclamation of January 5, 1838, by President Van Buren regarding the uprising in Canada. Oglesby claimed that since it called into attention domestic neutrality laws, it "foreshadowed" the manner that "recognition of insurgency" was granted later on. Oglesby, *supra* note 29, at 25. Bernard, however, seemed to have seen the same proclamation as a recognition of belligerency, albeit premature. Bernard, *supra* note 34, at 117–118 n. 2; Theodore Woolsey, *Our Duty to Spain,* 7 Yale Law Journal 101, 104 (1897).

thereafter be interpreted by courts.[87] Second, as opposed to belligerency recognition, there are no comprehensive authoritative statements regarding the implications of insurgency, and therefore these have to be gathered from scattered, sometimes contradictory practice and literature.

Indeed, if belligerency was an intermediate status between non-recognition and full recognition, insurgency was one that could be looked upon in several ways. One approach would view insurgency as mostly connoting limitations imposed by third-party states, in accordance with their domestic neutrality laws, resulting, perhaps, in liabilities for the insurgents but not for beleaguered governments. Insurgency could be seen, thus, as a de facto status emanating from the extension of domestic neutrality acts – hitherto applying only to inter-state wars or instances where belligerency was recognized[88] – also to prohibit support, namely by providing vessels, to non-recognized rebels. Such was the case of the 1817 amendment to the US Neutrality Act of 1794,[89] which was adopted under intense pressure from colonial Spain and Portugal, seeking to curtail the procurement of warships by rebelling colonies.[90] The amendment, for the first time, extended prohibitions enumerated in the Neutrality Act, previously applying only to "princes" or "states," also to cover support for an unrecognized "colony, district or people" involved in hostilities against any like entity in peace with the United States.[91] Chief Justice Marshall referred to the amendment as one that "adapts the previous laws to the actual situation of the world,"[92] by not requiring formal acts of recognition in order for neutrality acts to apply where de facto warfare exists.[93] Indeed, it could be argued that the decision to apply domestic neutrality acts did not result in

87 *See, e.g.*, O'Neill v. Central Leather Co., 87 N.J.L. 552, 553–554 (1915) (interpreting the declarations by President Wilson regarding the 1913–1914 strife in Mexico as inferring that the parties were in "actual war," albeit not recognized officially as belligerents; reversed in 246 U.S. 297 (1918), since the US already recognized the Carranza government as Mexico's government).

88 *See* Neutrality Act of 1794, §3 (prohibiting the fitting out of "any ship or vessel with intent that such ship or vessel shall be employed in the service of any foreign *prince or state* to cruise or commit hostilities upon the subjects, citizens or property of another *foreign prince or state* with whom the United States are at peace") (emphasis added) *see also id.* §5; The Estrella, 17 U.S. 298 (1819) (holding that the recognition of the belligerency of Bolivarian Venezuela has made it a belligerent state for the purpose of the US Neutrality Act of 1794).

89 *See* The Three Friends, *supra* note 15, at 498; on American neutrality laws and their relation to international law *see* Dumbauld, *supra* note 19, at 258–262.

90 The Three Friends, *supra* note 15, at 499.

91 Neutrality Act of 1817, §3. The British Foreign Enlistment Act of 1819 was modeled after the American law, as section 7 applied neutrality requirements to a wide variety of bodies. *See* The Three Friends, *supra* note 15, at 501.

92 The Gran Para, 20 U.S. 471, 489 (1822); *cited in* The Three Friends, *supra* note 15, at 499.

93 For a similar understanding, *see* the opinion of Chief Justice Fuller in Underhill v. Hernandez, 168 U.S. 250 (1897), *cited in* Wilson, *supra* note 72, at 51.

any formal international status, since their effects were mainly internal;[94] however, as aforementioned, domestic neutrality acts still had practical implications over insurgents, especially in an era in which international regulation of war was virtually non-existent.

The application of domestic neutrality laws to insurgencies was, for instance, a prominent feature of the US approach towards the conflict in Cuba (Ten Years' War) of 1868–1878. Throughout the conflict, President Grant found that the circumstances did not call for the recognition of belligerency, since the Cuban rebels failed to demonstrate a "de facto political organization,"[95] "organization of force" or "occupation of territory" sufficient to justify such recognition.[96] Still, the prohibitions of the Neutrality Act were applied, *at least* with regards to acts committed in favor of the insurgents.[97] The latter point demonstrates that the insurgency doctrine was used, at that stage, mainly to prevent disputes with the Spanish government. Accordingly, as expounded in an 1869 opinion by the Attorney General, it resulted in disadvantages for the Cuban insurgents but not for Spain.[98] While the uneven treatment of governments and insurgents could be legally challenged in light of the impartial language of the Neutrality Act,[99] the Attorney General's opinion clarified a main difference between the insurgency and belligerency doctrines, as understood at the time – according to which governments at peace with the neutral were entitled to some "preferential treatment" during insurgency.

The same logic could be read into the US Supreme Court decision in the case of *The Three Friends*.[100] There, the Court ruled that the Neutrality Act indeed applied to unrecognized groups "associated together in a common political enterprise, and carrying on hostilities against the parent country, in the effort to achieve independence."[101] However, in the case at hand, the Court ruled that the Neutrality Act prohibited assisting *rebels*. Thus, notwithstanding the symmetrical language of the Neutrality Act, and in conformity with view of the Attorney General expressed three decades earlier,[102] it is doubtful whether the Court would have been willing to recognize the *positive* rights of insurgents prior to belligerency recognition.[103]

94 Woolsey, *supra* note 86, at 103–104.
95 Annual Message of December 6, 1869, *cited in* Wilson, *supra* note 72, at 47.
96 Annual Message of December 7, 1875, *cited in* Wilson, *supra* note 72, at 47. Accordingly, for instance, American courts refused to recognize the standing of agents claiming to represent the rebelling Republic of Cuba. *See, e.g.*, The Hornet, 12 F. Cas. 529 (1870).
97 The Florida, 9 F. Cas. 321 (1871).
98 United States Attorney General, *Neutrality Act*, 13 U.S. Op. Atty. Gen. 177 (December 16, 1869) (asserting that equal treatment of governments and rebels is possible only after belligerency was recognized).
99 Neutrality Act of 1817, §3.
100 The Three Friends, *supra* note 15.
101 *Id.* at 499–500.
102 *See* the opinion of the Attorney General, *supra* note 98.
103 The Three Friends, *supra* note 15, at 502.

4.3 Insurgency as privilege

Other aspects of insurgency entailed several privileges to insurgents, even if indirectly. Namely, prominent authorities concluded that even absent recognition of belligerency, substantial *limitations* applied to *both* parties – equalizing, somewhat, the position of insurgents and governments. For instance, neither the government nor the insurgents could exercise the right to visit-and-search vessels of third states on the high seas, as this disruption of neutral trade was contingent upon the existence of formal war.[104] Furthermore, although insurgents could not proclaim a blockade – ostensibly since they lacked "responsible" prize courts[105] – the logic of reciprocity and reason was otherwise understood to require the observation of the laws of war by both parties.[106]

However, recognition of insurgency did in fact confer – even if indirectly – some *positive* rights upon rebels. They gained the right not to be considered pirates,[107] at least when acting within territorial waters under their control.[108] Perhaps reflecting a limited departure from the "amoral" thinking of the time, this was justified, sometimes, by "humanitarian" considerations – a "compromise principle which would elevate a political rebel to a plane higher than a pirate."[109] In addition, ports effectively controlled by insurgents could not be closed merely by decree of the recognized government, if not enforced by an effective blockade.[110]

The latter result of the recognition of insurgency, although not universally accepted,[111] was reflected in the practice of the US and Britain, as well as of other European powers.[112] Such was the case when Britain refused to recognize the belligerency of the rebels in the 1860–1862 conflict in New Grenada (modern Colombia and Panama),[113] while asserting nonetheless

104 Dickinson, *supra* note 59; Wilson, *supra* note 72, at 54.

105 *Id.* at 56–58.

106 *Id.* at 54.

107 President Cleveland, Annual Message of December 8, 1885.

108 Smith, *supra* note 51, at 25; O'Rourke, *supra* note 44, at 403.

109 *Id.*, at 403–404.

110 *Id.*; Wilson, *supra* note 72, at 57–58.

111 For instance, Latin American states, in general, did not accept this position. *See* Dickinson, *supra* note 59, at 70, 74–75. This is perhaps not surprising as the governments of these states, many times, were challenged by rebels. *See* for instance, the claim by Peru, during the insurrection of 1856–1858, according to which absent recognition of belligerency, US merchant vessels were obliged to abide to its closure of ports controlled by the rebels. *See* Oglesby, *supra* note 29, at 27–32.

112 The recognition of closure by decree evoked the old idea of "paper blockades," and thus was rejected in different instances by the US, European states and certain Arbitration panels. *See* Wilson, *supra* note 72, at 54–55, 58; Dickinson, *supra* note 59, at 74; Wheaton's, *supra* note 30, at 34 n.15, 688 n.239.

113 The conflict in New Grenada raged between 1860 and 1862 between the newly formed Grenadine Confederation and the seceding state of Cauca. The conflict ended in rebel victory and the formation of the United States of Colombia. *See* A Political Chronology of the Americas 75–76 (David Lea *et al.* eds., 2001).

that the government could not decree the closure of rebel-held ports.[114] The US adopted a similar position regarding the 1885 conflict in the United States of Colombia. When the Colombian government requested that the US respect the closure of Colombia's ports by decree, and treat opposition vessels as pirates, President Cleveland responded that these requests were inconsistent with international law, while stressing, conversely, that this did not "imply the admission of a belligerent status on part of the insurgents."[115]

Further "privileges" of insurgency were suggested by Lauterpacht. Thus, he argued that the recognition of insurgency could lead to the recognition of the insurgents also as de facto governments, at least regarding internal governing powers such as legislation (but not with regards to belligerent rights vis-à-vis third parties).[116] Essentially, Lauterpacht saw insurgency as an extremely flexible intermediate status between non-recognition and belligerency, conferring ad hoc rights and obligations to the parties as circumstances necessitated.[117]

Last – another possible way to frame the insurgency status is to consider it as similar, in essence, to belligerency, but without a formal recognition as such; or as a status similar to belligerency, that applied, however, only to actions taking place in the state's territory – both land and water.[118] The latter perception views insurgency as a "geographically constricted," or *territorial* version of belligerency.[119] The former approach corresponds, to some extent, to the declaratory theory of recognition, positing that rights of entities are accumulated through facts on the ground rather than through formal acts of recognition.[120] This approach can be exemplified in the 1928 case of the Oriental Navigation Company, arbitrated in front of the US–Mexico Claims Commission,[121] established to settle claims

114 Statement in the House of Commons, June 27, 1861, *cited in* Oriental Navigation Company, *infra* note 121, at 437; *see also* Wheaton's, *supra* note 30, at 687–688, n. 239; *but see* Dickinson, *supra* note 59, at 72–73 (maintaining that perhaps Lord Russell's statement failed to distinguish between insurgency and belligerency).

115 Annual Message of December 8, 1885; *see also* Dickinson, *supra* note 59, at 74. Many complex questions regarding the questions of blockade, insurgency and belligerency were never thoroughly clarified. For instance, whether a government's proclamation of a blockade results in automatic belligerency. *Id.* 70–76; *see also* Theodore S. Woolsey, *The United States and the Declaration of Paris*, 3 Yale Law Journal 77, 78 (1894) (arguing that by imposing a blockade on the South the North has itself recognized its belligerency); *see also* Woolsey, *supra* note 52, at 184.

116 Lauterpacht, *supra* note 31, at 279–294.

117 *Id.* at 270, 276–278.

118 As opposed to belligerent maritime actions that can interrupt commerce on the *high seas*. *See* Oglesby, *supra* note 29, at 103–104.

119 Neff, *supra* note 4, at 269–270.

120 For a survey of the constitutive and declaratory doctrines of recognition *see* Lauterpacht, *supra* note 31, at 2–3, 38–42; James Crawford, The Creation of States in International Law 1–17, 22–26 (2006); Thomas D. Grant, The Recognition of States 2–12 (1999).

121 The Oriental Navigation Company v. The United Mexican States (Docket No. 411, October 3, 1928), Claims Commission – U.S. & Mex., 23 American Journal of International Law 434 (1929).

resulting from the long running Mexican Civil War.[122] In April 1924, the American merchant vessel *Gaston* sailed from New Orleans to the Mexican port of Frontera. However, the Frontera port, along with other Mexican ports, was – at large – controlled by insurgents. During the Gaston's unloading, a Mexican government gunboat appeared, and ordered the Gaston to leave the port, since it was decreed closed. After warning shots were fired, the Gaston fled, leaving its cargo behind. The US claimed that the Mexican action was unlawful, since the port was in the hands of insurgents, and therefore could be closed only through an effective blockade, and not by mere decree.[123] Mexico claimed that it had full power to decree the ports closed according to its domestic law.

The Commission upheld, in principle, the view of the US, in line with the widespread understanding of the insurgency doctrine.[124] It ruled, however, that the mere presence of the Mexican gunship near the port during the Gaston's unloading, interrupted the insurgents' control over the port during that moment; and hence, Mexico was not in the wrong by acting against the Gaston, *notwithstanding* the absence of an effective blockade.[125]

This conclusion was challenged by the dissenting opinion of Commissioner Nielsen. Nielsen opined that in absence of an effective blockade, Mexico had absolutely no legal grounds to interfere in neutral commerce, regardless of the incidental presence of a Mexican gunship.[126] Of interest to us, however, was the link he made between the recognition of belligerency and the declaratory theory of recognition, which might account for the decline of the former doctrine.[127] Nielsen posited that no distinction has been made, in state practice, between ports controlled by recognized belligerents versus ports held by insurgents.[128] He thus argued that it is doubtful whether an affirmative act of recognition of belligerency was required in order for the rebels – indirectly – to attain some legal status. Just as states did not begin to exist strictly upon recognition, he asserted, so did the status of insurgents – although the recognition of belligerency does "entail important consequences."[129] While Nielsen did not say so

122 This instance took place in the era of the League of Nations, addressed in the next chapter, but because of its relevance for the understanding of the insurgency doctrine, it is nevertheless discussed here.

123 Oriental Navigation Company, *supra* note 121, at 434–435. For a summary of the facts *see also* Dickinson, *supra* note 59, at 69.

124 Oriental Navigation Company, *supra* note 121, at 435.

125 *Id.* at 436; *see also* Dickinson, *supra* note 59, at 77–78.

126 Oriental Navigation Company, *supra* note 121, at 437.

127 For a discussion of the relation between belligerency recognition and the declarative theory, *see* Thomas Baty, *So-Called "De facto" Recognition*, 31 Yale Law Journal 469, 470–472 (1922).

128 Oriental Navigation Company, *supra* note 121, at 439.

129 *Id.* at 440–441.

explicitly, a possible expansion of his argument – binding the status of insurgents with the declarative view of recognition – could result in the view that belligerency recognition had no substantial constitutive effects.[130]

5 The non-relation between belligerency, insurgency and consensual intervention

5.1 Belligerency, neutrality and consensual intervention in the war-prerogative era

Notably missing from our survey regarding the consequences of belligerency (or insurgency) recognition is the issue of consensual intervention. This, as we shall see, is not coincidental. Some modern commentators have identified two "opposing" approaches regarding this issue. One posits that upon recognition of belligerency, third states acquired a *duty* of neutrality. If such duty was assumed, intervention on behalf of both parties would be unlawful. The other approach asserts that upon such recognition – and *only* upon it – states gained the power to intervene on behalf of either party. The first approach, as elaborated shortly, presents a logical problem, which can be reconciled – if at all – if understood as relevant only since the prohibition on the use of force. The second, while seemingly present in the works of Oppenheim, is rather foreign to the general landscape of law prevalent in the era of the war-prerogative.

Doswald-Beck identified these supposedly opposing approaches:[131]

> [t]here is a widespread view that the traditional law favours intervention by invitation of the government but not by invitation of the rebels. The only situation where traditional texts *require* neutrality on the part of third States is on recognition of belligerency."[132]

Referring to Oppenheim, Doswald-Beck contrasted this position, noting that "there is also a view that recognition of belligerency turns a civil war into a real war and thus a third state can join either side or choose to remain neutral."[133]

130 Lauterpacht, alluded to this position, claiming that

> [s]tates may go very far in imposing upon themselves restraints indistinguishable in substance from duties of neutrality and in conceding to the contesting parties rights usually associated with belligerency proper. In that sense, but in no other, recognition of insurgency may be reared as a de facto recognition of belligerency.
>
> Lauterpacht, *supra* note 31, at 277.

131 Louise Doswald-Beck, *The Legal Validity of Military Intervention by Invitation of the Government*, 56 British Year Book of International Law 189 (1985).

132 *Id.* 196 (emphasis added).

133 *Id.* n. 40.

Perhaps following the same logic, Roth argued that recognition of belligerency imposed on third parties "an obligation of neutrality, and thereby, in theory, render[s] it unlawful for foreign states to provide war materiél to either side of the civil conflict, notwithstanding the requests of the recognized governments for assistance."[134] Like Doswald-Beck, Roth notes that while this was the "usual view," there is an "alternative view," according to which upon recognition of belligerency foreign states acquire the choice of "joining either side or remaining neutral."[135]

These modern understandings of traditional law merit clarification, since they do not expressly distinguish between the law *before* the prohibition on the use of force – during the war-prerogative era – and the law after it. Thus, they assume that there was a discrepancy between the "neutrality" that recognition of belligerency entailed, and an "alternative" view, that upon such recognition, a third party could intervene on behalf of either side of the conflict. An analysis of traditional law makes it clear, however, that such "competing" views were not substantively possible, and that in actuality neutrality and intervention were simply two alternative *choices*.

The root of the problem lies in the perception that recognition of belligerency required or obligated third parties to assume neutrality. However, as aforementioned, in the war-prerogative era, neutrality was not perceived as an obligation; it was simply a *status* that if states chose to adhere to, they could avoid being dragged into the conflict. In Hohfeldian terms, neutrality was a *privilege*, or a *liberty*, but not a duty.[136]

Granted, radical non-interventionists such as Bernard[137] opined that intervention in internal strife was universally prohibited, whether it was justified upon state interest or on party consent.[138] It seems that Bernard had drawn an implicit line between inter-state wars and internal conflicts, the latter imposing a restriction on the war-right of sovereigns that was non-existent in the former.[139] However, in hindsight, this approach can only be view as *de lege ferenda*, as there were no generally applicable legal norms, at the time, which could substantially restrict the war-prerogative. Thus, there could be no "true" obligations of neutrality regarding internal

134 Brad R. Roth, Governmental Illegitimacy in International Law 177 (1999).

135 *Id.* n. 149.

136 *See* Wesley Hohfeld, Fundamental Legal Conceptions (Arthur Corbin ed., 1978).

137 Bernard, *supra* note 9. We will return to Bernard's argument when we discuss strict-abstentionism in Chapter 6.

138 *Id.* at 10–23.

139 *Id.* at 21–22; *compare* Walzer, *supra* note 2, at 96–97. Walzer argues that although neutrality was always a choice regarding wars between *states*, in internal armed conflicts, when belligerency was recognized, there were good *ethical* reasons to make neutrality obligatory, to fulfill the principle of self-determination. However, it is doubtful that this notion is in accordance with the law of the time, *at least* until the 1928 Kellogg-Briand pact.

strife, since there was no law that prohibited states from ending their neutrality, if they were willing to face the consequences. As put by Oppenheim, "[d]uties of neutrality exist *so long only as a State remains neutral*."[140] A recognition of belligerency, then, would result in neutrality or in fact be prompted by a declaration of neutrality,[141] which states were required to observe in order not to be drawn in to the conflict; but this did not in fact mean that states could not intervene at will by shedding their neutral status.

Still another modern commentator held the view that in "pre-Charter international law," forcible intervention in favor of either side was prohibited when the conflict was prescribed as an "insurgency;" but "once a state of belligerency was recognized, an invitation to intervene or to offer assistance was legally valid, regardless of whether the inviting party was the previously-recognized government or the anti-government forces."[142] This position too reflects an intractable discrepancy. First, it also assumes the existence of a "duty" of neutrality when "insurgency" was recognized, disregarding the fact that neutrality was viewed as a choice; second, it accepts as obvious the position that recognition of belligerency affected the legality of consensual intervention. However, in the war-prerogative era, it made little sense to condition forcible intervention on any recognition of status, or upon consent.

Indeed, nineteenth-century writers such as Woolsey asserted that "no state is authorized to render assistance to provinces or colonies which are in revolt against the established government," as it violates the norm of non-interference;[143] and conversely – and here Woolsey contradicted his contemporary Bernard – that "there is nothing in the law of nations which forbids one nation to render assistance to the established government," as "[t]his aid is no interference."[144] Nevertheless, Woolsey too recognized, albeit with visible dissatisfaction, that this rule can be challenged by "the exercise of the war-right" of a sovereign state, and on justifications that "are more or less vague and under the influence of subjective opinion."[145] Positions such as Woolsey's, then, did little to bridge the gap between the principle of non-intervention and the sovereign right to wage war.

The same inconsistency can be found in the writings of Oppenheim – perhaps the foremost source for those connecting between recognition of belligerency and consensual intervention. While acknowledging that assisting governments, in general, is lawful "co-operation," Oppenheim argued that

140 2 Oppenheim, *supra* note 13, at §312.

141 *See* Smith, *supra* note 51, at 21.

142 Christopher J. Le Mon, *Unilateral Intervention by Invitation in Civil Wars: The Effective Control Test Tested*, 35 New York University Journal of International Law and Politics 741, 747–748 (2003).

143 Woolsey, *supra* note 57, §42.

144 *Id.*

145 *Id.* §43.

> [t]here is no doubt that a foreign State commits an international delinquency by assisting insurgents in spite of its being at peace with the legitimate Government. But matters are different after recognition. The insurgents are now a belligerent power, and the civil war is now real war. Foreign States can either become a party to the war or remain neutral, and in the latter case all duties and rights of neutrality devolve upon them.[146]

However, Oppenheim too did not explicitly reconcile the "international delinquency" of assisting rebels in spite of being at "peace" with the government, with his own realization that international law, at that time, could not and did not object "to States which are in conflict waging war upon each other instead of peaceably settling their difference." International law, he repeated the widely accepted view, merely regulated the conduct of hostilities.[147]

If we attempt to read Oppenheim's opinion regarding the aforesaid "international delinquency" in light of his position that war in itself was not prohibited, the conclusion must be that the delinquency of intervention prior to recognition of belligerency materialized only when the intervention was conducted through means historically considered as "short of war;" and if the actions in fact amounted to war, then they resulted in the termination of peace. The same consequence would occur when an intervention would be pursued *following* recognition of belligerency – here too, peace would be terminated. Therefore, the merits of Oppenheim's seeming distinction between forcible intervention prior recognition of belligerency and after it are unclear.

A precise understanding of belligerency and the question of intervention argues along the line that upon recognition, "states which did not *wish* to be treated as active participants in a war were obliged to assume the legal posture of neutrality."[148] Indeed, the "default" consequence – or perhaps, the *generator* – of the recognition of belligerency was the assumption of neutral status on part of the recognizing power.[149] However, owing to the war-prerogative, the result of neutrality did not mean that states were bound to non-interference in the conflict, should they choose to waive their neutrality.[150] The logical (and unsurprising) conclusion is that intervention on behalf of rebels was an "unfriendly" act towards the

146 2 Oppenheim, *supra* note 13, §298. Regarding forcible assistance to governments as "co-operation" *see* 1 Oppenheim, *supra* note 36, §134.

147 *Id.* §53.

148 Tom Farer, *Harnessing Rogue Elephants: A Short Discourse on Foreign Intervention in Civil Strife*, 82 Harvard Law Review 511, 511–512 (1969) (emphasis added); *see also* Evan Luard, Conflict and Peace in the Modern International System 154 (1968).

149 *See* Institut de Droit International, *supra* note 47; 2 Oppenheim, *supra* note 13, §308.

150 On the free choice between neutrality and belligerency *see* von Heinigg, *supra* note 14, at 544.

government; while intervention in support of the government was not. The former could, in effect, amount to a declaration of war, which resulted in severe consequences – but absent a specific treaty – not in *illegality*.

5.2 Consensual intervention as choice

In accordance with our discussion above, there are many examples, chiefly in American practice, that reinforce the conclusion that recognition of belligerency – or of insurgency, for that matter – was but simply *one* course of action available to third-party states, rather than a precondition for intervention. Nor was it a precondition for the recognition of the rebels as a government or as an independent state.[151]

This was evident already in US Supreme Court decisions concerning the Spanish Colonial Wars of 1810–1823. In *US v. Palmer*,[152] Chief Justice Marshall ruled that "[i]n such contests [internal conflicts] a nation may engage itself with the one party or the other – may observe absolute neutrality – may recognize the new state absolutely – or may make a limited recognition of it."[153] Limited recognition must have meant an intermediate position, such as recognition of belligerency or insurgency; however, it was not a precondition for intervention. The same logic was echoed in the contemporaneous Supreme Court decision in the case of the *Santissima Trinidad*, which dealt with the consequences of the recognition of the belligerency of the Spanish colonies:

> Each party is, therefore, deemed by us a belligerent nation, having, so far as concerns us, the sovereign rights of war, and entitled to be respected in the exercise of those rights. We cannot interfere to the prejudice of either belligerent without making ourselves a party to the contest, and departing from the posture of neutrality.[154]

It is evident from both of these decisions that the "limited" recognition of belligerency was an alternative to intervention, but not a necessary condition. As stated in the *Santissima Trinidad* decision, the consequence of intervention was merely departing "from the posture of neutrality," but not illegality.

In 1843, when opining on a long-running dispute between the US and Denmark regarding the treatment of British prize captured during the American Revolution, Henry Wheaton – one of the important

151 Theodore S. Woolsey, *Lecture on International Law*, 8 Yale Law Journal 387, 394 (1899) ("The topics here to be studied are called recognition of belligerency and of independence, the first a usual, though not a necessary, step to the second.")

152 16 U.S. 610 (1818).

153 *Id.* at 634.

154 The Santissima Trinidad, 20 U.S. 283, 337 (1822) (emphasis added).

international lawyers of the time – expressed this position clearly. He argued that states had three legal options regarding internal conflicts: either to remain "passive," while extending to both parties the rights of sovereign states during war; to recognize the opposition party as an independent state, and maintain neutrality; or, rather, to join in alliance with one party, thus becoming the other's enemy.[155] Wheaton stressed the amoral element in the third party's choice, and argued again, in 1846, that where a state decides to forcefully intervene, "the law of nations makes no distinction, in this respect, between a just and an unjust war."[156]

The wide spectrum of lawful possibilities enjoyed by states, even without recognition of belligerency, was reflected in the approach of the US towards the Cuban wars of the 1870s and 1890s, where Cuban opposition groups revolted against Spain. As President Grant stated in 1875:

> The recognition of independence or of belligerency being thus, in my judgment, *equally inadmissible*, it remains to consider what course shall be adopted should the conflict not soon be brought to an end by acts of the parties themselves, and should the evils which result therefrom, affecting all nations, and particularly the United States, continue. In such event I am of opinion that other nations will be compelled to assume the responsibility which devolves upon them, and to seriously consider the only remaining measures possible – mediation and intervention.[157]

Likewise, regarding the Cuban conflict of the 1890s, US President McKinley laid down the courses of action available to the US:

> [o]f the untried measures there remain only: Recognition of the insurgents as belligerents; recognition of the independence of Cuba; neutral intervention to end the war by imposing a rational compromise between the contestants, *and intervention in favor of one or the other party*. I speak not of forcible annexation, for that can not be thought of. That, by our code of morality, would be criminal aggression.[158]

Note, that President McKinley understood the different options available to the US as equal alternatives; thus, forcible intervention in favor of the opposition was viewed as a legal possibility – one which was actually *independent* of any previous recognition of belligerency, or of independence.[159] Belligerency recognition was therefore looked upon as an alternative to

155 *Cited in* Oglesby, *supra* note 29, at 4–5.
156 Wheaton's, *supra* note 30, at §23.
157 Annual Message of President Grant, *supra* note 52 (emphasis added).
158 Annual Message of President McKinley, *supra* note 52.
159 *See also* Beale, *supra* note 35, at 406.

harsher actions such as intervention or recognition of independence, but not a precondition for them.[160] Indeed, when intervention in Cuba finally took place in 1898 – in what became the Spanish-American War – no prior recognition of belligerency or of independence was extended. As a matter of fact, President McKinley stated explicitly that he would pursue the intervention without recognition of belligerency, which he saw as adding nothing in this context.[161]

Indeed, if a state was ready to actively and expressly support a party to an internal conflict, and was willing to pay the costs of war with the other party, there was no reason for it to limit itself to the recognition of belligerency. Instead, it could grant its ally staunch moral support by recognizing it as the lawful government or as an independent state. For instance, as early as in 1778, France recognized the US, before intervening on its behalf in the American Revolution, pursuant to a treaty of alliance between the parties.[162] Likewise, over a century later, the US intervened in the internal conflict in Colombia, in 1903, after recognizing Panama's independence without previously recognizing its belligerency.[163] Similarly, in the Spanish Civil War, Germany and Italy recognized the Franco regime, which they were forcibly assisting, as the "lawful" government, again without prior recognition of belligerency.[164] In sum, the discussion above demonstrates that intervention – upon consent or otherwise – was a matter of state-choice, and could not be understood as preconditioned by the prevailing legal doctrines of the time.

5.3 The secondary importance of the political rights of internal parties

If not the question of forcible intervention, what was the focus of the law of internal strife in the war-prerogative era? Indeed, the set of consequences of war, in the legal sphere, that so concerned the powers of the era, were quite different from the dominant concerns of contemporary international law. The main interest of states was to mitigate, or at least control, the effects of war over *neutral commerce*. The economic interests of external powers were paramount, rather than the political rights of the parties to the conflict themselves, which were at best secondary. This approach can be starkly contrasted with today's stated preoccupation with human rights, self determination and the protection of civilians. It can be

160 *Id.* at 407.

161 Message to the Congress, April 11, 1898. Notably, the intervention was presented as a neutral action to "stop the war," justified by *humanitarian* language and American interests. McKinley refrained from expressing preference towards the Cuban rebels, although they requested an American intervention. *Id.*; *see also* Walzer, *supra* note 2, at 102–104 (critiquing the humanitarian claims by the US as non-genuine).

162 Perkins, *supra* note 8, at ix–x; Alden, *supra* note 9, at 381. The treaty is available at http://avalon.law.yale.edu/18th_century/fr1788-2.asp.

163 Padelford, *supra* note 1, at 236.

164 *Id.*

demonstrated in an 1869 opinion of the US Attorney General regarding the Cuban conflict:

> The question of belligerency between organized communities is a question of fact, and may be one of the gravest facts upon which a nation is called to decide and act. The concession of belligerent rights ... necessarily involves serious restrictions upon the ordinary rights of the people of this country to carry on branches of manufacture and trade which are unrestricted in time of peace. To prevent our mechanics and merchants from building ships of war and selling them in the markets of the world, is an interference with their private rights which can only be justified on the ground of a paramount duty in our international relations; and however much we may sympathize with the efforts of any portion of the people of another country to resist what they consider oppression or to achieve independence, our duties are necessarily dependent upon the actual progress which they have made in reaching these objects.[165]

A few years later, President Grant, when explaining the US refrain from recognizing the belligerency of Cuban rebels, similarly emphasized the interests of *external* parties as a key determinant:

> The contest, moreover, is solely on land; the insurrection has not possessed itself of a single seaport whence it may send forth its flag.... No apprehension of any of those sudden and difficult complications which a war upon the ocean is apt to precipitate upon the vessels, both commercial and national, and upon the consular officers of other powers calls for the definition of their relations to the parties to the contest.[166]

Indeed, the secondary, if at all, importance of the rights of internal parties can explain why recognition of belligerent rights was generally contingent upon the recognizing power's substantial *interest* in doing so. As summarized by Dana, "[t]he reason which requires and can alone justify this step [recognition of belligerency] ... is, that its [the recognizing state's] own rights and interests are so far affected as to requite a definition of its own relations to the parties."[167] Meaning, internal rights and interests were insufficient for this purpose.

War indeed entailed consequences for neutral commerce. Mainly, the existence of *war* was a precondition for the application of maritime prize law, which had immense effects over the trade interests of the great naval powers. Thus, the distinction whether a state of war – or belligerency

165 United States Attorney General, *Neutrality Act*, 13 U.S. Op. Atty. Gen. 177, 180 (December 16, 1869) (emphasis added). For further discussion and analysis *see also* Woolsey, *supra* note 115.

166 Annual Message of December 7, 1875, *cited in* Wilson, *supra* note 72, at 47.

167 Wheaton's, *supra* note 30; *see also* Beale, *supra* note 35, at 407.

– existed, was one of great urgency to the trading naval powers. When major rebellions began to take place in the European colonies – for instance, the late eighteenth-century American Revolution or the early nineteenth-century Spanish Colonial Wars – a question of utmost importance was whether these amounted to wars, entailing all the maritime consequences of that status.[168]

In order to understand the wider context of the question, some elaboration is helpful. In traditional prize law, for instance, a belligerent vessel could legitimately visit-and-search a neutral vessel on the high seas, and – if caught carrying contraband (and prior to the Declaration of Paris of 1856, enemy property at large) destined to enemy territory – capture it. If a neutral vessel would breach or attempt to breach a blockade, it would suffer the same consequences, even on the high seas. In any case, capture would not transfer the title to the vessel or goods, until they were condemned following *in rem* adjudication in front of a prize court established by the belligerent. Furthermore, if the neutral would violate the terms of neutrality in a magnitude sufficient to render it an enemy belligerent by the "victim" state, vessels flying its flag could be captured on the high seas as enemy vessels, and condemned in front of prize courts, regardless of their destiny or cargo (however, if the *cargo* belonged to a neutral, only the *vessel* itself could be condemned and the cargo was released.)[169] However, the rights of belligerents to capture and condemn neutral vessels running a blockade or carrying contraband did not render the act of such vessels *illegal*; nor did it require third states to prevent such actions. Capture and condemnation was the only penalty incurred, and was viewed as no more of a calculated risk taken by the vessel's owner.[170]

In sum, it is in this context where traditional international law regarding internal conflicts developed, and not in the context of forcible intervention. The doctrines of recognition of belligerency, and – to a certain extent – of insurgency, were mainly concerned with effects over neutral commerce. The issue of consensual forcible intervention, conversely, was virtually non-existent in the discussion of the status of parties to an internal armed conflict, since, as aforementioned, use of force was a sovereign prerogative. Only since the creation of modern day *jus ad bellum* did the law on the use of force come to substantially affect the scope of this right, and thus, also, the legality of consensual intervention.

168 *See* Oglesby, *supra* note 29, at VI–VIII, 18–32. It is of interest that early colonial wars were considered internal conflicts. This is in stark contrast to colonial struggles of the modern era, which are viewed as international ones. This in itself, as we shall discuss in Chapter 9, demonstrates international law's shift to substantive considerations.

169 Perhaps with the exception of coast fishing vessels. *See* The Paquete Habana, 175 U.S. 677 (1900); for general prize law *see* Ex Parte Chavasse, *supra* note 33; and the High Court of Admiralty in The Helen, (1865–67) L.R. 1 (1865); The Santissima Trinidad, *supra* note 98; *see* also C. John Colombos, International Law of the Sea, 687 (6th ed., 1967).

170 The Helen, *supra* note 106, at 4.

However, since the status of parties to internal armed conflicts was indeed affected by these traditional doctrines, it is of much importance to understand the *considerations* that governed them. As we have noted, these were largely based on amoral considerations of effective control or similar concepts. We shall now turn to exemplify these dynamics as they unfolded in the American Civil War.

6 The amoral dynamics of the American Civil War

6.1 General

As discussed in section 3.1, the belligerency doctrine was born of necessity, throughout a series of eighteenth-century conflicts. However, it took a massive event such as the American Civil War to consolidate it. The American Civil War, as there is no need to elaborate, was prompted by the secession of the Southern States – organized as the Confederate States of America – mainly over the controversy between the parties over the institution of slavery.[171] Full blown conflict erupted in the battle of Fort Sumter of April 12, 1861, and when a blockade was proclaimed against Confederate ports by US President Lincoln a week later, the conflict immediately raised international concerns. As we shall see, the Confederacy was considered by the Union (albeit grudgingly), as well as by European powers, as a belligerent; the Confederacy saw itself as a state involved in an international war.[172]

The American Civil War constitutes the quintessential example of the recognition of belligerency as a mean to regulate the relations between external and internal parties. From our analysis until now, it is clear that the recognition of the rights of parties to internal armed conflicts was at large disconnected from any substantive or moral analysis – beyond the frequently stated condition that both parties must adhere to the laws of war, which were based on the concept of reciprocity between parties, and not concerned, at large, with a party's treatment of its *own* population. The American Civil War was one case where it was definitely possible to identify a glaring immorality – the institution of slavery[173] – and therefore, it best exemplifies the amoral approach of effectiveness-based doctrines towards the recognition of rights and powers of parties to internal armed conflicts.

6.2 Internal and external approaches

From the outset of the conflict, the US was caught in a bind. Simply put, it aspired to exercise belligerent powers against the South, without recognizing, sweepingly, the South's capacity to do the same. Thus, on one

171 For a factual summary and an extensive overview, *see* Wright, *supra* note 12.

172 *Id.* at 30–31.

173 *See, e.g.,* John Rawls, The Law of Peoples 38 (2001).

hand, the US saw utmost importance in preventing any legal status from the South; on the other, it had an interest in recognizing that the conflict was indeed a "war," mainly in order to impose a third-party binding blockade and to trigger the application of prize law on the high seas.[174]

In essence, the Union's approach amounted to a "half-hearted" acceptance that the conflict amounted to belligerency.[175] This explains, perhaps, the discrepancy between President Lincoln's blockade proclamation – according to which the Confederacy was merely "a combination of persons" engaged in insurrection entitled to no maritime rights[176] – and subsequent Supreme Court decisions that addressed the *belligerent* status of the South. However, as we shall shortly see, US Courts too were inconsistent, by recognizing belligerency only to the extent that it spawned rights for the US rather than for the Confederacy. Nonetheless, it is striking that Union courts, even when at large hostile to Confederacy belligerent rights, were careful to base their decisions on reasons of effectiveness and sovereignty, rather on any substantive judgment of the parties.

In the Prize Cases of 1862,[177] the Court had to grapple in detail with the question whether the Civil War constituted a *war* in the sense of international law, in which prize law applies.[178] The case involved an appeal by four merchant vessels that were captured by Union ships, to be condemned in a District Court sitting as a prize court. The claimants argued, *inter alia*, that the Union could not impose a blockade on the South with consequences in prize law, since the conflict was an insurrection rather than a war in the international or domestic sense.[179] The Court, in a majority ruling (5–4), rejected these claims, setting forth a territorial-effectiveness doctrine for the understanding of belligerent rights in civil wars:[180]

174 Wright, *supra* note 12, at 75; *see also* Bernard, *supra* note 34, at 159; Lauterpacht, *supra* note 31, at 243–244; John M. Taylor, William Henry Seward: Lincoln's Right Hand 179–180 (1991).

175 Wright, *supra* note 12, at 93–94. It should be added that the issue of belligerency did not arise in Confederate courts, since they operated under the assumption that the Confederacy was an independent state. *See id.* at 30–31; *see also* In the Matter of Finley, 60 N.C. 191 (1863); Russ v. Mitchell, 11 Fla. 80 (1864).

176 By the President of the United States of America – A Proclamation (April 19, 1861), *available at* www.historyplace.com/lincoln/proc-2.htm.

177 The Prize Cases, 67 U.S. 635 (1862); *see also* Ford V. Surget, 97 U.S. 594, 613–614 (1878) Wright, *supra* note 12, at 43–45; Smith, *supra* note 51, at 20.

178 It seems that nowadays, while it is reasonable that prize law is still relevant, to some degree, the existence of a state of war *stricto sensu* is not a condition for its application, as the concept of armed conflict substituted the term *war* in the classical sense. *See* Wolff Heintschel von Heinegg, *The Current State of International Prize Law*, *in* International Economic Law and Armed Conflict 33 (Harry H.G. Post ed., 1994).

179 The Prize Cases, *supra* note 177, at 642–643.

180 Justice Nelson, supported by Justices Catron, Clifford and Chief Justice Taney, opined in his dissenting opinion that "war" exists only after Congress recognizes it as such. Since this was not done until July 13, 1861, the Union's blockade, according to Justice Nelson, could not bind neutral vessels.

> The parties belligerent in a public war are independent nations. But it is not necessary to constitute war, that both parties should be acknowledged as independent nations or sovereign States. A war may exist where one of the belligerents, claims sovereign rights as against the other.... When the party in rebellion occupy and hold in a hostile manner a certain portion of territory; have declared their independence; have cast off their allegiance; have organized armies; have commenced hostilities against their former sovereign, the world acknowledges them as belligerents, and the contest a war.[181]

The Court thus vehemently rejected the notion that there is something inherent in internal armed conflicts which prevents them from being "wars," and the parties from being "enemies."[182] Furthermore, citing Vattel, the Court held that parties to a civil war ought to adhere to the laws of war, on counts of reason and reciprocity (stopping short of imposing a clear-cut legal obligation to do so); and that the existence of a civil war is a question of fact, notwithstanding formal declarations or the lack thereof, or the negative perception of one side regarding the other.[183] Thus, it concluded that the Union blockade was legal under international and domestic law, and that third parties must respect it to maintain their neutral status.[184] This conclusion was reaffirmed in further Supreme Court prize decisions throughout the Civil War.[185] However, the Court refrained from specifying the belligerent rights of the Confederacy, since what was discussed, to a large extent, were the belligerent rights of the *Union*. This approach was reflected in other rulings by the Court.[186]

Externally speaking, a prime concern of the Union was to prevent any status-conferring recognition of the Confederacy by foreign powers. However, when the Union blockade was imposed, the conflict immediately produced international effects that required maritime powers to take a stand.[187] On April 30, 1861, British Foreign Secretary Lord Russell learned that Fort Sumter had fallen into the hands of the Confederacy, and that President Lincoln had called out the national militia. Six days later, Lord Russell announced in Parliament that the Government came to the

181 The Prize Cases, *supra* note 177, at 666–667.

182 *Id.* at 670.

183 *Id.* at 667–669.

184 *Id.* at 671.

185 *See, e.g.*, The Circassian, 69 U.S. 135 (1864); The Admiral, 70 U.S. 603 (1865); The Thompson, 70 U.S. 155 (1865); The Bermuda, 70 U.S. 514 (1865). For cases regarding the belligerency in the split-state of Kentucky *see* Com. v. Holland, 1 Duv. 182 (1864); Martin v. Hortin 1 Bush 629 (1865).

186 *See also* The Lilla, 15 F. Cas. 525, 526, 529 (1862); affirmed in U.S. v. The Lilla, 26 F. Cas. 938 (1863).

187 *See* Bernard, *supra* note 34, at 130.

conclusion that the Confederacy must be treated as a belligerent.[188] After Confederate President Jefferson Davis invited private vessel owners to apply for letters of marque,[189] and President Lincoln proclaimed a naval blockade of the South, Queen Victoria proclaimed neutrality on May 13.[190] Notably, the proclamation warned British subjects from breaching neutrality laws – enforced domestically through the Foreign Enlistment Act of 1819[191] – *inter alia* by warning against

> fitting out, arming, or equipping any ship or vessel to be employed as a ship of war or privateer or transport, by either of the said contending parties; or by breaking, or endeavouring to break, any blockade lawfully and actually established by or on behalf of either of the said contending parties; or by carrying officers, soldiers, despatches, arms, military stores, or materials, or any article or articles considered and deemed to be contraband of war according to the law or modern usage of nations, for the use or service of either of the said contending parties.[192]

This declaration spawned an intense debate between the countries, in which Britain attempted to downplay its meaning, denying that it was a harbinger of recognition of independence, and labeling it as a mere technical "necessity," based upon a determination of a "fact." It was only designed to "explain to British subjects their liabilities."[193] The US agreed to this view in principle (meaning, presumably, the general concept of belligerency); however, it thought it was premature, as the recognition took place "before they [the South] had ever shown their capacity to maintain any kind of warfare whatever, except within one of their own harbours. ... It [Britain] considered them a marine power before they had even exhibited a single privateer."[194]

188 *Id.* at 13; Oglesby, *supra* note 29, at 34–35.

189 *Id.* at 35; *see also* Wright, *supra* note 12 at 46. President Davis invited "all those who may desire by service in private armed vessels on the high seas, to aid this Government in resisting so wanton and wicked an aggression." *See Important from Montgomery: Proposal to Issue Letters of Marque and Reprisal*, New York Times, April 18, 1861; *available at* www.nytimes.com/1861/04/18/news/important-from-montgomery-proposal-to-issue-letters-of-marque-and-reprisal.html; *see also* Bernard, *supra* note 34, at 78–79.

190 Oglesby, *supra* note 29, at 35.

191 *See* 2 Oppenheim, *supra* note 13, §311.

192 Royal Proclamation of May 13, 1861; *see also* Bernard, *supra* note 34, at 132. For an application of the Foreign Enlistment Act by British courts *see, e.g.*, Attorney-General v Sillim and Others Claiming the Alexandra, 176 E.R. 295 (1863).

193 Report of the meeting between of May 18, 1861 between John Francis Adams and US Secretary of State. Reprinted in Bernard, *supra* note 34, at 152–153, 155; for more on the Russell–Adams discussion, *see* Beale, *supra* note 35, at 413–414.

194 Bernard, *supra* note 34, at 154.

If framed in a normative way, it seems that the doctrinal dispute between the parties concerned the question whether a state could impose a third-party binding blockade and still claim, at the same time, that belligerency does not exist. It is clear that – contrary to the American view – Britain was prepared to recognize all the belligerent rights of the Confederacy, including rights in maritime prize law. The belligerency status of the Confederacy and questions regarding British neutrality were addressed by British courts in various instances, in which the belligerency of the South was not doubted.[195] In sum, by the time the war ended, both parties were in agreement on the general concept of belligerency recognition, and seem to differ solely on the question of its timing.[196]

France declared neutrality soon after the British declaration, on June 10, 1861; the majority of other states with interests in maritime trade followed suit in subsequent months.[197] The conservative powers of Europe, namely Russia, Germany and the Austro-Hungarian Empire denied any status from the South, due to particular interests and their general disapproval of revolutionary movements, reminiscent of the Holy Alliance's legitimism doctrine.[198]

6.3 The amoral application of law in the American Civil War

It is sometimes said that ethical questions should be judged in light of the prevailing norms of the time, and that one should be careful when attempting to "retrofit" contemporary norms to past events. In the mid-nineteenth century, however, there was already a widespread notion that slavery was immoral. Nonetheless, as we have seen, this fact did not affect, or in any case prevent, the majority of powers from adopting a neutral legal stance towards the American Civil War.

Thus, although slavery was abhorred in Britain of the nineteenth century, the issue of slavery did not affect its decision to adopt a neutral stance regarding the Civil War.[199] Throughout the war, Britain even considered, from time to time, the recognition of the Confederacy as a state, but ultimately decided to remain in the intermediate position of belligerency recognition.[200]

195 *See, e.g.*, Ionides v. Universal Marine Insurance, 143 E.R. 445 (1863); In re Tivnan, 122 E.R. 971 (1864); Hobbs v. Henning, 144 E.R. 317 (1864); Ex Parte Chavasse, 46 E.R. 1072 (1865); The Helen, (1865–67) L.R. 1 (1865).

196 *See* the 1865 correspondence between Adams and Russell, reprinted in Wheaton's, *supra* note 30, at 37–38 n. 15.

197 Wright, *supra* note 12, at 82.

198 *See* Chapter 1, sec. 2.2. *See also* Beale, *supra* note 35, at 414–417; Wright, *supra* note 12, at 82–83.

199 *Id.* at 80–81.

200 *Id.* at 50–51, n.24, 84.

So detached was the question of slavery from the policy of Britain and other European powers, that the US Congress had to remind them what was at stake. When France proposed to mediate between the parties – perhaps having in mind eventual Southern independence – the offer was rejected "promptly" by Lincoln; Congress, in a joint resolution of March 3, 1863,[201] emphasized that slavery was at the core of the conflict. Congress resolved that while the US could understand the wish of foreign powers to bring an end to the conflict, any offer of foreign "interference" in the struggle would be "so far unreasonable and inadmissible that its only explanation will be found in a misunderstanding of the true state of question, and of the real character of the war." The real character, as resolved by the Congress, was one in which the South was aspiring to "build a new Power whose corner-stone ... shall be slavery."[202]

In order to understand the amoral approach towards the American Civil War, it is illustrative to examine some of the powers' declarations of neutrality. Perhaps by nature, these were extremely technical, most very laconic, and addressed almost exclusively to the relevant state's citizenry by clarifying the adverse ramifications of breaches of neutrality laws. Some declarations notified that, in conformity with the Declaration of Paris, privateers of neither party would be admitted to their ports. None of the declarations referred to the issue of slavery or to other substantive questions, such as conformity to the laws of war. France addressed the fact that the Confederacy "claims" to be independent, without mentioning the merits, and proceeded to enumerate the neutrality provisions it will enforce.[203] Spain "resolved to maintain strict neutrality in the contest begun between the Federal States of the Union and the States confederated at the South."[204] Prussia laconically notified its merchants that "during the continuance of the conflict that has broken out among the North American States, the mercantile classes must abstain from all enterprises which are forbidden by the general principles of international law."[205] Belgium simply stressed its adherence to the Declaration of Paris.[206] The Netherlands followed the same route, and warned its merchants of losses due to "any violation of the obligations imposed on neutral Powers" in maritime law.[207]

The hypothetical question of consensual intervention in light of the South's slavery policies bothered John Stuart Mill, albeit from an ethical

201 Congressional Globe, 37th Congress, 3rd Session, p. 1497 (March 3, 1863), *available at* http://memory.loc.gov/ammem/amlaw/lwcglink.html.

202 *Id. see also* Wright, *supra* note 34, at 101–102.

203 Reprinted in Bernard, *supra* note 34, at 144.

204 *Id.* at 147–148.

205 *Id.* at 145.

206 *Id.* at 145–146.

207 *Id.* at 146–147. *See also* the declarations of Portugal, Hawaii, Bremen and Hamburg, *id.* at 148–150.

rather than legal point of view. After the Trent Affair of November 1861 – involving the US interception of a British vessel and the removal of Confederate officials – there was serious concern that Britain would intervene forcibly in favor of the Confederacy.[208] In an 1862 article, Mill denounced the immorality of any potential intervention of such nature.[209] Moreover, Mill was not entirely comfortable even with the recognition of the South's belligerency. He acknowledged the amoral aspect of this policy, but viewed it nonetheless as a result of "political" necessity:

> There is no denying that our attitude towards the contending parties (I mean our moral attitude, for politically there was no other course open to us than neutrality) has not been that which becomes a people who are as sincere enemies of slavery as the English really are.[210]

Mill saw the Trent Affair as "an indignity, and something more than an indignity, which not to have resented, would have been to invite a constant succession of insults and injuries."[211] However, he rejected any contention that belligerency recognition should lead to eventual forcible intervention. Mill strongly argued that it was inconceivable that Britain, which has long been active against slavery, "should have lent a hand to setting up … a powerful republic, devoted not only to slavery, but to pro-slavery propagandism." Thus, argued Mill, while Britain had the right to respond to the wrong inflicted upon it, the consequences would soon overshadow the initial objective:

> When the new Confederate States, made an independent Power by English help, had begun their crusade to carry negro slavery from the Potomac to Cape Horn, who would then have remembered that England raised up this scourge to humanity not for the evil's sake, but because somebody had offered an insult to her flag?[212]

Accordingly, Mill defended the policies of President Lincoln, which he saw as just in their essence. On counts of the wrongfulness of its cause – the perpetuation of slavery, he deduced that the South had no right to pursue secession:

> Secession may be laudable, and so may any other kind of insurrection; but it may also be an enormous crime. It is the one or the other, according to the object and the provocation. And if there ever was an

208 On the Trent Affair *see supra* note 55.

209 John Stuart Mill, *The Contest in America, in* III Dissertations and Discussions 179–205 (1867).

210 *Id.*

211 *Id.*

212 *Id.*

> object which, by its bare announcement, stamped rebels against a particular community as enemies of mankind, it is the one professed by the South.[213]

It was thus obvious that although he was willing to justify Britain's neutrality, Mill would not espouse any forcible support of the South – on *substantive* grounds. However, Mill's ethical position was foreign to international law of the time, which was controlled by the war-prerogative and rooted in considerations of effective control. Indeed, his reluctant acceptance of Britain's neutrality as a "necessary evil," highlighted the amoral characteristics of the doctrines of the time, in unambiguous moral circumstances.

213 *Id.*

5 Intervention and consent in the inter-war period and the fragmentation of traditional doctrines

1 The League of Nations system and the use of force: from the balance of power to the power of procedure

Following the trauma of World War I, public opinion in Europe and elsewhere was determined to limit the nineteenth century's balance of power approach towards the use of force. War, as a phenomenon, has come to be perceived as a product of misunderstandings between unaccountable leaders.[1] This perception was reflected in the Covenant of the League of Nations (LONS), adopted in 1919. A revolutionary document, the Covenant sought, for the first time, to prevent wars through an intricate system of *pacific settlement of disputes*, augmented by a *collective security* mechanism.[2] The idea behind the pacific settlement system was that war was an irrational act, often a product of miscalculations and ignorance. As such, it could be avoided by imposing a mandatory "cooling off" period, applied through complex bureaucratic procedures, and overseen by external actors. During this period, states would have the chance to regain rationality and reconsider their choices.[3] The pacific settlement approach was laid down in Articles 12, 13 and 15 of the Covenant, and was meant to be implemented through a combination of adjudication, arbitration and decisions by the Council of the LONS.[4]

Indeed, the Covenant presented new procedural-legal restrictions on the unfettered war-power of states, by creating a distinction between "legal

1 Alex J. Bellamy *et al.*, Understanding Peacekeeping 76 (2010).

2 On the LONS and the provisions surveyed here, *see generally*, Frederick Pollock, The League of Nations 112–155 (1920).

3 *See* Inis L. Claude, Swords into Plowshares: The Problems and Progress of International Organization 219–293 (1971).

4 For discussion of the pacific settlement system *see generally*, Manley O. Hudson, *The Permanent Court of International Justice*, 35 Harvard Law Review 245 (1922); *see* Reginald Berkeley, *The Work of the League of Nations*, 2 British Year Book of International Law 150, 159 (1921–1922).

and illegal wars."[5] States conducting illegal wars – meaning, undertaken in contravention of the pacific settlement procedure – would face the collective security mechanism set up in Articles 10, 11 and 16 of the Covenant.[6] As declared in Article 11, war was no more strictly a concern of the parties involved, but that of the whole League, which will take, accordingly, any action to safeguard peace.

However, the Covenant did not prohibit war per se, nor did it confine it only to cases of self-defense. Moreover, it did not create a *constitutional* restriction on war, since it applied only between member states.[7] The Covenant thus merely sought to inhibit war through the imposition of procedural requirements, reducing it to a measure to be taken only when other means were exhausted.[8] As such, the Covenant system had significant "gaps" that still allowed states to legally resort to war.[9] For instance, after a decision rendered through the pacific settlement mechanisms, states could still resort to war, as means of enforcement, after waiting for an additional three months. Furthermore, if the parties chose to submit a matter to the Council, the question of war-rights would be determined by the outcome of the process, which was subject to consensus-based decision making. If consensus was reached, the complying party was immune from war; however, war could be declared against the non-complying party, after the aforementioned three-months cooling period. Absent consensus, *both* parties could resort to war, presumably, again, after the cooling period.[10] Importantly, as provided in Article 15, if the Council found that a dispute has arisen from a matter "solely within the domestic jurisdiction"

5 Ian Brownlie, International Law and the Use of Force by States 57 (1963); *cited in* Stanimir A. Alexandrov, Self-Defense against the Use of Force in International Law 34 (1996). The distinction between legal and illegal wars sparked a debate regarding the freedom to assume neutral status. It was claimed, for instance, that where aggression occurs, traditional neutrality is irrelevant, and that some intermediate status between neutrality and participation in war must be recognized. *See, e.g.*, Edwin Borchard, *War, Neutrality and Non-Belligerency*, 35 American Journal of International Law 618 (1941).

6 *See generally* Arnold D. McNair, *Collective Security*, 17 British Year Book of International Law 150 (1936); John Fischer Williams, *Sanctions under the Covenant*, 17 British Year Book of International Law 130 (1936); Manley O. Hudson, *Amendment of the Covenant of the League of Nations*, 28 Harvard Law Review 903 (1925); L. Kopelmanas, *The Problem of Aggression and the Prevention of War*, 31 American Journal of International Law 244, 246 (1937); *See* Bellamy, *supra* note 1, at 78–79; Claude, *supra* note 3, at 255–269.

7 Yoram Dinstein, War, Aggression and Self-Defense 84 (5th ed. 2011). Thus, the right of war regarding non-members remained unaltered. This was of special importance as the emerging superpower – the US – was not a member, along with Germany and Japan. *See* McNair, *supra* note 6, at 156.

8 For a concise summary *see* Alexandrov, *supra* note 5, at 29–34; Myra Williams, Terrorism, War and International Law: The Legality of the Use of Force against Afghanistan in 2001 74–75 (2009).

9 Dinstein, *supra* note 7, at 83–84.

10 *See id.* at 83; Alexandrov, *supra* note 3, at 33, and the sources cited therein.

of a state, it would refrain from making recommendations – thus leaving the solution of the issue to states themselves, *including* through war.

These gaps could theoretically be utilized to justify forcible interventions in internal strife, even against governments. Thus, in the era of the LONS, consensual intervention in internal conflicts – even against governments – could be legal, as long as it conformed to the procedure outlined in the Covenant. However, it could be argued that interventions *in favor* of governments were completely uninhibited by the Covenant's procedure, assuming that these would be viewed as falling within the "domestic jurisdiction" of a party. Here, for the first time, a substantial, legally grounded argument could be set forth in favor of the principle of preference of governments in internal armed conflicts.

2 The Kellogg–Briand Pact: towards a universal prohibition on war

A per se abolishment of the right of war was introduced in international law only with the conclusion of the General Treaty for Renunciation of War as an Instrument of National Policy of 1928 (the Kellogg–Briand Pact),[11] which purported to mend the "gaps" in the Covenant system that contributed to its eventual failure.[12] The three-articled pact renounced war as an instrument of "national policy";[13] and required that the settlement of *all* disputes would only be pursued by pacific means.[14]

By World War II, the Pact had a record-setting membership of 63 states.[15] However – its novelty notwithstanding – it was not unflawed. First, it did not directly address the right of self-defense, although it was never doubted that it did not negate such a right; second, it left open for interpretation the question of what constitutes "national policy": as some claimed, the term did not include war as a sanction for violations of arbitration or judicial decisions (war as "international policy"); third, the Pact was not universal (although close to it);[16] and fourth, it did not address forcible acts that did not amount to formal war, in its traditional sense. In the era in which the distinction between acts of *war* and forcible acts

11 General Treaty for Renunciation of War as an Instrument of National Policy (Kellogg–Briand Pact), August 27, 1928, 94 L.N.T.S. 57.

12 McNair, *supra* note 6, at 156–157; on the failure of the League of Nations *see* Walter Schiffer, *The Idea of Collective Security, in* From Collective Security to Preventive Diplomacy 187 (Joel L. Larus ed. 1965); Gilbert Murray, *A League of Nations: The First Experiment, in* The Background and Issues of the War 49 (H.A.L. Fisher *et al.* eds., 1940).

13 Kellogg–Briand Pact, *supra* note 11, art. I.

14 *Id.* art. II.

15 Dinstein, *supra* note 7, at 85.

16 McNair, *supra* note 6, at 157.

short-of-war was of much importance, this was a substantial issue.[17] Thus, it is perhaps not surprising that in the 1930s, states often conducted hostilities without declaring war or referring to their actions as such.[18] This practice, an "unforeseen consequence of the Kellogg Pact,"[19] explains the eventual omission of the term "war" from the prohibition on the use of force set forth in the UN Charter.

The Kellogg–Briand Pact did not replace the Covenant of the LONS. It essentially caused states to lose their "residuary liberty to use war ... as an instrument of national policy,"[20] which was, as aforementioned, reserved to them in the Covenant. Attempts to harmonize the two instruments – in order to sanction wars that previously were not unlawful – did not materialize.[21]

3 The use of force in the inter-war period and consensual intervention: a departure from intervention as choice

By 1936, following the LONS' restriction on war and the Kellogg–Briand Pact's nascent prohibition on war, it was already safe to say that the old attitude towards war as a valid method of self-help, had given way to a new approach. Once a prohibition on war was put in place, it became valid to ask whether, and under what circumstances, consent can serve as an exception to this prohibition. It is at this point that the major set of questions regarding this issue was given real *legal* substance: if war, presumably between states, was no longer a legal "policy," does that mean that war conducted on *behalf* of a state, against opposition forces, is always a legal policy? Moreover, assuming the answer was positive, was the government of the state always presumed to be speaking in the name of the state, in a matter sufficient to allow it to consent to external intervention? Furthermore, it became relevant to ask whether the answers to these questions were determined by the effectiveness doctrine, or rather that another, alternative set of considerations emerged.

As part of these questions, traditional doctrines could also be assessed in light of the new legal environment. This potential change can be exemplified, for instance, in the Convention on Duties and Rights of States in the Event of Civil Strife, adopted at the International Conference

17 For these flaws *see* Dinstein, *supra* note 7, at 85–87 and the sources cited therein. For a more extensive analysis of the Pact, mainly in the context of the right to self-defense, *see* Alexandrov, *supra* note 5, at 51–76.

18 Oscar Schachter, *The Right of States to Use Armed Force*, 82 Michigan Law Review 1620, 1624 (1984); Philip M. Brown, *Editorial Comment: Undeclared Wars*, 33 American Journal of International Law 538 (1939).

19 *Id.* at 540.

20 *See* C.A.W. Manning, *The Proposed Amendments to the Covenant of the League of Nations*, 11 British Year Book of International Law 158, 159 (1930).

21 For the text of the proposed amendments *see id.* at 170–171.

of American States of 1928,[22] which must be read in light of the Kellogg–Briand Pact of the same year. Although the Civil Strife Convention was by no means universal, it allows us to draw a clearer picture of the understanding of the law of consensual intervention of the time. At large, the Convention enshrined the principle of "preferential treatment" for governments, at least until belligerency was recognized.[23] While this distinction had debatable legal consequences in the war-prerogative era, after the Kellogg–Briand Pact it seems that it could have substantive implications.

The five-articled Convention obliged states to prevent the inhabitants of their territory from participating in civil strife in another state; to disarm and intern rebels crossing their boundaries; and to "forbid traffic in arms and war material, except when intended for the Government, while the belligerency of the rebels has not been recognized, in which latter case the rules of neutrality *shall* be applied."[24] Recall that before the Kellogg–Briand Pact – and to a lesser extent before the Covenant of the LONS – neutrality was always a choice; recognition of belligerency was a method to express this choice, but it could always be departed from by sovereign decision to enter into war. However, by the time Civil Strife Convention was adopted, the war-prerogative of sovereigns was limited. Therefore, it seems that by that time, the recognition of belligerency and the resulting neutrality was the *farthest* a state could go if seeking to favor the opposition; any forcible intervention on behalf of the opposition would violate the nascent-limitations on the use of force, as long as the government was still recognized.[25]

The question, then, would remain whether government consent-power still remained, or was also limited. One approach could be that the preferential treatment of governments entailed also that they enjoyed unlimited powers to consent to external intervention. Another possible answer would be that the preference of governments was diminished when loss of territorial effective control occurred. This approach will be addressed in the next chapter. However, a different opinion emerged also, reflecting a movement towards a substantive approach towards the rights of parties to internal armed conflicts. In the inter-war period, self-determination became a dominant concept in international discourse, through the powerful advocacy of US President Woodrow Wilson.[26]

Self-determination enhanced the discussion of the norm of non-intervention, leading to ideas regarding intervention in internal conflicts

22 Convention on Duties and Rights of States in the Event of Civil Strife, February 20, 1928, 134 L.N.T.S. 45.

23 Hersch Lauterpacht, Recognition in International Law 231 (1948).

24 Civil Strife Convention, *supra* note 22, art. 1 (emphasis added).

25 *Compare* Michael Walzer, Just and Unjust Wars: A Moral Argument With Historical Illustrations 96–97 (4th ed., 2006).

26 *See* Joshua Castellino, International Law and Self-Determination 13–19 (2000).

that went beyond the developing law on the use of force. Lauterpacht, for instance, echoed the views expressed by Montague Bernard almost a century before,[27] seeing every such intervention as a "denial of the right of the nation to decide for itself – by a physical contest, if necessary, between rival forces – the nature and the form of its government."[28] Therefore, he perceived the "preferential treatment" of governments as very limited, essentially arguing for almost complete non-intervention, even without recognition of belligerency.[29] However, Lauterpacht departed, to an extent, from the effectiveness doctrine, implying a *substantive* analysis of parties:

> There must be definite limits to presumptions in favour of established governments so long as the international community has no such control over them as to secure effectively the fundamental rights of the individual and decent administration of the law.[30]

Lauterpacht's position can thus be seen as an early argument for a legal, substantive qualification of the "preferential treatment" of governments, in the era of the limitation on the use of force. These qualifications, and their different developments, will be addressed later on.

4 The Spanish Civil War and the crisis of the traditional law of internal armed conflict

The inter-war era, notwithstanding its legal achievements in limiting the lawfulness of war, was also a time of major crisis for the international system. The advent of ideologies with global aspirations – namely communism and fascism – gave rise to significant challenges to existing interstate relations.[31] The Spanish Civil War of 1936–1939 represented this ideological clash both internally and internationally. It erupted in July 1936, following the assassination of right-wing politician José Calvo Sotelo, allegedly by forces associated with the Spanish government. The conflict's roots can be found in attempted reforms by the Republican government, which aggravated a coalition of conservative forces, commonly known as the Nationalists. This coalition encompassed elements ranging from monarchists to fascists, comprising of industrialists, parts of the middle class, landowners and aristocrats. They were led by Spanish Army general Francisco Franco, who garnered most of the Army's support.

27 Montague Bernard, On the Principle of Non-Intervention (1860).
28 Lauterpacht, *supra* note 23, at 233.
29 *Id.*
30 *Id.* at 234.
31 H.A. Smith, *Some Problems of the Spanish Civil War*, 18 British Year Book of International Law 31 (1937).

Owing to their military might, the Nationalists rapidly took control over half of the country.[32] In October 1936, Franco appropriated the title of chief of the Spanish state.[33] By early 1939 the Republicans were on the brink of defeat. France and Britain recognized the Franco government on February 27, 1939;[34] and the Republican forces finally capitulated on March 31, 1939.[35]

The Republicans, in their effort, during the conflict, to counter the military advantages of the Nationalists, turned to arm peasants and workers, leading to full blown chaos in which each group fought for its own interests. Notwithstanding the conflict's root causes, the Nationalists' narrative was constructed upon the struggle against communism, while the Republicans saw themselves as confronting a dangerous fascist threat.[36] Accordingly, the conflict was not perceived as an isolated civil war, but – and as history soon proved, quite correctly – as one which involved forces that threatened the entire international order. Once the stakes were so high, it was not surprising that the traditional, effectiveness-based doctrines of international law regarding internal armed conflicts gave way to other approaches.[37]

The Spanish conflict was soon eclipsed by World War II, after which the world was fundamentally different, politically and legally. In this sense, it can be seen as one of the last major internal conflicts before the founding of the UN, signifying the closure of an era. However, the responses to the Spanish Civil War did foresee a major development in international law: the emergence of collective, formally organized reactions to internal armed conflicts. It was novel at being virtually the first internal conflict in which international institutions – whether ad hoc or permanent – played a substantial role, although they had limited effects in practice.[38] These dynamics were manifested in the involvement – however limited – by the LONS, and in the conclusion of a Non-Intervention Agreement (NIA) – in which parties pledged to refrain from support to either side. More than anything the reactions to the conflict reflected a system in transition, in

32 Norman J. Padelford, *International Law and the Spanish Civil War*, 31 American Journal of International Law 226, 226 (1937).

33 Ann Van Wynen Thomas and A.J. Thomas, Jr., *International Legal Aspects of the Civil War in Spain, 1936–1939, in* The International Law of Civil War 111, 111–112 (Richard A. Falk ed., 1972).

34 *Id.* at 160.

35 *Id.* at 118–119.

36 *Id.* at 112–113.

37 Smith, *supra* note 31, at 31.

38 Thomas and Thomas, *supra* note 33, at 175.

which traditional approaches, such as the belligerency doctrine, were largely set aside.[39]

In general, the debates that took place in the context of the Spanish conflict exemplify the intractable dilemmas regarding consensual intervention. One approach, suggested by scholars such as Lauterpacht, stemmed from a stringent perception of the principle of self-determination, and espoused an obligation amounting to *mandatory neutrality*, a concept that was now logically plausible, as a prohibition on the use of force was in place; another, as was unsurprisingly advanced by the Spanish government, argued for a *mandatory* preferential treatment of recognized governments, a claim augmented by the nascent laws on the use of force; yet another view, as presented by Mexico, argued for a *substantive* preference for the Spanish government, based on its democratic credentials.

The scope of the conflict and the inconsistencies of international reactions led some frustrated commentators to argue that the abandonment of old doctrines was due, and that collective mechanisms to address internal conflicts were required.[40] Others, conversely, heralded traditional international law, alleging that the some states' approaches toward the conflict were illogical, and highly contradictory to previous practice. Smith, for instance, lamented this development, warning that this deviation would be regarded, in the future, as a precedent, and – as he claimed with ample clairvoyance – will ultimately bring about what he saw as the destruction of the centuries-developed law regarding civil wars.[41]

4.1 Consensual intervention in the Spanish Civil War as an illegal use of force and the calls for substantive analysis of parties

During the course of the conflict, the Nationalists requested the support of fascist Italy and Nazi Germany. By the end of July 1936, both powers were involved in the conflict, by transfer of arms as well as by direct participation of their armed forces, concealed as "volunteers."[42] Authoritarian

39 Some claim that the belligerency doctrine was abandoned after the American Civil War, as recognition has not been granted since then. However, it was still prevalent in the debate surrounding the Cuban conflict of the late 1890s. It was also discussed in the scholarly debate regarding the Spanish Civil War. Thus, it was not completely abandoned, *although* recognition was denied. A decision that a certain situation does not merit a legal conclusion does not mean that the doctrine *itself* was abandoned, providing that the situation was evaluated in light of it. This appears to have changed to some extent in the Spanish Civil War and thereafter. *Compare* Roscoe R. Oglesby, Internal War and the Search for Normative Order 102–106 (1971).

40 Vernon A. O'Rourke, *Recognition of Belligerency and the Spanish War*, 31 American Journal of International Law 398, 413 (1937).

41 Smith, *supra* note 31, at 30–31.

42 Thomas and Thomas, *supra* note 33, at 113.

Portugal too supported the Nationalists with "volunteers" and arms, and allowed them to use Portuguese ports, namely for the transport of German aid.[43] The Republicans' calls for aid, however, were less successful. France and Britain denied a July 1936 request for aid, refusing to transfer arms to either side, while emphasizing, however, that neutrality law did not prohibit private dealers from providing arms to the Spanish government.[44] As we shall see, this too changed, later on, to the further detriment of the Spanish government.

The USSR covertly assembled international brigades to assist the Republicans through the Communist International (Comintern). Moreover, the USSR directly sent heavy military equipment to the Republicans, but not on a large scale,[45] and in no case comparable to the involvement of the fascist powers. By mid-1938, Communist aid to the Republicans all but ceased, as Stalin concentrated on the rising German and Japanese dangers.[46]

Throughout the conflict, the Spanish government repeatedly appealed, largely to no avail, also to the Council of the LONS, requesting it to act in the face of the German and Italian intervention. On November 27, 1936, Spain appealed to the Council, invoking Article 11 of the Covenant, labeling the German and Italian actions a "new form of aggression," whereby a state engaged in "war to all intents and purposes, but without declaring war, by ... giving military assistance to the rebels."[47] Reflecting the general notion of the time, in which internal conflicts were not per se viewed as international matters, Spain went to great lengths to convince the members that the conflict was indeed a threat to international peace, beyond the destruction suffered in Spain itself.[48] The League, however, failed to take significant action besides adopting a resolution supporting the Non-Intervention Agreement (NIA), which will be discussed in the next section.[49]

Other attempts to invoke Article 11 were made by Spain in 1937. Again, the Council failed to take significant action.[50] In September 1937, Spain managed to convince a majority of the Council to vote for a resolution recognizing that foreign forces were operating in Spain in *violation of*

43 *Id.* at 114.

44 *Id.* at 114–115. Recall that international neutrality law, in general, did not restrict private parties in their dealing with belligerents, but only states. Thus, states were not obliged to prevent individuals from transferring arms to belligerents. *See* Chapter 3, sec. 4.2.

45 Thomas and Thomas, *supra* note 33, at 118–119.

46 *Id.* at 118–119.

47 League of Nations Official Journal, January 1937, p. 8, *cited in* Norman J. Padelford, *The Non-Intervention Agreement and the Spanish Civil War*, 31 American Journal of International Law 578, 588 (1937).

48 Official Journal, *supra* note 47, at 8–9.

49 *Id.*; O'Rourke, *supra* note 40, at 410; Official Journal, *supra* note 47, at 18–19.

50 Thomas and Thomas, *supra* note 33, at 173–174.

international law, but lack of unanimity curtailed its adoption.[51] Indeed, since the conflict took place in an era in which aggression was already deemed illegal, it was possible at this stage to argue that the German and Italian intervention was illegal, *assuming* their recognition of the Franco regime, which was awarded in late 1936, was premature.[52] Further attempts by Spain to address the Council in 1938 failed to bring significant progress.[53]

After the conflict ended, most states recognized the Franco regime. Mexico was one of the few exceptions.[54] From the outset of the conflict, it maintained that a substantive view of the principle of non-intervention actually condoned supporting the Spanish government, since it was democratically elected. Accordingly, Mexico claimed that the NIA – essentially equalizing the status of the conflicting parties – was in itself an unlawful intervention: in its denial of rights from the Spanish government, it amounted to indirect support for the Nationalists. Mexico's objection to the NIA was unique at the time, due to its emphasis on democratic credentials as a justification for the preferential treatment of the Spanish Government.

Mexico furthermore argued that since the intervention by Germany and Italy constituted an aggression,[55] and also violated the principle of self-determination, the Franco regime could not be recognized – since it came to be by means contrary to the Covenant of the LONS and the Kellogg–Briand Pact. China, the USSR and New Zealand supported this view.[56] It could be said that the Mexican point of view was a harbinger of a new, substantive approach towards the law of internal armed conflicts and the law of consensual intervention in particular. We shall keep this in mind when examining, in the next chapters, these issues in the era of the UN Charter.

4.2 The non-intervention agreement and the fragmentation of traditional law

As aforementioned, the Spanish Civil War was unique in the fact that a non-intervention agreement between numerous states was formed, prohibiting states to intervene in favor of both parties to the conflict. The agreement was unprecedented on both the institutional and legal levels.

51 *Id.* at 174.

52 On November 19, 1936 – long before the end of the conflict – Germany and Italy recognized the opposition as the lawful government, "skipping" the intermediate status of belligerency or insurgency, and denying any belligerent rights of the Republicans. Padelford, *supra* note 32, at 237–239; O'Rourke, *supra* note 40, at 398.

53 Thomas and Thomas, *supra* note 33, at 175.

54 *Id.* at 161.

55 *Id.* at 118.

56 *Id.* at 161–163.

Institutionally, it set up a collective framework to govern the response of external parties to an internal conflict, signifying the movement towards the collectivization of the international system.[57] For instance, a Non-Intervention Committee was established to inquire violations of the agreement.[58] From a legal point of view, although thoroughly defied, the agreement presented a new approach towards the law of internal strife. As such, its lawfulness was heavily debated at the time.[59]

The NIA was initiated by Britain and France in August 1936, and was, in fact, comprised of declarations and exchanges of notes between participating states. It included a preamble, in which states pledged to abstain from all interference, direct or indirect, in the conflict, and three articles, in which they declared that they will prohibit all exportation of "arms, munitions and materials of war, as well as all airplanes ... and all ships of war" to Spanish territories. Furthermore, they agreed that participating states will inform each other on steps taken to enforce the prohibitions.[60]

Twenty-seven states made similar declarations. However, the declarations varied from each other. Some states, Italy and Germany notably among them, joined the agreement, but omitted the preamble, which prohibited *all* interference, arguably allowing them to undertake forms of intervention not specifically prohibited.[61] Both states promptly violated even their narrow declarations; the USSR also eventually violated its declaration.[62] Portugal also set forth a heavily qualified declaration, in which it set conditions for the realization of "the thought of non-intervention." Moreover, it declared that the recognition of belligerency of the parties, as well as of a new *government*, does not constitute intervention.[63]

Its wide variety of interpretations caused the NIA to be described as less of an "agreement" in the formal sense, but more of a "concert of policy"

57 Lauterpacht, *supra* note 23, at 254.

58 Padelford, *supra* note 47, at 586–587.

59 For a summary of the claims against the agreement *see* Thomas and Thomas, *supra* note 33, at 175–176.

60 Padelford, *supra* note 47, at 579–580.

61 These states, and others, attached interpretations, qualifications and reservations to their declarations. *See id.* at 580–581.

62 *See* Thomas and Thomas, *supra* note 33, at 115–117.

63 *Id.* at 116; Padelford, *supra* note 47, at 581–582. It should be noted that the US did not join the agreement, but pursued a policy of unilateral non-intervention based on its neutrality acts of 1935 and 1937. The latter laws extended to transfers of arms by private entities, applied also in internal conflicts, and prohibited interactions not only with the opposition but also with the government, even without belligerency recognition. *See* Edward Dumbauld, *Neutrality Laws of the United States*, 31 American Journal of International Law 258, 259 (1937); Thomas and Thomas, *supra* note 33, at 117; on the neutrality acts of 1935–1937 *see Neutrality Laws of the United States*, *supra* note 89, at 268–269; *see also* James Wilford Garner, *The United States Neutrality Act of 1937*, 31 American Journal of International Law 385 (1937).

based on unilateral declarations.[64] Indeed, it lacked a coherent binding mechanism for interpretation or enforcement, its application being effectively contingent upon the good will of states.[65] Nevertheless, 15 of the declarations were similar enough to form a common basis,[66] essentially, by imposing an arms embargo on both sides, which amounted, in practice, to an instrument of negative intervention.

A salient feature of the Spanish Civil War was states' use of "volunteers" in order to conceal their direct intervention. However, the agreement did not initially oblige the prevention of volunteering, in line with the traditional duty of neutrality, which extended only to the prevention of "organized expeditions" from the neutral's territory – but not to actions by individuals.[67] This loophole was used by all intervening parties, and most notably by Germany and Italy.[68] In early 1937, the members of the Non-Intervention Committee agreed to widen the agreement to include an explicit ban on volunteering.[69] An Observation Scheme, consisting of eight international agencies augmented by an international naval patrol, authorized to inspect merchant vessels, was set up to enforce the ban.[70] This ban could be viewed as a manifestation of states' due diligence requirements, regarding acts of individuals vis-à-vis internal conflicts in other states.[71]

From a legal point of view, the NIA could be seen as an undertaking by states to adopt an "enhanced" status of neutrality *without* recognizing the belligerent rights of either party, including those of the incumbent government.[72] This attitude deviated from prior practice, in which a formal declaration of neutrality was understood to constitute also a recognition of belligerency.[73] Indeed, the treatment of the parties' rights in the Spanish conflict reflected significant doctrinal fragmentation. Therefore, the agreement was not well received by some commentators of the time. Smith saw it as recognizing the "existence of a war," but disregarding its "logical

64 Padelford, *supra* note 47, at 598. It should be noted, however, the unilateral declarations may have binding powers in international law. *See* Krzysztof Skubiszewski, *Unilateral Acts of States*, *in* International Law: Achievements and Prospects 221, 224–226 (Mohammed Bedjaoui ed., 1991).

65 Padelford, *supra* note 47, at 580.

66 *Id.*

67 O'Rourke, *supra* note 40, at 409; Thomas and Thomas, *supra* note 33, at 176; Lauterpacht, *supra* note 23, at 234.

68 Thomas and Thomas, *supra* note 33, at 154–156, 164–166.

69 O'Rourke, *supra* note 40, at 410–411.

70 International Committee for the Application of the Agreement Regarding Non-Intervention in Spain, Resolution Relating to the Scheme of Observation of the Spanish Frontiers by Land and Sea (March 8, 1937) 31 American Journal of International Law, Supp. 163 (1937); Padelford, *supra* note 47, at 588–594. However, the patrol did not have an enforcement mandate – its vessels could not capture contraband. *See id.* at 595.

71 A classic early case can be found in the Alabama arbitrations. *See* Chapter 3, sec. 4.

72 *Compare* Padelford, *supra* note 32, at 234–235.

73 O'Rourke, *supra* note 40, at 409.

consequences."[74] He viewed the agreement as a "collective declaration of neutrality," and therefore of belligerency, *without* the recognition of the parties' belligerent rights, something which he found legally "difficult to understand."[75] This was the case, despite the view of some commentators that belligerency was recognized between the parties themselves.[76]

Indeed, recognition of belligerency was not extended to either party.[77] Britain, for instance, claimed that neither was a lawful belligerent,[78] and that in any case recognition was strictly a matter of discretion; it therefore disregarded the parties' attempts at imposing a blockade.[79] However, the denial of belligerent rights did not prevent Britain from concluding a commercial agreement with the Franco regime;[80] or from dealing with Franco's representatives, without granting them diplomatic status.[81] Moreover, British courts ruled that the government accorded de facto recognition to Franco, albeit with no belligerent status.[82] Regardless of the absence of belligerency recognition, Franco's regime was addressed by third states for protests, appeals and requests for guarantee of property.[83]

The Nationalists also enjoyed maritime privileges. When confronted with harassment of its merchant fleet, the US claimed – perhaps loyal to the insurgency doctrine – that the Spanish government could not close Nationalist ports by decree, absent an effective blockade, notwithstanding the absence of belligerency recognition of the rebels.[84] Moreover, states recognized the de facto power of the Nationalists over neutral merchant vessels *within* the territorial water of Spain,[85] while rejecting such powers on the high seas.[86] All in all, the aggregation of the unilateral approaches

74 Smith, *supra* note 31, at 26.

75 *Id.*, at 28–29; *see also* Thomas and Thomas, *supra* note 33, at 144–145.

76 Mainly on counts of their proclamation of blockades, and despite the fact that not all conditions for belligerency were met. *See* Padelford, *supra* note 32, at 227–232; *see also* Thomas and Thomas, *supra* note 33, at 122–140, 152–153; Smith, *supra* note 31, at 25, 27, 29; O'Rourke, *supra* note 40, at 412.

77 *Id.* at 404–405. The question of belligerency recognition was much debated in the negotiations between the parties to the Non-Intervention Agreement. On these efforts *see* Padelford, *supra* note 47, at 599–600.

78 The denial of belligerent rights from a government that itself employs belligerent means such as a blockade – thereby admitting the existence of a "war" – was contradictory to previous state practice. *See* Lauterpacht, *supra* note 23, at 193–199.

79 O'Rourke, *supra* note 40, at 401–402; Thomas and Thomas, *supra* note 33, at 153. The US held similar positions; Lauterpacht, *supra* note 23, at 250.

80 Smith, *supra* note 31, at 28.

81 Herbert W. Briggs, *Relations Officeuses and Intent to Recognize: British Recognition of Franco*, 34 American Journal of International Law 47, 48 (1940).

82 *Id.* at 47; Thomas and Thomas, *supra* note 33, at 158–159. For a concise summary of these cases *see* Lauterpacht, *supra* note 23, at 273.

83 Thomas and Thomas, *supra* note 33, at 142–143.

84 Padelford, *supra* note 32, at 230–233.

85 Lauterpacht, *supra* note 23, at 272–273.

86 Padelford, *supra* note 32, at 237.

relating to the Spanish Civil War – in addition to the NIA – resembled the recognition of insurgency, if one subscribes to a flexible perception of the doctrine.[87]

Beyond these doctrinal challenges, however, the major legal controversy spawned by the NIA – in the eyes of states and commentators – concerned the fact that it did not distinguish between the recognized government and the opposition. Accordingly, the Spanish government's main argument against the agreement was that it constituted, *in itself*, an act of intervention, by denying of "lawful" aid from an established government, thereby equalizing it with the rebels. The USSR, despite being a party to the agreement, partly joined this view, peculiarly arguing that it was a "breach of the principles of international law."[88] The same argument could be made, in principle, against the unilateral neutrality policy of the US.[89] For this reason, Turkey and Yugoslavia claimed that the agreement could "not constitute a precedent, or result in even the implicit recognition of a principle that a government can not render to a legal government ... aid in the struggle against rebellion."[90]

Some commentators thus viewed the NIA as contrary to international law, since it prohibited exports of arms to a state at peace with the participating parties. Padelford, for instance, argued that "[t]o apply to unrecognized and irresponsible rebels the same principles that are applicable to sovereign states and established governments is to encourage rebellion and disorder and to weaken public law and authority."[91] O'Rourke concurred, referring to the Convention on Civil Strife, which allowed, at least until belligerency was recognized, transfer of arms to governments but not to rebels.[92] Smith claimed, furthermore, that if states saw the conflict as "no more than an internal disorder," then the NIA was a "grave act of intervention" against the Spanish government.[93]

However, these positions were rather imprecise, as they did not sufficiently distinguish between *negative* and *positive* interventions.[94] As noted by Lauterpacht, in absence of a specific treaty, states were never obliged to freely trade with others, whether the latter were involved in an internal strife or not. Therefore, it was difficult to consider the NIA, being a case of negative intervention, as a violation of international law.[95] This conclusion

87 O'Rourke, *supra* note 40, at 404; Lauterpacht, *supra* note 23, at 272–274.

88 League of Nations Official Journal, Spl. Supp. No. 155, 17th Ordinary Session of the Assembly p. 49, *cited in* Padelford, *supra* note 47, at 585.

89 Thomas and Thomas, *supra* note 33, at 146; *see supra*, note 63.

90 Padelford, *supra* note 47, at 581.

91 *Id.* at 586 (emphasis added).

92 O'Rourke, *supra* note 40, at 409–410.

93 Smith, *supra* note 31, at 27–28.

94 *See* Chapter 2, sec. 3.

95 Thomas and Thomas, *supra* note 33, at 143; *see also* Lauterpacht, *supra* note 23, at 232 (note), 234 n. 1.

is relevant also today: there is no general rule of international law that prohibits states from limiting aid to beleaguered governments.

More controversially, and perhaps loyal to his general aversion to the "preferential treatment" of governments and support of the concept of self-determination, Lauterpacht saw the NIA as an evolvement towards a "workable rule of international law," that required neutrality towards *both* parties to an internal armed conflict, whether belligerency was recognized or not.[96] This position too, as we shall see, did not take hold in modern international law.

In general, and notwithstanding its novelty, the NIA failed to prevent aid from being rendered to either side: the definition of the term *indirect interference* was not agreed upon; the Committee dropped virtually all charges of violations brought in front of it; the Observation Scheme could be easily circumvented through ports of non-participating states; and at large, the agreement relied heavily on good will and cooperation of states, which were not, by way of understatement, well meaning partners.[97] More than anything, the NIA was made a travesty, as Italy and Germany relentlessly continued to send military aid to the Nationalists, while simultaneously participating in a naval patrol charged to prevent the exact same actions.[98]

Nonetheless, the debate regarding the NIA represented the ever-present dilemmas that still haunt the modern law of consensual intervention. Notably, it highlighted the question whether governments should always receive preferential treatment; and how are the rights of conflicting parties affected by substantive considerations such as the principle of self-determination or democratic credentials. In the next chapters, we shall analyze how these dilemmas have played out in the era of the UN Charter.

96 *Id.* at 233–234.

97 Padelford, *supra* note 47, at 578, 581, 587–588, 596–598, 603 (1937) (referring to the weaknesses of the agreement); *see also* O'Rourke, *supra* note 40, at 409.

98 Thomas and Thomas, *supra* note 33, at 156. For a succinct summary of the agreement's shortcomings *see id.* at 175–178.

6 The preference of governments

From dichotomy to rebuttable presumption

1 Enter the UN Charter: state consent as an exception to the prohibition on the use of force

After the Spanish Civil War, the belligerency doctrine has virtually disappeared from the international-legal discourse, leading some scholars to maintain that it has fallen into desuetude.[1] The subsequent catastrophe of World War II has further – and dramatically – changed the international system. Significantly, the tragedy led to an invigorated abolishment of the war-prerogative. Accordingly, Article 2(4) of the UN Charter famously states that

> All Members shall refrain in their international relations from the threat or use of force against the territorial integrity or political independence of any state, or in any other manner inconsistent with the Purposes of the United Nations.

Once a prohibition on the use of force was firmly set forth, the question of consensual intervention has gained substantive legal importance: if the use of force is prohibited in general, does consent provide for an exception to this rule? When addressing this question, it is imperative to recall that the prohibition on the use of force serves two mutually enforcing interests. It serves to minimize the catastrophes of war; but also to enforce the norm of non-intervention and to protect sovereignty, however we interpret the contents of these principles.[2]

Article 2(4), thus, prohibits the use of force "against the territorial integrity or political independence" of the state. Therefore, in theory, when an external actor uses force in the territory of another state in circumstances in which it is not acting against the latter's territorial integrity

1 Louise Doswald-Beck, *The Legal Validity of Military Intervention by Invitation of the Government*, 56 British Year Book of International Law 189, 197 (1985); Roscoe R. Oglesby, Internal War and the Search for Normative Order 100–108 (1971).

2 *See* Chapter 2, sec. 2.

or political independence, it is not, in general, in violation of Article 2(4).[3] Consensual intervention in favor of the "state" can be such a case, and thus can be viewed as an exception to the prohibition on the use of force.[4]

This understanding of the Charter's text can be deduced, nowadays, from four main sources: the UNGA's Definition of Aggression; the Kampala Definition of the Crime of Aggression; DASR; and the Draft Articles on Responsibility of International Organizations (DARIO).

Article 3(e) of the Definition of Aggression, which quite possibly reflects customary international law[5] – and in particular considering the fact that it was adopted as part of the Kampala Definition of the Crime of Aggression[6] – includes in the term "aggression" the following actions:

> [t]he use of armed forces of one State which are within the territory of another State with the agreement of the receiving State, in contravention of the conditions provided for in the agreement or any extension of their presence in such territory beyond the termination of the agreement.

Thus, the article recognizes, albeit indirectly, the *jus ad bellum* legality of forcible actions undertaken *in accordance* with the agreement of the "receiving" state – and could thereby exclude – from the term "aggression" and arguably also from the ambit of Article 2(4) of the Charter – instances of consensual interventions in internal conflicts.

Article 20 of DASR complements the Definition of Aggression, by precluding, in general, the wrongfulness of acts conducted with state consent:

> Valid consent by a State to the commission of a given act by another State precludes the wrongfulness of that act in relation to the former State to the extent that the act remains within the limits of that consent.[7]

A similar provision is included in Article 20 of the 2011 DARIO,[8] stipulating that valid consent to an act by an international organization precludes

3 *See* Oscar Schachter, *The Right of States to Use Armed Force*, 82 Michigan Law Review 1620, 1625–1626 (1984) (discussing the ambiguity of Article 2(4) of the Charter).

4 The same interpretation was used by some to justify unilateral humanitarian, *absent* state consent. However, this view is generally rejected. *See* Chapter 10, sec. 4.2.

5 Definition of Aggression, G.A. Res. 3314 (XXIX), ¶3(e), UN Doc A/9631 (December 14, 1974). Article 3(g) of the Definition, which is addressed in Chapter 3, sec. 2, was deemed by the ICJ as reflecting customary international law, and can serve as an indication for the customary nature of the other sub-articles of the Definition.

6 The Crime of Aggression, art. 8bis(g), Resolution RC/Res.6, RC/11 (June 11, 2010).

7 UN International Law Commission Draft Articles on Responsibility of States for Internationally Wrongful Acts, with Commentaries, art. 20 in Report of the International Law Commission, U.N. GAOR, 53d Sess., Supp. No. 10, A/56/20 (2001).

8 UN International Law Commission Draft Articles on the Responsibility of International Organizations, Yearbook of the International Law Commission (2011).

the wrongfulness of that act in relation to the consenting state. This provision might apply to interventions by regional organizations with "internal collective security" arrangements – or forward-looking intervention treaties – as these will be discussed later on.[9]

The term *valid* consent connotes two different meanings.[10] The first refers to free and genuine consent – meaning, that the consent is not coerced.[11] The second requires that the consent be expressed by a competent entity. Thus, a fundamental question concerns the determination of the entity speaking for the state in extreme situations, where a consensual forcible intervention is sought. Essentially, it asks whether intervention upon the consent of a beleaguered government is not actually per se conducted against the political independence of the state – under the assumption that the state is a "black box," the character of which must be determined only by its internal parties.[12] It is here where the normative duality of forcible interventions – meaning, their regulation by both the laws on the use of force and the principle of non-intervention – is at its most prevalent.

Two main approaches to this problem can be identified. The first, which is dominant mainly in the literature – and reflects a genuine will to limit the international use of force[13] – interprets the norm of non-intervention, and the related principle of self-determination, as entailing complete abstention from any intervention in internal strife, without much elaboration regarding the threshold of conflict required for such an obligation to apply. We shall call this view *strict-abstentionism.*[14] In fact, some strict-abstentionists set forth a very simple argument: they maintain that its mere request for assistance is sufficient to indicate that a government can no longer speak for the state.

The other approach, prevalent in practice and in international jurisprudence, identifies a *government preference*, recognizing, in principle, the power of governments to consent to forcible interventions, while illegalizing opposition consent. However, some of the proponents of the latter approach limit the government preference, in practice, in such a manner that it virtually merges with strict-abstentionism.

9 *See* Chapter 8.

10 As discussed also in Chapter 1, sec. 2.1.

11 *See id.*

12 On the "black box" approach to sovereignty *see* Helen Stacy, Human Rights for the 21st Century: Sovereignty, Civil Society, Culture 86–88 (2009).

13 *See, e.g.*, Quincy Wright, *Editorial Comment: United States Intervention in the Lebanon*, 53 American Journal of International Law 112, 122 (1959): "[t]he expediency of this rule is manifest not only to preserve the independence of states but also to prevent civil war from spreading into international war."

14 I do not label this approach as "non-interventionist" since even supporters of intervention, in the physical sense, will not claim that intervention in favor of governments is an intervention in the normative sense.

In this chapter, instead of subscribing to a dichotomistic abstention/preference distinction, we will revisit the approach suggested by Lauterpacht, identifying a rebuttable "presumption" in favor of governments.[15] This seems to be the conceptually clearest prism through which to evaluate the question of consensual intervention. Indeed, the mechanism of a presumption provides a framework that is not only doctrinally clearer, but practically more flexible – and thus more workable in the real world – than stringent formalistic approaches.

However, we will not yet address the circumstances that lead to the *rebuttal* of this presumption, whether based on tests relating to effective control or otherwise. We will only demonstrate, in this chapter, that such presumption is indeed reasonable, and is recognized in contemporary international law. The limits of this presumption will be addressed in subsequent chapters.

Nonetheless, in order to understand the approach towards the abstentionist/preference debate in the UN Charter era, it is helpful to first survey, rather briefly, the zero-sum Cold War dynamics that shaped the discourse on intervention throughout the first four decades of the Charter. The aspiration to "tame" these dynamics – and especially their often malicious nature – has greatly influenced the motivations of both the proponents of strict-abstentionism and of the government preference.

2 Containment, détente, roll-back: Cold War doctrines of intervention

Since World War II, the principle of effective control has been constantly challenged by competing, substantive doctrines for the evaluation of internal armed conflicts. For instance, in the context of decolonization, substantive analysis of conflicts – based on the principle of self-determination – led to the qualification of colonial struggles as closer to international conflicts, in contrast to the approach towards colonial wars of the nineteenth century, which were treated as internal conflicts controlled by the belligerency and insurgency doctrines.[16]

At the same time, owing to the Cold War dynamics, the general concern regarding the issue of intervention related to the attempts, by both sides, to minimize the adversary's influence. Indeed, even before the dust settled from World War II, the international community faced a bloc-related conflict in Iran (1946), in which the Soviet Union intervened in favor of

15 According to Lauterpacht, as we shall see, this presumption is very narrow. *See also* Schachter, *supra* note 3, at 1642.

16 *See* Chapter 9, sec. 2.1.

Kurdish nationalists;[17] a complex conflict in French Indochina between multiple armed groups, states and interveners, which lasted from 1946 until 1954, and sowed the seeds for the Vietnam War;[18] and a dramatic conflict in China, in which the nationalist government of the Republic of China (ROC) was ousted by communist revolutionaries, in 1949, to settle in the island of Taiwan (the birth of the "Two China Problem"). In the latter struggle the US favored the ROC,[19] and maintained its recognition as the lawful government of all of China; it concluded a mutual defense treaty with it in 1954;[20] and conducted joint training with its armed forces. The US withdrew its recognition of the ROC only in 1979, and the legal status of the Republic of China/Taiwan remains controversial and ambiguous to this day.[21]

The advent of Cold War-related conflicts demonstrate that the zero-sum reality of the post-war system, and the overwhelming bloc-interests at stake, could not be sufficiently addressed by traditional frameworks of neutrality, whether pursued through individual state choice, or by collective arrangements such as the Spanish Civil War's non-intervention agreement.[22] Accordingly, in the subsequent decades, American policy regarding the Soviet Union swung between containment, détente and roll-back, each influencing the US doctrines of intervention in their respective periods. These strategies were mirrored, at large, by like doctrines adopted by the Soviet Union. The practice of these doctrines, by both parties, frequently took the form of interventions and counter-interventions for the purpose of support or subversion of allied or opposing governments. In turn, the parties crafted – often *ex post* – legal arguments to justify their actions. As such, the Cold War ushered an era of international law in which the line between legality and narrow bloc-interests was notoriously blurry.

17 The USSR occupied, at the time, Northern Iran. The Kurdistan Democratic Party of Iran, supported by the USSR, collapsed after the USSR withdrew in mid-1946. *See* Massoume Price, Iran's Diverse People 185–188 (2005); Archie Roosevelt, Jr. *The Kurdish Republic of Mahabad, in* A People Without a Country 122, 125–129 (Gerard Chaliand ed., 1980). For the international reaction *see* S.C. Res. 2, U.N. Doc. S/RES/2 (January 30, 1946); S.C. Res. 3, U.N. Doc. S/RES/3 (April 4, 1946); S.C. Res. 5, U.N. Doc. S/RES/2 (May 8, 1946).

18 *See, generally*, Ronald Irving, The First Indochina War: French and American Policy, 1945–1954 (1975).

19 However, it seems that the US recognized, at least initially, the *insurgency* status of the communists (The People's Republic of China), as it denied the 1949 attempt by the ROC to impose a "paper-blockade" by decreeing all Chinese ports closed. *See* L.H. Woolsey, *Editorial Comment: Closure of Ports by the Chinese Nationalist Government*, 44 American Journal of International Law 350 (1950).

20 Mutual Defense Treaty between the United States of America and the Republic of China (December 2, 1954).

21 *See* Anthony A. D'Amato, International Law Studies 255–258 (1997). For an in-depth analysis of the Taiwan question *see, generally*, The International status of Taiwan in the New World Order: Legal and Political Considerations (Jean-Marie Henckaerts ed., 1996).

22 *See* Chapter 5, sec. 4.

The containment strategy, which endured, on-and-off, for decades, involved the support of *governments* allegedly challenged by pro-Soviet movements.[23] It can be best exemplified in the Truman Doctrine, designed, as phrased by President Truman himself, to "support free peoples who are resisting attempted subjugation by armed minorities or by outside pressures."[24] Containment was constantly rivaled by the détente and roll-back strategies, urging, respectively, the easing of tensions on the one hand versus positive, proactive support to anti-communist insurgents on the other.[25] The roll-back strategy was radical, in its explicit embrace of granting forcible aid to *opposition* groups, based on ideological considerations.[26]

The roll-back approach, although having earlier manifestations,[27] is famously associated with the Reagan Doctrine of the 1980s. Never formalized as a comprehensive doctrine, the Reagan Doctrine was mainly articulated by commentators.[28] It was based on President Reagan's pledge that the US would "stand by" its democratic allies to "defy Soviet supported aggression," while asserting that "support for freedom fighters is self-defense."[29] It was summarized by Jeane Kirkpatrick – one of its chief ideologues – as condoning support for insurgencies, including by military means, under certain circumstances:

> where there are indigenous opponents to a government that is maintained by force, rather than popular consent; where such a government depends on arms supplied by … foreign sources; and where people are denied a choice regarding their affiliations and future.[30]

23 Containment was based on deterrence and alliances with supporting governments. *See* Earl C. Ravenal, *The Requisites of Containment, in* Collective Defense or Strategic Independence? Alternative Strategies for the Future 273 (Ted Galen Carpenter ed., 1989).

24 *See* Special Message to the Congress on Greece and Turkey: The Truman Doctrine (March 12, 1947); The Truman Doctrine was the rationale for granting economic and military aid to the Greek government in 1947, in its struggle against pro-communist elements; it was also the basis for support granted to Turkey.

25 The Détente period usually refers to the relaxation of the American-Soviet tensions during the 1970s, ending in the Soviet invasion of Afghanistan. *See generally* Raymond L. Garthoff, Détente and Confrontation: American-Soviet Relations from Nixon to Reagan (1994). For the facts and effects of the Afghanistan invasion *see id.* at 977–1081.

26 Anthony S. Winer, *The Reagan Doctrine, the 2003 Invasion of Iraq, and the Role of a Sole Superpower,* 22 Law and Inequality 169, 189–190 (2004).

27 For instance, the restoration of the Iranian Shah in 1953. *See generally* Malcolm Byrne, *Introduction, in* Mohammad Mosaddeq and the 1953 Coup in Iran xiii (Mark J. Gasiorowski and Malcolm Byrne eds., 2004). Early manifestations of the roll-back approach can be found in the position of John Foster Dulles as expressed in 1949. *See* Foreign Policy Association, 29 Foreign Policy Bulletin 5 (1949).

28 Winer, *supra* note 26, at 182–186.

29 President's Address before a Joint Session of Congress on the State of the Union, 1985 Pub. Papers 135 (February 6, 1985); *cited in* Winer, *supra* note 26, at 178.

30 Jeane J. Kirkpatrick and Allan Gerson, *The Reagan Doctrine, Human Rights and International Law, in* Right v. Might: International Law and the Use of Force 19, 20 (Louis Henkin *et al.* eds., 1991).

Understood as such, the Reagan Doctrine was essentially one of consensual, ostensibly pro-democratic counter-intervention in internal armed conflicts, *in favor of opposition groups*. It was consensual, in the sense that it was *partial*: which means, that an intervention, a priori, must have received some consent of an indigenous party. As such, the Reagan Doctrine went further than the traditional counter-intervention doctrine – which we address later on – which generally served to justify intervention in favor of governments. The Reagan Doctrine was seemingly behind the support of the *mujahedeen* in Afghanistan, of UNITA in Angola, as well as the invasion of Grenada (to the extent that it was not conducted with governmental consent).[31] Perhaps the quintessential case of the Doctrine was the US aid to the Contras in Nicaragua.[32]

The American containment and roll-back approaches were paralleled, at large, by the Soviet Brezhnev Doctrine, which justified intervention to protect socialist regimes from internal challenges, and was sometimes extended to support for "national liberation movements" confronting non-socialist regimes.[33] In essence, like the Reagan Doctrine, it was a substantive approach towards internal strife, concerned not with democracy but with the promotion of Soviet-style socialism, which Brezhnev also linked to the principle of self-determination.[34] Soviet containment doctrine was employed in several instances up to the early 1980s.[35]

These Cold War doctrines reflected a significant rift between practice and traditional law, since by relying on substantive justifications – such as the promotion of democracy or socialism – they were contrary to the effectiveness principle and closer to legitimist approaches. However, considering the zero-sum character of the international system of the time, it comes as no surprise that rather than being conducted on a principled level, the contemporaneous legal debate regarding this issue was often

31 It should be noted that Jeane Kirkpatrick saw the Doctrine as irrelevant to the Grenada invasion since it was ostensibly an intervention with the consent of what the US saw as a legitimate authority. *See id.* at 19–20.

32 On these cases and others *see* James M. Scott, Deciding to Intervene: The Reagan Doctrine and American Foreign Policy (1996). On the Reagan Doctrine and international law *see* David J. Scheffer, *Introduction, in* Right v. Might, *supra* note 30, at 1, 11.

33 For comparison between the doctrines *see* William D. Rogers *et al.*, *The Brezhnev Doctrine and the Reagan Doctrine: Apples and Oranges?* 81 American Society of International Law Proceedings 561 (1987); W. Michael Reisman, *Allocating Competences to Use Coercion in the Post-Cold War World: Practices, Conditions, and Prospects, in* Law and Force in the New International Order 26, 34 (Lori Fisler Damrosch and David J. Scheffer eds., 1991); Winer, *supra* note 26, at 182; for a scathing critique of the comparison *see, e.g.*, Kirkpatrick and Gerson, *supra* note 30, at 28–33.

34 *See* Louis Henkin, International Law: Politics and Values 118–119 (1995).

35 *See generally* Matthew J. Ouimet, The Rise and Fall of the Brezhnev Doctrine in Soviet Foreign Policy (2003). Notably, the doctrine was at work in the Hungarian invasion of 1956 and Czechoslovakia in 1968. *See id.* at 4, 9–16.

merely a hollow pretext meant to justify these doctrines in specific instances.[36]

Accordingly, at different times, different legal justifications were tailored to match Cold War interventions. Containment interventions, such as the 1958 Lebanon intervention, and perhaps the 1983 Grenada invasion, were justified by the US on counts of government consent, enhanced by claims of counter-intervention. The invasion was also justified as an action taken to protect American nationals.[37] The Soviet Union explicitly cited government consent when justifying its 1968 invasion of Czechoslovakia; it went even further by arguing, along with its allies, that interventions upon request are not at all an issue to be discussed in the UNSC.[38] Support of opposition groups, and namely the American roll-back intervention in Nicaragua, was justified through a wide interpretation of the right of individual and collective self-defense (recall President Reagan's assertion that "support to freedom fighters is self-defense").[39] Such interventions were also vindicated, by American commentators, through a narrow construction of the prohibition on the use of force enshrined in Article 2(4) of the UN Charter.[40]

Interestingly, with regards to the intervention in Nicaragua, a split can be identified between the high-discourse of the Reagan Doctrine, in condoning support of "freedom fighters," and the actual legal justifications presented to the ICJ in the Nicaragua case. As we shall see, the US did not rely there on opposition consent or on democratic legitimism, but rather chose to set forth a less controversial claim: it advanced, mainly, a wide interpretation of the right to collective-self-defense in favor of neighboring El Salvador, rather than invoking a novel theory of intervention.[41] This raises doubt as to the extent the US itself saw the Reagan Doctrine – at its most extreme understanding – as compatible with positive international law. Indeed, as we shall demonstrate later, the Reagan Doctrine was

36 For a similar claim *see* the remarks by Louis Henkin in *Annual Dinner, American Society of International Law Proceedings, April 1–4 1992*, 86 Amerian Society of International Law Proceedings 501, 508 (1992); Louis Henkin, *The Invasion of Panama under International Law: A Gross Violation*, 29 Columbia Journal of Transnational Law 293 (1991).

37 *See* sec. 4.2.

38 1967 Yearbook U.N. 298–299.

39 State of the Union, *supra*, note 29.

40 *See* W. Michael Reisman, *Coercion and Self-Determination: Construing Article 2(4)*, 78 American Journal of International Law 642 (1984); Anthony D'Amato, *The Invasion of Panama was a Lawful Response to Tyranny*, 84 American Journal of International Law 520 (1990); *compare* Michael Byers and Simon Chesterman, "*You, the People*": *Pro-Democratic Intervention in International Law, in* Democratic Governance and International Law 259, 261–269 (Gregory H. Fox and Brad R. Roth eds., 2000). Kirkpatrick and Gerson even interpreted the UN Charter in light of the American Declaration of Independence. Kirkpatrick and Gerson, *supra* note 30, at 22–23, 25–26.

41 *See* sec. 4.3.

deemed unlawful by the ICJ, whether it was based on opposition consent or on a wide interpretation on the right of collective self-defense.[42] The Brezhnev doctrine, on the face of it, was also rejected by the international community, in light of the general condemnation of the Czechoslovakia invasion of 1968.[43] A UNSC Resolution condemning the invasion was rejected only on counts of a Soviet veto.[44]

While the collapse of the Eastern Bloc necessarily brought an end to the Brezhnev doctrine, the Reagan Doctrine can be linked to contemporary views supporting forcible unilateral pro-democratic intervention based on a "democratic entitlement," a concept which we discuss later.[45] The difference is that in the contemporary system, arguably, there is more space for a principled application of international norms. Nonetheless, during the Cold War, international lawyers had to struggle – perhaps in a "fighting retreat" – in their attempts to breathe order and principle into the blatantly self-interested dynamics of the time. This should be taken into consideration in our discussion in the following sections.

3 The strict-abstentionist approach

3.1 Strict-abstentionism

Article 3(e) of the Definition of Aggression, as well as Article 20 of both DASR and DARIO, refer to the consent of *states* as precluding aggression or wrongfulness. In the same vein, Article 2(4) of the UN Charter prohibits the use of force against *states.* This is not surprising, as the state is the basic legal personality in international law. However, it is not specified who is entitled to *speak* for the state and thus express *valid* consent to a forcible intervention, in a certain instance. As we shall see, the state is usually represented, in the international realm, by a government.[46]

However, a state and its government are not synonymous.[47] For this reason, it is equally unsurprising that in parallel to the understanding of Article 2(4) of the Charter as allowing for a "government preference," there has been a longstanding and persistent view suggesting that the

42 *See* Onder Bakircioglu, *The Right to Self-Defense in National and International Law: The Role of the Imminence Requirement,* 19 Indiana International and Comparative Law Quarterly 1, 36–37 (2009); Henkin, *supra* note 34, at 119; David Wippman, *Change and Continuity in Legal Justifications for Military Intervention in Internal Conflict,* 27 Columbia Human Rights Law Review 435, 457 (1996).

43 *See* Louis Henkin, *Use of Force: Law and U.S. Policy, in* Right v. Might, *supra* note 30, at 43–44.

44 1968 Yearbook U.N. 301–302.

45 Henkin, *supra* note 34, at 118–119; Winer, *supra* note 26, at 186–188.

46 *See* Settlers of German Origin in Poland, Advisory Opinion, 1923 P.C.I.J. 22 (ser. B) No. 6 (sept. 10); *cited in* Doswald-Beck, *supra* note 1, at 190.

47 Lassa Oppenheim, 1 International Law §75. 77 (2nd ed., 1912).

norm of non-intervention requires *strict-abstention* in cases of *purely* internal armed conflicts (as opposed to conflicts fomented and assisted by external "subversive intervention," in which counter-intervention was looked on favorably also by strict-asbtentionists).[48]

Strict-abstention was viewed as necessary both to ensure that the conflicting community will independently determine its own fate, and to minimize international use of force. The connection (or its absence) between this idea and the belligerency doctrine has been addressed thoroughly in Chapter 4; we have also discussed at length why such a perception, in the era of the war-prerogative, was very difficult to justify. Nevertheless, strict-asbtentionism stresses, when evaluating internal armed conflicts, the *uncertainty of the outcome* of the conflict as the driving force of abstentionism, rather than relying on formal distinctions such as the belligerency doctrine.[49] Indeed, once a prohibition on the use of force was set forth, a logical legal claim could be that in times of internal armed conflict, neither the government nor the opposition fully represent the state; and therefore forcible intervention on behalf of *either* party constitutes a "use of force against the territorial integrity or political independence" of the state, as well as a violation of the norm of non-intervention.[50]

If one subscribes to strict-asbtentionism, the question of threshold immediately arises: how to identify the circumstances in which such a duty of abstention materializes? Some strict-abstentionists provide a simple answer – the mere *request* for assistance establishes the conclusion that the government is no longer effective, and therefore does not possess the sovereign power to express valid consent.

The allure of strict-asbtentionism to international lawyers in the Cold War's zero-sum system was clear. However, it should be noted that the theoretical background of the approach is an orthodox – almost Darwinist – understanding of the concepts of non-intervention and self-determination, very much rooted in the idea of effective control over territory the sole source of sovereignty.[51] As such, it derives from the works of classic theoreticians. One of the most eloquent manifestations of this approach could be found in an 1860 work by Montague Bernard.[52] It is worthwhile to examine it in some detail, as it provides a clear rationalization for a robust version of

48 Wright, *supra* note 13, at 124.

49 *Id.* at 122.

50 *See, e.g.*, Antonio Cassese, International Law 371 (2005).

51 For a summary of strict-abstentionist and close approaches *see* John A. Perkins, *The Right of Counterintervention*, 17 Georgia Journal of International and Comparative Law 171, 183–195 (1987).

52 Montague Bernard, On the Principle of Non-Intervention (1860). The theoretical argument underlying Bernard's work is of contemporary interest, although, as discussed in Chapter 4, Bernard did not substantially explain the *legal* discrepancy between his rigid perception of non-intervention and the war-prerogative.

strict-abstentionism.[53] Bernard's argument retains its relevance, as his core claims have remained virtually unaltered in later works of strict-abstentionists.

Thus, Bernard saw non-intervention as a cardinal condition for the existence of a system of states,[54] and also as a utilitarian requirement:

> it [intervention] has a direct tendency to produce mischiefs worse than it removes. It encourages a proneness to resort to violent measures.... It destroys national self-respect and self-reliance. It interrupts the natural process by which political institutions are matured through the ripening of political ideas and habits. What it plants does not take root; what it establishes does not endure.[55]

Much of Bernard's reasoning, however, dealt with the rejection of consent, in its various forms, as a justification for intervention. First, he rejected the legality of forward-looking intervention treaties – not a rare occurrence throughout history[56] – which are concluded in advance for the "maintenance of a particular dynasty or of particular institutions."[57] Loyal to the understanding of governments as separate entities from states, he concluded that "no Government is authorized to degrade by compact the country it rules into a condition of real vassalage," unless it agrees, essentially, to waive its independence altogether.[58] He then proceeded to address the question of ad hoc intervention requested by a "legitimate" sovereign. Such cases, according to Bernard, could not exist since there was no such thing, in international law, as a "legitimate" ruler.[59] Furthermore, since he perceived sovereignty as a corollary of territorial effective control, the *mere request* for assistance indicated, in his eyes, the lack of effectiveness:

> [w]hat rights does he thus to act as sovereign who admits that he has ceased to be so, or that his sovereignty is (to say the least) in abeyance? How can he impersonate his people[,] who is begging the assistance of a foreign Power in order to reduce them to obedience?[60]

53 *Id.* at 5–8.

54 *Id.* at 9.

55 *Id.* at 9–10.

56 Bernard gives the examples of "ancient treaties" between Britain and Portugal, that were invoked in 1828 by Brazil (perhaps by a claim of succession), to secure British intervention in an internal struggle against Don Miguel; another example was the 1815 treaty between Austria and The King of the Two Sicilies. *Id.* at 14.

57 *Id.* at 11.

58 *Id.* at 14–15.

59 *Id.* at 15. The term "legitimate," used here by Bernard, should be read in the context of the nineteenth century debate between the legitimism doctrine and the effectiveness approach to sovereignty. *See* Chapter 1, sec. 2.2.

60 Bernard, *supra* note 52, at 16.

If intervention by sovereign consent was unlawful, does the right of consent belong to the "people" of the state? Here Bernard takes up an argument with Grotius, who argued, from a classical just-war perspective, that a *manifest* tyrant, committing atrocities against his own people, can be overthrown with the assistance of foreigners, but not in case of doubt.[61] Bernard rejected this position, claiming that it was based on "morality" rather than law, contending that it can never be objectively ascertained when a sovereign is beyond doubt a "manifest" tyrant.[62] He further rebuffed the claim that this problem can be solved by relying on the decision of the people, since it is never clear who the "people" are. Bernard's cold logic deduced that if by "people" we mean the "majority," the intervention would essentially be in favor of "a majority that is not strong enough to have its way" by imposing its will on the minority, a fact that contravened the principle of effectiveness.[63] Bernard thus directly challenged the majoritarian-democratic principle, first by pointing out the difficulty of ascertaining the majority's view, and even questioning whether a majority is entitled to "control the destiny of a nation" to begin with, again maintaining that governing power should be based strictly on effective control.[64]

Lastly, Bernard confronted the possible position that in the case of "civil war" states are free to intervene in favor of *both* parties, and specifically the position endorsed by Vattel, according to which the intervention must be conducted in favor of the *just* party.[65] Bernard responded by adopting a highly abstract view of the state, emphasizing that a state undergoing a "civil war" does not cease to be an integral state; and that the fact that it has no functioning sovereign does not mean that it is no longer "independent" in relation to other states. He thus concluded that foreign intervention, on counts of either side, "gives superiority to the side which would not have been uppermost without it, and establishes a sovereign, or a form of government, which the nation, if left to itself, would not have chosen."[66]

61 1 Hugo Grotius, The Rights of War and Peace, Book 2, Ch. 25, §8 (William Whewell trans. 1853):

> But the case [regarding intervention] is different if the wrong is manifest. If a tyrant like Busiris, Phalaris, Diomede of Thrace, practices atrocities towards his subjects, which no just man can approve, the right of human social connexion is not cut off... in such cases, what is not lawful to one person [the subject] may be lawful to another for him [the intervening power], if it be a case in which one can help another.

62 Bernard, *supra* note 52, at 17.

63 *Id.* at 17.

64 *Id.* at 17–18. Bernard seems to equalize effectiveness with "success achieved by unassisted effort."

65 *Id.* at 20–21; Emmerich De Vatell, The Law of Nations §§294–296 (1797), *available at* http://books.google.com.

66 Bernard, *supra* note 52, at 21. According to Bernard, one possible exception to this reasoning occurs when succession occurs – effectively creating two states – and thus the intervention ceases to be in the internal affairs of a state. *Id.* at 22.

Bernard's approach was clearly echoed in the works of later scholars. Hall and Wilson followed Bernard's logic – the former arguing that the mere fact "that it has been necessary to call in foreign help is enough to show that the issue of the conflict without it be uncertain,"[67] and the latter adding that in such cases the government is not the de facto power in the state.[68] Almost a century after Bernard, Lauterpacht presented a developed – and rather sophisticated – version of the strict-abstentionist principle, based on the principle of self-determination. He accepted, in general, the principle of government preference, which he saw as applying "so long as the lawful sovereign authority has not been definitely supplanted,"[69] and manifested through a "presumption in favour of established governments," which applied so long as the conflict was in progress.[70] However, since he saw the practical effects of this presumption as very limited, and in any case not extending beyond the duty of states not to prematurely recognize the opposition as a government or to permit hostile operations from their territories, Lauterpacht did not significantly depart from strict-abstentionsim.[71] He viewed any intervention beyond this narrow preference as a "denial of the right of the nation to decide for itself – by a physical contest, if necessary, between rival forces – the nature and the form of its government."[72]

Of particular interest to us is the fact that Lauterpacht injected substantive considerations into his limited, effectiveness-based view of the government preference principle, arguing that limitations on consent power of governments are due "so long as the international community has no such control over them as to secure effectively the fundamental rights of the individual and decent administration of the law."[73] This position can be understood as willing to recognize a more robust presumption in favor of governments, contingent upon the development of international human rights institutions.

The reliance on the idea of self-determination as a rationale for strict-abstentionism has understandably found its way into the works of predominant scholars of the Cold War and decolonization era. Brownlie, Bowett and Wright saw every external intervention in civil strife as contradicting

67 W.E. Hall, A Treatise on International Law 347 (8th ed. 1924); *cited in* Doswald-Beck, *supra* note 1, at 196; Wright, *supra* note 13, at 121–122.

68 George Grafton Wilson, International Law 93–94 (8th ed. 1922):

> The principle may now be regarded as established by both theory and practice that the invitation of neither party to a domestic strife gives a right to a foreign state to intervene, and that no state has a right to judge as to the merits of the contest.

69 Hersch Lauterpacht, Recognition in International Law 233 (1948).

70 *Id.* at 93–94.

71 *Id.* at 233.

72 *Id.*

73 *Id.* at 234; *see also* Chapter 5, sec. 3.

the right to self-determination.[74] Wright went as far as arguing that if intervention on part of any party be allowed, the "'right of revolution' implicit in the concepts of sovereignty and self-determination would be denied," and that therefore "[a] government beset by civil strife is not in a position to invite assistance in the name of the state."[75]

An approach similar to Lauterpacht's, endorsing a form of strict-abstentionism while hinting at a substantive analysis of the parties, was reflected in a 1975 resolution by the Institut de Droit International.[76] There, the Institute opined that in case of "civil war" – defined broadly as "any" internal armed conflict beyond "local disorder or riots," "[t]hird States shall refrain from giving assistance" to the parties,[77] and enumerated the actions that constituted such assistance.[78] However, three significant qualifications can be seen as challenging its distinction as strict-abstentionist.

First, the resolution excluded from the definition of civil wars "conflicts arising from decolonization."[79] The exclusion of colonial wars from the internal sphere is a generally accepted approach in international law, but this exclusion, in itself, was a development of the UN era – nowadays taken for granted – that reflected a movement away from effectiveness-based views of the international system.[80] Second, the resolution seems to have restricted its application only to certain internal armed conflicts, alluding to the need for the substantive analysis of conflicts. This was reflected in the preamble, stating that the Institute was "[r]eserving the study of issues arising from the danger of extermination of ethnic, religious or social groups or from other severe infringements of human rights during civil war."[81] Third, by excluding from its purview cases of "local disorder or riots," the resolution implicitly recognized government consent power in

74 Ian Brownlie, International Law and the Use of Force by States 327 (1963); Derek Bowett, *The Interrelation of Theories of Intervention and Self-Defense*, *in* Law and Civil War in the Modern World 38 (John Norton Moore ed., 1974); Quincy Wright, The Role of International Law in the Elimination of War 61 (1961); all *cited in* Doswald-Beck, *supra* note 1, at 200; *see also* Wright, *supra* note 13, at 120–121.

75 Wright, *supra* note 74, at 61, *quoted in* Doswald-Beck, *supra* note 1, at 200.

76 Institut de Droit International, The Principle of Non-Intervention in Civil Wars (August 14, 1975). A previous relevant resolution can be found in Institut de Droit International, Annuaire 18, 229 (1900).

77 *Id.* arts. 1(a), 2(a), 2(1). Interestingly, the Institute did not include loss of effective control as a precondition of the existence of "civil war" – by thus departing from the traditional belligerency doctrine.

78 *Id.* art. 2(2). Dinstein viewed this resolution as inconsistent with the understanding of international law and with state practice. Yoram Dinstein, War, Aggression and Self-Defense 119–120 (5th ed. 2011).

79 The Principle of Non-Intervention in Civil Wars Art, *supra* note 76, art. 1(2)(c).

80 As discussed in Chapter 4, colonial wars of the nineteenth century were viewed as *internal armed conflicts*.

81 The Principle of Non-Intervention in Civil Wars, *supra* note 76, prmbl. For an analysis of the resolution, *see* Schachter, *supra* note 3, at 1643.

such instances. In this sense, the 1975 resolution reflects the paradox plaguing some of the orthodox approaches towards intervention and consent: assuming, as these approaches generally do, that intervention should be restricted on counts of considerations of effectiveness – and that these serve best the principles of non-intervention and self-determination – it is unclear why a government which needs assistance in quelling mere local disorder, would be deemed as more effective than a government that requests support in a full scale "civil war." In other words, if we are serious about orthodox perceptions of non-intervention, we must prohibit intervention in full blown conflicts as well as in situations of local unrest.

A further resolution, adopted by the Institute in 2011 after much deliberation,[82] complements the 1975 resolution by addressing "military assistance" in situations "below the threshold of non-international armed conflict," as those were defined in Article I of Additional Protocol II to the Geneva Conventions.[83] In such cases – which include, *inter alia*, forms of local unrest and terrorism – the 2011 resolution asserts, and by thus explicitly ebbing away from strict-abstentionism, that military assistance may indeed be rendered upon request of a state.[84] Beyond the paradox mentioned in the previous paragraph, the 2011 resolution reflects only a slight step forward towards the understanding of consensual intervention: this is because it is silent on the question of intervention in situations that *do* cross the threshold of armed conflict as defined in Additional Protocol II. In addition, the resolution is also unclear with regards to intervention in strife of the type *not* falling within the confines of Additional Protocol II, but still amounting to non-international armed conflict, as widely defined in the *Tadic* case.[85]

Arguably, in those cases, the rather outdated resolution of 1975 still stands – and therefore, a significant opportunity to clarify this issue in light of contemporary developments was missed. Moreover, by referring to the definition of armed conflict found in Additional Protocol II – which requires loss of effective control on part of the government – the resolution, seemingly, refocuses on considerations of territorial effectiveness as determinants of consent power, perhaps without sufficient regard to the substantive considerations prevalent in contemporary discourse, as detailed shortly.

However, the resolution certainly constitutes a step forward by unequivocally declaring that at least in situations falling within its ambit, military assistance is prohibited when exercised in contravention of several substantive principles, such as "generally accepted standards of human rights."[86] This notion can be constructed to mean that military assistance rendered

82 Institut de Droit International, Military Assistance on Request (September 8, 2011).

83 *Id.* art. 2(1). On the relevance of Article 1 of Additional Protocol II *see* Chapter 2, sec. 4.

84 *Id.* arts. 2, 4(1).

85 *See* Chapter 2, sec. 4.

86 *Id.* art. 3(1).

in situations that do not amount to an armed conflict – of whatever type – must conform to law enforcement standards and cannot be conducted as combat operations.[87] Some of the further restrictions on consent power found in the resolution are addressed in other parts of this book.[88]

Returning to the strict-abstentionist debate – Cassese, too, adopted a rather complex approach. On the one hand, he conceded that "[s]tate practice makes extensive use of the consent exception"; on the other, he saw this practice as "hardly" conforming to present day international law.[89] He accepted that there are situations in which a government can authorize the deployment of forces on its territory, but qualified that "a State may not authorize another State to use force on its territory with a view to establishing control over the population of the consenting State."[90] Whether or not Cassese's approach can be described as strict-abstentionist depends on our interpretation of the phrase "establishing control." To the extent that Cassese meant *any* loss of control, he alluded to a strict-abstentionist approach. However, if by "establishing control" he implied, for instance, to extreme circumstances of state-failure, then he indeed accepted a qualified principle of government preference.

Strict-abstentionism has surfaced, rather recently, in the report of the Independent Fact-Finding Mission on the 2008 Conflict in Georgia. There, among its other claims, Russia argued that it had intervened in Georgia by invitation of South Ossetia – the secession seeking party.[91] The report noted that in "traditional writing," only the established and internationally recognized government could consent to forcible intervention. It argued, however, that the government preference approach was problematic, since it could lead to the "undesirable" result of states recognizing governments wantonly, as pretext for forcible intervention.[92] The report then proceeded to present a "new doctrine" – that as we seen, is hardly a novel one – according to which:

> in a state of civil war, none of the competing fractions can be said to be effective, stable and legitimate. Therefore, it is argued that the principle of non-intervention and respect of the international right to self-determination renders inadmissible any type of foreign intervention, be it upon invitation of the previous "old" government or of the rebels.[93]

87 For a discussion *see* Chapter 7, sec. 2.1.

88 Notable among these restrictions, found in Article 4(3), is that the existence of a forward-looking intervention treaty does not affect the necessity of ad hoc consent. This issue is discussed in Chapter 8.

89 Antonio Cassese, *supra* note 50, at 370.

90 *Id.* at 371.

91 *Independent International Fact-Finding Mission on the Conflict in Georgia*, Report (Vol. 2), at 276 (September 30, 2009) (*hereinafter* Georgia Report).

92 *Id.* at 277.

93 *Id.*

The report saw the principle of self-determination as "incumbent on peoples, and not on governments or on competing factions."[94] It then concluded that this approach is "prudent from a policy perspective;" that it is confirmed by state practice (without elaborating); and, accordingly, that South Ossetia's invitation could not have legalized the Russian intervention.[95] Nevertheless, the report was careful not to unequivocally and legally endorse either of the competing positions, since both positions – government preference and strict-abstentionism – deny, in general, intervention in favor of opposition parties. Thus, the report could avoid making a clear decision favoring one of the approaches over the other.

3.2 A critique of strict-abstentionism

While strict-abstentionism might seem initially compelling, it does not remain sound after a closer analysis. Barring the reference in the Report on Georgia, most of the positions expressly favoring this approach are products of the eras of decolonization and the Cold War. As such, they must be understood in light of their historical context. At the time, the international discourse was especially sensitive to attempts by colonial or ex-colonial powers to prop-up illegitimate governments in their present or former colonies, or to the manipulations of the rivaling blocs competing for global influence.[96] With the end of the Cold War, and considering the transformation of the principle of self-determination in the decolonized world – from one primarily concerned with achieving the independence of colonies, to one which connotes some form of democratic deliberation or political participation[97] – it is doubtful whether strict-abstentionist positions, as such, can remain unaltered.

Furthermore, even if one still subscribes to the effectiveness doctrine as the main source of sovereign power, the mere request for assistance is not an absolute proof that the government does not exercise effective control. For instance, one can imagine a situation in which a government requests the aid of a neighboring state, perhaps because the latter possesses capabilities that can help it quash the insurgency faster, or with less casualties; there are a myriad other possibilities in which a request for assistance will not necessarily connote that the government is no longer the de facto power. Perhaps, in legal terms, the mere request for assistance can serve as *evidence* for lack of effectiveness, but not more.

94 *Id.* n. 180.

95 *Id.* at 279.

96 *See, e.g.*, The Independent International Commission on Kosovo, The Kosovo Report 188–189 (2000).

97 *See* Thomas M. Franck, *The Emerging Right to Democratic Governance*, 86 American Journal of International Law 46, 52–56 (1992) (highlighting the post-decolonization development of the principle of self-determination into a "general notion of internationally validated political consultation" to be applied to all states). *See also* Chapter 9, sec. 2.

Strict-abstentionism seems to have also envisioned, in general, a simplistic understanding of internal armed conflicts, corresponding mainly to the classic scenario of a struggle for control over the state apparatus. In such cases, presumably, a coherent case can be made for non-intervention for the sake of fulfillment of the right to self-determination. However, as we saw in Chapter 2, the sheer complexity of contemporary internal conflicts rarely coincides with such simple models. Indeed, beyond the classic recognition of a counter-intervention exception,[98] strict-abstentionism does not address other complex scenarios.

For instance, strict-asbtentionism does not provide a satisfactory answer to struggles of secession, which challenge interests of the international community such as the principle of territorial integrity, that clash with strict-abstentionism's simplistic model of non-intervention. Moreover, it does not clarify the theoretical basis for abstention in instances where the conflict contains an element of irredentism. It further fails to lay down a rational position regarding situations in which armed groups are comprised of non-citizens whose actions cannot necessarily be imputed to external states – for instance, such as the Palestine Liberation Organization (PLO) in Lebanon during the Lebanese Civil War or the FDLR militias in Eastern DRC. In such cases the principles of non-intervention and self-determination lose some relevancy, being that some of the involved parties are external to the state's citizenry. It certainly cannot justify abstentionism in cases in which the opposition itself seeks to deconstruct the international order of states, such as when it is a part of a transnational network seeking to dismantle the state altogether (such as in the context of struggles against Al-Qa'ida and comparable groups).

Moreover, the concept of strict-abstentionism is questionable also in terms of its inner logic: while hailing its supposed neutrality, strict-abstentionism does not amount to non-intervention in the true sense. On the contrary, it is tantamount to the complete preference of the party which is *militarily stronger*, which is not a less of a moral judgment than *positive* forcible intervention. In essence, therefore, strict-abstentionism condones the view that the fulfillment of self-determination is a corollary of a party's capability to effectively use violence, while the principle is conversely understood, nowadays, to connote political participation.[99] In an era in which the international community is preoccupied with the protection of civilians, as discussed in Chapter 8, strict-abstentionism amounts to indifference, not to non-intervention. As such, strict-abstentionism is directly contradictory to emerging practice of the international system. For instance, the RtoP concept, which we address later on, is built on the

98 *See* Chapter 7, sec. 3.

99 For a comparable argument *see* David Wippman, *Military Intervention, Regional Organizations, and Host-State Consent*, 7 Duke Journal of Comparative and International Law 209, 220 (1996).

exact opposite premise – according to which the international community should be encouraged to assist a state that requests help in the face of mass atrocities, in order to allow it to exercise its responsibilities.[100]

Thus, and most importantly, the strict-abstentionist principle reflects a harsh interpretation of the right of self-determination and the norm of non-intervention, which perhaps was reasonable in the era of decolonization, but seems unfitting in contemporary international law. In particular, this is evident considering the disastrous consequences of the ostensible "neutrality and impartiality" assumed by the international community in the face of the mass atrocities in Rwanda (1994) and Srebrenica (1995).[101] Indeed, strict-abstentionism can lead to undesirable results in instances where atrocities are committed and the UNSC fails to act, or when it acts insufficiently.[102]

In light of all of the above, it is safe to say that the contemporary international system, with its various instruments that regulate intra-state conduct, is one in which "the impossibility of neutrality" prevails,[103] quite possibly rendering obsolete the concept of strict-abstentionism. However, this by no means implies that an "anything goes" approach, allowing parties to pick sides in internal conflicts as they wish, reflects current law or is desirable. Any analysis must recognize that governments, due to their status in international law, must enjoy *at least* a preliminary preference.

4 The rebuttable presumption in favor of governments

4.1 The government as the representative of the state

While the strict-abstentionist approach has been widely featured in the literature, it is strikingly scarce in the *opinio juris* of states. This fact has been true, of course, in the pre-Charter era, when the discourse emphasized the war-prerogative; as we shall see, this is also the case in contemporary practice. This is perhaps unsurprising, as *opinio juris* is conveyed primarily by governments; accordingly, any government that would advocate strict-abstentionism would thereby negate also its *own* ability to request external support, in time of need, and all this without any visible reciprocal advantage. Indeed, UNGA declarations on the issue of intervention have expressly referred to the prohibition on supporting rebels,

100 Under the "RtoP pillar" of "international assistance and capacity building." *See* Chapter 8, sec. 2.

101 *See* Anne Orford, International Authority and the Responsibility to Protect 8 (2011).

102 Georg Nolte, Eingreifen auf Einladung 607–628 (1999) (German). For an overview in English of Nolte's approach to consensual intervention *see* Bernd Martenczuk *Book Review: Eingreifen auf Einladung*, 11 European Journal of International Law 941 (2000).

103 *See* Orford, *supra* note 101, at 192–199.

while leaving the question of aiding governments, at most, vague.[104] Although states, and in particular those of the non-aligned bloc, frequently referred to the principle of non-intervention during the Cold War, they did not develop it so far as to negate the principle of government preference.

The strict-abstentionist approach, thus, is usually countered through the recognition of a "qualified" principle of government preference. This preference is, in essence, a rebuttable presumption, since virtually no contemporary source of international law condones an unlimited preference of governments in relation to external forcible assistance. We shall elaborate on the scope of the preference of governments – or the grounds for the rebuttal of the presumption – in later chapters.

The presumption in favor of governments is structured around the basic premise that the entity speaking for the state is the recognized and established government. The government is but the "human agent" of the abstract juridical personality which is the "state,"[105] and as such, it represents the latter in the international sphere.[106] When reading this principle in light of Article 2(4) of the UN Charter, Article 3(e) of the Definition of Aggression and Article 20 of the DASR and DARIO, it merits at least the *prima facie* presumption that a government speaks for the state when expressing consent to forcible intervention.[107]

Indeed, the International Law Commission (ILC) understood Article 20 of the DASR precisely in this way. In its discussion of the issue, the Commission analyzed state practice regarding consensual interventions in favor of governments, concluding that such consent has "nearly always" been invoked as a justification for them;[108] and that in the ensuing UN discussions, "no State contested the validity of the principle that the consent of the territorial State precluded – as a general rule – the wrongfulness of the sending of foreign troops into its territory." Rather, the disagreement usually revolved around the application of the principle in the specific circumstances.[109]

104 *See* Declaration on the Inadmissibility of Intervention in the Domestic Affairs of States and the Protection of their Independence and Sovereignty, G.A. Res 2131 (XX), U.N. Doc. A/6014 (December 21, 1965); Declaration on Principles of International Law concerning Friendly Relations and Co-operation among States, G.A. Res. 2625 (XXV), U.N. Doc. A/8082 (October 24, 1970); Declaration on the Inadmissibility of Intervention in the Domestic Affairs of States, G.A. Res. 36/103, U.N. Doc. A/36/51 (December 9. 1981); for an analysis of these declarations *see* Doswald-Beck, *supra* note 1, at 207–212.

105 M.J. Peterson, Recognition of Governments 20 (1997); *see also* Hans Kelsen, General Theory of Law and State 228 (1945).

106 Lauterpacht, *supra* note 69, at 87.

107 *See* Ademola Abass, *Consent Precluding State Responsibility: A Critical Analysis*, 53 International and Comparative Law Quarterly 211, 223–224 (2004).

108 Roberto Ago, 8th Rep. of the International Law Commission on State Responsibility, 2 Yearbook of the International Law Commission 31 (1979), U.N. Doc. A/CN.4/SERA/1979/Add.l.

109 *Id.* at 32; *see also* Nolte, *supra* note 102, at 634.

It is therefore well established that beleaguered governments can, in principle, consent to an external forcible intervention,[110] whether it amounts to a full-scale invasion such as was the case in the DRC,[111] or when it is limited to relatively narrow operations such as cross-border drone attacks.[112]

4.2 The presumption in favor of governments in practice

When analyzing state practice regarding consensual intervention in the UN Charter era, it is helpful to distinguish between the period of the Cold War era and the subsequent decades. During the Cold War, states did not object to the government preference principle, precisely because members of both blocs utilized it for their own benefit. After the Cold War – and *a fortiori* in the decolonized world – the eradication, at large, of classic bloc-rivalry, as well as the contemporary scarcity of "national liberation" struggles, significantly reduced the motivation of states to oppose consensual interventions to begin with.

Indeed, the proliferation of internal conflicts in ex-Yugoslavia and Africa, and the accompanying mass atrocities, shifted the international attention to the pursuit of stability. Attempts to mitigate the catastrophic results of internal strife were undertaken, many times, through active regional and international cooperation with beleaguered or transitional governments, or by international acquiescence to such actions when conducted by individual states. In a sense, in the post-Cold War world, the preference of governments has virtually come to be taken for granted.

110 *See, generally, id.* at 629–640 (1999); James W. Garner, *Editorial Comment: Questions of International Law in the Spanish Civil War,* 31 American Journal of International Law 66, 67 (1937); Pitman B. Potter, *Editorial Comment: Legal Aspects of the Beirut Landing,* 52 American Journal of International Law 727, 727–728 (1958); David Wippman, *Pro-democratic Intervention by Invitation, in* Democratic Governance and International Law, *supra* note 40, at 293, 294–297; Dinstein, *supra* note 78, at 119–120; Abass, *supra* note 107, at 223–225; Brad R. Roth, Governmental Illegitimacy in International Law 171, 181, 185–186, 284 (2000); Byers and Chesterman, *supra* note 40, at 287–288, 291; Schachter, *supra* note 3, at 1645; Jean d'Aspremont, *Legitimacy of Governments in the Age of Democracy,* 38 New York University Journal of International Law and Politics 877, 906–907 (2005); The Kosovo Report, *supra* note 96, at 193; Terry D. Gill, *Military Intervention at the Invitation of a Government, in* The Handbook of the International Law of Military Operations 229, 229 (Terry D. Gill and Dieter Fleck eds., 2010).

111 *See* Christine D. Gray, International Law and the Use of Force 70–71 (2008) (demonstrating that in general, in its approach towards the second Congolese conflict, the UNSC "took a clear position: aid to the government was permissible, intervention or force to overthrow the government was not"). *See also id.* at 73–74.

112 *See, e.g.,* Special Rapporteur on Extrajudicial, Summary or Arbitrary Executions, *Study on Targeted Killings,* Human Rights Council, ¶¶35, 37, U.N. Doc. A/HRC/14/24/Add.6 (May 28, 2010) (by Philip Alston); Michael N. Schmitt, *Drone Attacks under the Jus ad Bellum and Jus in Bello: Clearing the "Fog of Law,"* 13 Yearbook of International Humanitarian Law 311, 315 (2010).

The understanding of preference of governments, has been prevalent in state practice in the first decades of the UN system, although – and especially in the era of decolonization and at the height of the Cold War – frequently abused. However, interestingly, even in the most controversial cases of intervention, objecting states did not attack the principle of government preference itself. For instance, in 1957 the UK justified its intervention in Muscat and Oman in favor of the ruling Sultan and against the seceding Imamate,[113] as being "at the request of a friendly ruler."[114] The Arab states, in response, requested that the UNSC consider the intervention, but not on counts of their rejection of the principle of government consent. They claimed, rather, that the secession-seeking Imamate of Oman was an independent state, and therefore the intervention threatened *international* peace and security. The UK responded that the Sultan of Muscat was sovereign over Muscat as well Oman, and therefore was entitled to support in an "internal" issue. The UNSC accordingly refused to place the issue on the agenda.[115] Similar justification was made by the UK in relation to its 1958 intervention in Jordan.[116]

The 1958 American intervention in Lebanon, likewise, was justified upon the explicit consent of Lebanese President Chamoun, ostensibly in his struggle against subversive pro-Nasserite elements.[117] As such, this intervention was supplemented with the common Cold War era claim of "counter-intervention" as a supporting justification for government consent. This claim was controversially bound, in this case, to the invocation of "collective self-defense" justifications.[118] In an emergency meeting of the UNSC, the American and Lebanese representatives emphasized that US forces were invited by Lebanon. Two conflicting draft resolutions by the US and USSR were rejected by mutual veto; however the US resolution enjoyed a large majority of supporters.[119]

Further Cold War and colonialism-related examples of interventions justified, *inter alia*, on counts of government consent, are abundant. Such was the 1962 Egyptian intervention in Yemen,[120] the 1956 Soviet

113 *See* Husain M. Albahama, The Legal Status of the Arabian Gulf States 239–247 (1968).

114 Antonio Tanca, Foreign Armed Intervention in Internal Conflict 150–151 (1993); ILC Report, *supra* note 108, at 31 n. 132.

115 1957 Yearbook U.N. 56–58.

116 ILC Report, *supra* note 108, at n. 133.

117 *See* S.C. Res. 128, U.N. Doc. S/4023 (June 11, 1958); 1958 Yearbook U.N. 36–38.

118 *See* Wright, *supra* note 13, at, 113, 120. The US claimed that the 1958 Lebanon affair was an indirect-aggression, related to "communist" policies. *See id.* As we saw in Chapter 3, sec. 2.2, such actions have been rejected by the ICJ, in the Nicaragua case, as justifications for collective self-defense, since they were not viewed by the majority as "armed attacks." *See also* Cassese, *supra* note 50, at 364–365, 370.

119 1958 Yearbook U.N. 38–43; *see also* Tanca, *supra* note 114, at 153–154; ILC Report, *supra* note 108, at 31–32, n. 134.

120 Arthur Mark Weisburd, Use of Force: The Practice of States since World War II 184–186 (1997).

intervention in Hungary and the 1964 interventions of Belgium in Congo[121] and of France in Gabon;[122] France also invoked the consent justification in its 1958 Chad intervention, and in its 1979 operation in the Central African Republic.[123] The later cases were part of a general French policy of consensual interventions in former colonies, usually in favor of challenged governments. France's interventions were, in general, based on forward-looking intervention treaties concluded with ex-colonies.[124] Even the recent French participation in the 2011 operation in Côte D'Ivoire can be traced to such an agreement, in addition to a UNSC authorization.[125] The same principle can be found also in the UNSC's reaction to the multiple mid-1970s interventions in Angola, where a clear and explicit preference was given to the consensual (counter) interventions in favor of the MPLA government.[126]

The consent justification could be found also in the context of operations undertaken by regional powerbrokers. Syria, for instance, justified its 1976 intervention in Lebanon on counts of a Lebanese invitation.[127] India's massive 1987–1990 intervention in Sri Lanka, ostensibly to assist the government against the Tamil Tigers, was justified on counts of consent, "in response to a specific request from the Government of Sri Lanka, and in full conformity with international law,"[128] to the general acquiescence of the international community.[129]

To be sure, some interventions were widely condemned. However, the condemnations did not explicitly negate the notion of government preference, but rather focused on the specific circumstances. In April 1965, American forces intervened in the Dominican Republic, following heavy fighting between two contending governments. The American operation was endorsed by states party to the Organization of American States (OAS,) but explicitly supported in the UNSC only by the United Kingdom.[130] The US justified its intervention mainly on counts of protection of nationals abroad, but also argued that it had been "informed by the military

121 ILC Report, *supra* note 108, at 32.

122 Gray, *supra* note 111, at 85.

123 *Id.* at 85–86.

124 Nolte, *supra* note 102, at 297–364, 635–636.

125 *See* Chapter 9, sec. 1.3.

126 S.C. Res. 387, U.N. Doc. S/RES/287 (March 31, 1976) ("*[r]ecalling also* the inherent and lawful right of every State, in the exercise of its sovereignty, to request assistance from any other State or group of States"); Roth, *supra* note 110, at 285–289; *see also* 1976 Yearbook U.N. 171.

127 *See* Naomi Joy Weinberger, Syrian Intervention in Lebanon: The 1975–1976 Civil War 206–229 (1986).

128 Letter Dated 17 December 1987 from India to the President of the UNSC, UN Doc S/19354 (December 17, 1987).

129 Gray, *supra* note 111, at 86–87.

130 *Id.* at 91; 1965 Yearbook U.N. 140–155.

authorities" that its military assistance was required.[131] It further stressed the need to prevent the emergence of a communist government.[132]

The USSR and its allies argued that the intervention was, in essence, an attempt "to keep in power a dictatorship" which aimed to suppress a national liberation movement.[133] Other condemning states, it seems, denied the existence of consent, alleging that the US acted upon its "own assessment of the situation."[134] Generally, the colliding American, Soviet and non-aligned positions focused on the *nature* of the ostensibly consenting party, or on the question of the mere existence of consent, but did not advance a principled negation of the presumption in favor of governments. UNSC Resolutions 203 and 205 laconically called for a "strict cease-fire" without clarifying this matter.[135]

Similar positions were advanced regarding the 1968 Soviet invasion of Czechoslovakia, although it was not an intervention in an internal armed conflict per se. Among other justifications, the USSR invoked government consent. While the invasion was condemned by many states, the positions of the US, Canada, China, Denmark, Ethiopia and the UK involved the claim that the USSR failed to "document" the Czechoslovak consent.[136] The Czechoslovak representative also denied the existence of consent.[137] A draft resolution submitted by Denmark expressed "grave concern" that the Warsaw Pact troops entered Czechoslovakia "without the knowledge and against the wishes of the Czechoslovak Government."[138]

The 1983 American-led, post-coup intervention in Grenada – which was justified, *inter alia*, upon the invitation by the island's head-of-state, the Governor General[139] – was again widely condemned.[140] However, once

131 Letter Dated 29 April 1965 from the US to the President of the UNSC, U.N. Doc. S/6310 (29 April 1965). In the UNSC, the US changed the "requesting" entity from "military authorities" to "Dominican authorities." *See* 1965 Yearbook U.N. 141.

132 *See id.*

133 *Id.* at 140–141.

134 *See, e.g.*, the statement of Jordan, *id.* at 143.

135 S.C. Res. 203, U.N Doc. S/RES/203 (May 14, 1965); S.C. Res. 205, U.N. Doc. S/RES/205 (May 22, 1965).

136 1968 Yearbook U.N. 300.

137 *Id.* at 298–299.

138 1968 Yearbook U.N. 300.

139 1983 Yearbook U.N. 213. It was doubtful whether the Governor General, formally the viceroy of the Queen of England, was actually capable of speaking for the state. *See* Byers and Chesterman, *supra* note 40, at 271–272. There was also doubt whether the invitation was genuine, see Schachter, *supra* note 3, at 1644–1645; or whether it had any effect on the American decision to intervene to begin with. *See* Robert J. Beck, *International Law and the Decision to Invade Grenada: A Ten-Year Retrospective*, 33 Virginia Journal of International Law 765, 789–790 (1993).

140 The UNSC failed, in October 28, to adopt a draft resolution condemning the action in Grenada only due to a US veto. Yearbook U.N. 211 (1983). The UNGA, conversely, condemned the action as a "flagrant violation of international law." G.A. Res. 38/7, U.N. Doc. A/RES/38/7 (November 2, 1983); *see also* Byers and Chesterman, *supra* note 40, at 273.

more, the condemnation did not expressly involve a negation of the principle of government preference.[141] This might be partially explained by the fact that the eastern bloc, which led the condemnation of the invasion, could not seriously deny that Cuban troops were also present on Grenadian soil, themselves with the consent of the ousted government of Grenada.

Thus, France, for instance, argued that intervention was allowed "in response to a request from the legitimate authorities," but that such justification was not admissible in the specific case.[142] Seychelles recognized the "unquestionable right of any country to call on partners of its own choice for assistance" but emphasized that external states cannot intervene "if not requested to do so."[143] Grenada itself agreed that "intervention can come only if there is a request from a [OESC treaty] member Government."[144] Even Cuba, in an attempt to justify its own activities in Grenada, admitted – thus reinforcing the principle of government preference – that there was a presence of a "small military mission advising the Grenadian defense forces and giving assistance to the country."[145] To this claim, Jamaica answered that Cuban troops were not "properly there at the request of a legitimate government."[146] Indeed, many states invoked the general principles of non-use of force, non-intervention and self-determination in their statements regarding the Grenada issue,[147] but it is impossible to isolate these positions from the fact that the US-led intervention took place after a coup d'état was effectively

141 The American operation in Grenada raises an interesting question regarding the relations between regional organizations and external parties. The US justified its intervention, besides on counts of Grenadian invitation, *inter alia* on a request by the OECS. *See* 1983 Yearbook U.N. 213. Assuming *arguendo* that the OECS had authority to forcefully intervene in a member state (which was heavily debated), it is still questionable whether such authority allowed the regional organization to request assistance from an *external* party (here, the US). On the authority of the OECS *see* Byers and Chesterman, *supra* note 40, at 271–272; for the position of Mexico and an interesting statement by Nicaragua, *see* U.N. SCOR, 38th Sess., 2487th mtg. at 1–5, U.N. Doc. S/PV. 2487 (October 25, 1983); for the position of Grenada *see id.*, at 10. For the US position *see id.*, 19–20; Letter Dated 25 October 1983 from the Permanent Representative of the U.S. to the U.N. Addressed to the President of the Security Council, U.N. Doc. S/16076 (October 25, 1983).

142 Yearbook U.N. 212 (1983); U.N. SCOR, 38th Sess., 2489th mtg. at 15, U.N. Doc. S/PV.2489 (October 26, 1983).

143 *Id.* at 8.

144 S/PV.2487, *supra* note 141, at 10.

145 *Id.* at 13.

146 S/PV.2489, *supra* note 142, at 5.

147 1983 Yearbook U.N. 211–217.

completed – and against the will of the self-appointed junta – the consent of the Governor General notwithstanding.[148]

As aforementioned, when the Cold War ended, the discussion of intervention was largely freed from traditional bloc-influences, and the idea of government preference seems to have become taken for granted – subject to limitations explored in Chapter 7. Indeed, when the Economic Community of West African States (ECOWAS) intervened in Liberia in 1990, it cannot be disregarded that consent was expressed by the beleaguered (but still recognized) president, Samuel Doe.[149] Similarly, the ECOWAS 1997 intervention in Sierra Leone was, essentially, a unilateral intervention on behalf of what was perceived by the international community as a consenting government. The ECOWAS operation was authorized *ex post* by the UNSC.[150] Similarly, Senegal intervened in favor of the government of Guinea-Bissau in 1998, and was subsequently replaced by an ECOWAS force.[151]

In the year 2000, the presumption in favor of governments was enshrined in the Constitutive Act of the African Union. Article 4(j) entrenches, as a principle of the African Union, "the right of Member States to request intervention from the Union in order to restore peace and security."[152] This, indubitably, serves as powerful *opinio juris* regarding the principle of government preference, or, at least, a firm denial of the strict-abstentionist approach.

Examples of the presumption in favor of governments can also be found in the recent decade or so. Thus, the UK justified its 2000 intervention in Sierra Leone, *inter alia*, on its support of a "democratically

148 *See, e.g.*, the position of Guyana, that opposed the invasion, arguing that "when States arrogate to themselves the right to seek help to destroy the *Governments* of those States whose policies they find disagreeable, then who among us can feel safe?" [Emphasis added]. S/PV.2487, *supra* note 141, at 9. *See also* the position of Grenada, *id.* at 9–11; *compare* the position of Saint Lucia, the emphasized the consent of the Governor General. U.N. SCOR, 38th Sess., 2491st mtg. at 3, U.N. Doc. S/2491 (October 27, 1983).

149 *See* David Wippman, *Enforcing the Peace: ECOWAS and the Liberian Civil War, in* Enforcing Restraint: Collective Intervention in Internal Conflicts 157, 189 (Lori Fisler Damrosch ed., 1993); Ikechi Mgbeoji, Collective Insecurity: The Liberian Crisis, Unilateralism, and Global Power 77–78 (2003).

150 The Sierra Leone case is complex, as the consenting government was overthrown before the ECOWAS intervention, but it claimed strong democratic credentials – thereby raising the question whether democratically elected governments maintain their international status when deposed by *coups d'état*. *See* Byers and Chesterman, *supra* note 40, at 288–290. We discuss this issue in Chapter 9, sec. 1. It is worthwhile to note that I am not referring here to the 1994 Haiti intervention, since it was, from the outset, a multilateral Chapter VII action. *See* Wippman, *supra* note 110 at 293–294, 303–311 (addressing the cases of Haiti and Sierra Leone).

151 Gray, *supra* note 111, at 86.

152 Constitutive Act of the African Union, art. 4(j), July 11, 2000, 2158 U.N.T.S.. 3.

elected government" against rebel forces.[153] This justification was viewed favorably in a 2009 report by the UN Secretary General, which implied that consent is a legitimate alternative to UNSC authorization.[154] Similarly, the UNSC welcomed the 2002 intervention by France in Côte D'Ivoire, to the extent that it was conducted in favor of the government.[155] Moreover, as we shall demonstrate in Chapter 7, the international community clearly afforded preferred treatment to Ethiopia's 2006 intervention in favor of the TFG in Somalia, versus the negative approach towards Eritrea's involvement on behalf of the opposing Islamic Courts Union.[156]

In the multi-party conflict in DRC, the UNSC distinguished, at least most of the time, between the interventions on behalf of the government and those conducted, notably by Rwanda and Uganda, in support of the rebels.[157] In January-February 2009, in a surprising deal, Rwanda received the consent of the DRC to act against Hutu militias (FDLR) in East Congo, in a deal in which Rwanda was to cease supporting Laurent Nkunda of the CNDP. The joint operations resulted in Nkunda's arrest and the neutralization of the CNDP as a fighting force.[158] UN officials saw these actions positively, viewing the joint operations as creating "a new dynamic, which could have a significant and favourable impact."[159] They celebrated the "remarkable turnaround" in the DRC, commending the cooperating governments for their "courageous decision to overcome their previous distrust and to focus on common interests of the future."[160] There is no doubt that this generally supportive view of the operations was affected by the fact that they were conducted, *inter alia*, against "ex-génocidaires."[161] However, this alone does not undermine the presumption in favor of governments, but rather hints at its substantive application. It is worthwhile to mention, in this context, that the forcible Chapter VII operations of the UN mission in Congo, MONUC (and later MONUSCO), were conducted with the consent of the DRC's government and in "close cooperation" with it, suggesting that governmental consent plays a certain role even in extreme situations of state-failure.[162] Likewise, an illuminating example is

153 The other justifications were protection of British nationals, and to provide support for the UN peacekeeping force. *See* Gray, *supra* note 111, at 90–91.

154 *See* U.N. Secretary General, *Implementing the Responsibility to Protect: Report of the Secretary General*, ¶42, U.N. Doc. A/63/677 (January 12, 2009): "In 2000, with the consent of the Government, a modest British-led intervention force helped to protect Freetown ... and restore stability to the beleaguered West African State."

155 Gray, *supra* note 111, at 86.

156 *See* Chapter 7, sec. 2.4.

157 *See* Gray, *supra* note 111, at 68–73.

158 *See* Chapter 1, sec. 3.3.

159 U.N. SCOR, 64th Sess., 6083rd mtg. at 2, U.N. Doc. S/PV.6083 (February 17, 2009).

160 U.N. SCOR, 64th Sess., 6104th mtg. at 3, U.N. Doc. S/PV.6104 (April 9, 2009).

161 S/PV.6083, *supra* note 159, at 2.

162 Chapter 1, sec. 3.3.

the 2011 intervention by Kenya in Somalia – as discussed in Chapter 1 – arguably conducted pursuant to a joint communiqué between the two countries.[163]

The principle of government preference is also a key premise of American counterinsurgency operations (COIN) in Iraq and Afghanistan, a central operational pillar of which is the consent of local authorities.[164] After the 2003 invasion of Iraq, the UNSC recognized the Coalition Provisional Authority as the temporary de facto administrator of Iraq,[165] until a representative Iraqi government assumed responsibility.[166] The UNSC saw the establishment of an interim Iraqi government on June 30, 2004 as "the end of the occupation" and therefore the end of the administrative powers of the Coalition Authority.[167] On June 5, 2004, the prime minister of the interim government delivered a letter to the UNSC requesting the multinational force to stay in Iraq, thereby inviting Coalition forces to support the Iraqi government in the face of various insurgent groups. Accordingly, the UNSC authorized the presence of the Coalition forces on Iraqi soil.[168]

In December 2008, a SOFA was concluded between Iraq and the US, Article 4 of which provided that:

> [t]he Government of Iraq requests the temporary assistance of the United States Forces for the purposes of supporting Iraq in its efforts to maintain security and stability in Iraq, including cooperation in the conduct of operations against al-Qaeda and other terrorist groups, outlaw groups, and remnants of the former regime.[169]

163 Chapter 1, sec. 1.2.

164 *See, e.g.*, U.S. Army, Counterinsurgency ¶1–147, 2–36 (2006): "US forces committed to a COIN effort are there to assist a HN [host nation] government. The long-term goal is to leave a government able to stand by itself."

165 S.C. Res. 1483, U.N. Doc. S/RES/1483 (May 22, 2003).

166 S.C. Res. 1511, U.N. Doc. S/RES/1511 (October 16, 2003).

167 S.C. Res. 1546, U.N. Doc. S/RES/1546 (June 8, 2004).

168 Letter annexed to resolution 1546, *supra* note 167. Further Iraqi requests for the extension of the multinational forces' mandate were authorized in S.C. Res. 1637, U.N. Doc. S/RES/1637 (November 8, 2005); S.C. Res. 1723, U.N. Doc. S/RES/1723 (November 28, 2006); S.C. Res. 1790, U.N. Doc. S/RES/1790 (December 18, 2007); *See also* M. Cherif Bassiouni, *Legal Status of U.S. Forces in Iraq from 2003–2008*, 11 Chinese Journal of International Law 1, 7 (2010–2011): "The fact that the Council acted pursuant to a request by a member-state meant the foreign occupying forces became forces invited by a host state, thus giving their presence legitimacy under international law"; *compare* Tristan Ferraro, International Commission of the Red Cross, Expert Meeting: Occupation and Other Forms of Administration of Foreign Territory 27, 29 (2012) (debating whether the UNSC can determine the end of occupation in general and in the context of Iraq.)

169 Agreement between the United States of America and the Republic of Iraq on the Withdrawal of the United States Forces from Iraq and the Organization of their Activities during their Temporary Presence in Iraq, U.S.-Iraq, December 14, 2008; on the negotiation and content of the SOFA *see* Bassiouni, *supra* note 168, at 9–20.

In essence, the agreement changed the status of US forces in Iraq from operating under UN auspices to forces invited bilaterally to assist Iraq in its internal conflict.[170]

Furthermore, consent has been cited as a potentially lawful justification for ongoing American operations in Afghanistan, even by those who are generally reluctant to grant a carte-blanche for forcible actions in the context of the so-called "war on terror."[171]

Considering all of the above, it is hardly surprising that a 2010 UN report on the legality of "targeted killings," unequivocally stated that "[t]he proposition that a State may consent to the use of force in its territory by another State is not legally controversial."[172]

4.3 The presumption in favor of governments in ICJ decisions: a thin doctrine of government preference

The presumption in favor of governments has also resonated in the rulings of the ICJ. However, the treatment of this question has been rather thin and in no way reflects a comprehensive doctrine. In the *Nicaragua* case, the Court rejected the Reagan Doctrine by denying the possibility that aid to opposition groups could be justified on counts of the consent of the latter. Accordingly, it ruled that the customary principle of non-intervention did not prescribe a right for states to intervene in support of the opposition, on counts of specific "political and moral values."[173] Conversely, the Court held laconically that intervention on behalf of governments was permissible:

> it is difficult to see what would remain of the principle of non-intervention in international law if intervention, *which is already allowable at the request of the government* of a State, were also to be allowed at the request of the opposition. ... Such a situation does not in the Court's view correspond to the present state of international law.[174]

This position was expressed while the Court was entirely aware that an internal armed conflict "has continued and is continuing" in Nicaragua,[175]

170 *See* Letter Dated 7 December 2008 from the Prime Minister of Iraq addressed to the President of the Security Council, annexed to S.C. Res. 1859, U.N. Doc. S/RES/1859 (December 22, 2008).

171 *See, e.g., Rise of the Drones II: Examining the Legality of Unmanned Targeting: Hearings Before the Subcomm. On National Security and Foreign Affairs*, 111th Cong. (2010) (Statement of Mary Elen O'Connell) at 19.

172 *See, e.g.,* Study on Targeted Killings, *supra* note 112, ¶35, 37.

173 Military Aid and Paramilitary Activities in and against Nicaragua (Nicar. v. U.S.), 1986 I.C.J. 14 (June 27), ¶206.

174 *Id.* ¶246. For an analysis of the ruling *see* Gray, *supra* note 111, at 75–78.

175 Nicaragua, *supra* note 173, ¶58.

thereby clearly rejecting strict-abstentionism. However, while its treatment of the question sufficed to express the Court's recognition of the preference of governments, its laconic reasoning on this issue cannot be understood as recognizing that consent power is *limitless*.

Indeed, the Court held that the US, in its support of the Contras, has violated namely the prohibition on the use of force,[176] the norm of non-intervention[177] and the principle of territorial sovereignty.[178] However, it was careful not to craft a comprehensive doctrine of intervention. For instance, it noted it would only "define" the aspects of the principle of non-intervention that were relevant to the specific dispute.[179] It furthermore emphasized that the case did not concern "the process of decolonization,"[180] alluding, as emphasized critically by Judge Schwebel, that certain situations might be subject to different norms.[181] It moreover noted that in addition to the fact that it did not find in state practice a "new" exception to the principle of non-intervention, it was the US itself that refrained from arguing for a new interpretation of the concept, but rather chose to focus on "classic" justifications such as collective self-defense.[182] Thus, the Court was bound, to a large extent, by the limitations of the adversarial process – especially limited in this case, since the US did not participate in the main proceedings.[183]

It is for these reasons that the Court's addressing of the question of consensual intervention, as an issue independent from collective self-defense, was a one-paragraph treatment concealed in a ruling of 292 paragraphs.[184] It is worthwhile to note, furthermore, that the Court did not deal with the identification of the government capable of expressing consent, since this question was not in dispute. Therefore, the Court could not, and did not intend to, lay down a comprehensive doctrine of consensual intervention. It merely set forth the *prima facie* law of government preference.

If there could be any doubt that in the post-Cold War world, consensual intervention in favor of a government can, in principle, serve as an exception to the prohibition on the use of force – and even one that is taken for granted – it must be resolved by the 2005 decision of the ICJ in the DRC v. Uganda case.[185] There, the DRC argued that Uganda violated the laws on

176 *Id.* ¶238.
177 *Id.* ¶242.
178 *Id.* ¶251.
179 *Id.* ¶205.
180 *Id.* ¶206.
181 *Id.* ¶¶178–181 (Schwebel, J., dissenting).
182 *Id.* ¶¶207–209.
183 *Id.* ¶¶9–10 (the US decided not to participate in the proceedings after its jurisdictional objections were rejected).
184 *Id.* ¶246.
185 Armed Activities on the Territory of the Congo (D.R.C. v. Uganda), 2005 I.C.J. 168 (December 19).

the use of force and the norm of non-intervention in its operations in the DRC, in the course of the second Congolese conflict. In short, Uganda claimed that it was operating on Congolese soil since May 1997 with the consent of the DRC's government, while the latter claimed, conversely, that its consent was withdrawn in July 1998.[186]

The Court accepted, in general, that the DRC had withdrawn its consent, and thus held that Uganda violated international law by not removing its forces from the DRC's territory.[187] In its consideration of this issue, the Court must have, even if implicitly, accepted the perception that consensual forcible intervention in favor of governments, in the course of an internal armed conflict, is generally not unlawful.[188] Arguably, had the Court subscribed to a strict-abstentionist approach, it would have had to treat *any* intervention by Uganda as a violation of *jus cogens*, which it would then have to consider as one which is based on invalid consent.[189]

Indeed, the treatment of this issue in this ruling reflects the notion that government preference has become an almost trivial principle in the contemporary international system.

186 *Id.* ¶43.

187 *Id.* ¶¶51–54.

188 *Id.* ¶¶42–54. It should be noted, to complete the picture, that the fact that the DRC could consent to foreign intervention was not challenged by any party in this case; but from the language of the case it seems that it is a given that such intervention would not have been deemed illegal by the Court.

189 *See* Vienna Convention on the Law of Treaties, arts. 53, May 23, 1969, 1155 U.N.T.S. 331; ILC Draft and Commentaries, *supra* note 7, arts. 40–41.

7 The scope of government consent power

General thresholds

1 Intervention and consent in the twenty-first century: territorial effectiveness, mass atrocities and transnational terrorism

Having established that a presumption in favor of governments exists, we shall now turn to discuss the scope of this presumption, and accordingly, the principles that strengthen it or lead to its rebuttal. Recall that the debate regarding the NIA of the Spanish Civil War has clarified that the refusal by states to assist a beleaguered government does not in itself constitute a violation of the norm of non-intervention.[1] A further question is under what circumstances states are obliged *not* to assist such a government. In the era of the prohibition on the use of force, an intervention, in such cases, becomes both an illegal use of force and, in general, an unlawful intervention in internal affairs.

This latter question has gained acute importance in recent upheavals, notably when the international community is deadlocked, as is the case in the Syrian crisis. For instance, following a massacre allegedly committed by government forces in the town of Houla, Susan Rice, US ambassador to the UN, has criticized Russia for providing arms to the Al-Assad regime. However, she added that it was not "technically" a violation of international law "since there's not an arms embargo."[2] As we shall see in the following chapters, this reasoning – seemingly implying that in absent of a UNSC imposed arms embargo, support of governments is always permitted – is imprecise, if not erroneous altogether.

While a possible approach to the limitations on government consent power could be to read the traditional effectiveness-based doctrines into the contemporary prohibition on the use of force, the reality of law, as we shall see, has been more complex. Indeed, analysis of the presumption in favor of governments, through the prism of territorial effectiveness, has

1 Chapter 5, sec. 4.2.

2 Steven Lee Myers and J. David Goodman, *Clinton Says Russian Inaction May Lead to Syrian Civil War*, New York Times, May 31, 2012, *available at* www.nytimes.com/2012/06/01/world/middleeast/frustrated-clinton-says-russian-inaction-may-lead-to-syrian-civil-war.html.

been justified, throughout the twentieth century, on counts of the challenged regime's incapacity to represent the state, and the related principles of self-determination and of non-intervention.[3] Some equated the tests for the validity of consent with traditional tests for government recognition, asserting that "a regime may only be legally entitled to invite outside military help if it's a 'government' within the meaning of international law, and must therefore be in de facto control."[4]

However, the scope of loss of territorial effectiveness, supposedly meriting loss of consent power presents a difficult threshold question, which seems to have remained largely unresolved. The problem is further exacerbated since, in practice, loss of control over a significant part of a state's territory has not resulted in the withdrawal of recognition from beleaguered governments, as the latter, at least in the past, have normally retained *de jure* recognition until a *new* regime, which has gained control over the territory, has emerged.[5]

Moreover, the relation between consent power and the question of government recognition is in itself rather complex. While loss of recognition necessarily entails also the loss of consent power, the same is not true vice versa. When a government is in violation of international law, and for the purpose of continuing that violation it requests external assistance, its request can be powerless, in some cases, *although* the government retains recognition for other purposes.[6] Loss of recognition, however, might result in graver consequences for the previous government, as in such case it does not only lose consent power (negative result) but such power might be transferred to other groups (positive result). In this chapter, and in Chapters 8 and 9, attention will be largely given to the former situation, while the latter will be addressed in Chapter 10.

In any case, recent practice casts doubts regarding the centrality of loss of territorial effectiveness in the assessment of consent power. This process corresponds with two major intertwining – but distinct – characteristics of contemporary international dynamics. The first concerns the increasing preoccupation of the international community with the protection of civilians, in light of the tragic internal conflicts of the past two decades. This issue will be extensively discussed in Chapter 8. The second concerns the struggle against transnational terrorist entities, which dominated, at least, the first decade of the millennium. The latter's relation to consent power is manifested in contemporary COIN operations, and in particular where transitional governments are formed following international, internal or mixed armed conflicts.

3 *See* Louise Doswald-Beck, *The Legal Validity of Military Intervention by Invitation of the Government*, 56 British Year Book of International Law 189 (1985).

4 *Id.* at 195–196.

5 *Id.* at 197–200.

6 *See* David Wippman, *Military Intervention, Regional Organizations, and Host-State Consent*, 7 Duke Journal of Comparative and International Law 209, 215–216 (1996).

For instance, the Bonn Agreement, concluded under UN auspices to set up an interim authority after the fall of the Taliban, included a request by the Afghan delegations for an establishment of an international security force.[7] The UNSC endorsed the Bonn Agreement as a whole, and specifically noted the Afghan request in Resolution 1386, establishing the International Security Assistance Force, which was mandated to work in "close consultation" with the Afghan authorities.[8] Similarly, in June 2004 Coalition forces have received the consent of the interim Iraqi government concerning their operations against various armed groups. Iraq's consent was granted once again, with the conclusion of a bilateral Status of Forces Agreement in 2008 with the United States.[9] Although arguments could be made that the Afghan and Iraqi authorities were coerced, or that they did not exercise territorial effectiveness, the matter passed with general international acquiescence.

In the same vein, arguably, loss of significant territorial control does not hinder the potential consent, although not publicly admitted, apparently given by Pakistan to US drone attacks conducted on its territory, possibly in the context of Pakistan's conflict with the Tehrik-e-Taliban and the US struggle against Al-Qa'ida.[10] Furthermore, it seems that Yemen has retained in its consent power, vis-à-vis Saudi Arabia, in 2009's "Scorched Earth" campaign against Houthi rebels, although the former have gained control over territory in Northern Yemen.[11] In sum, in the context of the international struggle against terrorism – to the extent the aforementioned conflicts qualify as such – government consent power has virtually become taken for granted, loss of control notwithstanding.

In light of the above, it seems that another set of considerations constitutes the "active agents" that define government consent power. Whatever these may be, an underlying notion of our analysis is that such rules should not, in general, aspire to predetermine the regime of the target state, nor, *a fortiori*, to set up a utopian society. Rather, a workable, relatively objective and agreed-upon standard to assess consent power – as discussed in Chapter 8 – could be the principle of protection of civilians. Any further goal, such as the establishment of a democratic system, can and should be the concern of an inclusive post-conflict reconstruction process.

7 Agreement on Provisional Arrangements in Afghanistan Pending the Reestablishment of Permanent Government Institutions, annex I ¶3, U.N. Doc S/2001/1154 (December 5, 2001); *see also* Letter Dated 19 December from the Permanent Representative of Afghanistan, U.N. Doc. S/2001/1223 (December 19, 2001).

8 S.C. Res 1386 prmbl., U.N. Doc. S/RES/1386 (December 20, 2001).

9 *See* Chapter 6, sec. 4.2.

10 Laurie R. Blank and Benjamin R. Farley, *Characterizing U.S. Operations in Pakistan: Is the United States Engaged in an Armed Conflict?* 34 Fordham International Law Journal 151, 154–159, 183–184 (2010).

11 Ian Black, *Arab Governments Move to Ease Yemen Crisis*, The Guardian, October 5, 2008, *available at* www.guardian.co.uk/world/2009/oct/05/arab-governments-yemen-crisis; on the Houthi conflict in general *see* International Crisis Group, Yemen: *Defusing the Saada Time Bomb* 2–4, ICG Middle East Report No. 86 (May 27, 2009).

2 Threshold questions

2.1 Towards an internal jus ad bellum *and the reversal of traditional paradigms*

For the presumption in favor of governments to materialize, there is a general threshold question that has to be answered first: simply put, whether the *internal* resort to force by the territorial government is legal. Indeed, the term *jus ad bellum* usually refers to the resort to force in the *international* realm. Accordingly, Article 2(4) of the UN Charter applies to the use of force between *states.* Internal armed conflicts, conversely, were traditionally viewed as controlled mainly by domestic law.[12] Thus, a state's resort to force against its nationals – in contradistinction, to some extent, to the *jus in bello* of internal armed conflicts[13] – was not considered a subject of international law. Therefore, it was impossible to suggest that there was an international law, comparable to *jus ad bellum*, governing the internal resort to force.

However, since the conclusion of the main instruments of the international law of human rights – namely the International Covenant on Civil and Political Rights (ICCPR)[14] – the relations between the state and individuals under its control, in all aspects, have become a concern of international law. Significantly, the ICCPR enshrines the inherent and non-derogable right to life, which prohibits the *arbitrary* deprivation of life;[15] in addition, it prescribes various "due process" conditions for the administration of criminal law,[16] which are derogable, "to the extent strictly required," only "[i]n time of public emergency which threatens the life of the nation."[17]

IHRL thus regulates the use of state violence against those within the state's territory or subject to its jurisdiction.[18] As such, it can be viewed as establishing an international law of *jus ad bellum* – or, perhaps, *jus contra bellum* – within the boundaries of the state. However, since human rights law does not pinpoint the "vanishing point" in which states can resort to internal "hostilities", the logical conclusion is that resort by states to extrajudicial

12 *See* Christine Gray, International Law and the Use of Force 67 (2008); Francçois Bugnion, *Jus ad Bellum, Jus in Bello and Non-International Armed Conflicts*, 6 Yearbook of International Humanitarian Law 167 (2003).

13 The traditional view of the *jus in bello* of internal conflicts, as we saw, was based on "reciprocity and reason" rather than on law. *See* Chapter 4, sec. 3. However, contemporary IHL binds also parties to internal conflicts. *See* Prosecutor v. Tadic, Case No. IT-94-1-I, Decision on Defence Motion for Interlocutory Appeal on Jurisdiction ¶¶100–127 (International Criminal Tribunal for the Former Yugoslavia, October 2, 1995).

14 International Covenant on Civil and Political Rights, December 16, 1966, 999 U.N.T.S. 171.

15 *Id.* arts. 4(2), 6(1).

16 *Id.* arts. 9, 14.

17 *Id.* art. 4(1).

18 *Id.* art. 2(1).

military force against members of their populations is impermissible absent circumstances that amount to internal armed conflicts, as these were discussed in Chapter 2. Namely, these refer to the existence of organized armed groups that violently challenge the authority of the government, in a manner that compromises its ability to apply its domestic criminal law. Otherwise, the conduct of the state is regulated by the law of human rights *alone*, in which lethal use of force is regulated by rules of engagement applicable in the context of law enforcement.[19] Conversely, when an internal armed conflict exists, "internal" *jus in bello* applies,[20] allowing the government to use lethal force against members of organized armed groups or, at least, civilians directly participating in hostilities, while accepting proportional incidental harm inflicted on non-participating civilians.[21] In essence, therefore, only in the context of an internal armed conflict could Article 6(1) of the ICCPR, prohibiting the arbitrary deprivation of life, be interpreted in reference to norms of international humanitarian law.[22]

The determination of the existence of non-international armed conflict has been an exceptionally controversial issue in recent years, especially in the context of the US-led "global war on terror."[23] We shall not attempt to resolve this question here. However, it is of special significance to the law of consensual intervention since the legality of the resort to force by a territorial government necessarily affects the legality of forcible actions conducted by an external, consensual intervener. It is a fundamental principle of law, and therefore of the regulation of consensual intervention, that a state cannot abrogate its international obligations by inviting a third-party to act in its territory; and, accordingly, that an external intervener cannot conduct activities that the territorial

19 *See* Special Rapporteur on Extrajudicial, Summary or Arbitrary Executions, *Study on Targeted Killings*, Human Rights Council, ¶¶31–33, U.N. Doc. A/HRC/14/24/Add.6 (May 28, 2010) (by Philip Alston).

20 This conclusion applies in any case, without prejudice to the question of the application of IHRL during armed conflicts. *See generally* International Humanitarian Law and Human Rights Law: Towards a New Merger in International Law (Roberta Arnold and Noëlle Quénivet eds., 2008).

21 *See* Nils Melzer, International Commission of the Red Cross, Interpretive Guidance on the Notion of Direct Participation in Hostilities under International Humanitarian Law 27–36 (2009); *compare* Kenneth Watkin, *Opportunity Lost: Organized Armed Groups and the ICRC "Direct Participation in Hostilities Interpretive Guidance,"* 42 New York University Journal of International Law and Politics 641 (2010).

22 Legality of the Threat or Use of Nuclear Weapons, Advisory Opinion, 1996 I.C.J. 226 (July 8), ¶25; *see also* Schmitt, *supra* note 20, at 53.

23 *See, e.g.*, Rosa Ehrenreich Brooks, *War Everywhere: Human Rights, National Security and the Law of Armed Conflict in the Age of Terrorism*, 153 University of Pennsylvania Law Review 675 (2004); Mary Ellen O'Connell, *When is War Not a War? The Myth of the Global War on Terror*, 12 ILSA Journal of International and Comparative Law 5 (2006); Noam Lubell, Extraterritorial Use of Force against Non-State Actors 112–121 (2010).

state is prohibited from undertaking itself.[24] According to this logic, if the territorial state is party to human rights conventions, the intervening state is bound to them automatically. If not, the intervening party, assuming it is a party to such conventions, may still be bound through extraterritorial application, even if operating through the "consent invitation or acquiescence" of the host state.[25] Therefore, in cases where human rights law prohibits the internal use of force – for instance, in absence of an internal armed conflict between at least two organized armed parties – it necessarily follows that consensual forcible intervention is also prohibited.

This distinction is especially evident in instances, such as have taken place in the events of the Arab Spring, in which some states resorted to force against largely unarmed protesters, in gross violation of IHRL.[26] For instance, in February 2011, protests erupted in the Gulf state of Bahrain, immediately facing harsh repression, including by the Bahraini military.[27] Since it is obvious that there was no internal armed conflict, it is reasonable that according to IHRL, the use of force by Bahrain – to the extent that it exceeded law enforcement operations – was unlawful. On March 15, pursuant to a request by Bahrain, the Gulf Cooperation Council (GCC) sent forces into the state, comprised predominantly of Saudi troops.[28] Assuming that the resort to force by Bahrain was illegal, any support rendered by GCC troops to Bahraini operations was unlawful as well.[29] Perhaps, without exhausting the argument on this specific case, the most that the GCC could do is assist the Bahraini government in law enforcement operations, subject to IHRL.

Therefore, when assessing the legality of consensual interventions, it must be determined a priori that an internal armed conflict exists in the state to begin with, and that an "armed conflict" is not proclaimed as a

24 *See* John L. Hargrove, *Intervention by Invitation and the Politics of the New World Order*, *in* Law and Force in the New International Order 113, 116–117 (Lori F. Damrosch and David J. Scheffer eds., 1991); Wippman, *supra* note 6, at 209, 215; *see also* Institut de Droit International, Military Assistance on Request, art. 7 (September 8, 2011).

25 *See* Al-Skeini v. UK, European Court of Human Rights (2011) ¶135.

26 *See, e.g.*, Anthony Shadid, *Security Forces Kill Dozens in Uprisings Around Syria*, New York Times, April 22, 2011, *available at* www.nytimes.com/2011/04/23/world/middleeast/23syria.html. It should be noted that later on, the Syria crisis has developed into a full fledged armed conflict.

27 *Bahrain Activists in "Day of Rage,"* Aljazeera English, February 14, 2011, *available at* http://english.aljazeera.net/news/middleeast/2011/02/2011214925802473.html; *see also Bahrain Troops "Fire on Crowds,"* B.B.C. News, February 18, 2011, *available at* www.bbc.co.uk/news/world-middle-east-12509658.

28 *Saudi Soldiers Sent into Bahrain*, Aljazeera English, March 15, 2011, *available at* http://english.aljazeera.net/news/middleeast/2011/03/2011314124928850647.html.

29 *See* Bahrain Unrest: U.N. Rights Chief Criticises Crackdown, B.B.C. News, March 17, 2011, available at www.bbc.co.uk/news/world-middle-east-12769168.

pretext to abrogate international human rights obligations and to suppress non-violent dissent. The armed conflict precondition was summarized succinctly by O'Connell, in a 2010 statement in front of the US House of Representatives:

> Even in places like Yemen and Pakistan, where there is armed conflict going on, the United States would only have the right to use combat drones in the armed conflicts that those governments are participating in, and not in some rogue operation of our own that has nothing to do with what those governments are trying to accomplish.[30]

And elsewhere, in a similar vein:

> There is a very key and often overlooked distinction. The invitation has to be to participate in the armed conflict that the government of the country is participating in. So Yemen right now is facing insurgencies.... If they had asked us, the United States, to be also involved, we could use military force there, on their invitation, in their armed conflict. But what we have done [in 2002] ... this attack was not part of any armed conflict that the Yemeni authorities were involved in.... So even having consent in that case is not sufficient.[31]

This position is of course without prejudice to the question whether a state, not involved itself in an internal armed conflict, can consent to external attacks conducted against elements in its territory, as part of some paradigm of self-defense exercised by the attacking state – provided that we are willing to view such instances as lawful self-defense to begin with. This justification has been cited by the Obama administration, several times, as a legal basis for transnational drone attacks against individuals.[32] In practice, however, it seems that in many of these cases, when the non-state actor operates from within the target-state's territory against the latter's will, the latter would become, at some stage, itself involved in an internal armed conflict against the targeted entity. These could be the

30 Rise of the Drones II: Examining the Legality of Unmanned Targeting, Hearing Before the Subcommittee on National Security and Foreign Affairs of the Committee on Oversight and Government Reform, House of Representatives, 11th Congress 2nd Sess. (2010) 19 (Statement of Mary Elen O'Connell).

31 *Id.* at 51; *see also* id. at 63; compare Institut de Droit International, Military Assistance on Request art. 2(1) (September 8, 2011).

32 *See, e.g.,* Eric Holder, Speech at Northwestern University School of Law (March 5, 2012), available at http://opiniojuris.org/2012/03/05/ag-holders-national-security-speech-text; *see also* 1 John O. Brennan, The Ethics and Efficacy of the President's Counterterrorism Strategy, speech delivered at the Woodrow Wilson International Center for Scholars (April 30, 2012), available at www.wilsoncenter.org/event/the-efficacy-and-ethics-us-counterterrorism-strategy.

dynamics concerning American drone strikes in Yemen and Somalia, and also in Pakistan – to the extent that it consented to such strikes.

Indeed, armed conflict as a precondition for the legality of consensual intervention contradicts traditional writing, according to which intervention was *prohibited* when internal strife amounted to a "civil war." However, these claims are actually on different levels. While the contemporary armed conflict precondition stems from considerations of human rights, the "civil war" limitation, as we shall see, was actually concerned with diminished sovereign power caused by loss of territorial effectiveness. This change in focus can be explained by the fact that in contemporary law, human rights and the protection of civilians have moved to the center stage, shifting the understanding of sovereignty as territorial effectiveness to a concept based on other, substantive considerations. If we interpret the concepts of effectiveness and sovereignty in light of the principle of protection of civilians, this incompatibility, to some extent, is reconciled. We shall discuss this in Chapter 8.

It should be added, however, that while the armed conflict precondition is the rule, complex scenarios can occur, particularly where "failed states" are involved. Consensual support to governments in law enforcement, naturally, does not require the existence of an armed conflict. However, in the context of the fight against maritime piracy off the coast of Somalia, the line seems to have been blurred. In May 2012, for the first time, European forces (EU NAVFOR) have conducted an aerial attack – labeled as a "disruption action" – against alleged "pirate equipment" on the Somali coastline.[33] Beyond the pure *jus in bello* problems raised by the action – and notably whether "pirate equipment" can, in any situation, amount to legitimate military objectives as these are defined under IHL – the action by EU NAVFOR gives rise to significant human rights law questions with regard to the resort to force. In justification of the operation, EU NAVFOR referred to UNSC Resolution 1851, which authorized – with the TFG's consent – "all necessary measures" for the suppression of piracy in Somalia;[34] and the "full support" of the TFG for the specific operation.[35] In intra-EU law, the operation was authorized by a 2012 Decision by the Council of the European Union, adopted with the TFG's consent, to conduct a "military operation," including on the coastal territory of Somalia, in support of UNSC Resolution 1851.[36] While consent of the TFG formed part of the general legal basis for the attack, its main grounding is ostensibly found in Resolution 1851. However, the Resolution reiterated that counter-piracy measures must conform to applicable IHL *and* IHRL,

33 Press Release, EU Naval Force Delivers Blow against Somali Pirates on Shoreline (May 15, 2012), www.eunavfor.eu/2012/05/eu-naval-force-delivers-blow-against-somali-pirates-on-shoreline.

34 S.C. Res. 1851, U.N. Doc. S/RES/1851 ¶6 (December 16, 2008).

35 Press Release, *supra* note 33.

36 Council Decision 2012/174/CFSP of 23 March 2012, O.J. L 089, 27/3/2012 p. 69–71.

thereby creating a vague normative situation. Furthermore, the Resolution also referred to the UN Convention on the Law of the Sea (UNCLOS) – which approaches piracy from a law enforcement perspective –[37] as the "legal framework applicable to combating piracy."[38]

This Resolution thus reverts us to the question whether absent an armed conflict – and assuming that Somali pirates do not constitute an organized armed group – IHRL can allow forcible acts such as the ones conducted by EU NAVFOR. It is for this reason, perhaps, why EU NAVFOR emphasized that its operation targeted only objects – by thus being "merely an extension" of regular disruption actions at sea – and that no injury to persons occurred.[39] This reasoning raises a host of problems that we shall not address here. It would be best, of course, that future UNSC resolutions do more to clarify unique situations such as these.

2.2 The legal irrelevance of the term "civil war" as negating consent power

The most common restriction, in the literature, on government consent power relies on some ambiguous notion of loss of territorial effectiveness. This approach usually accepts the "theoretical" right of governments to consent to forcible intervention, but immediately qualifies it in light of considerations of territorial effectiveness. The threshold is sometimes defined through the use of the term "civil war," to connote situations in which consent power is negated, as opposed to situations of "local unrest," in which consent power stands. Gray, for instance, concedes that government consent power exists, and has been "taken for granted" since 1945. However, she restricts it only to instances of "domestic unrest," arguing that the norm of non-intervention negates it in when "civil wars" occur.[40] This position was based, *inter alia*, on a 1984 UK Foreign Policy Document advocating this approach,[41] and can be found in the works of other commentators.[42]

Arguably, the term "civil war" is sometimes used, in these sources, in the generic sense. However, since it had, at least in the past, significant legal meaning (as expressed in the belligerency doctrine), the use of the term can lead to confusion. Furthermore, it seems incompatible with

37 UNCLOS, art. 105.

38 S.C. Res. 1851, *supra* note 4, prmbl.

39 Press Release, *supra* note 33.

40 Gray, *supra* note 12, at 80, 85.

41 U.K. Materials on International Law, 57 British Year Book of International Law 614 (1986).

42 Ann van Wynen Thomas and Aaron Joshua Thomas, Non-Intervention: The Law and its Import in the Americas 94 (1956), cited in Doswald-Beck, *supra* note 3, at 196; Oscar Schachter, The Right of States to Use Armed Force, 82 Michigan Law Review 1620, 1645 (1984).

modern law, even beyond the reversal discussed in the previous section. For instance, preconditioning government consent power on the absence of "civil war" contradicts the approach of the Nicaragua court, where the preference of governments was manifest – although it was clear that the Nicaraguan situation was beyond the threshold of "domestic unrest." The Contras operated an armed force of 30,000; the conflict in Nicaragua resulted, between 1980 and 1989, in over 40,000 casualties; it had major internal and external effects.[43] And still, the Court did not at all imply that consent power was annulled only on counts of the scale of the conflict.

Gray concedes that the "civil war" threshold is difficult to apply, since states – involved and uninvolved alike – are reluctant to admit that the "legal" threshold of "civil war" has been crossed.[44] As we saw in previous chapters, this difficulty has been a constant feature of the treatment of internal strife since the nineteenth century. In essence, then, relying on the distinction between "domestic unrest" and "civil war" reverts international law to the largely unhelpful discourse of the belligerency doctrine. Just as recognition of belligerency was extremely rare, so it is expected that a positive recognition that a "civil war" exists, in its traditional legal sense, will not be a common occurrence.[45]

Furthermore, the distinction between situations of "war" and those that do not amount to it seems foreign to contemporary law, which emphasizes the factual terms *use of force* and *armed conflict* rather than the technical-legal term of "war."[46] This is a prominent characteristic of both the spheres of *jus ad bellum*[47] and of *jus in bello*.[48] It reflects the attempt to prevent the circumvention of legal obligations through the denial that a legal state of war exists.[49] In light of this development, it is unreasonable that "war" remains a dominant legal term only when assessing the question of consensual intervention.

However, it is possible to reconcile this anomaly, with a slight adjustment of the terms. It seems that when commentators use the term "civil war" as a limitation for consent power, they actually allude to the loss of effective control that "civil war" supposedly entails, rather than to the term "war" in the technical sense. For instance, Schachter uses the term "civil war" interchangeably with terms relating to territorial effectiveness. While

43 *See* Karl R. DeRouen and Heo Uk, Civil Wars of the World: Major Conflicts since World War II 552–553 (2007).

44 Gray, *supra* note 12, at 82.

45 As opposed to the incentive of states to admit that a factual situation of an armed conflict exists. Compare Chapter 2, sec. 4.

46 *Id.*

47 As Article 2(4) of the UN Charter refers to use of force and not to wars. *See* Schachter, *supra* note 42, at 1624.

48 As Common Article 2 to the Geneva Conventions applies in war as well as in "any other armed conflict."

49 *See* Philip M. Brown, Editorial Comment: Undeclared Wars, 33 American Journal of International Law 538 (1939).

sometimes using the "civil war" threshold, he also suggests a clearer contention, asserting that when conflict occurs "on a large scale involving a substantial number of people or control over significance of the country" the preference of government should be revoked.[50] Therefore, in essence, the "active agent" in the negation of consent power, according to this approach, is the loss of territorial control. Thus, limitations on government consent power of this kind should be framed as limitations based on *territorial effectiveness*, rather than limitations based on the confusing classification of a conflict as a "civil war."

In this sense, the position of Wright, according to which "a government, even if generally recognized, cannot speak for the state if it is not *in firm possession of the state's territory*,"[51] represents a doctrinally clearer phrasing, since it highlights territorial effectiveness rather than the technical definition of the conflict as a "war." This is not to say that the territorial effectiveness test is in itself coherent. On the contrary: as mentioned in Chapter 6, it can prove quite paradoxical. For instance, under the territorial effectiveness tests governments could request assistance in the face of "unrest." However, it is unclear why a state, which cannot even deal alone with unrest, would be deemed more effective, in the territorial sense, than a state that requires assistance in the face of a major insurrection.

2.3 The failed state threshold: no government – no preference

A possibly workable threshold – related but distinct from traditional territorial effectiveness tests – is the "failed state" standard. Such a test, at least, provides relatively tangible parameters – although these too suffer from ambiguity, since there is no formal legal definition of the term "failed state." However, at least for the purpose of the assessment of consent power, a failed state can be identified as one in which there is total or near total breakdown of the institutions guaranteeing law and order, even *within* territories controlled by different factions; moreover, a failed state does not have a body capable of representing it internationally by possessing *any* form of legitimacy, be it based on territorial effectiveness, democratic representation or otherwise.[52] In this sense, a failed state is different than the traditional case of "civil war" in which *some* territorial effectiveness is lost in favor of opposition groups.

Indeed, in a situation where it is obvious that there is simply no functioning government at all – which is *at least* capable of expressing a coherent position regarding the conflict – and the state is torn by fluid and unstable warring factions, it is a necessary logical and legal consequence

50 Schachter, *supra* note 42, at 1642.

51 Quincy Wright, United States Intervention in Lebanon, 53 American Journal of International Law 112 (1959), cited in Doswald-Beck, *supra* note 3, at 196. (emphasis added).

52 *See, e.g.*, Daniel Thürer, The "Failed State" and International Law, 81 International Review of the Red Cross 731 (1999).

that – absent unique circumstances – there will be no government preference. If there is no entity physically capable of representing the state internationally, there is no entity that can conclude agreements that form the basis for consensual interventions (or to withdraw from such agreements).

Note that this approach does not attribute significant *normative* value to territorial effectiveness: it merely argues that in a "true" failed state scenario there is absolutely no party that can physically express coherent will. In such cases, it is reasonable that the question of intervention be resolved by the UN or regional organizations, either with UNSC authorization in accordance with Article 53 of the Charter,[53] or, in absence of UNSC authorization, by relying on forward-looking intervention treaties, assuming that these are generally valid.[54] A failed state, in this sense, can be roughly analogized to an unconscious patient undergoing an operation: she has previously authorized the encroachment of her personal autonomy manifested in the operation, but does not possess, in real-time, the physical capacity to withdraw her consent.

Interventions in failed state scenarios – whether based on UNSC authorization or forward-looking treaties – should immediately aim to provide protection to civilians.[55] In parallel to achieving this goal – as might be deduced from state practice – the interveners, in such cases, seek to identify the parties that are capable of concluding an agreement that would reasonably reflect the collective will of the state,[56] thereby, at least *de jure*, rescuing the state from its "failed" status and initializing a transitional period. This is not merely a descriptive analysis of practice: it also seems to best promote the norm of non-intervention. An example for such a role played by a regional organization, in relation to a failed state situation, could be the actions undertaken by ECOWAS in Liberia, after the assassination of President Samuel Doe.[57]

A different but related situation can take place when there are, in principle, functioning institutions, but the various functions of government are split between warring factions, resulting in a conflict between the state institutions themselves. An example of this scenario could be when a president and a prime minister head different factions (for instance, the 1960 Kasavubu-Lumumba conflict in Congo, and to an extent, the Lebanese

53 Wippman, *supra* note 6, at 231.

54 *See* Chapter 8, sec. 3.2; compare Tristan Ferraro, International Commission of the Red Cross, Expert Meeting: Occupation and Other Forms of Administration of Foreign Territory 23 (2012).

55 We shall elaborate on the principle of protection in Chapter 8.

56 David Wippman, Treaty-Based Intervention: Who Can Say No? 62 University of Chicago Law Review 607, 628 (1995).

57 For a detailed survey *see* David Wippman, Enforcing the Peace: ECOWAS and the Liberian Civil War, in Enforcing Restraint: Collective Intervention in Internal Conflicts (Lori Fisler Damrosch ed., 1993) 157, 169–178.

Civil War of 1975–1976).[58] Such situations result, much like in the failed state scenario, in the default of the *de jure* entity of government and thus require a flexible, case-by-case approach by the international community,[59] in which some analysis of the internal-constitutional order of the state cannot be avoided.

In any case, it should be taken into account that – whether pursuing an intervention or not – the contemporary international system does not in practice permit, for long, the *de jure* situation of "failed states;" instead, it prefers to grant recognition to transitional governments, even if – as we shall see – the latter do not exercise territorial effectiveness. It seems that the international legitimacy of such entities rests on the fact that they are products of multilateral reconciliation processes, or otherwise have future prospects to end the conflict and thus promote the protection of civilians. Especially relevant for us is the fact that such governments have also been recognized as possessing consent power. We shall demonstrate this notion in the context of the quintessential failed state – Somalia.

2.4 Beyond the failed state threshold: recognition, intervention, and the role of the UNSC in Somalia

After the 1991 ousting of longstanding autocrat Siad Barre, Somalia has descended into total anarchy. The fractioning of the various militias led, by 1992, to mass killings, starvation and other atrocities.[60] After failing to secure peace and having suffered heavy losses, UN forces withdrew from Somalia in March 1995, in a rare admission of defeat.[61] Somalia has remained in chaos since. Ceasefires and transitional governments did not hold. A regionally sponsored effort, the National Reconciliation Process, resulted in the October 2004 establishment of the Transitional Federal Government (TFG). Exercising no control over Somali territory, but supported by regional powers Ethiopia, Kenya and Uganda, the TFG was initially based in Kenya.

The TFG was controversial from its inception, as the transitional parliament elected a warlord, Abdillahi Yusuf Ahmed, as interim president. Yusuf established a loyalist cabinet, marginalizing and alienating other power wielders – especially those related to Islamist movements shunned

58 Regarding Congo, *See* Anne Orford, International Authority and the Responsibility to Protect 80–87 (2011). Regarding Lebanon, *see* generally Naomi Joy Weinberger, Syrian Intervention in Lebanon: The 1975–1976 Civil War (1986).

59 This was indeed the approach undertaken by the UN in the context of the 1960 situation in Congo. *See* Orford, *supra* note 58, at 82–84.

60 *See* David D. Laitin, Somalia: Civil War, and International Intervention, in Civil Wars, Insecurity and Intervention 146, 147–148 (Barbara F. Walter et al. eds., 1999).

61 *See* S.C. Res. 954, U.N. Doc. S/RES/954 (November 4, 1994).

by Ethiopia.[62] Soon after his election, while his government was still in Kenya, Yusuf appealed for forcible intervention by the African Union (AU) and the UN in order to enter and gain control over the territory of Somalia. The international community, at that stage, was reluctant.[63] In subsequent months, however, the international community gradually and cautiously recognized the TFG.[64]

The TFG entered Somalia in June 2005, amidst a rift among its members, between President Yusuf and representatives of local Mogadishu groups, themselves very loosely aligned, and united only in their rejection of Ethiopian involvement. Because of this split, the TFG could not enter Mogadishu – the traditional capital of Somalia – and had to settle in the city of Jowhar.[65] One of the disputes between the parties related to Yusuf's appeal to the AU and the Horn of Africa's sub-regional organization, the Intergovernmental Authority on Development (IGAD), for assistance. Needless to say, the TFG was completely ineffective at the time. Nevertheless, its request was endorsed by all IGAD members, except Eritrea, and also by the African Union's Peace and Security Council (AUPSC).[66]

However, any intervention in Somalia required UN authorization, because of the longstanding UNSC comprehensive arms embargo.[67] Accordingly, in July 2005 the AU requested the UNSC to grant an exemption from the sanctions regime, a request that was, at that stage, denied. This demonstrates that consensual intervention can be thwarted by a binding UN sanctions regime and reflects a significant limitation on the presumption in favor of governments.[68]

The union of Islamist movements, known as the Islamic Courts Union (ICU) – and the radical jihadist elements within them[69] – emerged in 2005 out of the power vacuum. In June 2006, following heavy fighting in Mogadishu – and while the ranks of the TFG were split – the ICU took control over most of the capital and its surroundings, defeating the US-backed and short-lived Alliance for Restoration of Peace and Counter-Terrorism (ARPCT), which was composed, *inter alia*, of non-Islamist elements of the

62 *See* International Crisis Group, Somalia: Continuation of War by Other Means? 1–5, ICG Africa Report No. 88 (December 21, 2004); International Crisis Group, Can The Somali Crisis Be Contained? 3–4, ICG Africa Report No. 116 (August 10, 2006).

63 Continuation of War by Other Means? *supra* note 62, at 10–11.

64 *Id.* at 18–19. *See also* S.C. Res. 1587, U.N. Doc. S/RES/1587 (March 15, 2005) (commending the support given to the TFG; expecting further steps by it to establish effective governance in Somalia).

65 Can the Somali Crisis be Contained? *supra* note 62, at 4.

66 *Id.*

67 S.C. Res. 733, U.N. Doc. S/RES/733 (January 20, 1992).

68 *See* U.N. Charter, art. 2(5).

69 On the Jihadi elements within the ICU *see* Can The Somali Crisis be Contained? *supra* note 62, at 10–11.

Mogadishu groups. The ICU's victory has placed Mogadishu, for the first time since 1991, under a unified authority.[70]

At the time of the ARPCT defeat, the TFG controlled virtually no territory in the state and had no reasonable prospects to attain such control.[71] By this time international calls to lift the sanctions regime increased, in order to permit assistance to the TFG, and deployment of international forces – although it was rather the ICU that was the most effective force in South Somalia. In parallel, Ethiopian troops were starting to be seen in the Baidoa area (then seat of the TFG), and more were amassed on the border.[72]

As the TFG and its Ethiopian allies were poised for a decisive battle against the ICU, the UNSC authorized international intervention by the IGAD Peace Support Mission in Somalia (IGASOM), while urging dialogue between the TFG and the ICU, and stressing that the Traditional Federal Institutions offered the only route to achieve stability in Somalia. While attempting to maintain a neutral language, IGASOM was mandated to protect the seat of the TFG and to train its security forces. Strictly to that end, the UNSC lifted the arms embargo.[73] It did not explicitly call for the withdrawal of Ethiopian forces.

In December 2006, the Ethiopian army, acting without explicit UNSC authorization and claiming *inter alia* that it was acting in self-defense against "terrorists,"[74] scored an initial military victory over the ICU, with the consent of the TFG and in cooperation with its forces, enabling the TFG to enter Mogadishu. However, the victory resulted in the ICU's splintering into several groups, including Al-Shabaab, a radical group allegedly associated with Al-Qa'ida.

Despite its limited victory, the TFG was unable to substitute the ICU in terms of effective control.[75] In February 2007, the UNSC authorized the deployment of AU troops in Somalia (African Union Mission to Somalia –AMISOM), instead of IGASOM, with a similar mandate – essentially, to support the TFG.[76] Soon enough, the Somali situation deteriorated, as a decentralized Islamist insurgency spread. By 2009, the TFG had control only over Baidoa and certain parts of Mogadishu – and that too depended on strong Ethiopian support. The Islamist splinter groups gradually returned to control almost as much territory as they did prior to the Ethiopian intervention. Under these circumstances, Ethiopia withdrew in 2009,

70 *Id.* at i, 1, 9–14.

71 *Id.* at 8–9.

72 *Id.* at 22.

73 S.C. Res. 1725, U.N. Doc. S/RES/1725 (December 6, 2006).

74 *See* U.N. SCOR, 61st Sess., 5614th mtg. at 3, U.N. Doc. S/PV.5614 (December 26, 2006).

75 International Crisis Group, Somalia: The Tough Part is Ahead 1–2, ICG Africa Briefing No. 45 (January 26, 2009).

76 S.C. Res. 1744, U.N. Doc. S/RES/1744 (February 21, 2007).

leaving the TFG to rely only on the limited capacity of AMISOM for support.[77]

The international response to the intervention by Ethiopia was largely one of acquiescence. During the height of the fighting, in the end of December 2006, the UNSC issued a Presidential Statement urging dialogue, in which Ethiopia was not condemned nor even mentioned.[78] Furthermore, the UNSC's December 2006 decision[79] to lift the arms embargo in order to enable IGASOM – in which Ethiopia is a dominant member – to operate in Somalia, can be seen as a tacit encouragement for Ethiopia's actions. The first action by the UNSC regarding Somalia, after the major battles of late 2006, was two months later: in Resolution 1744, the Council mandated AMISOM, "welcomed" Ethiopia's decision to withdraw, and "underlined" that AMISOM would create the conditions for a full withdrawal.[80] It seems reasonable to assume that Ethiopian forces, to a large extent, paved the way for the deployment of the AU forces that still, as of December 2012, uphold the existence of the Somali authorities.

Eritrea, which supported the TFG's opponents, received a wholly different treatment. A traditional enemy of Ethiopia, Eritrea sought to curb the latter's ambitions in Somalia by supporting the ICU and, after its dissolution, the Islamist factions. For instance, during 2005 and 2006, Eritrea delivered arms shipments to the TFG's rivals.[81] Recall that in international law, arms transfers to opposition groups can amount to forcible intervention, and thus the Eritrean actions could constitute a forcible consensual intervention in favor of an opposition group.[82] The UNSC, in Resolution 1907, demanded that "Eritrea cease all efforts to destabilize or overthrow, directly or indirectly, the TFG" and imposed sanctions on it.[83]

Despite its lack of control, the TFG continued to entrench its position vis-à-vis the international community as the only viable and recognizable government of Somalia. As the TFG's foreign minister remarked earnestly, "It can be argued that the *very existence* of the TFG, under the circumstances, is a clear plus."[84] It is doubtful that the "very existence" standard is suitable, in all cases, to replace the territorial effectiveness test in the context of recognition and consensual intervention. What is clear, however, is that territorial effectiveness was entirely absent from the

77 International Crisis Group, Somalia: To Move Beyond the Failed State i–ii, ICG Africa Report No. 147 (December 23, 2008).

78 S.C. PRST 59, U.N. Doc. S/PRST/2006/59 (December 22, 2006).

79 S.C. Res. 1725, *supra* note 73.

80 S.C. Res. 1744, *supra* note 76.

81 Can the Somali Crisis be Contained? *supra* note 62, at 20.

82 *See* Military Aid and Paramilitary Activities in and against Nicaragua (Nicar. v. U.S.), 1986 I.C.J. 14 (June 27), ¶238, 247.

83 S.C. Res. 1907, S/RES/1907 (December 23, 2009).

84 U.N. SCOR 65th Sess., 6407th mtg. at 7, U.N. Doc. S/PV.6407 (October 21, 2010) (emphasis added). Note that in September 2012 new Somali authorities replaced the TFG, as Somalia's transitional period ended.

discourse of government recognition in the Somali context, and in the analysis of the capacity of the rival forces to request, consent or acquiesce to external forcible support.[85] It follows that simple territorial effectiveness thresholds are not sufficient to explain modern international practice regarding government consent power, and that other considerations come into play.

3 Counter-intervention: a defense claim for loss of effective control over territory

Even those that limit consent power to situations that do not amount to "civil wars," or otherwise base such limitations on territorial effectiveness standards, usually concede that when a civil war, or loss of territorial effectiveness, is fomented by external intervention, the government too is entitled to receive assistance.[86] This is the well-established doctrine of "counter-intervention" which, as noted in Chapter 6, has been frequently invoked (and abused) in the Cold War era.[87] Indeed, even when one subscribes to a very strict understanding of the concept of consensual intervention – meaning, to strict-abstentionism – there is merit in the idea of counter-intervention. This is because when the opposition receives external assistance, it could be said that the first interveners – and the opposition, should it gain control over the state – are *estopped* from invoking the principle of non-intervention against other intervening powers. In addition, from the internal standpoint, the political independence of the peoples in the conflicting state has already been compromised by the first intervention, and therefore the counter-intervention cannot be seen, in itself, as a violation of the norm of non-intervention.

The counter-intervention doctrine is usually understood as permitting intervention in favor of governments. However, approaches such as the 1980's Reagan Doctrine, as discussed in Chapter 6, sought to expand it to justify counter-intervention on behalf of opposition groups.[88] As aforementioned, this idea is in direct contravention to the prohibition on the use of force, and was rejected in the Nicaragua ruling.[89]

While the counter-intervention doctrine certainly maintains its theoretical vigor, in practice, it was particularly important in the colonial and

85 *See also*, in this context, the 2012 Kenyan intervention in Somalia, undertake, inter alia with reference to the TFG's consent, as discussed in Chapter 1, sec. 1.2.

86 *See* Gray, *supra* note 12, at 92–98; *see* generally Wright, *supra* note 51.

87 See, generally, John A. Perkins, The Right of Counterintervention, 17 Georgia Journal of International and Comparative Law 171, 171–173 (1987); for a summary of some Cold War era consensual interventions augmented by claims of counter-intervention *see* Doswald-Beck, *supra* note 3, at 213–242.

88 *See also* Perkins, *supra* note 87, at 221–224 (supporting counter-intervention in favor of insurgents).

89 Chapter 6, sec. 4.3.

Cold War eras, in which many internal conflicts were actually proxy wars in the struggle between the main powers, or concealed attempts to preserve colonial rule.[90] Nevertheless, in legal terms, the claim of counter-intervention can still be raised both by beleaguered governments and intervening powers as a defense-claim, when confronted with effectiveness-based rebuttals of the presumption in favor of governments.[91]

It should be added that a formalistic reading of the counter-intervention principle might lead to the conclusion that any such action must be proportional to the original intervention.[92] Ethically, as suggested by Walzer, counter-intervention aims at "preserving the balance, restoring some degree of integrity to the local struggle."[93] Thus, according to this logic, if the first intervention included a non-forcible act such as transfers of funds, so must the counter-intervention be limited to such acts. The Nicaragua Court alluded to this principle.[94] However, it did so in the context of *cross-border* counter-interventions – instances in which a state, or its ally, claims the right to intervene in another state, in response to an intervention by the latter in its own or in *another state's* internal affairs. This differs from situations in which a counter-intervention is pursued strictly within the territory of the victim state.

In instances where the first intervention amounts to a "less grave" use of force, such as arms transfers, the Court took an even narrower approach, ruling that "less-grave" forcible interventions, which are not "armed attacks," do not justify a response consisting of "less grave" forcible interventions by the victim state's allies into the territory of the first intervening state; the rationale being that any use of force, grave or less grave, is conditioned upon the occurrence of an "armed attack."[95] In essence, such understanding of the counter-intervention doctrine results in its complete merger with the idea of collective self-defense, since it allows for forcible cross-border counter-intervention only when the first intervention amounts to an armed attack by the intervening state.

It is doubtful, however, whether the rationale requiring strict proportionality in counter-intervention can unequivocally apply also to counter-interventions that take place strictly within the territory of the victim state.

90 On the Cold War "proxy-war" phenomenon *see* Ann Hironaka, Neverending Wars: The International Community, Weak States and the Perpetuation of Civil War 104–130 (2005). A classic case for an attempt to preserve colonial domination through "internal" conflicts is the Katanga affair of 1960. *See* Orford, *supra* note 58, at 69–79.

91 But *see* Schachter, *supra* note 42, at 1642.

92 *See* Perkins, *supra* note 87, at 178–180.

93 Michael Walzer, Just and Unjust Wars 97 (4th ed, 2006).

94 Nicaragua, *supra* note 82, ¶210.

95 *Id.* ¶¶211, 247–249. For a similar view *see* Schachter, *supra* note 42, at 1643; but *see* John Norton Moore, The Secret War in Central America and the Future of World Order, 80 American Journal of International Law 43, 105–106 (1986). For the distinction between "grave" and "less-grave" uses of force *see* Chapter 3, sec. 2.2.

This is so, since such a limitation will essentially terminate the presumption in favor of governments, by effectively equalizing its position to the externally supported opposition. Furthermore, there is also no conclusive evidence in state practice that counter-interventions have been required to mirror the scope of the first intervention.[96]

The "territorial" limitation on counter-intervention, set forth by the Nicaragua majority, was heavily challenged in the dissenting opinion of Judge Schwebel, not only on counts of his objection to the characterization of "indirect aggression" as not amounting to an "armed attack,"[97] but also by his understanding of state practice as allowing counter-interventions to "spill" over to the territory of the first intervener.[98] The gist of this controversy is rooted in the understanding of the distinction between the related – but different – claims of counter-intervention and collective self-defense.

The right of collective self-defense, as enshrined in Article 51 of the UN Charter, is usually understood as the right of states to request assistance against an *external* armed attack, whether committed by a state or, possibly, by a non-state actor.[99] The counter-intervention doctrine, conversely, connotes a situation in which a government requests external intervention to suppress an *internal* element *supported* by an *external* party, perhaps through "less grave" uses of force. To the extent, however, that the involvement of the external party in the actions of the internal element amounts to an armed attack, and is of such character that it creates state-attribution, then the claim of counter-intervention merges with the claim of collective self-defense.[100] In such cases, it is both logical and reasonable that the assisting state, as part of the collective self-defense operations, can attack the territory of the external state.[101] It is plain that such operations must adhere to the proportionality and necessity limitations on the exercise of self-defense enshrined in customary international law.[102] Thus, the legality of a counter-intervention that "spills" into the first intervening state's territory is influenced by our perception of what constitutes an armed attack.

96 Schachter, *supra* note 42, at 1644.

97 Nicaragua, *supra* note 82, ¶¶174–176.

98 *Id.* ¶¶217–220 (Scwebel, J., dissenting).

99 The question of the right to self-defense, as enshrined in Article 51, against armed attacks by non-state actors in the course of a transnational armed conflict, is controversial. The majority opinion of the ICJ, in the Wall advisory opinion, was that such right against non-state actors, and in particular in cases of occupation, does not exist. Legal Consequences of the Construction of a Wall in the Occupied Palestinian Territory, Advisory Opinion, 2004 I.C.J. 136 ¶139 (July 9) (Koroma, J.). Judge Higgins, in her separate opinion, rejected this interpretation. *Id.* ¶¶33–34 (Higgins, J.) For a critique of the reasoning of the majority *see* Sean D. Murphy, Self-Defense and the Israeli Wall Advisory Opinion: An Ipse Dixit from the ICJ? 99 American Journal of International Law 62 (2005).

100 *See* Oscar Schachter, International Law in Theory and Practice 159 (1991).

101 *See* Perkins, *supra* note 87, at 207–209.

102 On these principles *see, e.g.,* Yoram Dinstein, War, Aggression and Self-Defense 242–278 (5th ed. 2011).

Another parallel that can be drawn from the proximity of collective self-defense and counter-intervention is the requirement of consent. Just as collective self-defense, as held in Nicaragua, requires consent by the attacked state, the question of counter-intervention must be analyzed through the framework of consent: a state that embarks on a counter-intervention must also have the genuine consent of the "victim" government. Indeed, this notion runs contrary to the idea, sometimes invoked, of counter-intervention as a "right" or "entitlement" of third states.[103] However, such reasoning belongs to an era in which internal conflicts were analyzed mainly according to their effects over external parties, or on counts of some vague normative meaning attributed to the "global balance of power."[104] Nowadays, in the era of the prohibition on the use of force, intervention can be judged only in terms of conferral of authorization or, as we shall see, on counts of "responsibility" – and not in terms of a "right" of an intervener. Since the legality of intervention, almost always,[105] must be a corollary of the rights of the internal entities, a "right" of counter-intervention cannot be asserted in a paternalistic fashion, independent from the consent of the internal actors.[106] As such, intervention should always be analyzed in terms of principal-agency relationship, rather than strictly as a relationship between two (or more) parties bearing "regular" and equal contractual rights.[107]

Last – and importantly – the traditional doctrine of counter-intervention cannot be used as a valid defense claim when the challenges to the government preference are based on *substantive* issues, as opposed to claims based on the technical loss of territorial effectiveness. For instance, if a government commits mass atrocities, it would not be able to rely strictly on the doctrine of counter-intervention as a source of consent power. This conclusion is augmented, of course, when the first intervention was authorized by a Chapter VII resolution – as was in the case of Libya in 2011.[108]

103 *Compare* Perkins, *supra* note 87, at 171–173 (and the sources cited therein).

104 *Compare id.* at 180–183, 195.

105 A possible exception is the right to intervene for the protection of nationals abroad, which is based on the interests of the intervener rather than on those of the territorial state; and the right of self-defense against non-state actors.

106 *Compare* Wippman, *supra* note 6, at 220–221. Moreover, a violation of the balance of power cannot be viewed, in itself, as a breach of an *erga omnes* obligation entitling external parties to intervene when not requested to do so. *Compare* Perkins, *supra* note 87, at 211–212.

107 *See* Chapter 1, sec. 2.1.

108 *See* Chapter 10.

8 From effective control over territory to effective protection of civilians

1 The emergence of protection of civilians as a fundamental principle of international law

With the collapse of the Iron Curtain, and the initial embrace of liberal-democracy by the ex-eastern bloc states, the promotion of "democracy" has become predominant in the international discourse on intervention.[1] Gradually, however, the mass atrocities of the 1990s forced a robust pre-occupation with the protection of civilians, a concept more basic and primordial.[2] The question of democracy and intervention will be mainly addressed within our debate of "democratic entitlement" in Chapter 9. However, we will do so in light of the realization explored in this chapter: that the principle of protection of civilians ("the principle of protection") has been elevated, in the last two decades, to a paramount principle of international law.

The rise of the principle of protection is mainly a product of recent decades. For instance, a striking aspect of the early instruments of IHL, such as those adopted in the Hague conferences of 1899 and 1907, is the absence of explicit reference to the protection of civilians in armed conflicts. However, the reality of warfare throughout the twentieth century has changed radically. The percentage of civilian deaths in armed conflicts – and particularly in internal conflicts – steadily climbed up to an overwhelming majority by the 1990s.[3] The increasing practical need for protecting civilians has been supplemented by changes in the understanding of different international norms. These changes have been labeled as

1 *See* Gregory H. Fox and Brad R. Roth, *Introduction: The Spread of Liberal Democracy and its Implications for International Law, in* Democratic Governance and International Law 1, 1–25 (Gregory H. Fox and Brad R. Roth eds., 2000); Tom J. Farer, *Humanitarian Intervention Before and After 9/11, in* Humanitarian Intervention: Ethical, Legal and Political Dilemmas 53, 56 (J.L. Holzgrefe and Robert O. Keohane eds., 2003).

2 *See* Ruti G. Teitel, Humanity's Law 3–4 (2011).

3 Simon Chesterman, *Introduction: Global Norms, Local Contexts, in* Civilians in War 1, 1–2 (Simon Chesterman ed., 2001).

a "humanization" of law[4] – perhaps giving rise to a corpus of "humanity law"[5] – a process in which humanitarian considerations have gained increasing prominence within the balance of the competing interests protected in various legal arrangements. Throughout the twentieth century, and in particular in the last decades, this process can be exemplified in several milestones.

First, the principle of protection has been enshrined in the fourth Geneva Convention of 1949, and significantly in the Additional Protocols of 1977,[6] particularly in the basic principles of distinction and proportionality.[7] Second, the binding nature of IHL in internal armed conflicts has been clearly established. Traditionally, the application of the "laws of war" in internal armed conflict has been seen as voluntary, to be applicable only on counts of "reciprocity and reason,"[8] or as binding only in cases of belligerency recognition.[9] Common Article 3 of the Geneva Conventions, supplemented by Additional Protocol II, have entrenched the binding application of *at least* the basic norms of IHL to all internal armed conflicts.[10] In this context, although Common Article 3 and Additional Protocol II are thin instruments in comparison to those regulating international armed conflicts, there is growing convergence between the customary norms covering all kinds of conflicts – international, transnational or internal – and especially those of a humanitarian nature.[11] This convergence is evident, for instance, in the study of the International Committee of the Red Cross on customary IHL, where many of the customary rules have been found, in essence, equally applicable to all conflicts.[12]

Third, since the 1948 Universal Declaration of Human Rights and, more significantly, since the coming into force of major human rights conventions (the International Covenant on Civil and Political Rights

4 *See* Theodor Meron, *The Humanization of Humanitarian Law*, 94 American Journal of International Law 239 (2000).

5 See generally Teitel, supra note 2.

6 See Karma Nabulsi, Evolving Conceptions of Civilians and Belligerents: One Hundred Years after the Hague Peace Conferences, in Civilians in War, supra note 3, at 9.

7 Protocol Additional to the Geneva Conventions of 12 August 1949, and Relating to the Protection of Victims of International Armed Conflicts (Protocol I), June 8, 1977, arts. 50–51, 1125 U.N.T.S. 3.

8 See The Prize Cases, 67 U.S. 635, 667–669 (1862).

9 See supra, Chapter 4, sec. 3.2.

10 Prosecutor v. Tadic, Case No. IT-94-1-I, Decision on Defence Motion for Interlocutory Appeal on Jurisdiction ¶¶96–97 (International Criminal Tribunal for the Former Yugoslavia October 2, 1995); Anthony Cullen, The Concept of Non-International Armed Conflict in International Humanitarian Law 25–113 (2010).

11 On the convergence between regimes regulating international and internal armed conflicts *see* Tadic, *supra* note 9, ¶¶100–127; on transnational armed conflicts, *see* Noam Lubell, Extraterritorial Use of Force against Non-State Actors 131–134 (2010).

12 See, generally, Jean-Marie Henckaerts and Louise Doswald-Beck, International Commission of the Red Cross, Customary International Humanitarian Law (2007); *see also* Meron, *supra* note 4, at 261–263.

(ICCPR) and the International Covenant on Economic, Social and Cultural Rights (ICESCR)), the obligation to protect human rights has for the first time enshrined the protection of *individuals* – rather than sovereigns – in the international realm.[13] In this context, and supplementing the convergence between the *jus in bello* applicable to international and internal conflicts, another normative convergence has emerged: the drawing closer of IHL and IHRL.[14] In the *Nuclear Weapons* advisory opinion, the ICJ has ruled that IHL and IHRL are not mutually exclusive, and that IHRL, as the *lex generalis,* applies also during armed conflict. The same notion was expressed, in the context of occupation, in the *Wall* advisory opinion and in the case of DRC v. Uganda.[15]

Recent literature points out the difficulties in the application of the *lex generalis/lex specialis* distinction, and suggests that IHRL be seen instead as *complementary* to IHL.[16] However we see the specific nature of the relation between IHL and IHRL, it is clear that their dual-application reflects that the protection of individuals has become an integral, predominant part of the law of armed conflict at large; and accordingly – and perhaps more obviously – also of the law of internal armed conflict.[17]

Fourth, the preoccupation with the protection of civilians is expressed in the development of international criminal law, through the establishment of ad hoc international tribunals in the former Yugoslavia (ICTY) and Rwanda (ICTR), and the permanent International Criminal Court, all mandated to adjudicate crimes by and against individuals.[18]

Fifth, since the 1990s, UNSC practice has reflected a widening interpretation of the Council's mandate – authorizing the imposition of enforcement measures, inter alia, in cases of threat to the peace – as extending to

13 *See, e.g.,* The Independent International Commission on Kosovo, The Kosovo Report 168–169 (2000).

14 For an in-depth analysis of this process *see* Meron, *supra* note 4, at 244–247, 266–273.

15 Legality of the Threat or Use of Nuclear Weapons, Advisory Opinion, 1996 I.C.J. 226, ¶25 (July 8); Legal Consequences of the Construction of a Wall in the Occupied Palestinian Territory, Advisory Opinion, 2004 I.C.J. 136, ¶106 (July 9); Armed Activity on the Territory of the Congo (D.R.C. v. Uganda), 2005 I.C.J. 168, ¶¶216–220 (December 19).

16 Noëlle Quénivet, The History of the Relationship Between International Humanitarian Law and Human Rights Law, in International Humanitarian Law and Human Rights Law: Towards a New Merger in International Law 1, 9–10 (Roberta Arnold and Noëlle Quénivet eds., 2008).

17 For an analysis of IHRL and IHL in internal armed conflicts *see* Lindsay Moir, The Law of Internal Armed Conflict 193–210 (2003). Such dual-application is more "obvious" in internal conflicts since in such contexts the question of extra-territorial application of human rights law does not surface. *See, e.g.,* Wall Opinion, *supra* note 15, at ¶¶109–112.

18 On the International Criminal Court, *see* generally William A. Schabas, An Introduction to the International Criminal Court (2011).

situations that are largely confined to the borders of a single state, such as internal armed conflicts.[19]

Sixth, in the last decade, African regional organizations – that operate in the most strife-torn parts of the world – have increasingly stressed the concept of "non-indifference" to mass atrocities, as supplementing the norm of non-intervention. For instance, as discussed in Section 3.3, Article 4(h) of the Constitutive Act of the African Union, and its subsequent protocol, authorize the Union to intervene in member states in cases of mass atrocities.[20]

By the late 1990s, thus, the principle of protection has broken the boundaries of IHL, and began to emerge as a general principle of the international system. The atrocities in Iraq (1991), Rwanda (1994), Bosnia (Srebrenica, 1995) and Kosovo (1998)[21] – the latter resulting in NATO's controversial unilateral intervention – have brought the principle of protection, and its means of implementation, to the forefront of international concern. Indeed, NATO's bombing campaign in Kosovo has been a watershed moment regarding the principle of protection.[22] After Kosovo, it became obvious, in light of the previous failures of the international system,[23] that a robust international consideration of the question of civilian protection must take place; and that otherwise, the entire order of the UN Charter would be put at risk. This development was the backdrop to the intense debate regarding the concept of unilateral *humanitarian intervention*, which will be addressed in Chapter 10. Significantly, the atrocities committed in the 1990s have compelled the international community – now largely free from zero-sum Cold War considerations – to distance itself from the idea that "impartiality" towards internal crises was an absolute value, and to recognize that there are indeed instances in which local parties can be identified, in principle, as aggressors and victims.[24] The

19 Report of the International Commission on Intervention and State Sovereignty, The Responsibility to Protect ¶4.23, 6.16 (2001) [hereinafter ICISS Report]; Georg Nolte, Secession and External Intervention, in Secession: International Law Perspectives 65, 67 (Marcelo G. Kohen ed., 2006); Anne Orford, International Authority and the Responsibility to Protect 168–169 (2011).

20 *See also* U.N. Secretary General, Implementing the Responsibility to Protect: Report of the Secretary General, ¶8 U.N. Doc. A/63/677 (January 12, 2009).

21 U.N. Secretary General, Report of the Secretary General to the Security Council on the Protection of Civilians in Armed Conflict ¶31 U.N. Doc. S/1999/957 (September 8, 1999).

22 *See* The Kosovo Report, *supra* note 13, at 191; *see also* Jane Stromseth, Rethinking Humanitarian Intervention: The Case for Incremental Change, in Humanitarian Intervention: Ethical, Legal and Political Dilemmas, *supra* note 1, at 232, 232–233.

23 *See, e.g.*, Report of the Independent Inquiry into the Actions of the U.N. during the 1994 Genocide in Rwanda, U.N. Doc. S/1999/1257 (December 15, 1999); U.N. Secretary General, Report of the Secretary General Pursuant to General Assembly Resolution 53/35: The Fall of Srebrenica, U.N. Doc. A/54/549 (November 15, 1999).

24 *See* Orford, *supra* note 19, at 8; *see also* The Kosovo Report, *supra* note 13, at 189–190; Jennifer Welsh, Civilian Protection in Libya: Putting Coercion and Controversy Back into RtoP, 25 Ethics and International Affairs 1, 4–6 (2011).

decline of the notion of impartiality has intertwined with the shift in the function of international bodies, taking place since the 1960s, from serving mainly as treaty-making forums to resembling, to some extent, an international executive or *administrative* system.[25] In recent years, literature has taken this process a step further: identifying the emergence of similar transnational "administrative" relations between states themselves and between states and citizens of *other* states.[26]

In light of the processes outlined above, the UNSC has considered, since 1999, the protection of civilians in armed conflicts as a thematic issue.[27] Reports by the UNSG, submitted as part of these discussions, have identified the principle of protection as a main tenet of international peace and security, and recommended various measures to be taken by the UNSC to promote this principle, including, in certain situations, forcible enforcement measures.[28] The reports have thus urged the promotion of a "culture of protection," focused on the individual rather than on the state, whose "primary function" is to ensure the security of the civilian population.[29] They presented a "roadmap" for the promotion of protection,[30] and have recognized that the principle of protection emerges from a wide body of positive international law, comprising of IHL, international criminal law, IHRL and refugee law.[31] All in all, the UNSG's reports contain over a hundred recommendations for the promotion of protection,[32] which are categorized according to "five core challenges" required to be met in order to ensure the *effective protection* of civilians.[33]

Some of the UNSG's recommendations were reflected in general and forward-looking UNSC resolutions such as resolutions 1265 (1999), 1296 (2000), 1674 (2006), 1738 (2006) and 1894 (2009). Significantly, resolution 1296 affirmed that peacekeeping forces should be granted mandates

25 For a detailed account of this process *see* generally Orford, *supra* note 19.

26 As part of the idea of Global Administrative Law *see* sec. 2.2.

27 S.C. Prst. U.N. Doc. S/PRST/1999/6 (February 12, 1999).

28 Report of the Secretary General, *supra* note 21, ¶¶27–28, 35–67; endorsed in S.C. Res 1265, U.N. Doc. S/RES/1265 (September 17, 1999).

29 U.N. Secretary General, Report of the Secretary General to the Security Council on the Protection of Civilians in Armed Conflict ¶¶1–5, 7, U.N. Doc. S/2001/331 (March 30, 2001). For subsequent reports *see* U.N. Doc. S/2002/1300 (2002); S/2004/431 (2004); S/2005/740 (2005); S/2007/643 (2007); S/2009/277 (2009); S/2010/579 (2010).

30 U.N. Secretary General, Report of the Secretary General to the Security Council on the Protection of Civilians in Armed Conflict ¶6, U.N. Doc. S/2002/1330 (November 26, 2002).

31 U.N. Secretary General, Report of the Secretary General to the Security Council on the Protection of Civilians in Armed Conflict ¶34, U.N. Doc. S/2005/740 (November 28, 2005).

32 U.N. Secretary General, Report of the Secretary General to the Security Council on the Protection of Civilians in Armed Conflict ¶9, U.N. Doc. S/2009/277 (May 29, 2009).

33 U.N. Secretary General, Report of the Secretary General to the Security Council on the Protection of Civilians in Armed Conflict ¶43, U.N. Doc. S/2010/579 (November 11, 2010).

to actively protect civilians in danger.[34] Accordingly, mandates of numerous peacekeeping operations were broadened to include such activities.[35] Resolution 1674 reaffirmed the principle of protection, the broadening of mandates of UN missions, and for the first time, endorsed the "responsibility to protect" (RtoP) doctrine – which we shall discuss later on.[36]

Since the principle of protection itself is theoretically free from "political" pretext (as it is not necessarily connected to a specific form of government), it enjoys relatively wide credibility across states with different political cultures and systems.[37] The "primary" legal validity of the principle of protection – in distinction from the "secondary" methods to *implement* it, which remain controversial – has thus emerged as a rare normative consensus in the international community.[38] Indeed, the major disagreement does not concern the validity of the principle itself, but is reflected, for instance, in China and Russia's persistent positions that the principle should not, in general, be promoted through forcible intervention.[39]

In light of all of the above, it seems that collective *opinio juris* has elevated, in the last two decades, the principle of protection of civilians to the same plateau of basic principles of international law such as sovereignty, territorial integrity, non-intervention and the prohibition on the use of force, effectively complementing and redefining them.

Indeed, the principle of protection has affected UNSC authorized interventions conducted, in practice, in favor of beleaguered governments. As such, it has direct bearing on our understanding of the law of consensual intervention. For instance, in 2009, forcible support given to the DRC by UN Forces (MONUC) was heavily criticized, due to the Congolese military's alleged involvement in serious IHL violations. In response, the UNSG instructed MONUC not to support DRC forces where there are grounds to believe that IHL and IHRL violations will take place and to only support operations that were jointly planned.[40] A subsequent UNSC resolution urged the DRC to "effectively protect" the civilian population;[41] and mandated MONUC, in cooperation with the DRC, to ensure such effective protection, strictly conditioning MONUC's support upon the former's compliance with international law.[42]

34 S.C. Res. 1296, U.N. Doc. S/RES/1296, ¶13 (April 19, 2000).

35 *See* U.N. Secretary General, Report of the Secretary General to the Security Council on the Protection of Civilians in Armed Conflict ¶8, U.N. Doc. S/2004/431 (May 28, 2004).

36 S.C. Res. 1674, U.N. Doc. S/RES/1674, ¶4 (April 28, 2006).

37 Compare Alex J. Bellamy, Responsibility to Protect 26–57 (2009).

38 *See* Thomas G. Weiss, RtoP Alive and Well after Libya, 25 Ethics and International Affairs 1, 5(2011); Jennifer Welsh, *supra* note 24, at 1.

39 *See, e.g.*, U.N. SCOR, 54th Sess., 3977th mtg., U.N. Doc. S/PV.3977, 14–15, 29–30 (February 2, 1999).

40 U.N. Doc. S/2010/579, *supra* note 29, ¶¶63–64.

41 S.C. Res 1906, ¶3, U.N. Doc. S/RES/1906 (December 23, 2009).

42 *Id.* ¶22.

In addition, the UN is undertaking a process to outline general "conditionality policies" regarding forcible support granted to governments by UN forces, in order to ensure the protection of civilians.[43] This process implies that intervention, in contemporary international law, is intertwined with the concept of effective protection of civilians. Indeed, beyond the obvious moral virtues of the principle, it is also a relatively definable, objective and tangible threshold for the assessment of internal armed conflicts.

2 From effective control to effective protection: protection as a component of sovereignty

2.1 The emergence of the responsibility to protect

Until now, we have mainly demonstrated the international preoccupation with the principle of protection. In parallel, a no-less important development has been taking place – *effective protection* has come to be viewed as an integral component of sovereignty, through the concept of the Responsibility to Protect (RtoP).[44]

The 1999 NATO intervention in Kosovo has not only invigorated the international consideration of civilian protection as a concept, but also the debate regarding the means for the principle's enforcement – namely, concerning the legality or legitimacy of unilateral humanitarian intervention. In response to calls by UNSG Kofi Annan, Canada has established the International Commission on Intervention and State Sovereignty (ICISS), mandated to clarify the connection between intervention, civilian protection and sovereignty.[45] ICISS published its landmark report in 2001, calling for the endorsement of the concept of RtoP.[46] Echoing the influential ideas of Francis Deng, the report's main premise was its reading of the UN Charter, and its understanding of emerging state practice, as connoting a shift in the perception of sovereignty: "*from sovereignty as control to sovereignty as responsibility.*"[47]

This "responsibility," according to the ICISS report, is to "protect" human security; it lies first and foremost with the territorial state, but when the latter is unable or unwilling to fulfill it, or is itself perpetrating atrocities against individuals under its control, the responsibility shifts to the international community. The responsibility, according to ICISS, is

43 S/2010/579, *supra* note 29, ¶65.

44 On the nuances in the UN discourse between Protection of Civilians (PoC) and RtoP *see* Welsh, *supra* note 24, at 2–3.

45 For the background on ICISS and its discussions, *see* Bellamy, *supra* note 37, at 35–51.

46 ICISS Report, *supra* note 19, at 1–3.

47 *Id.* ¶2.14. This concept was first proposed, in such words, in Francis Deng et al., Sovereignty as Responsibility 1–2 (1996). For a wider discussion of the principles of the ICISS Report *see* generally Gareth Evans, The Responsibility to Protect: Ending Mass Atrocity Crimes Once and For All (2008).

comprised of three elements: the responsibility to prevent, to react and to rebuild.[48] These responsibilities, and in particular the responsibility to react, override the norm of non-intervention, in the strict understanding of the term, in cases of violence that "shock the conscience of mankind."[49] Accordingly, the report laid down six criteria for military intervention, which correspond, at large, to classic just-war theory conditions.[50]

Under the "just-cause" condition for intervention, the report referred to cases of large-scale loss of life or ethnic cleansing, actual or *apprehended.*[51] Significantly, such cases include, *inter alia,* "state collapse" that leads to starvation or "civil war," and overwhelming natural or environmental catastrophes.[52] Moreover, the report stressed that causes for intervention do not distinguish between state action, deliberate inaction or failure.[53] However, the report excluded, as grounds for *military* intervention, violations of human rights falling short of "outright killing or ethnic cleansing," such as systematic racial discrimination, or the overthrow of democratic regimes.[54]

The report acknowledged that forcible intervention as part of the RtoP concept must be authorized by a Chapter VII UNSC resolution.[55] However, it recognized the problematic "capricious use" of the Permanent Five's veto power as a major potential inhibition to international action.[56] It then proceeded to suggest modes of action "when the Security Council fails to act." These included UNGA actions under the "Uniting for Peace" procedure,[57] which could add "a high degree of legitimacy" (in distinction from legal authorization) to military intervention;[58] and actions by regional organizations, that receive *ex post* authorization by the UNSC, such as was the case regarding the 1990s ECOWAS interventions in Liberia and Sierra Leone.[59]

The Commission then issued two "important messages" to the UNSC:[60] first, that if it fails to act, it is inevitable that concerned states will act

48 ICISS Report, *supra* note 19, at ¶¶2.29–2.33.
49 *Id.* ¶4.13.
50 *Id.* ¶4.16 et seq. These criteria are right authority; just cause; right intention; last resort; proportional means and reasonable prospects.
51 *Id.* ¶4.19.
52 *Id.* ¶4.20.
53 *Id.* ¶4.22.
54 *Id.* ¶¶4.25–4.26. Interestingly, regarding cases of coup d'états against democratic government, the Report recognizes that in such cases the overthrown government may request forcible intervention. This situation is discussed in Chapter 9.
55 *Id.* ¶¶6.14–6.15.
56 *Id.* ¶6.20.
57 *Id.*; Uniting for Peace, G.A. Res. 377(V), U.N. Doc. A/377 (November 30, 1950).
58 ICISS Report, *supra* note 19, ¶6.30.
59 *Id.* ¶¶6.31–6.35. It should be noted that nowadays, actions by regional organizations can be viewed as consensual interventions based on forward-looking intervention treaties, in regions where such are concluded. *See* sections 3.3–3.4.
60 ICISS Report, *supra* note 19, ¶6.38.

unilaterally, a process which will potentially lead to adverse results; and second, that if such interventions are successful, the credibility of the UN as a collective system will be seriously damaged.[61]

Some of the ICISS Report's recommendations were included in the conclusions of the UN's High Panel on Threats, Challenges and Change of 2004. In particular, the Panel endorsed "the emerging norm that there is a collective international responsibility to protect, exercisable by the UNSC authorizing military intervention as a last resort," in cases of mass atrocities.[62] The general idea of the RtoP concept has been endorsed unanimously in Paragraphs 138–139 of the 2005 World Summit Outcome Document (WSOD), adopted by the General Assembly.[63] Paragraph 138 refers to the responsibility of the individual state, and Paragraph 139 refers to situations in which a state fails to fulfill its responsibilities, and these shift to the international community, acting through the UN.

Paragraph 138 thus recognizes that each state has the responsibility to protect its populations from genocide, war crimes, ethnic cleansing and crimes against humanity ("the four crimes"); and that the international community should "encourage and help States to exercise this responsibility." By focusing strictly on the four crimes, and excluding, for instance, "natural or environmental catastrophes," the WSOD has narrowed the concept as it was presented in the ICISS report. Paragraph 139 acknowledges that when states manifestly fail to protect their populations from the four crimes, the responsibility extends to the international community, acting through the UN, including – as a last resort – by forcible measures authorized by the UNSC. As opposed to the ICISS Report, paragraph 139 excluded an explicit reference to *apprehended* failure to protect as a potential cause for intervention, although it includes a pledge to assist "those which are under stress before crises and conflicts break out." Notably, paragraph 139 lacks any reference to the UNSC's "capricious veto" problem, and thus reaffirms the Council's monopoly over the authorization of forcible intervention.[64]

Its limitations notwithstanding, the adoption of the WSOD solidified the understanding of sovereignty as the responsibility to effectively protect civilians.[65] It is for this reason that it was heralded by the UNSG as a "cardinal achievement" of particular significance.[66] However, this process was

61 *Id.* ¶¶6.39–6.40.

62 Note by the Secretary General ¶203, U.N. Doc. A/59/565; *see also* U.N. Secretary General, In Larger Freedom: Towards Development, Security and Human Rights for All ¶135, U.N. Doc. A/59/2005 (March 21, 2005).

63 2005 World Summit Outcome, G.A. Res. 60/1, U.N. Doc. A/60/L.1 (September 15, 2005).

64 This reflects the concerns of many states that RtoP would be used to disguise the controversial claim that a "right" of extra-charter humanitarian intervention be recognized. *See* Orford, *supra* note 19, at 24–25.

65 Implementing RtoP, *supra* note 20, at ¶10.

66 U.N. Doc. S/2007/643, *supra* note 29, ¶11.

not uncontroversial. For instance, it was only after six months of intense debate in which reluctant states, such as China and Russia, expressed discomfort with the concept, that paragraphs 138–139 of the WSOD were endorsed in UNSC Resolution 1674 of 2006.[67] Moreover, in 2006–2007, the RtoP concept has been heavily questioned in UN forums, namely by some Arab and Asian states, in particular regarding the events in Sudan.[68] Nevertheless, the principle was reaffirmed in UNSC Resolution 1706 concerning Darfur;[69] and in subsequent years it seems that RtoP came to be generally accepted.[70]

In parallel, many states – both developed and developing, and in particular African states – began to refer to RtoP in their statements in front of various forums.[71] In 2009, in Resolution 1894 concerning the protection of civilians, the UNSC once again reaffirmed paragraphs 138–139 of the WSOD.[72] In the same year, the UNGA debated the RtoP concept and called for its continuing consideration.[73] The implementation of the concept was further discussed in "informal dialogues."[74] As part of this process, the UNSG issued annual reports regarding the implementation of the RtoP concept. In his 2009 report, UNSG Ban Ki-moon phrased RtoP as encompassing three pillars: (1) the protection responsibilities of the state; (2) international assistance and capacity building (which, of course, augments the concept of government consent power); and (3) the issue of timely and decisive response, which encompasses both non-forcible to forcible measures.[75] His 2012 report, "focusing on timely and decisive response,"[76] noted that in recent years "the responsibility to protect has been invoked in more situations than ever before,"[77] and emphasized that the concept also places an onus on the international

67 S.C. Res. 1674, *supra* note 36.

68 *See* Alex J. Bellamy, Global Politics and the Responsibility to Protect 28–31 (2011). Interestingly, it seems that the Arab States, acting through the Arab League, have in practice endorsed the idea of RtoP, for instance, when suspending Syria from the League and issuing an ultimatum to the Assad regime during the Syrian conflict of 2011–2012. *See* Arab League Deadline for Syria Action Passes, B.B.C. News, November 19, 2011, www.bbc.co.uk/news/world-asia-15802312.

69 S.C. Res. 1706, U.N. Doc. S/RES/1706 (2006) (August 31, 2006); *see also* Implementing RtoP, *supra* note 20, ¶¶1–3.

70 Bellamy, *supra* note 68, at 31–36.

71 *Id.* at 17–19.

72 S.C. Res. 1894, U.N. Doc. S/RES/1894 (November 11, 2009).

73 G.A. Res. 63/308, U.N. Doc. A/RES/63/308 (October 7, 2009).

74 U.N. Secretary General, The Role of Regional and Subregional Arrangements in Implementing the Responsibility to Protect, U.N. Doc. A/65/877 (June 28, 2011).

75 Implementing RtoP, *supra* note 20, ¶11; *see also* The Role of Regional and Subregional Arrangements, *supra* note 74.

76 U.N. Secretary General, Responsibility to Protect: Timely and Decisive Response, U.N. Doc. A/66/874 (July 25, 2012).

77 *Id.* ¶49.

community – including while intervening under Chapter VII – to exercise "responsibility while protecting."[78]

Indeed, in 2011 RtoP has been first incorporated into significant, operational UNSC resolutions. It has been referred to in resolutions concerning the 2011 crisis in Libya, *inter alia* authorizing forcible intervention,[79] as well as in the resolution reiterating the mandate for forcible actions in Côte d'Ivoire.[80] These will be discussed later in this work. For now, suffice it to say that in both cases, the mandates granted for the protection of civilians were interpreted widely – too widely in the eyes of some[81] – resulting eventually in the removal of an unrecognized leader (in Côte d'Ivoire),[82] and the widespread withdrawal of recognition from another, eventually leading to his ouster (in Libya).[83] It is also of special significance that Resolution 1973, authorizing intervention in Libya, was the first time that forcible intervention in an internal armed conflict, for the sake of civilian protection, was authorized *against* the will of a functioning government.[84]

2.2 The normative significance of RtoP: affecting effectiveness

RtoP undoubtedly presents a rather thin legal framework, surrounded by an environment of robust policy considerations. As noted by the UNSG, paragraphs 138–139 of the WSOD reflect *already existing* principles and obligations of international law regarding protection of civilians.[85] Moreover, the paragraphs do not challenge the monopoly or the wide discretion of the UNSC regarding the authorization of forcible action. Thus, there is considerable disagreement whether RtoP has any novel legal-

78 A concept introduced by Brazil. *Id.* ¶¶50–58.

79 S.C. Res. 1970, U.N. Doc. S/RES/1970 (February 26, 2011) (imposing sanctions on Libya); S.C. Res. 1973, U.N. Doc. S/RES/1973 (March 17, 2011) (authorizing forcible intervention in Libya); *see also* Michael W. Doyle, The Folly of Protection, Foreign Affairs (March 20, 2011), www.foreignaffairs.com/articles/67666/michael-w-doyle/the-folly-of-protection; but *see* Welsh, *supra* note 24, at 1.

80 S.C. Res. 1975, U.N. Doc. S/RES/1975 (March 30, 2011) (recalls and stresses the mandate of the force in Cote d'Ivoire to protect civilians). RtoP language has also been used in a Draft Resolution concerning the situation in Syria, vetoed by Russian China. *See* Draft Resolution by France, Germany, Portugal and the U.K., U.N. Doc. S/2011/612 (October 4, 2011).

81 For a discussion *see* Mehrdad Payandeh, The U.N., Military Intervention and Regime Change in Libya, 52 Virginia Journal of International Law 355, 383–391 (2012).

82 Xan Rice and Nicholas Watt, Ivory Coast's Laurent Gbagbo Arrested, Guardian, April 11, 2011, www.guardian.co.uk/world/2011/apr/11/ivory-coast-former-leader-arrested.

83 Sebnem Arsu and Steven Erlanger, Libya Rebels Get Formal Backing, and $30 Billion New York Times, July 15, 2011, www.nytimes.com/2011/07/16/world/africa/16libya.html.

84 *See* Alex J. Bellamy, Libya and the Responsibility to Protect: The Exception and the Norm, 25 Ethics and International Affairs 1, 1 (2011).

85 Implementing RtoP, *supra* note 20, ¶¶2–3.

normative significance.[86] For instance, the responsibility of third parties to "prevent and to punish" genocide is already well established in international law;[87] similarly, states are also already obliged to "ensure respect" for the laws of the Geneva Conventions.[88] Some commentators therefore went as far as concluding that RtoP is merely "political rhetoric."[89]

Furthermore, RtoP has been criticized substantively from various angles. On the one hand, it has been labeled as ambiguous lip-service that will not promote international efforts against atrocities; on the other, it was attacked as a new cover for imperialist interventionism.[90] Some have even blamed the concept for *promoting* genocide by creating a moral hazard.[91] However, these critiques are not particularly well based. The "lip-service" claim seems to contradict emerging international practice, such as in the case of Libya, and perhaps also in Kenya.[92] The accusations of "imperialism" seem contradictory to the fact that African states – hardly the usual suspects for neo-imperialism – have been major supporters of RtoP;[93] it also cannot serve to explain the Arab League's support of the 2011 RtoP intervention in Libya.[94] Last, the moral hazard argument can serve to reject any form of international involvement which deviates from a *laissez faire* approach towards mass atrocities, and in any case has not been empirically validated.[95]

Although novel legal obligations, in the strict sense, are not explicitly entrenched in "official" RtoP documents, the concept still has potential

86 *See* Carlo Focarelli, The Responsibility to Protect Doctrine and Humanitarian Intervention: Too Many Ambiguities for a Working Doctrine, 13 Journal of Conflict and Security Law 191 (2008); Amrita Kapur, Humanity as the A and Ω of Sovereignty: Four Replies to Anne Peters, 20 European Journal of International Law 560 (2009); for a summary of these claims *see* Orford, *supra* note 19, at 22–24.

87 Convention on the Prevention and Punishment of the Crime of Genocide, art. I, December 9, 1948, 78 U.N.T.S. 277.

88 Common Article I, Geneva Conventions of 1949.

89 Carsten Stahn, Responsibility to Protect: Political Rhetoric or Emerging Legal Norm? 101 American Journal of International Law 99 (2007); *see also* Simon Chesterman, "Leading from Behind": The Responsibility to Protect, the Obama Doctrine and Humanitarian Intervention after Libya, 25 Ethics and International Affairs 1, 3 (2011).

90 Orford, *supra* note 19, at 22–23 (addressing such arguments); *see* generally Ramesh Thakur, The Responsibility to Protect: Norms, Laws and the Use of Force in International Politics ch. 10 (2010).

91 For a critical response to the "moral hazard" claim *see* Bellamy, *supra* note 68, at 71–73.

92 *See* Serena K. Sharma, The 2007–08 Post-Election Crisis in Kenya: A Success Story for the Responsibility to Protect? in The Responsibility to Protect: From Principle to Practice 27 (Andre Nollkaemper and Julia Hoffman eds., 2012).

93 The AU adopted a common position endorsing the RtoP concept. *See* African Union, The Common African Position on the Proposed Reform of the U.N.: The Ezulwini Consensus (March 7–8, 2005); cited in Orford, *supra* note 19, at 19; *see also* Ademola Abass, The African Union and the Responsibility to Protect: Principles and Limitations, in The Responsibility to Protect: From Principle to Practice, *supra* note 92, at 132.

94 Weiss, *supra* note 38, at 5.

95 Bellamy, *supra* note 68, at 73–74.

for legal significance.[96] First, it serves as a clear-cut statement by the international community that internal situations, even when lacking tangible cross-border effects, are indeed of international interest, and are also within the mandate of the UNSC.[97] As such, RtoP, although expressed in a non-binding UNGA resolution, reflects an interpretation of the UN Charter that arguably ends the longstanding debate regarding the relations between UNSC authority – considered by some to extend only to issues of *international* peace and security – and *internal* crises such as internal armed conflicts. Likewise, it reinforces the understanding of the interaction between enforcement measures and the norm of non-intervention, enshrined in Article 2(7) of the UN Charter, as not precluding Chapter VII actions regarding internal conflicts. Orford, borrowing from H.L.A. Hart, labels this aspect of RtoP as a "power-conferring" form of law, which allocates jurisdiction or power – in the administrative sense – rather than a "duty imposing" norm.[98]

Second, RtoP can serve to aggregate and consolidate various existing international norms of civilian protection under a common theoretical wing – where the concept of sovereignty as responsibility is understood as a basic principle to which major *interpretational* value should be attributed.[99] This value can serve, for instance, to advance the equal and like application of the principle of protection to *all* types of armed conflicts: international, internal or transnational.

Third, RtoP explicitly shifts the debate from the permissive "rights" of external parties – namely, the "right to intervene" – to *responsibilities* accrued towards the civilian population of the target state. Thus, in contradistinction to the doctrine of "humanitarian intervention," discussed in Chapter 10, RtoP refocuses the attention on the rights of internal parties.[100] This is indeed an important development: even the proponents

96 For a detailed discussion of the various aspects of this question, *see* generally The Responsibility to Protect and International Law (Alex J. Bellamy et al. eds., 2010); Cristina G. Badescu, Humanitarian Intervention and the Responsibility to Protect 130–135 (2010); The Responsibility to Protect: From Principle to Practice, *supra* note 92, chs. 6–10.

97 Previously, there was a tendency by some commentators to justify UNSC action with regards of internal situations on counts of cross-border flow of refugees. *See* J.L. Holzgrefe, The Humanitarian Intervention Debate, in Humanitarian Intervention: Ethical, Legal and Political Dilemmas, *supra* note 1, at 15, 42–43.

98 *See* Orford, *supra* note 19, at 25–27; for the traditional approach, compare Lori Fisler Damrosch, Commentary on Collective Military Intervention to Enforce Human Rights, in Law and Force in the New International Order 219 (Lori Fisler Damrosch and David Scheffer eds., 1991); compare also Doyle, *supra* note 79.

99 Compare Orford, *supra* note 19, at 42–108.

100 On humanitarian intervention as a "right" *see* Dino Kritsiotis, *Reappraising Policy Objections to Humanitarian Intervention*, 19 Michigan Law Review 1005, 1027 (1998); *compare* ICISS Report, *supra* note 19, at ¶¶2.28–2.29.

of the "right of humanitarian intervention" define it as an "imperfect right" possessed by the intervener,[101] which is closer, in legal theory, to a "freedom" – since it is not accompanied by a clearly defined obligation owed by anyone.[102] The definition of humanitarian intervention as a "freedom" is inconsistent with a principled approach that should be the basis of any legal doctrine of intervention.[103] Therefore, RtoP's emphasis on the term "responsibility" potentially provides a more principled framework, less sensitive to the whims or self-arrogated "rights" of external parties.[104] In essence, it reflects a transition from a perception of the international community as comprised of self-interested unitary actors, acting to fulfil their "rights" – perhaps in a manner similar to individuals acting in the realm of private law[105] – to a system in which actors on the international level play a role which is closer to that of an administrative or executive function, perhaps acting as public-global trustees.[106]

Fourth, and most significant to our context, RtoP solidifies the understanding of the international community that sovereignty means *responsibility* rather than the ability to exercise territorial effective control. As such, it can alter our understanding of the concept of recognition in international law, as well as other concepts of law that traditionally attribute much importance to territorial effectiveness. Accordingly, it can explain and justify substantive preference given to one side over the other in an internal armed conflict.[107] We shall explore this notion in the next sections.

In sum, RtoP, in its legal sense, is a concept that represents the aggregation of all existing normative and institutional obligations enshrining the basic principle of protection of civilians; serves to bridge between these obligations and the understanding of sovereignty and its traditional corollary of non-intervention; and clarifies the authority to act in accordance with the emerging "administrative" role of international bodies.

101 *See* Holzgrefe, *supra* note 97, at 24 n. 40.

102 *See* Wesley Hohfeld, Fundamental Legal Conceptions (Arthur Corbin ed., 1978).

103 On the need to adopt a principled approach in this context *see* The Kosovo Report, *supra* note 13, at 190–192.

104 Thomas Poole, *Sovereign Indignities: International Law as Public Law,* 22 European Journal of International Law 351, 353–354 (2011) (explaining, albeit critically, the concept of "responsibility" as a characteristic of administrative functions).

105 A notion classically expressed in the famous Louts case. S.S. Lotus (Fr. v. Turk.) 1927 P.C.I.J. Ser. A-No. 10 (September 7).

106 *See* Orford, *supra* note 19, at 42–47; in this sense, the discourse of "responsibility" can be placed within the emerging perception of global administrative law (GAL). *See* Benedict Kingsbury *et al.*, *The Emergence of Global Administrative Law,* 68 Law and Contemporary Problems 15, 17 (2005); *see also* Eyal Benvenisti, *Sovereigns as Trustees of Humanity: The Minimal Other-Regarding Obligations,* SSRN Working Paper (June 11, 2011), *available at* http://papers.ssrn.com/sol3/papers.cfm?abstract_id=1863228; *see also* Jeremy Waldron, The Rule of International Law, 30 Harvard Journal of Law and Public Policy 15 (2006); *compare* Poole, *supra* note 104, at 351.

107 Orford, *supra* note 19, at 9–10.

2.3 Absence of effective protection and negation of government consent power

With the transformation of sovereignty – from a term connoting effective physical "control" over territory, which generates, in and of itself, a right to exercise *further* control, to one that spawns a responsibility to protect civilians – change must also follow in the understanding of *normative* effectiveness: meaning, control of the type that positively affects the recognition of rights and powers of entities engaged in internal armed conflicts.[108] Since effectiveness, as a technical term, is necessary for any entity's mere physical capacity to protect civilians, the concept of sovereignty as responsibility compels us to *reformulate* the doctrine of effectiveness rather than to abandon it.[109] Thus, the perception of effectiveness can be shifted from its traditional understanding as connoting *effective control over territory*, to one which refers to the *effective protection of civilians*. In this sense, the effective control and effective protection principles share one characteristic: both focus chiefly on the way power is used rather on the way it was initially appropriated.[110]

For instance, while autocracy was always a feature of the Al-Assad regime in Syria, its international legitimacy, in the strict sense, was never substantially challenged. Only after its military crackdown in the context of the uprising of 2011–2012 – allegedly amounting to a violation of the protection principle[111] – did the US, Canada and major EU powers assert that the regime has "lost its legitimacy," and that Al-Assad "can no longer claim to lead the country."[112] Turkey – previously a staunch ally of Al-Assad – went further by issuing a stern warning to the latter, threatening that "[i]f these operations do not stop there will be nothing left to say about the

108 Interestingly, this notion has been experienced at the grassroots level. As noted in the US Army's counterinsurgency manual, "In the eyes of some, a government that cannot protect its people forfeits the right to rule. Legitimacy is accorded to the element that can provide security, as citizens seek to ally with groups that can guarantee their safety." U.S. Army, Counterinsurgency ¶1–43 (2006).

109 *Compare* Martti Koskenniemi, The Politics of International Law 46 (2011).

110 For this distinction *see* Jean d'Aspremont and Eric De Brabandere, *The Complementary Faces of Legitimacy in International Law: The Legitimacy of Origin and the Legitimacy of Exercise,* 34 Fordham International Law Journal 190 (2010).

111 *See, e.g.*, U.N. Human Rights Council, *Report of the Independent International Commission of Inquiry on the Syrian Arab Republic,* ¶126, U.N. Doc. A/HRC/19/69 (February 22, 2012) (finding that the Syrian Government "has manifestly failed in its responsibility to protect its people").

112 Chris McGreal and Martin Chulov, *Syria: Assad Must Resign, Says Obama,* Guardian, August 18, 2011, www.guardian.co.uk/world/2011/aug/18/syria-assad-must-resign-obama; *Canada PM Joins Obama in Calling for Syrian Leader to Resign,* Wall Street Journal, August 18, 2011, http://online.wsj.com/article/BT-CO-20110818–710297.html.

steps that would be taken."[113] Here, we see that the attitude towards the Syrian regime was shaped, in general, in light of its exercise of power rather than on counts of its longstanding autocratic nature. The same dynamic was also prevalent concerning the autocratic Al-Qadhafi regime in Libya. Only during the 2011 internal armed conflict, and following the atrocities committed against civilians, Russia, the US and the UK claimed that the regime has "lost legitimacy."[114] While these declarations did not amount, at the time, to a formal withdrawal of recognition – they nevertheless highlighted the role of effective protection as a main component of legitimacy.[115]

Thus, effective protection can be a major factor when assessing the rights and powers of parties to internal armed conflicts;[116] among these powers, the absence of effective protection can adversely affect the government's legal capacity to express consent to external intervention. The perception of sovereignty as responsibility challenges therefore the traditional doctrines, discussed in previous chapters, which limit government consent power strictly on counts of territorial effective control, while providing a relatively tangible standard for the analysis of governmental behavior. Territorial effective control, conversely, can affect consent power only to the extent that it reflects the actual or potential exercise of effective protection of the civilian population.

However, it should be emphasized, that the concept of effective protection does not substitute the consent of the governed as a source of sovereign legitimacy; as discussed in section 2.5, it is merely a key consideration when considering *intervention.*

2.4 Effective protection and augmentation of government consent power

The notions of effective protection and RtoP, it should be emphasized, do not serve only to *limit* governmental consent power. Pillar 2 of the RtoP concept ("international assistance and capacity building"), as suggested by the UNSG and reflected in paragraph 138 of the WSOD, revolves around

113 Zvi Bar'el and Reuters, *Turkey FM Issues "Final Words" Calling on Syria to Halt Violent Crackdowns,* Haaretz, August 15, 2011, www.haaretz.com/news/middle-east/turkey-fm-issues-final-words-calling-on-syria-to-halt-violent-crackdowns-1.378777; *Arrest Warrant Shows Gaddafi Lost Legitimacy,* Reuters, June 27, 2011, www.reuters.com/article/2011/06/27/us-libya-usa-whitehouse-idUSTRE75Q51A20110627.

114 Henry Meter, *Russia Says Qaddafi Has Lost Legitimacy to Govern, Joining Support of NATO,* Bloomberg, May 27, 2011, www.bloomberg.com/news/2011–05–27/russia-seeking-to-negotiate-qaddafi-exit.html; *William Hague: "Gaddafi's Regime Has Lost Legitimacy,"* B.B.C. News, March 29, 2011, www.bbc.co.uk/news/uk-12901453/.

115 On the distinction between longstanding autocracies such as Syria or Libya, and revolutionary autocracies *see* Chapter 9, sec. 1.2.

116 For a comparable analysis, grounding the rights of parties in internal armed conflicts on counts of protection, *see* Orford, *supra* note 19, at 109–139 (linking this concept to works by Thomas Hobbes and Carl Schmitt).

an opposite premise: that states should assist other states in fulfilling their duties under RtoP.[117] This notion was already implied in the 2000 Kosovo Report, which viewed humanitarian intervention, when conducted with government consent, as raising "no legal problem."[118]

It is not hard to imagine a situation, for instance, in which a government that exercises, in general, effective protection – or at least shows reasonable prospects and motivation to do so – is confronted by an opposition group that is regularly engaged in atrocities, and has also caused the government to lose some territorial effective control.[119] In such cases, should a government request forcible support, the international community – separately and together – might acquire some *responsibility* to assist it;[120] in any case, it would be fully justified in doing so. Some have even gone as far as arguing that the state itself has the responsibility to request assistance in such circumstances.[121] Significantly, such responsibilities to assist may arise even before UNSC action. This is since Paragraph 138 deals with state responsibilities prior to UN involvement. This conclusion is fortified by the fact that in the global consultations preceding the ICISS report, it was widely recognized that when the UNSC fails to act in the face of atrocities, host-state consent – and in particular when given to regional organizations – provides an alternative legal justification for intervention.[122]

For the existence of such a consent-augmenting situation, in which external parties may accrue the responsibility to assist, the consenting government need not be a perfect democracy. It suffices that it protects civilians in the specific context. This is evident in contemporary dilemmas. For instance, in July 2011, the UN declared that a famine existed in Somalia.[123] However, since 2009, an opposition group – Al-Shabaab – has banned food aid from areas under its control.[124] In these circumstances, and although Somalia is ruled, *de jure*, by a territorially ineffective government, should the latter request help to secure the delivery of aid, it is

117 *See* Bellamy, *supra* note 68, at 37–38. As stated in ¶138 of the WSOD, *supra* note 63: "[t]he international community should, as appropriate, encourage and help States to exercise this responsibility."

118 The Kosovo Report, *supra* note 13, at 193.

119 A possible example is the Ugandan Lord's Resistance Army. An arrest warrant against five Lord's Resistance Army was issued by the ICC in late 2005. *See* Press Release, Warrant of Arrest Unsealed against Five LRA Commanders (October 13, 2005). The UNSC has also named the LRA specifically as a target of enforcement operations. *See* S.C. Res. 1991, U.N. Doc. S/RES/1991 (June 28, 2011) ¶¶13–14.

120 Bellamy, *supra* note 37, at 23, 147–149; Bellamy, *supra* note 68, at 37–38.

121 *See* Bellamy, *supra* note 37, at 150 (citing UN officials that have expressed this idea.)

122 *Id.* at 47–48. The consultations involved academics, government representatives and NGOs. *Id.* at 38.

123 *U.N. Declares Somalia Famine in Bakool and Lower Shabelle*, B.B.C. News, July 20, 2011, www.bbc.co.uk/news/world-africa-14211905.

124 *Somali Islamists Maintain Aid Ban and Deny Famine*, B.B.C. News, July 22, 2011, www.bbc.co.uk/news/world-africa-14246764.

reasonable that a claim regarding its territorial ineffectiveness will not be heard, since the issue of protection of civilians is at stake. This situation can be a prime example in which effective protection trumps territorial ineffectiveness.

This notion constitutes, therefore, a complete reversal of the traditional territorial effective-control doctrine: if, in the past, lack of such effective-control was seen as a liability, in the contemporary system, in some cases, it might be understood as generating a certain *entitlement* for assistance.[125] It all rests upon the question whether the government requests assistance for the purpose of fulfilling its protection responsibilities.

2.5 Effective protection, human rights and democracy: protection now, democracy later

In essence, the reliance on the principle of protection as a determinant of consent power is closely related to human rights and "democracy" thresholds. However, it remains significantly different. Indeed, human rights are indivisible, but most of them are not absolute. Some can be derogated from in times of emergency, providing that the derogation is proportional and non-discriminatory.[126] Others are subject to intricate internal balancing with other rights and public interests.[127] Because of their complex nature, it is almost certain that all states can be deemed, in certain aspects, violators of human rights. It is thus doubtful whether a vague invocation of the general concept of "human rights" can affect the laws on the use of force. As noted by Henkin, in another context, "if it were permissible to remedy them [violations of human rights] by external use of force, there would be no law to forbid the use of force by almost any state against almost any other."[128] For similar reasons, the implementation of a human right in a specific instance necessarily draws us into extensive debates about cultural and political context, whether we like it or not.[129]

125 Whether such entitlement creates a "perfect" or "imperfect" obligation, or, in legal terms, a right that creates a legal claim vis-à-vis a specific actor, is a complex question that will not be addressed here. Suffice it to realize that loss of effectiveness is no longer considered a liability for the sake of consent power. On perfect and imperfect duties *see* Holzgrefe, *supra* note 97, at 26 n. 40.

126 International Covenant on Civil and Political Rights art. 4(1), December 16, 1966, 999 U.N.T.S.. 171.

127 *See, e.g., id.* art. 19, protecting the right to freedom of expression, which contains both the entrenchment of the right, and its lawful limitations.

128 Louis Henkin, How Nations Behave: Law and Foreign Policy 145 (1979); *cited in* Holzgrefe, *supra* note 97, at 24.

129 *See generally* Negotiating Culture and Human Rights (Lynda S. Bell *et al.* eds., 2001); Allen Buchanan, *The Legitimacy of International Law, in* The Philosophy of International Law 79, 94–96 (Samantha Besson and John Tasioulas eds., 2010).

The principle of protection, conversely, focuses on the core values that law protects during armed conflict. In this sense, it is minimalist.[130] In contrast to human rights law, it does not aspire to create an ideal society, or even an entirely decent society; it aspires to put an expedient end to atrocities. This in no way implies that protection trumps the consent of the governed as the main source of sovereignty. Indeed, effective protection, in the narrow sense, cannot and should not be viewed as the ultimate sought-after end result for the relevant internal order. It does not aim to establish an absolutist Leviathan designed to protect the lives of otherwise rights-less subjects.[131] It is merely the minimum result sought *during* an internal armed conflict, when the protection of civilians is the primary objective of the international community. Indeed, as phrased already in the eighteenth century by Vattel, "the flames of discord and civil war are not favourable to the proceedings of pure and sacred justice: more quiet times are to be waited for."[132]

It is in this context that we should understand also the role of *democracy* and the question of consensual intervention, as opposed to the role of protection of civilians. While the establishment of substantive democracy must be a main element of post-conflict rebuilding, at the time of intervention, effective protection should be the main guiding principle.[133] Indeed, effective protection can be also rationalized on the premise that those who protect civilians during conflict are more likely to establish or maintain a democratic, human rights protecting government afterwards. We shall elaborate more on the connection between these values in Chapter 9.

The two-tiered, "protection now, democracy later," approach of the international community can be exemplified in the UNSC's treatment of the 2011 intervention in Libya. It is revealing, in this regard, to compare Resolution 1973, authorizing forcible intervention *during* the Libyan armed conflict, and Resolution 2009, adopted after the fall of the Al-Qadhafi regime, which mainly dealt with the post-conflict period.[134]

130 *Compare* Michael Walzer, *The Argument about Humanitarian Intervention*, 49(1) Dissent (2002) (arguing that humanitarian interventions are best served by a "minimalist version of human rights," regarding which there is sufficient understanding across the globe). It might be interesting to compare between the notion of effective protection as a condition for consent power and the Rawlsian idea of "decent peoples." *See* John Rawls, The Law of Peoples 59–78 (1999).

131 On the relation between Hobbesian theory and the principle of protection *see* Orford, *supra* note 19, at 109–125.

132 Emmerich De Vatell, The Law of Nations ¶295 (1758, 1797).

133 In the RtoP discourse, promotion of democracy can be perhaps considered a part of the international community's "responsibility to rebuild". *See* Bellamy, *supra* note 37, at 59. On related questions of transitional strategies *see, e.g.*, Michael W. Doyle and Nicholas Sambanis, Making War and Building Peace: U.N. Peace Operations 303–334 (2006); *see also* Jus Post Bellum: Towards a Law of Transition from Conflict to Peace (Carsten Stahn and Jann K. Kleffner eds., 2008).

134 S.C. Res 1973, *supra* note 79; S.C. Res. 2009, U.N. Doc. S/RES/2009 (September 16, 2011) ¶20.

Resolution 1973, while authorizing the use of all necessary measures to protect civilians (excluding occupation)[135] did not bind – beyond vaguely referring to the need to respond "to the legitimate demands of the Libyan people" – the objectives of subsequent military operations with the enforcement of electoral democracy.[136] Resolution 2009, conversely, greatly emphasized the promotion of democracy and human rights. It reaffirmed that the UN should "lead the effort of the international community in supporting the Libyan-led transition and rebuilding process aimed at establishing a democratic, independent and united Libya," and further stressed the need for "a commitment to democracy, good governance, rule of law and respect for human rights."[137]

Similarly, the 32-state Contact Group on Libya, in a July 2011 statement recognizing the opposition as the government of Libya, seemed to have granted its recognition based on considerations of protection of civilians, while reserving the development of representative government to a later stage.[138] It is thus clear that the Council, and the international community, saw the protection of civilians as the key factor in the moment of intervention, while leaving the question of democracy to the post-conflict environment, where deliberation and other non-forcible processes prevail.

3 Effective protection and withdrawal of consent

3.1 Withdrawal of consent as a near-absolute right

The discussion of the scope of consent power necessarily entails also the analysis of the capacity to *withdraw* such consent. This issue is relevant when consent is given ad hoc, but is more acute in situations in which consent was given through a general, forward-looking intervention treaty. As we shall see, the concept of effective protection – besides affecting consent-capacity – can also play a role in the assessment of withdrawal-capacity.

Recall, that Article 3(e) of the Definition of Aggression provides that the term *aggression* includes "[t]he use of armed forces of one State which are within the territory of another State with the agreement of the receiving State, in contravention of the conditions provided for in the agreement or any extension of their presence in such territory beyond the termination of the agreement."[139] Thus, when consent is withdrawn, and

135 *Id.* ¶4.

136 *Id.* ¶2.

137 S.C. Res. 2009, *supra* note 134, prmbl., ¶2.

138 Republic of Turkey, Ministry of Foreign Affairs, Fourth Meeting of the Libya Contact Group Chair's Statement, 15 July 2011, Istanbul, *available at* www.mfa.gov.tr/fourth-meeting-of-the-libya-contact-group-chair_s-statement_-15-july-2011_-istanbul.en.mfa.

139 Definition of Aggression, G.A. Res. 3314 (XXIX), ¶3(e), UN Doc A/9631 (December 14, 1974).

absent other justifications such as self-defense, the principal-agent relation between the parties lapses, and the intervention becomes an act of aggression.

An illustrative example can be found in the events that unfolded in the second Congolese conflict of 1998. As discussed in Chapter 1,[140] on July 27, 1998, President Kabila "terminated" the consensual presence of Rwandan forces in the DRC, proclaiming that "[t]his marks the end of the presence of all foreign military forces in the Congo."[141] Rwanda and Uganda, present in the DRC since the first Congolese conflict, refused to withdraw their forces, leading to the eruption of major hostilities. On these counts, the DRC sued Uganda in the ICJ, and claimed, *inter alia*, that Uganda's actions constituted aggression.[142]

It was not contested that Kabila consented to the Rwandan and Ugandan intervention.[143] However, the parties were at odds regarding the existence of consent following Kabila's declaration of July 27. Uganda claimed that the declaration did not explicitly mention the withdrawal of Ugandan forces, but was addressed only to Rwandan forces, and thus was not sufficient to constitute a withdrawal of consent.[144] The ICJ rejected this claim, holding that absent any specific terms, "no particular formalities" are required for a withdrawal of consent to forcible intervention.[145] The Court also stressed that the original consent given to Uganda was not "open ended." The Court held that "at the latest" the DRC's consent was withdrawn by August 8, 1998 (two weeks after Kabila's somewhat ambiguous declaration), when the DRC openly accused Uganda of invading its territory.[146]

When reading the Court's treatment of the issue of consent, the question arises whether a case exists, in which consent can indeed be "open ended." The answer seems to be negative. Dinstein, for instance, argues that withdrawal is always possible, even in breach of a previous treaty – as long as the state still has an effective government capable of withdrawing the consent. His conclusion is based on the logic of effectiveness, and the peremptory *jus cogens* status of the prohibition on the use of force. Once the consent is withdrawn, the argument goes, a violation of Article 2(4) occurs *notwithstanding* any treaty, since treaty provisions cannot contravene *jus cogens*.[147] A comparable claim was made, for instance, by Cyprus, when

140 *See* Chapter 1, sec. 3.2.

141 Armed Activities on the Territory of the Congo (D.R.C. v. Uganda), 2005 I.C.J. 168 (December 19) ¶49.

142 *Id.* ¶¶43, 45.

143 *See id.* ¶43.

144 *See id.* ¶50.

145 *Id.* ¶51.

146 *Id.* ¶¶52–53.

147 Yoram Dinstein, War, Aggression and Self-Defense 122–124 (5th ed. 2011).

Turkey invoked the 1960 Treaty of Guarantee to justify its 1974 invasion of Cyprus.[148]

Wippman similarly argues that authorizations of forcible intervention are agreements of a special type: they concern the core of a state's sovereignty and independence, and since they deal with the use of force, they also affect the interests of the international community as a whole. Thus, an implicit "right of revocation" should be read into any intervention agreement.[149] Indeed, these positions correspond with the view expressed in Chapter 1, according to which intervention treaties, in essence, create a revocable principal-agent relationship.[150] However, as we shall see in section 3.5, the principle of effective protection, just as it affects consent power, can also have bearing on withdrawal power.

3.2 Consent and forward-looking intervention treaties

The question of withdrawal of consent is especially challenging in the context of *forward-looking intervention treaties*. Such agreements are ones in which states, whether acting bilaterally or within the framework of a regional organization, grant external parties a forward-looking permission to intervene forcefully in their territories, in the event that certain *internal* circumstances occur. It is important to distinguish between such agreements and collective self-defense agreements, such as North Atlantic Treaty, which strictly address *external* threats to a member state.[151]

Forward-looking intervention treaties have been common since the eighteenth century, shifting forms along with the changes in the international system.[152] Nowadays, the internal circumstances addressed by such treaties may refer, namely, to instances where a government commits mass atrocities; when a democratic regime is overthrown; when state-failure occurs; or, in less frequent cases, when parties seek an external guarantor for an internal settlement.[153] In general, the rationale of such treaties is to allow reliance on past-consent, in times of crisis, to justify forcible intervention – usually by a regional organization – *absent* UNSC authorization.

Such treaties differ from agreements based on ad hoc consent. They are special in the sense that as opposed to the latter, they are not concluded in relation to a specific event in real-time. They are potentially

148 David Wippman, *Treaty-Based Intervention: Who Can Say No?* 62 University of Chicago Law Review 607, 644 (1995); Treaty of Guarantee, 1960, 382 U.N.T.S. 3.

149 *See* David Wippman, *Pro-democratic Intervention by Invitation, in* Democratic Governance and International Law, *supra* note 1, at 293, 315.

150 Chapter 1, sec. 2.1; *see also* Institut de Droit International, Military Assistance on Request art. 5 (September 8, 2011).

151 *See, e.g.*, North Atlantic Treaty art. 5, April 4, 1949, 34 U.NT.S. 243.

152 *See* Wippman, *supra* note 148, at 613–615.

153 The famous example being the 1960 Cyprus Treaty of Guarantee. *See* Wippman, *supra* note 148, at 633.

applicable to future, hypothetical events. Therefore, they purport to bind the will of current as well as *future* governments. Granted, this is a common occurrence in treaties in general – indeed, the basic rule of continuity of international obligations is founded on this premise[154] – however, it raises unique problems in the context of the use of force.

To be sure, there is considerable debate regarding the legal validity of forward-looking intervention treaties, and in particular concerning the question whether they are void *ab initio* as violations of *jus cogens* norms.[155] The debate recognizes that states have the power to limit their sovereignty by treaty – and can even agree to cease to exist as separate entities by merging with other states. However, the critics ask, does it follow that states can also limit their sovereignty by granting a forward-looking permit for intervention, *irrespective* of the will of a later government in real-time?[156] Indeed, by utilizing *past* consent to intervene forcibly against the ostensible will of the state in real-time, such agreements can be criticized as condoning, in advance, a breach of Article 2(4) of the UN Charter, and thus are contrary to the law on the use of force. Any past consent notwithstanding, these treaties envision a situation in which a forcible intervention will take place absent *real-time* consent.[157] Hence, the argument goes, the treaty *itself* is null and void, as a contravention of *jus cogens.*[158] Furthermore, the critics claim, complete subordination of the state's "political destiny" to foreign powers is in direct conflict with the principle of self-determination.[159]

Notwithstanding the theoretical complexity of the dilemma regarding the *ab initio* validity of forward-looking intervention treaties, the practical problem concerning such treaties can arise mainly in real time, when a government seeks to withdraw its consent in light of an impending

154 The continuity principle binds successor states; *see, e.g.*, Vienna Convention on Succession of States in Respect of Treaties, August 23, 1978, 1946 U.N.T.S. 3; *a fortiori* that it binds new governments. This principle stems from the general separation between internal circumstances and international obligations. *See* The Tinoco Case (Great Britain v. Costa Rica), 1 R.I.A.A. 375, 377, (1923); Vienna Convention on the Law of Treaties arts. 27, May 23, 1969, 1155 U.N.T.S. 331; UN International Law Commission Draft Articles on Responsibility of States for Internationally Wrongful Acts, with Commentaries, art. 3, in Report of the International Law Commission, U.N. GAOR, 53rd Sess., Supp. No. 10, A/56/20 (2001); a possible exception for continuity of governmental obligations is the *odious debt* doctrine. *See* The Tinoco Case, *supra* at 394; Seema Jayachandran and Michael Kremer, *Odious Debt* 96 American Economic Review 82 (2006) (discussing odious debt in the context of the Saddam Hussein regime in Iraq).

155 *See* Wippman, *supra* note 148, at 610–611.

156 *See* Brad R. Roth, *The Illegality of "Pro-Democratic" Invasion Pacts, in* Democratic Governance and International Law, *supra* note 1, at 312–313; *see also* Wippman, *supra* note 148, at 616–620.

157 Louise Doswald-Beck, *The Legal Validity of Military Intervention by Invitation of the Government,* 56 British Year Book of International Law 189, 244–250 (1985).

158 *See* Wippman, *supra* note 149, at 313.

159 *See* Roth, *supra* note 156, at 329, 342.

intervention, and not in the moment of the conclusion of the treaty. Thus, focusing on the capacity of withdrawal in certain circumstances, rather than on the theoretical question of invalidity, allows us to better center the discussion on the core issues of practical importance.[160]

Thus, withdrawal of consent can occur, in practice, in two main situations. In the first, a government might withdraw its past consent in the face of an approaching intervention. In such cases, the question is confined to the capacity of governments – in general and specifically – to do so. This remains the sole question until, for some reason, the government ceases to be recognized, after which it obviously loses its capacity of withdrawal. A prime example of the latter situation is when a government refuses to step down following democratic elections, in which case the international community might withdraw its recognition and transfer it to the elected individual or party.[161] A second situation arises when a government is overthrown, and the de facto junta now claims to have withdrawn the consent of the previous regime. Here, it has to be first determined whether the *junta* is recognized as the new government. If it is not, then the question of withdrawal-capacity is quashed.

The question of real-time withdrawal of consent raises seemingly intractable dilemmas. On the one hand, as aforementioned, withdrawal of consent is virtually an absolute right, and thus, an implicit right of revocation should be read into intervention treaties. These considerations, perhaps, led the Institut de Droit International to opine, in a 2011 resolution, that ad hoc consent is required notwithstanding prior, treaty-based consent – at least in the circumstances addressed by the resolution.[162] On the other hand, the main objective of such agreements is precisely to negate this power in certain situations;[163] a fact that cannot be taken lightly considering that arrangements of this type have been concluded in recent years – as is demonstrated in the next section – by major regional and subregional organizations. Nonetheless, at least in a pure "failed state" scenario, in which no entity would be otherwise capable of expressing ad hoc consent, the case is theoretically simpler: since when there is no government physically capable of withdrawing previous consent, the past-consent remains as it stands. Indeed, if one assumes that in a failed state situation valid consent is impossible, one must reach the same conclusion regarding the power to *withdraw* previous consent.[164] In these instances, the intervening party may be looked upon as acting in trusteeship for the state, until a representative government emerges. In sum, forward-looking intervention

160 *Compare* Wippman, *supra* note 148, at 623.

161 *See* the discussion regarding Côte d'Ivoire, in Chapter 9, sec. 1.3.

162 Military Assistance on Request, *supra* note 50, arts. 4(3), 5. For a discussion of the resolution *see* Chapter 6, sec. 3.1.

163 *See* text accompanying note 150.

164 *See* Dinstein, *supra* note 148, at 122–124; *see also* Chapter 7, sec. 2.3.

treaties remain controversial. As will be suggested later on, however, the concept of effective protection can play a clarifying part in the analysis of this question.

3.3 Forward-looking intervention treaties in Africa

Significant practice of forward-looking intervention treaties can be found, nowadays, in Africa. In the past two decades, such agreements were concluded on the bilateral as well as regional African levels. The Nigerian intervention in Sierra Leone in 1997, in favor of the ousted (and democratically elected) President Ahmed Kabbah, is a prime example of an intervention based on a bilateral forward-looking agreement.[165] In 1997, Sierra Leone and Nigeria signed a Status of Forces Agreement, granting Nigeria the "right" to use force to assist Sierra Leone against "internal or external threats."[166] On May 26, 1997, one day after a junta forced him to flee to Guinea, President Kabbah requested Nigeria to intervene in his favor. Nigerian forces responded, but retreated after confronted with stiff resistance by the junta.[167] Eventually, ECOWAS forces intervened also, by ad hoc request of Kabbah, and expelled the junta.[168]

The Nigerian intervention in Sierra Leone represents the classic dilemma of forward-looking intervention treaties, being a seemingly pro-democratic intervention against the will of a de facto junta – a "revolutionary autocracy," as we shall label such regimes later on.[169] It sheds light, as we shall see in Chapter 9, on the dynamics of forward-looking treaties and recognition, since President Kabbah was still the internationally recognized ruler of the state during the intervention, although he was ousted from the state's territory.[170]

In the first decade of the twenty-first century, forward-looking intervention treaties have become a central pillar of African regional security

165 Other examples are agreements between Senegal, Guinea and Guinea-Bissau, which led to the former's intervention in the latter in 1998. *See* Jeremy Levitt, *African Interventionist States and International Law*, *in* African Interventionist States 15, 28 (Oliver Furley and Roy May eds., 2001).

166 *See id.*, at 24 (quoting from the Status of Forces Agreement Between the Government of the Federal Republic of Nigeria and the Government of the Republic of Sierra Leone Concerning the Provision of Military and Security Assistance to the Republic of Sierra Leone, 1997).

167 *See id.*, at 23.

168 *See id.*, at 23, 25–26. The intervention of ECOWAS here was conducted before the adoption of the ECOWAS Protocol, discussed *infra*; the same is true regarding ECOWAS' intervention in Liberia in 1990. *See* David Wippman, *Enforcing the Peace: ECOWAS and the Liberian Civil War*, *in* Enforcing Restraint: Collective Intervention in Internal Armed Conflicts 157, 166–167 (Lori Fisler-Damrosch,ed., 1993).

169 On the distinction between established and revolutionary autocracies *see* Chapter 9, sec. 1.2.

170 *See* Levitt, *supra* note 165, at 24.

arrangements. Article 4(j) if the Constitutive Act of the African Union, adopted in 2001, entrenches the right of Member States to request intervention from the Union. In addition, Article 4(h) establishes, as a basic principle of the Union, its "right" to "intervene in a Member State pursuant to a decision of the Assembly in respect of grave circumstances, namely war crimes, genocide and crimes against humanity."[171] Note that, excluding "ethnic cleansing," the acts enumerated in Article 4(h) are similar to those referred to in paragraph 138 of the WSOD.[172]

Article 4(j) of the Protocol Relating to the Establishment of the Peace and Security of the African Union, adopted in 2002 (AU Protocol),[173] reflects the arrangement set forth in Article 4(h) of the Constitutive Act. Accordingly, the AUPSC is authorized to recommend to the AU Assembly to undertake intervention, in the enumerated cases,[174] *without* the consent of the target state, which is excluded from voting.[175] The Council is mandated to "take initiatives and action" regarding potential or "full blown" conflicts,[176] and for that purpose the Protocol establishes an "African Standby Force."[177] Interestingly, forcible intervention strictly on pro-democratic grounds (when a *coup d'état* occurs), in absence of other "grave circumstances," is not mandated by the Protocol. In such cases, resort will be to non-forcible measures.[178] This distinction reflects the process outlined above, in which in the moment of intervention, considerations of protection might be of more acute importance than those of electoral democracy.[179] However, in such cases, as we shall see in Chapter 9, since the ousted government might retain its recognition, its consent can authorize, perhaps, such intervention; furthermore, "grave circumstances" are likely to accompany many instances of anti-democratic *coups d'états*.[180]

Intervention treaties can be found also on the African sub-regional level: the 1999 ECOWAS Protocol Relating to the Mechanism for Conflict Prevention, Management, Resolution, Peace-Keeping and Security (Lomé Protocol) sets forth such an arrangement.[181] Articles 21 and 22 permanently

171 Constitutive Act of the African Union arts. 4(h), 4(j), July 11, 2000, 2158 U.N.T.S.. 3. It should be noted, that although it is a significant legal instrument, Article 4(h) has not been invoked as of April 2012. *See* Weiss, *supra* note 38, at 3.

172 This does not imply that the AU excluded ethnic cleansing from the scope of Article 4(h), as the article refers to "grave circumstances" in general.

173 Protocol Relating to the Establishment of the Peace and Security of the African Union, July 9, 2002.

174 *Id.* art. 7(1)(e).

175 *Id.* art. 8(9).

176 *Id.* arts. 9, 15.

177 *Id.* art. 13(1).

178 *Id.* art. 7(1)(g). However, in such cases, since the ousted government might retain its recognition, its consent can legitimize such intervention.

179 *See* sec. 2.5.

180 Chapter 9, sec. 1.

181 ECOWAS Protocol Relating to the Mechanism for Conflict Prevention, Management, Resolution, Peace-Keeping and Security, December 10, 1999 [hereinafter *Lomé Protocol*].

establish the ECOWAS cease-fire Monitoring Group (ECOMOG), a standing intervention force available for immediate deployment. Article 25 stipulates the conditions in which the intervention "mechanism" will apply; among them are instances of "internal conflict" that "threatens to trigger a humanitarian disaster" or that "poses serious threat to peace and security in the sub-region"; and – as opposed to the AU Protocol – "an overthrow or attempted overthrow of a democratically elected government." Importantly, the authority to "initiate" "all forms" of intervention is delegated, in Articles 10 and 26, to various ECOWAS organs, even against the will of the target state or de facto regime.

3.4 Forward-looking intervention treaties as alternatives to security council action

Both protocols discussed above challenge the UNSC's monopoly on the authorization of forcible intervention. This is since they can be reasonably interpreted as mandating that in the event of withdrawal of consent by a de facto ruling government, ECOWAS and the AU would still have the power to intervene forcibly, even without UNSC authorization. As such, these protocols imply that in the eyes of African regional organizations, consensual intervention, based on past consent, can serve as an alternative to UNSC action in extreme cases, namely when the protection of civilians is required.

Accordingly, while the Lomé Protocol is "mindful" of the UN Charter and namely of Chapters V, VI and VII,[182] reaffirms the commitment of ECOWAS members to the "principles" of the Charter,[183] and pledges to "cooperate" with the UN,[184] it does not explicitly precondition action upon prior UNSC authorization. It merely requires a "report" to be submitted to the United Nations.[185] Elsewhere, in Article 52, it provides that "[i]n accordance with Chapters VII and VIII of the UN Charter, ECOWAS shall *inform* the UN of any military intervention undertaken in pursuit of the objectives of this Mechanism,"[186] perhaps alluding to the obligation set forth in Article 54 of the UN Charter. The latter requires that regional organizations inform the UNSC of their activities for the maintenance of international peace and security. However, Article 54 of the Charter does not refer to forcible measures, which *ipso facto* can only be prescribed by the UNSC. Arguably, thus, the Lomé Protocol seeks to "reverse" the presumption of illegality of the use of force embodied in the UN Charter:

182 *Id.* prmbl.

183 *Id.* art. 2.

184 *Id.* art. 52.

185 *Id.* art. 27.

186 For an analysis of the Lomé Protocol's relation to the limitations imposed by the UN Charter, *see* Ademola Abass, Regional Organisations and the Development of Collective Security: Beyond Chapter VIII of the UN Charter 163 (2004).

while Chapter VII is understood to require an explicit UNSC authorization prior to the use of force, the Lomé Protocol's Article 52 suggests that by default, ECOWAS is authorized to intervene forcibly; it will only *inform* the UNSC, which will only consider the decision *ex post*. The Protocol does not explicitly state what will be the reaction of ECOWAS if the UNSC demands it to halt its intervention.

This approach is echoed also in the AU Protocol. Much like the Lomé Protocol, it acknowledges that the UNSC "has the primary responsibility for the maintenance of international peace and security," but does not explicitly subject AU interventions to UNSC authorization.[187] It merely stipulates that the AUPSC shall "cooperate and work closely" with the UNSC.[188] Essentially, this can only be understood as a mechanism for the AU to retain the authority to intervene in "grave circumstances," where the UNSC fails to act. As is the case with the similar arrangement in the Lomé Protocol, these provisions can place the AU in direct conflict with the UN Charter, in cases where AU intervention is pursued against the will of the targeted government – meaning, where the government, assuming it is recognized, *withdraws* its forward-looking consent – and UNSC authorization to intervene is absent.

Over the years, various attempts have been made to justify unilateral forcible actions by regional organizations by noting, for instance, that such actions have been, at times, approved *ex post* by the UNSC, as was arguably the case in Liberia in 1992–1993 and Sierra Leone in 1997–1999.[189] Furthermore, it was claimed that unilateral regional actions do not amount to "enforcement actions" under Article 53 of the UN Charter, which always require UNSC authorization – but rather that they are actions "relating to the maintenance of international peace and security as are appropriate for regional action" as prescribed in Article 52.[190] However, Article 52 qualifies that such actions be "consistent with the Purposes and Principles of the United Nations." This qualification, reasonably read in light of the purposes of the Charter, clearly subjects Article 52 actions to the prohibition on the use of force.

It is high time for a principled treatment of this question, going beyond *ex post* justification or ad hoc attempts of creative interpretation of the UN

187 *See* Jean Allain, *The True Challenge to the U.N. System of the Use of Force: The Failures of Kosovo and Iraq and the Emergence of the African Union, in* 8 Max Planck Yearbook of United Nations Law 237, 265–266, 284–289 (Armin von Bogdandy and Rüdiger Wolfrum eds., 2004).

188 A.U. Protocol, *supra* note 173, art. 17(1).

189 *See, e.g.*, ICISS Report, *supra* note 19, ¶¶6.5, 6.35; Farer, *supra* note 1, at 69. Note that the Sierra Leone operation was conducted in favor of a democratically elected, and thus *recognized* government. *See* the discussion in Chapter 9, sec. 1.2; *see also* Thomas M. Franck, *Interpretation and Change in the Law of Humanitarian Intervention, in* Humanitarian Intervention: Ethical, Legal, and Political Dilemmas, *supra* note 1, at 204, 221–224.

190 *See* Farer, *supra* note 1, at 72–74, referring to an argument presented by Sean D. Murphy.

Charter. In this context, the African challenges to the UNSC can be reconciled, to some extent, if we adopt an approach according to which when a government fails to exercise effective protection, it suffers the loss of sovereign power to withdraw previous consent given in the context of forward-looking intervention treaties. This possibility is discussed in the next section.

3.5 RtoP, effective protection and withdrawal of consent

As with consent power at large, there are several prisms through which the power to withdraw consent can be analyzed. Of course, a traditional approach can precondition this capacity on considerations of effective control, or to bind withdrawal power to the distinct but related failed state threshold.[191] Other prisms through which to assess this question can be substantive. One, which is analyzed in Chapter 9, is through the principles of democratic legitimacy. Here, the argument will be that a junta that overthrows a democratically elected government will be devoid of power to withdraw its consent from an intervention treaty.[192]

The latter construction can be based on two justifications: the first simply relies on the plain language of a treaty that explicitly authorizes pro-democratic intervention, assuming that we are willing to accept the general legality of such agreements. A second justification can be based on the acknowledgment of a customary "democratic entitlement," which couples sovereignty with electoral democracy, in a manner strong enough to negate a regime's power to withdraw the state's consent, or, perhaps, to negate the regime's recognition.[193] A robust version of this approach might argue for the negation of withdrawal power even in *absence* of an overthrow of an elected government – and merely on counts of a regime's autocratic nature. In this sense, the discussion merges with our analysis of democracy and consent power, and the distinction between "established" and "revolutionary" autocracies, as presented in Chapter 9.[194]

Yet another view analyzes the background of the specific intervention treaty. Wippman, for instance, proposes a model of "concurrent consent," that takes into consideration the political divisions within a state,[195] in light of the fact that in many states, the population is so divided that it cannot be looked upon as a single political community.[196] Thus, he concludes that in cases when intervention treaties are a part of an agreed settlement of a

191 Chapter 7, sec. 2.3, *supra* sec. 3.2.

192 *See, e.g.*, Wippman, *supra* note 148, at 608; David Wippman, *Military Intervention, Regional Organizations, and Host-State Consent*, 7 Duke Journal of Comparative and International Law 209, 218–220 (1996).

193 *See* Thomas M. Franck, *The Emerging Right to Democratic Governance*, 86 American Journal of International Law 46 (1992).

194 Sec. 1.2.

195 Wippman, *supra* note 148, at 611.

196 *Id.* at 612.

severe inter-communal conflict, consent can only be withdrawn through joint-action of the relevant communities, and not by a government per se.[197] However, such a standard naturally applies only in specific cases, and does not resolve cases of intervention treaties in other contexts. Moreover, and importantly, while the concurrent consent model seems to be fair, it does not itself prejudge important substantive questions, namely, whether the analysis changes if one of the parties to the communal settlement is engaged in mass atrocities or other grave violations of international law.

The protection principle, and the understanding of sovereignty as responsibility, can assist us in laying down a workable doctrine in this context. Just as lack of effective protection results in the negation of government consent power, it can also be viewed as negating *withdrawal* power. The underlying principle is simple: in cases where a government cannot express consent – meaning, as discussed in section 2.4, when it fails to exercise effective protection – it will also lack the sovereign power to withdraw previous consent. As phrased by Bellamy:

> [a]lthough military deployments for R2P [RtoP] purposes benefit from host state consent, once they are in place they should prioritise civilian protection over the need to maintain host government support in cases where one cannot be established except at the expense of the other.[198]

Indeed, the act of withdrawal, in itself, is an act of sovereignty. Therefore, in situations in which at least some sovereign power is lost due to a failure to effectively protect civilians, the capacity to withdraw previous consent might diminish. Conversely, the capacity of withdrawal would only exist in those cases in which a government exercises effective protection: meaning, where it fulfils its responsibility to protect. This analysis, beyond providing conceptual clarity, also serves to reconcile between intervention treaties and the *jus cogens* prohibition on the use of force: since the target government would not have the sovereign power to withdraw consent, the previous consent remains, and the intervention will therefore not be considered as conducted against the will of the state.

This approach can also assist us in the assessment of the withdrawal power of a de facto junta that has overthrown a democratically elected government, as further discussed in Chapter 9. Since, in many cases, the junta – even if otherwise recognized, which is not obvious – would resort to grave human rights violations in order to secure its power (thus failing to exercise effective protection), it is reasonable to presume that in many instances, the junta will lack the power to withdraw its consent.

197 *Id.* at 612, 623–632, 646–653.

198 Bellamy, *supra* note 37, at 148; *but see* Military Assistance on Request, *supra* note 150, art. 4(3).

4 Failure to exercise effective protection: the threshold question

As in many questions of law, the concept of effective protection presents a threshold question: what scale of a violation triggers the loss of consent (or withdrawal) power. The question might be formulated as such: while it is true that a state must abide by *all* of its obligations, it is obvious that not *any* violation of international law automatically results in loss of consent power. For instance, even a generally law-abiding military can violate international law, at some point, during an armed conflict. While there is no doubt that even small-scale and non-recurring violations must be addressed, the question is what level of violations entails a degree of loss of sovereign-power that negates a government's consent capacity altogether.

The answer is found within the ICISS Report, the WSOD, as well as in the inherent characteristics of the crimes enumerated in the RtoP doctrine. Thus, the ICISS report expressly refers to "large scale" loss of life or ethnic cleansing as failures to fulfill sovereign responsibility.[199] Similarly, Paragraph 139 of the WSOD mentions the "manifest" failure of protection as a cause for forcible enforcement measures – which must mean acts that are either large-scale or systematic enough to usher the conclusion that a government is generally failing its obligations.[200]

This threshold can also be deduced from the components of the crimes enumerated in the WSOD, as these can be found also in the ICC Statute.[201] Regarding "war crimes," while even a single act of wilful killing, for instance, constitutes a war crime, the Statute stipulates that the ICC shall have jurisdiction "in particular" when war crimes are "committed as part of a plan or policy or as part of a large-scale commission of such crimes."[202] Regarding "crimes against humanity" – ethnic cleansing, functionally, falling within this category of crimes – these are per se "widespread or systematic."[203] The same is true for genocide, which is by nature widespread and systematic as it is committed against a national, ethnical, racial or religious group.[204]

This conclusion is augmented when analyzing consent power in light of IHRL. Since, as aforementioned, human rights are inherently complex, it

199 ICISS Report, *supra* note 19, ¶¶4.19–4.21.

200 W.S.O. Document, *supra* note 63, at ¶139. The "manifest" threshold, as a cause for the rebuttal of the presumption in favor of governments, can be traced back to the seventeenth-century writings of Grotius. 1 Hugo Grotius, The Rights of War and Peace, Book 2, Ch. 25, §8 (William Whewell, trans. 1853)

201 Rome Statute of the International Criminal Court, July 17, 1998, 2187 U.N.T.S. 90.

202 *Id.* art. 8(1).

203 *Id.* art. 7(1).

204 *Id.* art. 6.

is inconceivable that a single case or minor cases of human rights violations would suffice to negate consent power. Thus, when analyzing the international effects of human rights violations, the threshold of "gross and large-scale" violations has emerged as a parameter for substantial international action.[205] Such violations, unsurprisingly, correspond to a large extent to actions that violate the protection principle as outlined in the WSO Document.[206]

Last, the problem of ascertaining when gross, grave, widespread or systemic breaches of the principle of protection occur, and the accompanying question of "who decides," are inherent in the international system in the absence of a collective, objective and universally binding adjudication mechanism.[207] International law is constantly struggling to find the balance between its (still) decentralized, auto-interpretive nature on the one hand,[208] and its growing preoccupation with universal ideas on the other. This problem is persistent in all aspects of international law, and cannot be exhausted here. However, the proliferation of mass media, including through ubiquitous availability of new-media online instruments; the institutionalization of international fact-finding missions conducted by the UN and other international organizations;[209] and the increasing role played by regional organizations[210] can account for enhanced transparency in the international system, that potentially allows for sounder judgments regarding the existence of gross, grave, widespread or systemic breaches of the principle of protection. As noted in the ICISS Report, while disagreements on the existent of large-scale violations of the principle of protection can occur in "marginal cases," most cases will not – hopefully – generate major disagreement,[211] assuming that the international community will act in good-faith.

205 *See, e.g.*, U.N. Commission on Human Rights, *Definition of Gross and Large-Scale Violations of Human Rights as an International Crime*, ¶¶12–22, U.N. Doc. E/CN.4/Sub.2/1993/10 (June 8, 1999).

206 W.S.O. Document, *supra* note 63.

207 *See, e.g.*, Hersch Lauterpacht, Recognition in International Law 234 (1948); Orford, *supra* note 19, ch. 4.

208 On the problem of auto-interpretation *see* Hersch Lauterpacht, The Function of Law in the International Community 189–191 (1933); Leo Gross, *States as Organs of International Law and the Problem of Autointerpretation*, *in* Leo Gross: Essays on International Law and Organization 367 (1984).

209 *See* Théo Boutruche, *Credible Fact-Finding and Allegations of International Humanitarian Law Violations: Challenges in Theory and Practice*, 16 Journal of Conflict and Security Law 105, 107 (2011).

210 *Compare Libya and the Responsibility to Protect: The Exception and the Norm*, *supra* note 85, at 4.

211 ICISS Report, *supra* note 19, ¶4.22.

5 Other positive legal mechanisms for the negation of consent in absence of effective protection: *jus cogens*, IHL, IHRL and international criminal law

In previous sections, we have discussed the principle of protection of civilians and its normative expression in the RtoP doctrine. As aforementioned, a part of RtoP's significance is in its reflection of a transition to an "administrative," rather than "rights"-based outlook regarding the question of intervention. However, even if one rejects the view that RtoP has any significant normative value, and that it elevates the principle of protection to the level of an integral component of sovereignty, violation of the principle of protection can still lead to the invalidation of consent power. If forced to categorize these different mechanisms, the argument from RtoP is based on "public law" principles, stemming from the limitations of sovereign power in international law. The following mechanisms, conversely, are rooted in more traditional notions, perceiving the relations between states as parallel to those between private individuals, or on individual criminal liability.

As we have seen, the RtoP doctrine, as formulated in the WSOD, concerns the protection of civilians threatened by four types of atrocities: genocide, war crimes, ethnic cleansing and crimes against humanity.[212] Unsurprisingly, the prohibitions on such acts also constitute peremptory norms of international law, or *jus cogens*.[213] It is a well established principle that acts that are contrary to *jus cogens* are invalid: thus, Article 53 of the VCLT invalidates treaties conflicting with such norms.[214] This provision is complemented by Article 41(2) of DASR, providing that no state shall recognize situations created by serious breaches of peremptory norms, nor assist in maintaining that situation. Significantly, a similar article is found in DARIO.[215] Therefore, when a government that fails to exercise effective protection, as formulated in the WSOD and entrenched in *jus cogens*, invites a state or a regional organization to intervene on its behalf, whether through a treaty, in the

212 W.S.O. Document, *supra* note 63, ¶138.

213 *See* Antonio Cassese, International Law 202–203 (2005); *see also* DASR with Commentaries, *supra* note 154, art. 40, ¶¶3–4.

214 Vienna Convention on the Law of Treaties, *supra* note 155.

215 DASR with Commentaries, *supra* note 154; UN International Law Commission Draft Articles on the Responsibility of International Organizations, Yearbook of International Law Commission art. 42(2) (2011). The Vienna Convention itself does not enumerate which norms constitute *jus cogens*, nor is there anywhere else an authoritative list of such norms. Over the years, various sources referred to the prohibitions on aggression, colonialism, slavery, genocide, apartheid, torture, and forms of racial discrimination as *jus cogens*; violation of general rules of self-determination, fundamental principles of humanitarian law and massive pollution have also been mentioned. *See* Cassese, *supra* note 212, at 202–203; *compare* DASR with Commentaries, *supra* note 154, at 112–113.

strict sense, or through any type of other agreement,[216] the invitation is invalid. Importantly, this is true even absent a UNSC resolution to that effect.

A state that acts upon such consent, notwithstanding its invalidity, and chooses to intervene in favor of the perpetrating government, is itself in violation of international law, as it violates the obligation not to render assistance to violations of *jus cogens*. Thus, it can be subjected to various non-forcible sanctions imposed unilaterally or by regional organizations. States indeed have a right to sanction other states that assist in violations of *jus cogens*, since such violations are considered to be *erga omnes*, meaning, owed to the entire international community.[217] Furthermore, according to Article 41(1) of DASR, states are *obliged* to cooperate, through lawful means, to bring an end to violations of peremptory norms of international law. Imposition of non-forcible sanctions does not require UNSC authorization, and therefore they undoubtedly constitute lawful means to confront the violation.[218]

The notion of *jus cogens* has also implications on the capacity to withdraw consent, in the context of forward-looking intervention treaties, when a government commits mass atrocities. Indeed, where a government withdraws its consent in order to enable it to commit actions in violations of the *jus cogens* norms that are also reflected in the principle of protection, the instrument of withdrawal *itself* can be viewed as an action designed to breach *jus cogens*. In such cases, third parties – states and international organizations alike – are obliged not to recognize the withdrawal.[219] Indeed, not only is the instrument of withdrawal itself considered a violation of *jus cogens*, it is arguable – without exhausting this issue – that the mere acceptance of such instrument can be viewed as rendering aid or assistance in maintaining that situation, as prohibited, essentially, in DASR. This conclusion applies, naturally, also to the regional organization empowered to authorize a forcible intervention in a forward-looking intervention treaty. In sum, in cases in which a government violates its responsibility to protect, it will not possess the sovereign power to

216 On the classification of consensual interventions – whether based on treaties or otherwise, *see* Eliav Lieblich, *Intervention and Consent: Consensual Forcible Interventions in Internal Armed Conflicts as International Agreements*, 29 Boston University International Law Journal 337 (2011).

217 Case Concerning The Barcelona Traction (Belgium v. Spain), 1970 I.C.J. Rep. 3, ¶¶33–34 (February 5); Wall Opinion, *supra* note 15, ¶155.

218 *See* Lori Fisler Damrosch, *Politics Across Borders: Nonintervention and Nonforcible Influence over Domestic Affairs* 83 American Journal of International Law 1 (1989); Sarah H. Cleveland, *Norm Internalization and U.S. Economic Sanctions* 26 Yale Journal of International Law 1 (2001).

219 DASR with Commentaries, *supra* note 154, art. 41(2); Articles on Responsibility of International Organizations, *supra* note 216, art. 42(2).

withdraw from a forward-looking intervention treaty – since its act of withdrawal itself will be invalidated.

Violations of the protection principle during internal armed conflicts are necessarily violations of IHL. While considerations of *jus in bello* are traditionally – and rightfully so – separated from those of *jus ad bellum*,[220] violation of the protection principle might raise the veil between these separate spheres, at least with regard to the question of consent power. This result can be affected through Common Article 1 of the Geneva Conventions, obliging states "to respect and to ensure respect" for the conventions, in all circumstances.[221] Common Article 3, which applies to internal armed conflicts, is among those provisions which the respect of must be ensured. The ICJ, in the *Wall Advisory Opinion*, interpreted Common Article 1 as not only requiring states to act positively in the face of violations committed by their armed forces, but as applying also in the relations between the conflicting state and *external* states. Meaning, IHL imposes an independent *erga omnes* obligation on uninvolved parties to ensure compliance by the conflicting states, *inter alia* by withholding any aid or assistance to violators of IHL.[222]

A further instrument that can render instances of consensual intervention unlawful can be found in Article 2 of the ICCPR, requiring member states to "to respect and to ensure to all individuals within its territory and subject to its jurisdiction the rights recognized in the present Covenant."[223] A state that embarks on an intervention pursuant to consent by a state that fails to exercise effective protection, and crossing the threshold discussed above, might be in violation of its obligations under IHRL, either through extra-territorial application of the latter, or by serving as an agent of the consenting state, thereby acquiring all of the latter's human rights obligations.[224]

Last, individuals ordering consensual interventions in favor of entities in violation of the protection principle might accrue criminal liability. The complexities of this issue merit a study of their own. In our context, it suffices to mention the 2012 conviction of ex-Liberian president, Charles Taylor, in the Special Court for Sierra Leone (SPCSL). Taylor was convicted on counts of aiding and abetting – including by operational support and

220 *See* Robert D. Sloane, *The Cost of Conflation: Preserving the Dualism of Jus ad Bellum and Jus in Bello in the Contemporary Law of War*, 34 Yale Journal of International Law 48, 48 (2009).

221 On Common Article 1 and RtoP *see* Hanna Brollowski, *The Responsibility to Protect and Common Article 1 of the Geneva Conventions and Obligations of Third States*, *in* The Responsibility to Protect: From Principle to Practice, *supra* note 92, at 93.

222 Wall Opinion, *supra* note 15, ¶¶158–159.

223 ICCPR, *supra* note 126, art. 2.

224 On the extraterritorial application of human rights law *see, e.g.*, Wall Opinion, *supra* note 15, at ¶¶109–112. On its application during armed conflict *see* Chapter 7, sec. 2.1.

provision of military personnel – the commission of crimes by the Sierra Leonean Revolutionary United Front (RUF) and the Sierra Leonean junta (Armed Forces Revolutionary Council (AFRC)).[225] Taylor was sentenced to 50 years in prison. In his sentencing, the Court mentioned the extra-territorial aspect of Taylor's actions, being acts of intervention, as an aggravating factor.[226]

225 Prosecutor v. Taylor, Case No. SCSL-03–1-T, Summary of Trial Chamber Judgment ¶¶66–99 (Sp. Crt. for Sierra Leone, April 26, 2012).

226 Prosecutor v. Taylor, Case No. SCSL-03-1-T, Sentencing Judgment ¶27, part IV (Sp. Crt. for Sierra Leone, May 30, 2012).

9 Consent power, democracy, human rights and self-determination

1 Consent by non-democratic regimes: democracy and protection

1.1 The presumption in favor of governments in democratic and non-democratic regimes

Having discussed, in the previous chapter, the centrality of the protection of civilians in the contemporary law of consensual intervention, we shall now place it in the context of other substantive concepts that may be used to assess parties to internal conflicts. As we shall see, it seems that nowadays many aspects of these concepts, in essence, "collapse" into the principle of protection.

Thus, it is beyond doubt that during internal conflict, genuine democratic governments enjoy a strong presumption in their favor, since substantive democracies necessarily exercise effective protection over their civilians, through their internal mechanisms for the protection of human rights. It can be said that just as substantive democracies are better at maintaining peace between them, they are more likely to maintain peace between their citizens.[1] Therefore, to deny a democratic government's consent power will require a very high evidentiary threshold pointing that it does not fulfill its protection responsibilities.

Considering this assumption, do *non*-democratic regimes enjoy, at all, the presumption in favor of governments in the context of consensual intervention? All other things equal, it seems that the answer is positive, even if the presumption will be less forceful. It cannot be denied that non-democratic regimes participate in the international system, including in bodies such as the UNSC, that they enjoy the principle of sovereign equality,[2] and that states do not withdraw previously granted recognition from

1 *See, generally,* Michael W. Doyle, Liberal Peace: Selected Essays (2011).
2 U.N. Charter, art. 1(2).

long-established non-democratic governments.[3] Therefore, it would be an exercise in wishful thinking to argue that under international law, such regimes a priori lack consent power. Instead, a more nuanced approach is required.

For instance, it is helpful to look at the case of Yemen. The authoritarian regime of Ali Abdullah Saleh faced mass protests in the Arab Spring of 2011, to which the regime responded with a deadly crackdown. Eventually, Saleh resigned as part a regional transitional plan.[4] Simultaneously, Yemen has been involved in a conflict with elements allegedly tied to Al-Qa'ida.[5] It is fairly reasonable that Saleh's unlawful response to the Arab Spring protests – regarding which he did not possess consent power – does not also entail that the regime lost its consent power with regards to actions against Al-Qa'ida, to the extent that it was genuinely involved in an armed conflict against it. Thus, the position of non-democratic regimes vis-à-vis the question of consensual intervention is more complex. Any attempt at its articulation requires a further inquiry into the different aspects of such regimes.

1.2 The electoral aspect: the distinction between "established" and "revolutionary" autocracies

Any discussion of the role of democracy in the context of intervention merits the clarification of the basic components of democracy. The first relates to its procedural (or formal) *electoral* aspect. The other connotes the protection of *human rights*, which is a precondition for the existence of *substantive* democracy.[6] Regarding the electoral aspect, it seems – when analyzing the conduct of the international community – that a clear-cut distinction is drawn between longtime "existing" non-elected regimes ("established autocracies") on the one hand, versus regimes that have *overthrown* an elected government or otherwise fail to respect the ballot ("revolutionary autocracies"). While established autocracies are not per se excluded from the international system, revolutionary autocracies are

3 *See* Sean D. Murphy, *Democratic Legitimacy and Recognition, in* Democratic Governance and International Law 123, 143–146 (Gregory H. Fox and Brad R. Roth eds., 2000).

4 *See* Brian Whitaker, *Yemen's Ali Abdullah Saleh Resigns – But it Changes Little*, Guardian, November 24, 2011, www.guardian.co.uk/commentisfree/2011/nov/24/yemen-ali-abdullah-saleh-resigns; *see also* S.C. Res. 2014, U.N. Doc. S/RES/2014 (October 21, 2011) (endorsing the transition plan outlined by the GCC).

5 *See, e.g., Yemenite Troops Target Al-Qaeda*, Al-Jazeera, January 5, 2010, *available at* www.aljazeera.com/news/middleeast/2010/01/201015132832598600.html.

6 On substantive democracy, *see* Gregory H. Fox and Georg Nolte, *Intolerant Democracies, in* Democratic Governance and International Law, *supra* note 3, at 389, 401–405; Aharon Barak, Proportionality: Constitutional Rights and Their Limitations 218–220 (2012).

ostracized and sometimes face a forcible intervention.[7] This might be especially true when the elections have been internationally supervised.

Indeed, even the proponents of the general legal right to democratic governance – the "democratic entitlement" – demonstrate their arguments by referring to revolutionary autocracies, rather than to longstanding unelected regimes.[8] Thus, the 1964 British intervention upon the request of ousted President Nyerere of Tanganyika is an early case of an intervention against a revolutionary autocracy.[9] The 1994 international intervention in Haiti, the 1996 French intervention in the Central African Republic, and the 1997 ECOWAS operation in Sierra Leone in 1997–1998 are paradigmatic post-Cold War examples.[10] The refusal of Laurent Gbagbo to step down following elections in Côte d'Ivoire, and the forcible international reaction of 2011 constitutes a recent case.[11] Furthermore, upon the March 2012 coup in Mali, in which elected president Toure was ousted by a military junta, ECOWAS and the AU imposed sanctions on the junta, while ECOWAS discussed the deployment of its regional Standby Force in the country. Soon thereafter the parties reached an agreement according to which Toure will resign and the junta will hand over control to interim institutions.[12] Their differences notwithstanding, in all of these cases, clear

7 In the Inter-American system, for instance, a 1992 amendment to the Charter of the Organization of American States (OAS) authorized the OAS to suspend a state "whose democratically constituted government has been overthrown by force." Protocol of Amendment to the Charter of the Organization of American States "Protocol of Washington", art. 9 (December 14, 1992). *See also* The Inter-American Democratic Charter, arts. 19, 21 (2001). Recently, UNASUR (Union of South American Nations) has also adopted a protocol authorizing sanctions in such cases. *See* Protocolo Adicional Compromiso con la Democracia, *available at* www.unasursg.org/index.php?option=com_content&view=article&id=292&Itemid=340; in Africa, see Article 25 of the ECOWAS Protocol Relating to the Mechanism for Conflict Prevention, Management, Resolution, Peace-Keeping and Security, December 10, 1999. In recent years, ECOWAS has suspended several states on considerations of democratic elections – Niger, Guinea (2009), Côte d'Ivoire (2010) and Mali (2012). For official ECOWAS press releases by year *see* http://news.ecowas.int/presselist.php.

8 *See* Murphy, *supra* note 3, at 146–151 (critiquing the notion of the democratic criterion for recognition).

9 *See* David Wippman, *Pro-Democratic Intervention by Invitation, in* Democratic Governance in International Law, *supra* note 3, at 293, 300.

10 *See* Thomas M. Franck, The Emerging Right to Democratic Governance, 86 American Journal of International Law 46, 47 (1992); Murphy, *supra* note 3, at 146–147; *see also* Gregory H. Fox and Brad R. Roth, Introduction: The Spread of Liberal Democracy and its Implications for International Law, in Democratic Governance and International Law, *supra* note 3, at 1, 3; Wippman, *supra* note 9, at 300.

11 S.C. Res. 1975, U.N. Doc. S/RES/1975 (March 30, 2011).

12 Press Release, ECOWAS Joint Chiefs of Defense Staff Hold Emergency Meeting on Mali Crisis (April 5, 2012), available at http://news.ecowas.int/presseshow.php?nb=098&lang=en&annee=2012; *see also* A.U. Peace and Security Council Communique, PSC/PR/COMM.(CCCXVI) (April 3, 2012), available at http://au.int/en/dp/ps/sites/default/files/psc%20comm%20mali%2003–04–2012.pdf; Mali Leader Resigns Ahead of Power Transfer, Al-Jazeera, April 8, 2012, available at www.aljazeera.com/news/africa/2012/04/201248172256860746.html.

preference was given to largely ineffective, democratically elected governments, over revolutionary autocracies that exercised at least some de facto power.

It is possible to justify the distinction between established and revolutionary autocracies on both practical-political and legal-theoretical levels. Practically, the international community will descend into chaos if all non-elected regimes be suddenly stripped of their powers, not to mention, of course, that it is politically impossible. Legally, such a distinction is reasonable, since when an elected government is overthrown, we can positively claim that the people have been forcibly deprived of their system of choice – since there is no democracy without the consent of the governed. Conversely, this claim can be at least doubtful in societies where no electoral-democracy was ever established. In this sense, the removal of an elected government can be viewed as an outrage on the principle of self-determination, according to its contemporary understanding as connoting political participation.[13] Moreover, in cases of revolutionary autocracies it is easier to distinguish between the "democratic" and "non-democratic" party, which can be a difficult task in other situations.

Revolutionary autocracies can be further broken down into two categories: the first concerns situations where an autocrat appropriates power through a *coup d'état* against an elected government (the 1991 Haiti and 1997 Sierra Leone scenarios). The second refers to rulers who refuse to *step down* following elections (the 2010 Côte d'Ivoire scenario). While both situations raise the same theoretical questions regarding the relations between de facto and *de jure* regimes, the latter poses, at least from a classic effective-control point of view, a more significant challenge. This is because in such cases, intervention would be undertaken in favor of a ruler that has *never* exercised effective control over the state, which perhaps amounts to a more dramatic external involvement.

Furthermore, both scenarios pose the same perplexing problem of categorization: namely, whether consent expressed by ineffective elected governments is considered "governmental" or rather, conversely, as *opposition* consent. Here the question of consensual intervention merges with the question of recognition of revolutionary autocracies. A model strictly based on territorial effective control would have to result in the contention that pro-democratic interventions – as these were conducted – were undertaken in the support of the opposition. Paradoxically, this would be a more revolutionary claim than the assertion that the revolutionary autocracies, in these cases, were not recognized to begin with and, thus, the interventions were in support of governments. Thus, it seems that the international community prefers the second contention, by withholding

13 *See* sec. 2.2.

recognition from revolutionary autocracies and maintaining the recognition of the *de jure* elected regime.[14] The 2011 intervention in Côte d'Ivoire illuminates this trend.

1.3 Côte d'Ivoire 2011 – coupling substantive democracy with civilian protection

In November 2010, Côte d'Ivoire held its first presidential elections since 2000, when Laurent Gbagbo came to power through questionable elections. The 2010 elections, monitored by the UN as part of the long peace-process in the country, resulted in the victory of Alassane Ouatarra. However, the state's Constitutional Council, controlled by Gbagbo loyalists, invalidated hundreds of thousands of votes, to proclaim Gbagbo as the winner with 51.4 percent of the vote. Grave political violence ensued as Gbagbo resorted to violent measures to stay in power.[15] Despite Gbagbo's position, Ouattara has been widely recognized as the *de jure* president by regional and international actors. Thus, the UNGA accepted the credentials of his ambassador on December 23, 2010.[16] Likewise, ECOWAS has quickly recognized Ouattara and suspended Côte d'Ivoire from the decision making bodies in the organization until Gbagbo stepped down. The AU too suspended the participation of Côte d'Ivoire in the organization.[17]

These international reactions have taken place regardless of the fact that, at the time, Ouattara had taken refuge in a hotel in Abidjan under the protection of UN peacekeeping forces (UN Operation in Côte d'Ivoire (UNOCI)), completely unable to exercise control over the country, and that Gbagbo, conversely, remained in firm control of the state's elite security units as well as various militias.[18] Ouattara has managed, however, to strike an alliance with a former rebel group, the Forces Nouvelles (FN), by appointing its leader as prime minister and minister of defense. FN forces were located, however, in a geographically distanced area in the north of the country and were thus physically separated from the president-elect.[19]

14 For a detailed analysis of practice in this context *see* Jean d'Aspremont, Responsibility for Coups D'état in International Law, 18 Tulane Journal of International and Comparative Law 451, 455–468 (2010); *see also* Gregory H. Fox, The Right to Political Participation in International Law, 17 Yale Law Journal 539 (1992). Relating to Haiti and Sierra Leone, *See, e.g.*, Wippman, *supra* note 9, at 301–311.

15 *See* International Crisis Group, Côte d'Ivoire: Is War the Only Option? 1–9, ICG Africa Report No. 171 (March 3, 2011).

16 G.A. Res 65/237, U.N. Doc. A/65/237 (December 23, 2010).

17 Is War the Only Option? *supra* note 15, at 12–14; Decision of the African Union Peace and Security Council (December 9, 2010).

18 Is War the Only Option? *supra* note 15, at 10.

19 *Id.*

On December 20, 2010, the UNSC condemned the attempt to "usurp the will of the people" and welcomed the non-forcible measures adopted by ECOWAS and the African Union.[20] It recalled the previous authorization given to UNOCI to use all necessary means to carry out its mandate, including for the protection of civilians, and requested UNOCI to support, *in coordination* with Ivorian authorities, the provision of security for the government and "key political stakeholders." It furthermore extended the longstanding authorization given to the French Forces already present in the country to support UNOCI.[21] The French Forces, it should be noted, intervened in the conflict in Côte d'Ivoire in September 2002, on the basis of a 1961 mutual defense pact and apparently for the purpose of protection of French nationals.[22] Thus, in essence, the first presence of the French Forces in the country was a consensual intervention based on a forward-looking intervention treaty. Since their 2002 intervention, the French Forces have remained in Côte d'Ivoire and have been involved in robust peacekeeping operations. The UNSC, at the time, welcomed the French operation and authorized the presence of French troops, in support of ECOWAS troops, in February 2003.[23] The mandate of the French Forces has since been modified to complement and support the UN peacekeeping forces, and extended periodically thereafter.[24]

Thus, when the events of 2011 unfolded, a significant presence of foreign forces was already on the ground in Côte d'Ivoire. Therefore, UNSC Resolution 1975 of March 30, 2011, which used explicit RtoP language, served mainly as a blunt identification of the culprit – Laurent Gbagbo. The Resolution identified Ouattara as the president of Côte d'Ivoire, "as recognized by ECOWAS, the AU, and the rest of the international community"; specifically condemned Gbagbo for not stepping down; called upon all of the Ivorian institutions to yield to Ouattara's authority; and demanded that Gbagbo immediately lift the siege of the Golf Hotel, where Ouattara had taken refuge.[25] It furthermore condemned all atrocities committed in the course of the turmoil.[26] However, the resolution alluded to UNOCI's "impartial" mandate to protect civilians, perhaps implying, that in terms of *forcible enforcement*, it remained "neutral" regarding the parties' conflicting claims concerning the elections, reserving any forcible actions only to the extent needed to protect civilians.[27]

20 S.C. Res. 1962, U.N. Doc. S/RES/1962 (December 20, 2010).

21 *Id.* ¶¶14, 15, 17.

22 France-Diplomatie – Political Relations, available at www.diplomatie.gouv.fr/en/country-files_156/cote-ivoire_191/france-and-cote-ivoire_2426/political-relations_6122/index.html.

23 S.C. Res. 1464, U.N. Doc. S/RES/1464 (February 4, 2003).

24 *See, e.g.*, S.C. Res. 1479, U.N. Doc. S/RES/1479 (May 13, 2003); S.C. Res. 1528, U.N. Doc. S/RES/1528 (February 27, 2004); S.C. Res. 2000, S/RES/2000 (July 27, 2011).

25 S.C. Res. 1975, U.N. Doc. S/RES/1975 (March 30, 2011), ¶¶1, 3, 4, 11.

26 *Id.* ¶5.

27 *Id.* ¶6.

Resolution 1975 was adopted two days after Ouattara launched a wide scale attack against Gbagbo, utilizing the forces of his northern FN allies.[28] Since it authorized UNOCI "to prevent the use of heavy weapons against the civilian population,"[29] there was significant leeway to construct the resolution as mandating a proactive military campaign against Gbagbo. Accordingly, the UN and French Forces deployed attack helicopters against his forces. The foreign forces were instrumental in the FN's assault on Abidjan, and on April 11, 2011, Gbagbo was arrested by forces supporting Ouattara.[30]

Two significant lessons can be learned from the Gbagbo affair. First, that revolutionary autocracies, even those that do not engage in a positive *coup d'état*, but simply refuse to step down following elections, are not likely to be recognized as governments, including for the purpose of consent (or withdrawal) power. As recent practice reveals, the ousted or denied elected government will typically retain or gain recognition – as was in the cases of Haiti, Sierra Leone[31] and Côte d'Ivoire. Thus, it is reasonable that "pro-democratic" interventions against revolutionary autocracies are essentially interventions in favor of governments, and are thereby positioned within the theoretical sphere of the preference of governments. This is true both when the intervention was pursued absent *ex ante* UNSC authorization (Sierra Leone),[32] and in cases where such authorization was granted (Haiti,[33] Côte d'Ivoire). It should be noted however, that the Sierra Leone intervention was conducted by a regional organization, and not by a single state, which might account for the operation's enhanced legitimacy and its implied *ex post* endorsement by the UNSC.[34]

The second lesson is that regardless of the consequentially pro-democratic nature of the intervention, and the wide condemnation of Gbagbo's actions, the forcible acts against the latter were conducted primarily under the banner of "civilian protection," and not under a mandate to enforce *electoral* democracy. This fact demonstrates the coupling of the principle of civilian protection and *substantive* democracy, as illustrated in the next section, and correlates with the prevalence of the protection principle over other considerations.

It seems thus, that contemporary practice points to the following trends: revolutionary autocracies are denied recognition, and therefore do not

28 International Crisis Group, A Critical Period for Ensuring Stability in Côte D'Ivoire, ICG Africa Report No. 176 (August 1, 2011).

29 S.C. Res. 1975, *supra* note 24, ¶6.

30 A Critical Period for Ensuring Stability, *supra* note 28, at 1–2.

31 Wippman, *supra* note 9, at 301, 304.

32 Wippman, *supra* note 9, at 304–306; Michael Byers and Simon Chesterman, "You, the People": Pro-Democratic Intervention in International Law, in Democratic Governance and International Law, *supra* note 3, at 259, 288–290.

33 *Id.* at 284–288.

34 Wippman, *supra* note 9, at 311.

enjoy consent power; ousted elected governments, conversely, retain recognition and therefore might possess consent power,[35] *at least* for the immediate period following their loss of control.[36] However, the Sierra Leone intervention, which is a paradigmatic case in which consent has been used as one justification for a pro-democratic unilateral intervention,[37] involved a regional organization. While there is no inherent differentiation between the *jus ad bellum* applicable to regional organizations as opposed to that applying to single states, the former enjoy wider credibility as collective decision making instruments.[38] Therefore, consensual interventions pursued by regional organizations, in such scenarios, are likely to be more widely accepted.

1.4 Established autocracies facing a genuine pro-democratic insurrection: deconstructing the "democratic entitlement"

What is the law in instances in which a longstanding and established autocracy is challenged by a democratic opposition? Any approach that seeks to evaluate consent power according to the democratic credentials of the opposition requires, as a preliminary condition, the difficult determination that the latter is genuinely willing and able to "deliver" its promise. Mere claims by armed opposition that it is "democratic" are certainly not enough, considering the scope of the term's abuse by various groups. Moreover, since internal armed conflict is a fundamentally undemocratic phenomenon – as it substitutes political deliberation with violence – it is extremely difficult, in most cases, to identify genuine democratic tendencies among the conflicting parties (in contradistinction, perhaps, to cases of revolutionary autocracies, where a genuine democratic government previously existed). This dilemma is ever present when assessing external intervention in armed strife: it was prevalent, for instance, in the debate surrounding US support of the Contras,[39] as well as the nature of the rebelling forces during the Arab Spring in Libya[40] and Syria.[41]

Assuming a case where we can clearly establish that a non-democratic regime is challenged by a genuinely pro-democratic opposition, the question whether the regime's non-democratic nature affects its consent power

35 Compare Report of the International Commission on Intervention and State Sovereignty, The Responsibility to Protect ¶4.26 (2001).

36 Wippman, *supra* note 9, at 302–303.

37 *Id.* at 308–309.

38 *See, e.g.*, ICISS Report, *supra* note 35, ¶¶6.31–6.32; The Independent International Commission on Kosovo, The Kosovo Report 195 (2000).

39 *See* Robert Kagan, A Twilight Struggle: American Power and Nicaragua 1977–1990 355 (1995).

40 *See, e.g.*, Jon Lee Anderson, Who are the Rebels? The New Yorker, April 4, 2011, www.newyorker.com/talk/comment/2011/04/04/110404taco_talk_anderson.

41 *See* generally International Crisis Group, Syria's Phase of Radicalisation, ICG Middle East Briefing No. 33 (April 10, 2012).

can be viewed as intrinsically woven with the debate whether, and to what extent, "democracy," as a system of governance, is a right under international law, and what are the remedies for its violation.[42] This notion has been famously phrased by Franck as a "democratic entitlement."[43] However, while the latter concept has certainly affected the understanding of international law in recent decades, there is still no consensus that it has galvanized, as such, as an unequivocal rule of customary international law[44] – *a fortiori* as one which would strip established autocracies from *jus ad bellum* rights.[45] As some argue, this is especially true since the concept of democracy itself is not authoritatively defined, as such, in international law.[46] With the multitude of political systems and their intricacies, it is sometimes difficult to objectively pinpoint which government represents a "true" democracy, and to what extent.[47]

Indeed, if we limit the "democratic entitlement" to the narrow, procedural requirement of "free and fair elections" and majority rule, it loses much of its appeal – since free and fair elections are not sufficient, in themselves, to secure human rights. However, if we understand the entitlement as connoting also substantive democracy, we must recognize that the latter is comprised of numerous rights and interests that are not absolute, and are therefore subject to unique balancing in different societies, in accordance with their cultures and circumstances.[48] It is in this context where there is constant tension – whether justified or not – between the proponents of the democratic entitlement and those that suspect that the idea is yet another method to perpetuate "western" hegemony, in a manner at odds with the concept of non-intervention, as it is sometimes understood in the developing world.[49]

42 Fox and Roth, *supra* note 10, at 10–11.

43 Franck, *supra* note 10; *see also* Christina M. Cerna, Universal Democracy: An International Legal Right or the Pipe Dream of the West? 27 New York University Journal of International Law and Politics 289 (1995); Steven Wheatley, Democracy, Minorities and International Law 128–140 (2005). For an updated analysis *see* Susan Marks, What Has Become of the Emerging Right to Democratic Governance? 22 European Journal of International Law 507 (2011).

44 Steven Wheatley, Democracy in International Law: A European Perspective, 51 International and Comparative Law Quarterly 225 (2002); Gregory H. Fox, The Right to Political Participation in International Law, in Democratic Governance and International Law, *supra* note 3, at 48, 69; *see also* Marks, *supra* note 43, at 511–513 (and the sources cited therein).

45 Although a regime's non-democratic nature might suffer reduced consent power due to the norm of non-intervention. *See* Chapter 3, sec. 1.

46 Fox, *supra* note 44, at 48–49; *see also* Marks, *supra* note 43, at 511–512, 522; *see also* 2005 World Summit Outcome, G.A. Res. 60/1, ¶135, U.N. Doc. A/60/L.1 (September 15, 2005).

47 Marks, *supra* note 43, at 511–512; *see also* Martti Koskenniemi, Intolerant Democracies: A Reaction, 37 Harvard International Law Journal 231, 231–232 (1996).

48 Compare Barak, *supra* note 6, at 220–221.

49 *See* Franck, *supra* note 10, at 78, 82; Koskenniemi, *supra* note 47, at 231–232.

Some, while admitting that the democratic entitlement has indeed taken form in the last two decades, argue that the ongoing economic crisis in the western world, the growing global security concerns and the rise of authoritarian superpowers could undermine the establishment of the democratic entitlement in the near future. They identify a process in which the overarching idea of "democracy," in its procedural sense, is marginalized in favor of a pragmatic analysis of a government's adherence to basic human rights standards.[50] According to this view, in certain situations – among them when consensual intervention is sought – the question whether a government has been democratically elected is secondary to the question of how the government exercises its powers. In the eyes of this approach, the latter, but not necessarily of the former, can result in the "disqualification" of consent.[51]

It is beyond this work to add to the robust literature on the democratic entitlement. Instead, we can constructively focus on the rights constituting the "compounds" of democracy. Indeed, rather than stressing the concept of "democracy" as such, it is helpful to emphasize the various rights that comprise it – thereby "returning" the elusive concept of "democracy" to the realm of positive IHRL.[52] From here, it is only a short theoretical distance to reach the conclusion that substantive democracy and the concept of effective protection are merging together, at least during internal armed conflicts when intervention is assessed.

Setting aside the complexities of the right to free and fair elections as enshrined in Article 25 of the ICCPR,[53] the truth remains that autocratic regimes are virtually always violators of *other* well founded norms of IHRL. Indeed, repression is a precondition to secure and protect autocracy. It is here that the discussion of the "democratic entitlement" can receive significant legal augmentation: as aforementioned, democracy, in its substantive sense, does not only connote (procedural) electoral rights and majority rule[54] – but is comprised also of a bundle of (substantive) rights that must supplement it,[55] the chief of them being the right to life.[56] Thus, while "democracy" in itself is controversial as a "right" in international law,

50 Jean d'Aspremont, The Rise and Fall of Democracy Governance in International Law: A Reply to Susan Marks, 22 European Journal of International Law 549 (2011).

51 *See* Jean d'Aspremont and Eric De Brabandere, The Complementary Faces of Legitimacy in International Law: The Legitimacy of Origin and the Legitimacy of Exercise, 34 Fordham International Law Journal 190, 209–210; Jean d'Aspremont, Legitimacy of Governments in the Age of Democracy, 38 New York University Journal of International Law and Politics 877, 906–909 (2005).

52 *See* Cerna, *supra* note 43, at 328; *see also* d'Aspremont, *supra* note 50, at 559–560.

53 International Covenant on Civil and Political Rights art. 25, December 16, 1966, 999 U.N.T.S.. 171; Fox, *supra* note 43, at 55–59.

54 *See* Marks, *supra* note 42, at 511–512.

55 *See* Thomas Franck, Legitimacy and the Democratic Entitlement, in Democratic Governance and International Law, *supra* note 3, at 25, 25–26.

56 ICCPR, *supra* note 52, art. 5.

many of its substantive elements are enshrined in positive international law. Some of these rights – though not all – are integral also to the concept of effective protection as a source of sovereign power. Therefore, when assessing the consent power of established autocracies, in the context of an internal armed conflict, the focus should not be solely on their autocratic, non-elected nature, but rather on the gross violations of legally protected human rights, amounting also to a breach of the principle of protection, that such regimes almost always commit when attempting to preserve their rule. Indeed, it is theoretically possible that an autocracy will exercise effective protection over civilians, perhaps in line with the Rawlsian idea of "decent hierarchical peoples."[57] However, it is hard to imagine a situation in which an autocracy would deal with mass dissent without either succumbing, or, ultimately, breaching the protection principle. This tendency of such regimes has been clearly demonstrated in the events of the Arab Spring in Libya and Syria.

This approach for the assessment consent power seems prudent. Since at issue is the lawfulness of forcible intervention, with all of its political and humanitarian consequences, it makes sense – at least when assessing a possible intervention – to shy away from sweeping ideological terms and to focus, borrowing from d'Aspremont and De Brabandere, on the way the consenting government exercises its power, rather on that power's origins. Namely, as discussed at length in Chapter 8, this exercise of power will be judged according to the notion of protection of civilians, which offers a widely accepted standard, at least in principle, for the assessment of parties to an internal armed conflict.[58] It is also conceptually easier to judge, during armed conflict, a party's adherence to its protection responsibilities, as opposed to its promotion of democratic governance. Indeed, the immediate concern of the international system, during internal conflict, should be to prevent or swiftly respond to humanitarian crises, rather than to secure a complex democratic system, which is best reserved to the lengthy process of post-conflict institution building. This approach seems to correlate with the contemporary "protection now, democracy later" practice of the UNSC.[59]

However, as aforesaid, since it is likely that autocratic regimes will rarely exercise their power in accordance with the principles of effective protection, the presumption in their favor would be naturally weaker, and would require meticulous review by international actors.

57 *See* John Rawls, The Law of Peoples, §8 (1999).

58 d'Aspremont, *supra* note 50, at 559–560; d'Aspremont & De Brabandere, *supra* note 51.

59 Chapter 8, sec. 2.5.

2 Deprivation of self-determination and consent power

2.1 Self-determination in the colonial context: the exclusion of struggles from the internal realm and the question of forcible intervention

Self-determination is universally accepted as a basic principle of international law, entrenched in Article 1(2) of the UN Charter as one of the organization's purposes. Nonetheless, the meaning of the principle has not been constant. On the contrary, it has evolved and changed significantly throughout the twentieth century. It has developed from the Wilsonian model, based on the protection and self-governance of minorities in post-World War I Europe; to a central principle during decolonization in Africa and Asia in the post-World War II world; and, in its latest form, to the contemporary concept of internal self-determination, as discussed in section 2.2.[60] Underlying self-determination's development is its longstanding, inherent tension with the principle of territorial integrity, chiefly concerning the right of secession. These issues have been robustly addressed in the literature.[61] We shall only discuss them here in the context of their possible effects over consent power.

As aforementioned, much of the consideration of self-determination, in the first decades of the UN, took place in relation to the process of decolonization.[62] It is imperative to note, in this regard, that the normative treatment of colonial wars in the UN era constituted, in itself, a significant departure from the traditional perception of sovereignty as a corollary of effective control. Recall that in the nineteenth century, colonial wars – such as the Cuban conflicts – have been generally looked upon as "regular" cases of internal strife, where the colonized party was perceived as seeking secession from an empire.[63] This has changed remarkably in the UN era. Indeed, during decolonization, latter-day colonial powers such as Portugal sought to maintain the distinction of colonial wars as internal

60 *See* Franck, *supra* note 10, at 52–56.

61 *See* generally Antonio Cassese, Self-Determination of Peoples: A Legal Reappraisal (1995); Karen Knop, Diversity and Self-Determination in International Law (2002). For a concise history of the principle *see* Joshua Castellino, International Law and Self-Determination 7–43 (2000); compare Christian Tomuschat, Secession and Self-Determination, in Secession: International Law Perspectives 23, 37–38 (Marcelo G. Kohen ed., 2006); *see also* Independent International Fact-Finding Mission on the Conflict in Georgia, Report (Vol. 2), at 135–136 (September 30, 2009); Allen E. Buchanan, Justice, Legitimacy and Self-Determination: Moral Foundations for International Law 331–426 (2004).

62 *See, e.g.*, Legal Consequences for States of the Continued Presence of South African in Namibia (South West Africa) Notwithstanding Security Council Resolution 276 (1970), Advisory Opinion, 1971 I.C.J. 16, ¶¶52–53 (June 21).

63 *See* generally Chapter 4; compare ICRC, Commentary on the Additional Protocols of 8 June 1977 to the Geneva Conventions of 12 August 1949 ¶89 (Yves Sandoz et al. eds. 1987).

64 Castellino, *supra* note 61, at 27–31.

struggles for secession. However, the international community unequivocally rejected this stance.[64]

In its 1960 Declaration on the Granting of Independence to Colonial Countries and People, the UNGA called for the cessation of "all armed action or repressive measures" directed against dependent peoples, while still reaffirming that any disruption of a state's territorial integrity is incompatible with the UN Charter.[65] In this sense, the Declaration, and subsequent resolutions,[66] clearly established that in the context of decolonization, the question of self-determination is distinct from the issue of secession, and that colonial wars, thus, do not challenge the principle of territorial integrity. The 1970 Declaration on Friendly Relations explicitly reaffirmed this notion, by declaring that territories under colonial rule have a "separate and distinct status" from the administering state.[67] With this, the Declaration clarified that the issue of secession, in the internal sense, is irrelevant to the question of decolonization. This determination corresponds with the approach expressed in the (controversial) Article 1(4) of Additional Protocol I, which provides that struggles against colonial domination, alien occupation and racist regimes, in the exercise of the right of self-determination, are to be considered *international* armed conflicts in the context of IHL.[68]

In the UN era, thus, colonial struggles have been *excluded* from the internal realm, and were therefore no longer understood as secession conflicts. Instead, they were treated as belonging to a separate category of struggles for self-determination, which were closer, in their nature, to *international* conflicts. The exclusion of colonial wars from the internal sphere and their possible transfer to the realm of external *jus ad bellum*, necessarily removed them also, in the context of consensual intervention, from the paradigm of the preference of governments – resulting therefore in the negation of colonial powers' consent capacity.[69] This conclusion was expressed in the Declaration on Friendly Relations, which proclaimed that states have a duty to refrain from any forcible action which deprives peoples of their right to

65 Declaration on the Granting of Independence to Colonial Countries and Peoples, G.A. Res. 1514, ¶4, 7, U.N. Doc. A/1514 (December 14, 1960).

66 *See, e.g.*, G.A. Res. 1541, U.N. Doc. A/1541 (December 15, 1960).

67 Declaration on Principles of International Law concerning Friendly Relations and Co-operation among States, Principle 5¶6, G.A. Res. 2625 (XXV), U.N. Doc. A/2625 (October 24, 1970).

68 Protocol Additional to the Geneva Conventions of 12 August 1949, and Relating to the Protection of Victims of International Armed Conflicts (Protocol I), June 8, 1977, art. 1(4), 1125 U.N.T.S. 3; *See* Commentary on The Additional Protocols, *supra* note 63, 41–55. On the US objections to the article *see* Martin D. Dupuis et al., A Workshop on Customary International Law and the 1977 Protocols Additional to the 1949 Geneva Conventions, 2 American University Journal of International Law and Policy 415, 463–464 (1987).

69 *See* David Wippman, Military Intervention, Regional Organizations, and Host-State Consent, 7 Duke Journal of Comparative and International Law 209, 215 (1997).

70 Declaration on Friendly Relations, *supra* note 67, Principle 5¶5.

self-determination,[70] and in the demand from states, in other resolutions, to cease any support rendered to colonial powers.[71]

The Declaration went, however, a step further, by stating that "such peoples" "are entitled to seek and to receive support in accordance with the purposes and principles of the Charter."[72] This vague phrasing – as will be further discussed in Chapter 10[73] – raised questions regarding the lawfulness of *forcible* support to peoples struggling for self-determination. Indeed, for the same reasons that Article 1(4) of Additional Protocol I was (and remains) controversial, the question whether such conflicts, sometimes labeled as "wars of national liberation," spawned also the right to receive forcible support – perhaps comparable to collective self-defense rights of states – remained unresolved.[74] This controversy was exemplified in a *dictum* in the *Nicaragua* case, implying that colonial struggles might be analyzed under a separate paradigm of intervention. This idea was vehemently rejected in the dissenting opinion of Judge Schwebel.[75]

Accordingly, when attempting to circumscribe the means for the *implementation* of self-determination, the Declaration on Friendly Relations plunged into nearly unworkable incoherence, characteristic of Cold War era compromises.[76] One key problem concerned the nature of its application to non-colonial instances. Thus, it enumerated the possible routes for the implementation of self-determination as consisting of the establishment of an independent state; association or integration with an independent state; or any other political status chosen by the people.[77] However, since it stipulated that self-determination was not strictly limited to instances of colonialism – by acknowledging that the principle applied to "all peoples"[78] – it remains unclear whether these methods of implementation referred only to situations of decolonization or otherwise.

The situation was further complicated by Principle 5¶7 of the Declaration, qualifying that the latter could not be construed as challenging the territorial integrity of independent states, which comply with the principles of equal rights *and* self-determination.[79] It can be inferred from this statement, by way of negation, that the territorial integrity of states that *do*

71 G.A. Res 2105, ¶11, U.N. Doc. A/2105 (December 20, 1965).

72 Declaration on Friendly Relations, *supra* note 67, Principle 5¶5; *see also* G.A. Res. 2105, *supra* note 71, ¶10.

73 Sec. 2.3.

74 *See* Yoram Dinstein, War, Aggression and Self-Defense 70–73 (5th ed. 2011); Julius Stone, Hopes and Loopholes in the 1974 Definition of Aggression, 71 American Journal of International Law 224, 233–237 (1977).

75 Military Aid and Paramilitary Activities in and against Nicaragua (Nicar. v. U.S.), 1986 I.C.J. 14 (June 27), ¶206; compare id. ¶1, ¶¶178–181 (Schwebel J., dissenting).

76 *See* Georgia Report, *supra* note 61, at 138.

77 Declaration on Friendly Relations, *supra* note 67, Principle 5¶4.

78 *Id.* Principle 5¶1.

79 *Id.* Principle 5¶7.

not comply with these principles is not an absolute value. Furthermore, Principle 5¶7 can hardly be understood as applying strictly to colonized peoples, since its reference to "equal rights" alludes to a wider spectrum of situations. In particular, the qualification of the principle of territorial integrity, implied in Principle 5¶7, could be relevant to racist regimes which are not per se colonialist – apartheid South Africa being the most clear-cut historical example.[80]

The Declaration's potential qualification of the principle of territorial integrity, also in some non-colonial situations, could arguably be construed as opening the door for the possibility of *remedial secession*, as the term is discussed in the next section. However, the Declaration quickly contradicted this thought, in Principle 5¶8, proclaiming that states shall refrain from any action aimed to disrupt the territorial integrity of *any* other state.[81] This last Principle, however, can be interpreted as applying to any instance *not* covered by previous paragraphs, ostensibly allowing support to secessionist groups in certain circumstances. Therefore, the ambiguity regarding the treatment of secession in the Declaration on Friendly relations remains.[82]

2.2 Relevance in the decolonized world: internal self-determination, remedial secession, civilian protection and consent power

The principle of self-determination, although prevalent in the discourse on decolonization, is not limited only to this specific context. It is also entrenched as an internationally protected human right. Accordingly, Common Article 1 of the ICCPR and the ICESCR provides that the principle applies to *all* peoples, whether or not under foreign domination. However, there is significant difference in the application of the principle in the colonial versus the non-colonial contexts. While peoples under colonial rule would have a right to establish independent states, in already established and independent states, conversely, self-determination is limited to *internal* application. In practice, the immediate meaning of this qualification, as we shall see, is that in the decolonized world, the principle of self-determination does not in general spawn a positive right of secession, even if not prohibiting it per se.[83]

80 *See* Ioana Cismas, Secession in Theory and Practice: The Case of Kosovo and Beyond, 2 Goettingen Journal of International Law 531, 546–547 (2010).

81 Declaration on Friendly Relations, *supra* note 67, Principle 5¶8.

82 *See* Georgia Report, *supra* note 61, at 137–138.

83 Franck, *supra* note 10, at 58–59; Castellino, *supra* note 61, at 31–34; for an overview of self-determination outside the colonial context *see* Reference re Secession of Quebec, [1998] 2. S.C.R. 217 (Can.). Arguably, international law does not prohibit secession; *see* Request for an Advisory Opinion of the ICJ on the Question "Is the Unilateral Declaration of Independence by the Provisional Institutions of Self-Government of Kosovo in Accordance with International Law?" Written Statement of the United Kingdom 87–93 (April 17, 2009), available at www.icj-cij.org/docket/files/141/15638.pdf.

Thus, the contemporary discussion of the principle of self-determination has become somewhat narrower. The principle is now commonly analyzed under the concept of internal self-determination, meaning, the application of the right within the boundaries of an existing independent state. This concept derives from the practical understanding that the international system could not withstand the perpetual fragmentation created by infinite claims for secession, and that the principles of territorial integrity and *uti possidetis* – meaning, the respect of colonial borders as they were at the time of independence[84] – must counterbalance the right to self-determination.

The notion of internal self-determination has been viewed by some, in the past, as synonymous with non-intervention. Indeed, self-determination as been cited as a key justification for strict-abstentionism.[85] However, the rationale of internal self-determination has been understood, by most contemporary scholars, as being based on some form of a right to political participation.[86] When equating internal self-determination with political participation, the discussion of self-determination merges, to a large extent, with the debate surrounding the existence of a democratic entitlement and its effect on government consent power. In this sense, our conclusions regarding the relations between democracy and consensual intervention are applicable also in the context of the interaction between internal self-determination and intervention: both should be analyzed according to the substantive human rights violations that usually accompany their deprivation; when such violations amount to a breach of the principle of effective protection by the government, the latter loses its sovereign power to request assistance – or to withdraw previous consent – during an internal armed conflict.

However, the question of internal self-determination spawns another dilemma, concerning the *positive* consequences of its breach. Due to the prevalence of the principle of territorial integrity, as aforementioned, self-determination in the decolonized world is to be fulfilled within the framework of the state. It is thus clear that a right of forcible, unilateral, non-consensual secession cannot be an inherent component of the right

84 *See* Suzanne Lalonde, Determining Boundaries in a Conflicted World: The Role of Uti Possidetis 4 (2002).

85 *See* Chapter 6, sec. 3. *See also* Louise Doswald-Beck, The Legal Validity of Military Intervention by Invitation of the Government, 56 British Year Book of International Law 189, 200 (1985).

86 *See* David Raič, Statehood and the Law of Self-determination 237–238 (2002), and the sources cited therein, in n. 42.

of internal self-determination.[87] This conclusion is merited both in light of the substantive meaning of the principle of internal self-determination,[88] and on counts of the dangerous practical implications of the recognition of a right to secede.[89] Accordingly, and at least since the early 1960s, when the international community adopted a strong anti-secessionist approach in the context of the Katanga affair,[90] it can be definitely said that state practice has not recognized a right of secession based *strictly* on the notion of internal self-determination.[91]

Regarding the question of consensual intervention, the implication must be that – absent violations of the protection principle – a claim cannot be made for the negation of government consent power when the latter is facing an armed secessionist movement, when the secessionists' claims are based *solely* on an alleged deprivation of internal self-determination. It could be further prescribed that, all other things equal, any loss of territorial effective control resulting from such actions cannot be used as a claim against the government's consent power. If, however, the conflict is not one of secession, but for control over the state apparatus, any limitation on consent power justified on counts of a violation of internal self-determination should be analyzed according to the same principles outlined in the discussion regarding the democratic entitlement.

It is in this context that the unresolved issue of "remedial secession" has to be addressed. Until now, we have generally discussed the effects of "regular" violations of internal self-determination over government consent power. However, the idea of remedial secession, a term first used by Buchheit,[92] suggests that in exceptional circumstances a group might be entitled – in accordance with international law – to be considered as having a right to secede, as a *remedy* for grave and massive violations of human rights directed against it in a discriminatory fashion.[93] Thus, while for the purpose of consent power internal self-determination largely

87 Internationally recognized secession can be a product of an agreement. This agreement can be the result of an internal armed conflict or not; the key issue is that the secession is validated, in relation to the international community, by consent of the rump state. *See* the secession of South Sudan in July 2011, following a referendum. Compare Dapo Akande, The Newly Independent State of South Sudan – Should We Rethink the Right to Secession? European Journal of International Law: Talk (July 15, 2011), www.ejiltalk.org/the-newly-independent-state-of-south-sudan.

88 *See* Emilio J. Cárdenas and Maria Fernand Can as, The Limits of Self-Determination, in The Self-determination of Peoples: Community, Nation, and State in an Interdependent World 101, 110–112 (Wolfgang Danspeckgruber ed., 2002).

89 Tomuschat, *supra* note 61, at 24–25.

90 *See* Georg Nolte, Secession and External Intervention, in Secession: International Law Perspectives 65, 67–70 (Marcelo G. Kohen ed., 2006).

91 For a summary of practice, *see* Tomuschat, *supra* note 61, at 27–34.

92 Lee Buccheit, Secession: The Legitimacy of Self-Determination 222–223 (1978).

93 Tomuschat, *supra* note 61, at 35; *see also* Buchanan, *supra* note 61, at 247–248 (on the meaning of the remedial aspect of the right).

merges with the question of substantive democracy, the doctrine of remedial secession is directly related to the notion of effective protection of civilians. Importantly, this supposed right will apply also in the non-colonial context, meaning, where self-determination is usually strictly internal.

Frequently referred to as based on Principle 5¶7 of the Declaration on Friendly Relations,[94] the doctrine of remedial secession has received much support in legal literature, but scant support, if at all, in state practice.[95] In recent times, the issue has been most heavily debated in the context of Kosovo's struggle to secede from Serbia. In response to mass atrocities conducted by the Serbian army in 1998–1999, NATO launched a unilateral bombing campaign against Serbia, which led to the establishment of a UN Interim Administration (UNMIK), supplemented by a NATO-dominated security presence (KFOR), mandated in UNSC Resolution 1244.[96] In practice, the international civil and military presence in Kosovo amounted to a transfer of control over the territory to the international community.[97] Following a long stalemate in the final-status negotiation between representatives of Kosovo and Serbia,[98] Kosovo declared independence on February 17, 2008,[99] to be recognized, as of December 2012, by 96 states.[100]

The debate regarding remedial secession in the case of Kosovo revolves around the question whether such right exists in international law to begin with; and if not, whether the Kosovo case sets any legal precedent for such a right; or rather, as commonly claimed by states that have recognized Kosovo, the recognition of Kosovo is merely a *sui generis* case, its unique circumstances negating any potential precedential, norm-creating value.[101]

The *sui generis* argument is best exemplified in the positions expressed in the dramatic UNSC discussion taking place a day after Kosovo's declaration of independence.[102] There, the UK recalled that the Council, in

94 *See supra*, text accompanying nn. 77–81.

95 For a summary of opinions in the literature *see* Alexandra Xanthaki, Indigenous Rights and United Nations Standards 141–142 (2007); Georgia Report, *supra* note 61, at 138; Tom J. Farer, Humanitarian Intervention Before and After 9/11, in Humanitarian Intervention: Ethical, Legal and Political Dilemmas 53, 57 (J.L. Holzgrefe and Robert O. Keohane eds., 2003).

96 S.C. Res. 1244, U.N. Doc. S/RES/1999 (June 10, 1999).

97 *See* K. William Watson, When in the Course of Human Events: Kosovo's Independence and the Law of Secession, 17 Tulane Journal of International and Comparative Law 267, 269–274 (2008).

98 *See* Report of the Special Envoy of the Secretary-General on Kosovo's Future Status, 2, U.N. Doc. S/2007/168 (March 26, 2007).

99 Cismas, *supra* note 80, at 577–578.

100 For an updated list of states that have recognized Kosovo, including the texts of the recognitions, *see* www.kosovothanksyou.com.

101 Cismas, *supra* note 80, at 581–586; for an overview of the *sui generis* debate *see Georgia Report, supra* note 61, at 139–140.

102 U.N. SCOR, 63rd Sess., 5839th mtg., U.N. Doc. S/PV.5839 (February 18, 2008).

Resolution 1244, took an "unprecedented step" by depriving Serbia of its control over Kosovo, in response to its attempt to expel the Albanian population from Kosovo in 1999. It argued that these events "shape" the current situation.[103] It blamed Serbia for the collapse of negotiations, and repeated the claim that the situation is *sui generis*.[104] The US presented similar reasoning, claiming that the declaration of independence was a "logical, legitimate and legal response" considering the circumstances. However, it too stressed that its uniqueness negates the situation of any precedential value.[105] Croatia followed the same route,[106] and so did France.[107]

The *sui generis* argument regarding Kosovo, thus, is based on a three-pronged set of justifications. First, it refers to the "unprecedented step" taken by the UNSC in Resolution 1244, in its decision to de facto remove Kosovo from Serbian control; second, it relies on the Serbian attempts to expel the Albanian population; and third, it points out the ongoing failure of the negotiations between the parties.

However, an analysis of the argument reveals that it does not convincingly establish a rational basis for a *sui generis* claim. The reliance on past "unprecedented" actions by the UNSC as connoting the situation's uniqueness is somewhat of an *ipse dixit*, due to its circular reasoning (requiring us to accept the false statement that since the international community acted unprecedentedly, the situation does not constitute a precedent for future actions by the international community). Furthermore, the argument fails to explain why it is inconceivable that similar circumstances might take place again, in the face of mass atrocities elsewhere; or in other places where negotiations fail to achieve a political solution.[108] Indonesia, for instance, rejected the *sui generis* argument, rightly asserting "that all issues that are on the agenda of the Council have their own unique character," and called for the continuance of negotiations.[109] Similarly, other states, namely Russia and China, were not convinced by the *sui generis* argument and warned against the future implications.[110] The 2010 ICJ advisory opinion regarding Kosovo's declaration did not clarify these issues, as it rendered a very narrow opinion merely legalizing the *act* of Kosovo's declaration of independence, without grappling with the substantive question of remedial secession.[111]

103 *Id.* at 12.
104 *Id.* at 13–14.
105 *Id.* at 18–19.
106 *Id.* at 16.
107 *Id.* at 19–20.
108 For similar critique, *see* Cismas, *supra* note 80, at 585–586.
109 S/PV.5839, *supra* note 102, at 11.
110 *Id.* at. 6–8.
111 Accordance with International Law of the Unilateral Declaration of Independence in Respect of Kosovo, Advisory Opinion, 2010 I.C.J. 141 (July 22).

Even if we are willing to accept the notion that a positive right of "unilateral" remedial secession exists,[112] it is obvious that such right does not materialize under "regular" circumstances of deprivation of internal self-determination, in the form of denial of political participation. Such an extreme result would be problematic when offered as a remedy for a violation of such an ambiguous norm.[113] Indeed, even the unilateral NATO intervention in Kosovo was based on the atrocities committed by Serbia, and not the right to self-determination, in its narrow sense, of Kosovo.[114] Accordingly, in its report on the 2008 Russia–Georgia conflict, the International Fact-Finding Mission concluded that although Georgia has violated, for a time, the internal right of self-determination of the people of South Ossetia and Abkhazia, the latter were not entitled to secede.[115]

Struggles for secession, could be, however, affected by the principle of protection of civilians, even if one does not recognize the doctrine of remedial secession as such. Indeed, if secession is sought as a response to mass atrocities, as was the case in Kosovo, or in instances of other "grave and massive" human rights violations,[116] government consent power can be negated – a fact that can indirectly assist the seceding party. Here, our analysis merges, to a large extent, with the discussion in Chapter 8 regarding the principle of protection of civilians, and its implementation through the RtoP doctrine.[117] Whether secessionist forces are entitled – should the idea of remedial secession be accepted – also to a positive right of *remedial forcible intervention* in the form of the power to request external assistance – is a complex question, on the seam between the concept of humanitarian intervention and recognition, which will be addressed in the next chapter. What is clear, however, is that a government that actively disregards the principle of protection of civilians will lose its consent power when facing a secessionist movement, whether we accept the concept of remedial secession or not.

112 *See* Tomuschat, *supra* note 61, at 38–44.

113 On the high threshold of violations required for remedial secession *see* Cismas, *supra* note 80, at 544–546; Buccheit, *supra* note 92, at 223; *compare* Allen Buchanan, *Uncoupling Secession from Nationalism and Intrastate Autonomy from Secession*, *in* Negotiating Self-Determination 81, 84 (Hurst Hannum and Eileen Babbitt eds., 2006).

114 Farer, *supra* note 95, at 57.

115 *Georgia Report*, *supra* note 61, at 145–146, 147.

116 Tomuschat, *supra* note 61, at 35.

117 *Compare id.* at 41–42 (paralleling the question of remedial secession and humanitarian intervention).

10 Consent by opposition groups

Between recognition and humanitarian intervention; between legality and legitimacy

1 Framing the discussion: between recognition, humanitarian intervention and self-defense

Previous chapters analyzed the scope of the principle of government preference. However, the negation of government consent power does not necessarily entail its *positive* transfer to opposition groups. Indeed, positive forcible support of opposition groups during internal strife has been a longstanding question of international law. During the Cold War, this issue underlined the controversial Brezhnev and Reagan doctrines; it was also a prevalent question in the context of decolonization, and specifically, regarding the support of peoples struggling for self-determination.[1]

An analysis of state practice in terms of support to opposition groups is a problematic exercise. Because of their *prima facie* illegality and reasons of political prudence, states will rarely admit, in specific cases, that they are substantially engaged in such activities[2] – even when it is otherwise a matter of declared policy.[3] Instead, the question can be discussed through a three-tiered, principled approach. First, we must ascertain whether an intervention is in fact in favor of the opposition, or rather it is a "regular" case of intervention in support of a government. For instance, if the intervention followed the recognition of the benefited group as a government or a state, it might not at all be a question of intervention in favor of the opposition. Second, and conversely, if the benefited group is unrecognized to begin with, or recognized unlawfully only as a pretext, any unilateral forcible support given to it – unless it can be separately justified as an act of self-defense – is a *prima facie* violation of the laws on the use of force and the norm of non-intervention. Third, in such cases, if humanitarian justifications are invoked, we may inquire as to the potential role of

1 Chapter 6, sec. 2.

2 Christine D. Gray, International Law and the Use of Force 105–107 (2008).

3 For instance, it is interesting to compare between the legal justifications given by the US to its actions in Nicaragua (collective self-defense), and the various expressions of the Reagan Doctrine, which ostensibly condoned the support of opposition "freedom fighters." *See* Chapter 8, sec. 2.

consent in the legitimization[4] of such an intervention within the paradigm of *unilateral humanitarian intervention.*

As in cases of government consent, self-defense actions by third-party states can amount, in practice, to interventions in support of opposition groups involved in a separate armed conflict against the allegedly aggressor government. An example can be found in the 2001 US invasion of Afghanistan, undertaken as self-defense following the September 11th attacks.[5] In the initial stages of operation Enduring Freedom, Coalition forces de facto supported the Northern Alliance in its armed struggle against the Taliban regime,[6] assuming, for the sake of the example, that the latter could indeed be considered the government of Afghanistan, although it was never recognized by the vast majority of states.[7]

However, as opposed to government consent, that – as we saw in Chapter 1 – can augment controversial self-defense claims against non-state actors,[8] support granted to opposition groups in the wider context of self-defense actions does not produce the same effect. On the contrary, it can potentially transform an otherwise legal self-defense action into an unlawful intervention. This is because regime change, assuming it is sought by the opposition and supported by the intervening state, is not necessarily a valid objective of self-defense actions, in light of the *jus ad bellum* principles of necessity and proportionality. Nevertheless, the assessment of the relations between self-defense, opposition consent and regime change can only be conducted on a case-by-case basis, upon analysis of the gravity of the threat posed to the self-defending intervener by the attacking regime.[9] Since this is primarily a question of the law of self-defense, we shall not analyze it further here.[10]

4 The term "legitimate," as opposed to "legal," is used here generically, referring to acts that are not legal per se but may be justified or excused on some other basis. For a discussion of the term "legitimacy" in various international legal aspects *see* Brad R. Roth, Governmental Illegitimacy in International Law Ch. 2 (2001); Thomas Franck, The Power of Legitimacy among Nations (1990).

5 S.C. Res. 1368, U.N. Doc. S/RES/1368 (September 12, 2001); S.C. Res. 1373, U.N. Doc. S/RES/1373 (September 28, 2001).

6 Laurie R. Blank and Benjamin R. Farley, *Characterizing U.S. Operations in Pakistan: Is the United States Engaged in an Armed Conflict?* 34 Fordham International Law Journal 151, 179–180 (2010); Michael N. Schmitt, *Targeting and International Humanitarian Law in Afghanistan,* 85 International Legal Studies Series U.S. Naval War College 307, 308–309 (2009).

7 The UN continuously refused to accept the credentials of the Taliban government upon its taking power in 1996. *See, e.g.,* 1996 Yearbook U.N. 1482; 2000 Yearbook U.N. 1369.

8 Sec. 1.2.

9 For an ethical analysis of regime change and *jus ad bellum see* Michael Walzer, Just and Unjust Wars ix–xviii (4th ed., 2006).

10 *See* Theresa Reinold, State Weakness, Irregular Warfare, and the Right to Self-Defense Post-9/11, 105 American Journal of International Law 244, 268 (2011) (addressing the question of regime change within the proportionality requirement of the law of self-defense).

Like self-defense, not every case of humanitarian intervention – as we shall discuss the concept later on – warrants regime change.[11] However, in light of the concept of sovereignty as *responsibility*, it seems intuitively right that contributing to regime change – *inter alia* through support of the opposition – can be, generally, more reasonable in cases of internal mass atrocities, than in most instances of "pure" inter-state self-defense.

2 Government and opposition: distinction, interaction and the basic rule against the forcible support of opposition groups

2.1 The distinction between government and opposition

The legality of any forcible act in favor of a party *recognized* by the intervener as a government or as an independent state raises an immediate question in the law of recognition. If the recognition itself is lawful, then the intervention is in support of a government, and should thereafter be analyzed according to the limits of the presumption in favor of governments. If the conflict is one of secession, and the opposition is lawfully recognized as a separate state, then the act is not an intervention in an internal armed conflict but rather a participation in an international one.

Of course, the recognition of governments and states is one of the perpetual problems of international law. Intrinsically woven with it is the question of "who decides," in a particular instance, whether a party is duly recognized.[12] Indeed, absent binding collective mechanisms, recognition is highly prone – as we shall see – to abuse. However, the primary distinction between recognized and non-recognized entities, in the context of the law on the use of force, remains theoretically sound nonetheless. While this postulation merits a study of its own, we assume that nowadays,

11 *See* James Pattison, The Ethics of Humanitarian Intervention in Libya, 25 Ethics and International Affairs 1, 3–4 (2011).

12 It is in this context where the longstanding argument between the declarative and constitutive doctrines of recognition takes place. This work will not add to the abundance of scholarship regarding this question. *See* Hersch Lauterpacht, Recognition in International Law 2–3, 38–42 (1948); James Crawford, The Creation of States in International Law 1–17, 22–26 (2006); Thomas D. Grant, The Recognition of States 2–12 (1999). We adopt, as a given, the contemporary opinion that recognition has both declarative and constitutive elements. *See, e.g.*, Crawford, *supra* note 12, at 23; Grant, *supra* note 12, at 19, 71–73. The dual nature of recognition seems especially true considering the recent debates on questions of recognition, both in the context of Palestine, and in the Arab Spring. *See* John Quigley, The Statehood of Palestine: International Law in the Middle East Conflict (2010) (making the case that Palestine is a state); but *see* The Office of the Prosecutor, International Criminal Court, Situation in Palestine (April 3, 2012) (asserting that the Prosecutor cannot decide that Palestine is a state absent such a determination by relevant UN bodies, or by the Court's Assembly of State Parties). On recognition in the context of the Arab Spring, *see* next sections.

recognition is more likely to be internationally accepted – and in particularly in the context of intervention – when conducted through universal or regional bodies. For instance, UN membership or acceptance of credentials, can serve as acts of recognition enjoying enhanced legitimacy;[13] positions of regional organizations, as we saw in the context of the 2011 Gbagbo affair, can also play a substantial role.[14]

Conversely, any intervention on behalf of a group not fully and completely recognized as the lawful government or as a separate state is an intervention on behalf of an opposition group. Indeed, this definition provides some conceptual clarity. However, as a mirror image of the question of recognition of governments, it presents the same practical difficulties. Here, too, the absence of a collective mechanism for recognition can result in abuse, or in anomalous situations where recognition is granted to opposition groups by certain states but not by others[15] – as is the case today regarding Kosovo, Abkhazia and South Ossetia.[16] In other instances, such as in the 2011 Libyan conflict, recognition can be a "rolling" affair, some states being quicker to recognize the opposition as the government than others.[17]

Since we define the "opposition" negatively – meaning, as the party not recognized as a government – it is worthwhile to ask whether there are also *positive* criteria for the identification of opposition groups. Essentially, the existence of an internal armed conflict, as defined in Chapter 2, requires the existence of "organized armed groups."[18] The same threshold of "organization" that is used to ascertain whether an internal armed conflict exists is key for the identification of the opposition in a certain instance – *a fortiori* for viewing it as a valid interlocutor to promote the protection of civilians. Of course, the opposition can often consist of fragmented groups, constantly shifting alliances and splintering into smaller groups, thereby making it impossible to treat it as a unified body capable of expressing any kind of collective will. However, in certain instances, loosely aligned opposition groups were relatively quick to form quasi-representative bodies, such as the Libyan National Transitional Council;[19] the Syrian National Council, established in September 2011, attempted to

13 Roth, *supra* note 4, at 126.

14 Chapter 9, sec. 1.3.

15 Compare, Antonio Cassese, International Law 74 (2005); Grant, *supra* note 12, at 19–22. Compare Lauterpacht, *supra* note 12, at 53–54.

16 *See, e.g.,* Rein Müllerson, Precedents in the Mountains: On the Parallels and Uniqueness of the Cases of Kosovo, South Ossetia and Abkhazia, 8 Chinese Journal of International Law 2 (2009).

17 *See* sec. 2.2.

18 Sec. 2.

19 International Crisis Group, Popular Protest in North Africa and the Middle East (V):Making Sense of Libya 24–26, ICG Mid. East/North Africa Report No. 107 (June 6, 2011).

play the same role, to a lesser degree of success on the ground, at least as of December 2012.[20] Such bodies purport to represent the general interest of the opposition in front of the international community.[21] As we shall see, if they are sufficiently organized, and exercise or seek to exercise effective protection of civilians, or are confronting government forces that do not do so, the international community might be willing to engage such opposition groups – and perhaps even to recognize them.

2.2 Effective protection and non-forcible interaction with opposition groups

Consistent with our analysis in Chapter 8, the concept of effective protection can trump considerations of territorial effective control also in the context of the international community's will to *engage* with opposition groups prior to official recognition. Here, we do not yet ask whether forcible intervention on behalf of such groups is lawful, but merely the interaction of external parties with such groups.

In a manner reminiscent of – yet differing from – the traditional insurgency doctrine,[22] intermediate situations in which external parties engage opposition groups, on different levels, occur also in contemporary practice. For instance, Turkey has maintained contact with Syrian opposition groups during the 2011–2012 Syrian uprising[23] prior to official recognition; it moreover cooperated to a certain extent with armed Syrian groups, namely the Free Syrian Army.[24] A similar position was taken by France,

20 Syrian Opposition Unveils Council Names, B.B.C. News, September 16, 2011, available at www.bbc.co.uk/news/world-middle-east-14929813. In December 2011, the Syrian National Council pledged to unify with other groups and to promote democratic transition. *See* David Batty, Syrian Opposition Groups Unite to Chart Roadmap to Democracy, Guardian, December 31, 2011, available at www.guardian.co.uk/world/2011/dec/31/syria-opposition-plan-democratic-future. The study of how and when organized opposition groups form political wings, or when they enter into political participation, is a science in itself. *See, e.g.,* Benedetta Berti, Armed Groups as Political Parties and Their Role in Electoral Politics: The Case of Hizballah, 34 Studies in Conflict and Terrorism 942 (2011).

21 For instance, on January 21, 2012, the Syrian National Council requested the League of Arab States to refer the Syrian crisis to the UNSC. *See* Opposition Urges Arab League to Refer Syria to U.N., Reuters, January 21, 2012, available at http://af.reuters.com/article/commoditiesNews/idAFL6E8CL0AH20120121.

22 Chapter 4, sec. 4.

23 *See* Peter Harling and Sarah Birke, Beyond the Fall of the Syrian Regime, Middle East Research and Information (February 24, 2012), available at www.merip.org/mero/mero022412.

24 Dominic Evans, Turkey Holds Talks with Syrian Opposition Council, Reuters, October 18, 2011, www.reuters.com/article/2011/10/18/us-syria-idUSTRE79H3VB20111018; Liam Stack, In Slap at Syria, Turkey Shelters Anti-Assad Fighters, New York Times, October 27, 2011, available at www.nytimes.com/2011/10/28/world/europe/turkey-is-sheltering-antigovernment-syrian-militia.html?_r=3&hp.

admitting that it was "helping" the opposition and "encouraging them to get organized."[25] Britain sent a special envoy to the Syrian opposition, and other countries urged various Syrian groups to cooperate with each other.[26] US Secretary of State Hillary Clinton has also met the Syrian opposition, calling it a "leading and legitimate representative of Syrians seeking a peaceful democratic transition"[27] – a statement short of full recognition, but undoubtedly one of support.[28] The Syrian opposition was also a party to failed Arab League reconciliation processes,[29] and was mentioned in the 2012 Six-Point peace plan outlined by Kofi Annan, acting as a joint envoy of the UN and the Arab League.[30]

All of these interactions were met with general international acquiescence. Indeed, following vetoes exercised by China and Russia in relation to any condemnation of the Syrian regime in the UNSC,[31] many dozens of states participated in anti-regime summits under the auspices of the "Friends of the Syrian People" framework, where the Syrian opposition presented reports regarding the situation on the ground, and eventually received recognition "as the legitimate representative of the Syrian people."[32] The Friends' Group also pledged to set up a Sanctions Working Group to monitor sanctions against the regime and, importantly, to grant financial support "to meet the needs of the Syrian people,"[33] which is likely

25 Khaled Yacoub Oweis, Russia Stands by Assad as Pressure Mounts on Syria, Reuters, November 17, 2011, available at www.reuters.com/article/2011/11/17/us-syria-idUSL5E7MD0GZ20111117.

26 Syria's Opposition Gaining Ground, The Economist (December 17, 2011), available at www.economist.com/node/21541847.

27 Karen DeYoung, Clinton Meets with Syria Opposition, Washington Post, December 6, 2011, available at www.washingtonpost.com/world/middle_east/clinton-meets-with-syria-opposition/2011/12/06/gIQApzQ9ZO_story.html.

28 Britain made a similar declaration. *See* Martin Chulov and Matthew Weaver, Saudi Arabia Backs Arming Syrian Opposition, Guardian, February 24, 2012, available at www.guardian.co.uk/world/2012/feb/24/saudi-arabia-backs-arming-syrian-opposition.

29 Syria "Violence Defies Peace Deal," Al-Jazeera English, November 4, 2011, available at http://english.aljazeera.net/news/middleeast/2011/11/201111381935847935.html.

30 S.C. Prst. 2012/6, U.N. Doc. S/PRST/2012/6 (March 21, 2012) (endorsing and outlining the Six Point plan); S.C. Prst. 2012/10, U.N. Doc. S/PRST/2012/10 (April 5, 2012) (calling on the parties to adhere to the plan).

31 *See* infra, n. 140.

32 Friends of Syria Group Recognizes Opposition Coalition, Reuters, December 12, 2012, available at http://www.reuters.com/article/2012/12/12/us-syria-crisis-idUSBRE8AJ1FK20121212; *see also* Full Text of the Chairman's Conclusions of the International Conference of the Group of Friends of the Syrian People ¶4, 10 (April 1, 2012), available at www.fco.gov.uk/en/news/latest-news/?view=News&id=749074282.

33 *Id.* ¶¶17–18.

34 Chapter 2, sec. 2.

35 Chapter 1, sec. 1.2; Jeffery Gettleman, Ethiopian Troops Said to Enter Somalia, Opening New Front Against Militants, New York Times, November 20, 2011, available at www.nytimes.com/2011/11/21/world/africa/ethiopian-troops-enter-somalia-witnesses-say.html.

channeled through the Syrian opposition. A comparable international reaction took place, as we shall shortly see, during the 2011 Libyan conflict.

In the past – as we have detailed in Chapter 4 – the rigid belligerency doctrine, and to a large extent also the flexible insurgency doctrine, made the interaction with opposition groups contingent mainly upon their attainment of a degree of territorial effective control. Furthermore, underlying these doctrines was, in general, a notion of neutrality between the conflicting parties. However, it seems that nowadays the interaction is influenced – once the uprising becomes substantial – primarily by considerations of effective protection, shedding the pretense of neutrality or "impartiality." Accordingly, the more that opposition groups are deemed as violators of the protection principle, the more the international community might be willing to rely on territorially ineffective governments. Conversely, the more a government violates the principle of protection, the international community might be more willing to give credit to relatively ineffective opposition groups, as potential fulfillers of the responsibility to protect. In other cases, any substantial *positive* interaction with opposition groups might amount to a violation of the norm of non-intervention.[34]

In order to exemplify this notion it is revealing to juxtapose the treatment, in recent times, of opposition groups in Somalia versus their treatment in Libya. As detailed in Chapter 7, the Transitional Federal Government (TFG) of Somalia has retained its international recognition, including in the context of consent power, although it barely controlled any territory. It has received the forcible support of Ethiopia 2006, and again in late 2011, when it also received support from Kenya;[35] likewise, the UNSC has emphasized its support of the TFG in many resolutions. Conversely, the opposing Al-Shabaab militia, accused of links with Al-Qa'ida and of obstructing humanitarian aid, has not, in general, received any intermediate recognition by the international community – despite controlling vast parts of Somalia. Furthermore, Eritrea was punished for supporting the group and its predecessor, the Islamic Courts Union.[36]

Regarding the 2011 Libyan conflict, the reaction has been the exact opposite. First, many states have engaged the Libyan opposition, prior to full recognition, as legitimate "political interlocutors" with which dialogue can be conducted.[37] For instance, in March 2011, the US appointed a Liaison to the Libyan rebels, in order to "determine how the United States could help them."[38] This approach is reminiscent of the flexible

36 On these dynamics regarding Somalia *see* Chapter 7, sec. 2.4; Chapter 8, sec. 2.4; Chapter 1, sec. 1.2.

37 *See* Stefan Talmon, Recognition of the Libyan Transitional Council, 15 Amerian Society of International Law Insights (June 16, 2011), www.asil.org/insights110616.cfm.

38 Helene Cooper, U.S. to Name a Liaison to Libyan Rebels, New York Times, March 11, 2011, available at www.nytimes.com/2011/03/12/world/africa/12policy.html?_r=3&hpw.

insurgency doctrine, except for the significant fact that it reflects a preference of the opposition on *substantive* grounds, rather than on counts of territorial effectiveness.

Second, the intermediate status of the Libyan opposition can be demonstrated in the unusual circumstances of the UNSC debate of February 26, 2011.[39] In mid-February 2011, protests against the Al-Qadhafi regime erupted, spreading westward from the eastern city of Benghazi.[40] As the regime responded forcefully, key Libyan diplomats resigned or sided with the opposition. On February 21, Libya's deputy ambassador to the UN called for Al-Qadhafi's resignation, proclaiming that the delegation serves the Libyan people, and not the regime.[41] So did Libya's delegations to the UN Human Rights Council and the Arab League.[42] On February 25, the same "former" representative of Libya, appearing in the UNSC, appealed for support, calling for a "swift, decisive and courageous resolution."[43] A day later, the UNSC adopted Resolution 1970, recalling "the Libyan authorities' responsibility to protect its population," imposing sanctions and referring the situation to the Prosecutor of the ICC.[44] As the resolution imposed an arms embargo on Libya, it *a fortiori* prohibited any forcible support of the regime, thereby unequivocally negating the government preference.[45]

Significantly, the resolution – and the circumstances of its adoption – exemplifies the international readiness to interact with opposition groups, where the government violates the principle of protection. Accordingly, although the Libyan delegation ceased to represent the Al-Qadhafi regime, the resolution noted the letter of the Permanent Representative of Libya, in which he expressed *support* for UNSC action.[46] In his statements, the representative of Libya thanked the Council for the resolution and commended it as a "sincere attempt to protect civilians." He expressed

39 See, in this context, Eliav Lieblich, Consensual Intervention and the Responsibility to Protect, in The Responsibility to Protect: From Theory to Practice 141, 149–150 (Andre Nollkaemper and Julia Hoffman eds., 2012).

40 Timeline: Six Remarkable Days in Libya, C.N.N., February 20, 2011, http://articles.cnn.com/2011–02–20/world/libya.protests.timeline_1_anti-government-protesters-pro-government-security-forces/2?_s=PM:WORLD.

41 Libyan U.N. Diplomats: Al-Qadhafi Should Resign, C.B.S. News, February 21, 2011 www.cbsnews.com/stories/2011/02/21/501364/main20034507.shtml.

42 Libyan Delegation to U.N. Rights Council Resigns, Haaretz, February 25, 2011, available at www.haaretz.com/news/international/libyan-delegation-to-un-rights-council-resigns–1.345713.y 2011.

43 U.N. SCOR, 66th Sess., 6490th mtg. at 5, U.N. Doc. S/PV.6490 (February 25, 2011).

44 S.C. Res. 1970, U.N. Doc. S/RES/1970 (February 26, 2011).

45 *See* U.N. Charter art. 2(5).

46 S.C. Res. 1970, *supra* note 44, prmbl; Letter dated 21 February 2011 from the Chargé d'affaires a.i. of the Permanent Mission of the Libyan Arab Jamahiriya to the United Nations addressed to the President of the Security Council, U.N. Doc. S/2011/102 (February 22, 2011).

confidence that it will bring "a definite end to the fascist regime that is still in place in Tripoli."[47]

Although Resolution 1970 did not yet authorise a forcible intervention – this happened in Resolution 1973, adopted a few weeks later, which led to Al-Qadhafi's ouster[48] – it demonstrates that in cases of loss of effective protection, support for the opposition can affect decision-making in the Council. This notion was reflected in statements by several Council members. While China referred laconically to the "special situation in Libya" as grounds for its support for the resolution,[49] other states were less ambiguous. India stated that the position of the Libyan delegation "strengthened" its support for the resolution.[50] Nigeria declared that the Libyan delegation's stance and the "cries of help of the Libyan people" persuaded it to vote positively.[51] Brazil stated that it gave "due regard" to the requests by the delegation.[52] South Africa and France went further. The former declared that the Council "responded swiftly and resolutely" to the call of the Libyan delegation.[53] France welcomed the fact that the Council has "unanimously and forcefully responded" to the Libyan appeal.[54]

It is inconceivable that the members of the Council were not fully aware of the peculiar situation. It is equally implausible that they were willingly engaged in a joint violation of international law, in such a public international forum. There can thus be little doubt that the failure of the Al-Qadhafi regime to effectively protect its civilians resulted in some de facto status granted to the opposition in front of the Council; this was true although the Al-Qadhafi regime was still considered by the Council as the "authority" in Libya, and the credentials of the Libyan National Transitional Council were accepted by the UNGA only months later.[55] Although the circumstances above were unique, and are rather unlikely to be repeated in an exact manner, they arguably reflect a general trend in the law of internal armed conflict.

Nonetheless, the decision of the international community to engage opposition groups, without recognizing them as governments, cannot in itself grant them the power to consent to forcible intervention. However, from the case of Libya we can learn two main things: first, that opposition consent can play a role in UNSC considerations; and second, that protection of civilians plays a prominent role in the will of states to deal with the opposition in specific instances.

47 U.N. SCOR, 66th Sess., 6491st mtg. at 7, U.N. Doc. S/PV.6491 (February 26, 2011).

48 S.C. Res. 1973 ¶4, U.N. Doc. S/RES/1973 (March 17, 2011); *see also* Chapter 1, sec. 4.1.

49 S/PV.6491, *supra* note 47, at 4.

50 *Id.* at 2.

51 *Id.* at 3.

52 *Id.* at 7.

53 *Id.* at 3.

54 *Id.* at 5.

2.3 The basic rule: forcible intervention in favor of opposition groups as an unlawful use of force

As evident from the prohibition on the use of force as entrenched in Article 2(4) of the UN Charter, and as was ruled in the Nicaragua case,[56] any unilateral intervention in an internal armed conflict justified strictly on counts of opposition consent – and absent a credible self-defense claim by the intervener – is a *prima facie* violation of the norm of non-intervention and the prohibition on the use of force. Accordingly, the Declaration on Friendly Relations proclaims that:

> Every State has the duty to refrain from organizing, instigating, assisting or participating in acts of civil strife or terrorist acts in another State or in organized activities within its territory directed towards the commission of such acts, when the acts referred to in the present paragraph involve a threat or use of force.[57]

The Declaration further declares that "no State shall organize, assist, foment, finance, incite or tolerate subversive, terrorist or armed activities directed towards the violent overthrow of the regime of another State, or interfere in civil strife in another State."[58] Additionally, Article 3(g) of the 1974 Definition of Aggression – reflecting customary international law – defines as aggression indirect forcible intervention in the form of "the sending by or on behalf of a State of armed bands, groups, irregulars or mercenaries, which carry out acts of armed force against another State of such gravity as to amount to the acts listed above, or its substantial involvement therein."[59] The same formula has been adopted in the 2010 Kampala definition of the crime of aggression.[60]

However, the nature of the prohibition on supporting opposition groups has not always been entirely clear. As we saw in Chapter 9, the era of decolonization ushered in a robust debate regarding the relation between the principle of self-determination and the use of force. A product of this era, Article 7 of the Definition of Aggression created a rather complex normative situation:

55 G.A. Res. 66/1A, U.N. Doc. A/RES/66/1A (September 16, 2011).

56 *See* Chapter 6, sec. 4.3.

57 Declaration on Principles of International Law concerning Friendly Relations and Co-operation among States, Principle 1¶9, G.A. Res. 2625 (XXV), U.N. Doc. A/2625 (October 24, 1970).

58 *Id.* Principle 3¶2.

59 Definition of Aggression, G.A. Res. 3314 (XXIX), UN Doc A/9631 (December 14, 1974). Article 3(g) of the definition was considered by the ICJ, in the Nicaragua case, as a customary norm. Military Aid and Paramilitary Activities in and against Nicaragua (Nicar. v. U.S.), 1986 I.C.J. 14 (June 27), ¶195.

60 The Crime of Aggression, art. 8bis(g), Resolution RC/Res.6, RC/11 (June 11, 2010).

> Nothing in this Definition … could in any way prejudice the right to self-determination, freedom and independence, as derived from the Charter, of peoples forcibly deprived of that right and referred to in the Declaration on Principles of International Law concerning Friendly Relations and Cooperation among States in accordance with the Charter of the UN, particularly peoples under colonial and racist regimes or other forms of alien domination: nor the right of these peoples to struggle to that end and to seek and *receive support*, in accordance with the principles of the Charter and in conformity with the above-mentioned Declaration.[61]

Presumably, then, the Definition allows for the provision of positive support to opposition groups, in the circumstances enumerated. These circumstances encompass struggles against three distinct (but potentially overlapping) forms of oppression: colonial regimes, racist regimes, and "other forms" of alien domination.[62] Indeed, as we have seen, anti-colonial struggles have been excluded from the realm of internal strife, and in any case are of less contemporary significance.[63] Cases of "alien domination," while differing from usual forms of occupation, are also not internal.[64] The third instance, however, refers to "racist regimes," a term that can include regimes that are *not* colonialist or alien, but are still "racist." In essence, then, of the three scenarios mentioned in Article 7, struggles against "racist regimes" could theoretically fall within the paradigm of internal armed conflicts. In such instances, Article 7 can be construed as recognizing that opposition forces, in *internal* conflicts against racist regimes, are entitled to seek and receive support. In this sense, the Article represents a move towards substantive analysis of opposition groups, permitting their support on counts of the *nature* of their struggle.

However, much like the Declaration of Friendly relations, the Definition of Aggression is an ambiguous document. A typical document of the Cold War era UN, its adoption by consensus required a high degree of normative vagueness.[65] Accordingly, Article 7 does not explicitly refer to the right of peoples to use *force*, but rather to their "struggles," thereby alleviating some states' concerns that the article would be perceived as

61 Definition of Aggression, *supra* note 59, art. 7.

62 *See* the comparable provision in Protocol Additional to the Geneva Conventions of 12 August 1949, and Relating to the Protection of Victims of International Armed Conflicts (Protocol I), June 8, 1977, art. 1(4), 1125 U.N.T.S. 3.

63 Chapter 9, at sec. 2.1.

64 Such cases are different by not being restricted to occupation of a territory of a state. *See* ICRC, Commentary on the Additional Protocols of 8 June 1977 to the Geneva Conventions of 12 August 1949 ¶112 (Yves Sandoz et al. eds., 1987) (discussing the concept of "alien occupation").

65 *See* Julius Stone, Hopes and Loopholes in the 1974 Definition of Aggression, 71 American Journal of International Law 224, 225, 233–237 (1977).

recognizing a positive right to engage in armed resistance and receive support.[66] Moreover, as the Definition of Aggression subjects itself both to the Declaration of Friendly Relations and to the principles of the UN Charter, the scope of the right of peoples to "seek" and "receive" support is rather unclear, in particular regarding to the power to request *forcible* support. In light of the supremacy of the *jus cogens* prohibition on the use of force, the correct interpretation of the Article would be that at least to the extent that it encompasses situations that could be qualified as "internal" – i.e., racist regimes – any right to seek and receive support would have been limited to non-forcible measures.[67]

In the decolonized world, the significance and controversy surrounding Article 7 is of less importance.[68] Notably, the Article does not address one of the most burning issues of the contemporary system – the protection of civilians, and whether mass atrocities could affect, in any way, the power to consent to and receive forcible assistance.

3 Consensual intervention and recognition

3.1 State recognition, remedial secession and remedial intervention

As discussed in Chapter 9, the question of remedial secession remains controversial in international law. Naturally, if we reject this doctrine to begin with, it is obvious that secessionist claims cannot alter the opposition's lack of consent power. However, if we do accept the plausibility of remedial secession, does it follow that the seceding-seeking party also attains the right of "remedial forcible intervention"?

The answer is rather simple, at least in legal-theoretical terms. It involves a two-stepped approach, requiring first to address the issue as a question of state-recognition; and in the second stage, as a case of collective self-defense. Indeed, the remedy offered by the doctrine of remedial secession is the *recognition* of the seceding party as a state, and not the unilateral forcible intervention on its behalf.[69] After such recognition is granted, however, the conflict is no longer one between a "government" and "opposition" groups, but rather one between two states. In this stage, it becomes an *international* armed conflict, in which the seceding state,

66 *Id.* at 233–234.

67 *See* Yoram Dinstein, War, Aggression and Self-Defense 72–73 (5th ed. 2011); Nicaragua, *supra* note 59, ¶¶178–181 (Schwebel J., dissenting). It is noteworthy that the ICISS Report expressly referred to situations of "racist regimes" as not justifying forcible intervention. *See* Report of the International Commission on Intervention and State Sovereignty, The Responsibility to Protect ¶4.25 (2001).

68 *See, e.g.,* Mary Ellen O'Connell, Regulating the Use of Force in the 21st Century: The Continuing Importance of State Autonomy, 36 Columbia Journal of Transnational Law 473, 476 (1997).

69 *See* Chapter 9, sec. 2.2.

if attacked by the rump-state, can theoretically invoke the right of collective-self-defense as enshrined in Article 51 of the UN Charter.[70] In such cases, the right of the seceding state to request forcible support is not controlled by the principle of government preference, but rather by the *jus ad bellum* law of self-defense.

This analysis raises acute problems in the law of state recognition. Of course, as in questions of recognition at large, the absence of a collective recognition mechanism is prone to abuse, during secession struggles, by interested external parties. For instance, on August 26, 2008, Russia unilaterally recognized secession-seeking Abkhazia and South Ossetia as states independent from Georgia, shortly after Russian forces invaded the breakaway territories.[71] In addition to justifying its initial operations in Georgia as self-defense actions[72] – a claim partially vindicated by a fact-finding mission – Russia based its recognition of the breakaway territories on the notion of remedial secession. Thus, it argued that:

> Constantly trying to use brutal military force against the very ethnic groups whom he purportedly wanted to see as a part of his state, [Georgian President] Mr. Saakashvili left them with no other choice but to seek ways to ensure their security and the right to self-determination as independent nations. In this respect the Decrees issued by President Dmitry Medvedev of the Russian Federation recognising Abkhazia's and South Ossetia's independence offered the only opportunity to save the lives of people and prevent further bloodshed in the Transcaucasian region.[73]

After its recognition of the breakaway territories, Russia has proceeded to justify its operations on counts of the right of *collective* self-defense.[74] Whatever the legal merits of the Russian position in this context – and considering these were rejected by the fact-finding mission[75] – the dynamics of the Russia–Georgia conflict clearly represent the dangers of unilateral state-recognition granted as a pretext for intervention justified thereafter as an act of collective self-defense. However, these "secondary" concerns in themselves do not challenge the "primary" theoretical soundness of such claims, should we accept the doctrine of remedial secession.

70 Compare Michael Byers and Simon Chesterman, Changing the Rules about the Rules? Unilateral Humanitarian Intervention and the Future of International Law, in Humanitarian Intervention: Ethical, Legal and Political Dilemmas 177, 182 (J.L. Holzgrefe and Robert O. Keohane eds., 2003).

71 Independent International Fact-Finding Mission on the Conflict in Georgia, Report (Vol. 2), at 28, 44, 209–217 (September 30, 2009).

72 *Id.* at 189.

73 *Id.* at 190.

74 *Id.* at 280.

75 *See* id. at 141, 281–282.

Recent practice – and in particular the robust involvement of regional organizations in internal conflicts, and the general international deference to their views, can perhaps alleviate these concerns.[76]

In any case, as regarding government and belligerency recognition, the traditional law of state recognition is based on standards of effective control, as provided for in Article I of the Montevideo Convention of 1933. In order to be considered a state – the controversy regarding the constitutive versus declarative approaches notwithstanding[77] – the entity had to possess a *permanent population*; *a defined territory*; a *government*; and the *capacity to enter into relations with other states*.[78] Before discussing these criteria in the context of remedial secession, it should be emphasized that there is a general decline in their predominance with regards to recognition of *new* states. Most notably during the dissolution of Yugoslavia and the USSR, numerous substantive criteria for recognition have emerged. For instance, the European Communities' Guidelines on the Recognition of New States in Eastern Europe and in the Soviet Union[79] provided a substantive framework for the recognition of new states. By moving away from a formal, effectiveness-based process of recognition to a value-based assessment, the Guidelines reflected a significant reform to traditional recognition law.[80] Thus, the Guidelines maintained that the EC will adhere to "normal standards of international practice" concerning recognition, but set forth additional conditions – relating to the principles of self-determination; democracy; respect for the UN Charter; minority rights; territorial integrity; and non-aggression.

In a similar manner, the mere idea of remedial secession presupposes the possibility of a *substantive* analysis of the parties, since it connotes a right of secession independent from considerations of effective control, but based on the protection of civilians. For instance, if we consider the Kosovo case as an example of remedial secession, we must agree that the

76 *See, e.g.*, the heavy involvement of the European Communities in the recognition of states following the dissolution of Yugoslavia; and the general international deference to the position of the AU on the question of Somaliland and its attempt at secession from Somalia. Roland Rich, Recognition of States: The Collapse of Yugoslavia and the Soviet Union, 4 European Journal of International Law 36, 42 (1993); Benjamin Farley, Calling a State a State: Somaliland and International Recognition, 24 Emory International Law Review 777 (2011).

77 *See supra*, note 12.

78 Convention on the Rights and Duties of States (Montevideo Convention) December 26, 1933, art. I, 165 L.N.T.S. 19; Lauterpacht, *supra* note 12, at 26. On the Montevideo Convention and its relation to prevalent perceptions of statehood as effective control, *see* Grant, *supra* note 12, at 5–12; Sean D. Murphy, Democratic Legitimacy and Recognition, in Democratic Governance and International Law 123, 125 (Gregory H. Fox and Brad R. Roth eds., 2000).

79 E.C. Declaration on the Guidelines on the Recognition of New States in Eastern Europe and in the Soviet Union (December 16, 1991).

80 *See* Rich, *supra* note 76, at 42, 56; on the EC Guidelines in the context of democracy as a recognition criterion *see* Murphy, *supra* note 79, at 132–139.

existence or inexistence of territorial effective control in the hands of the Kosovar authorities was not a dominant consideration in the eyes of the international community. In fact, neither the opponents nor the proponents of Kosovo's statehood, regardless of their stance regarding its precedential value, referred explicitly to territorial effectiveness as a justification for their positions.[81]

Likewise, the principle of territorial integrity – which generally rejects the possibility of secession – must presuppose that secession does not connote automatic recognition *even* in cases where the seceding party fulfills the Montevideo criteria. Otherwise, the principle of territorial integrity would be rendered utterly meaningless. We can see this tendency in the case of Somaliland: while that breakaway territory of Somalia generally fulfills the Montevideo conditions for statehood,[82] as of December 2012 Somaliland was not officially and fully recognized by any state. Instead, the international community has opted to maintain the recognition of Somalia in its previous borders, administered through completely ineffective governments. Western powers, in general, are reluctant to extend recognition to Somaliland before the AU takes such a step, which it is reluctant to make.[83]

It is obvious, then, that the Montevideo criteria do not reflect the complex balancing of interests required to address the question of secession: in regular struggles for secession, the principle of territorial integrity seems to trump the Montevideo effectiveness criteria; if, conversely, one adopts the doctrine of remedial secession, then the guiding principle for recognition *must* be the protection of civilians – since that principle forms the basis of the doctrine to begin with.

Nevertheless, even if we do accept the doctrine of remedial secession in principle, when states intervene in favor of a secession-seeking party *prior* to full and official state recognition, as was the case in Kosovo, or when recognition is merely a pretext for intervention – as in the Russia-Georgia conflict – then the intervention is a *prima facie* violation of the prohibition on the use of force. If justified on humanitarian grounds, then the discussion falls within the ambit of the humanitarian intervention question, which we will address in section 4.

3.2 Recognition of the opposition as the government

As discussed in section 2.1, once opposition groups are recognized as governments, any consent they grant must be analyzed according to the presumption in favor of governments. The question of government

81 *See* U.N. SCOR 63rd Sess., 5839th mtg. U.N. Doc. S/PV.5839 (February 18, 2008).

82 Farley, *supra* note 76.

83 *Id.* at 809–815; Human Rights Watch, Hostages to Peace: Threats to Human Rights and Democracy in Somaliland 51–55 (July 13, 2009).

recognition differs from state recognition in secession struggles, since the former does not challenge directly the principle of territorial integrity. However, despite this difference and others, they are similar in two main aspects: both spheres of recognition traditionally rely on criteria of territorial effectiveness;[84] and regarding both there is an inherent potential for abuse emanating from the absence of collective recognition mechanisms. This danger has been consistent throughout the decades, as government recognition was granted or otherwise manipulated as pretext for forcible interventions. This was definitely the case of the 1936 recognition of the Franco regime as the government of Spain by Nazi Germany and Fascist Italy;[85] possibly with regards to the 1962 Egyptian recognition granted to the ineffective Yemen Arab Republic;[86] and arguably in the case of the 1983 American reference to the invitation of Grenada's Governor General as one justification for its intervention there.[87] This potential for abuse persists also in present times.

In any case, traditionally, opposition groups that managed to wield "effective power, with a reasonable prospect of permanency, over the whole – or practically the whole – territory of the State" were seen as entitled to recognition.[88] Thus, as long as the conflict was in progress, their recognition as governments was perceived as contrary to international law.[89] Like in the context of state recognition, this test was not concerned with substantive considerations.[90] Nor, in general, was the consent of the governed a necessary condition for recognition – although some, such as Lauterpacht, viewed such consent as an indication that effective control indeed exists.[91]

Indeed, the question of recognition of insurgents as governments has troubled international lawyers for centuries. Lauterpacht, for instance, adopted an intricate theory of de facto versus *de jure* recognition, positing that opposition groups could be granted de facto recognition as the governments of the territories they control, but as long as the conflict continued, they could not be recognized as *de jure* governments.[92] Whatever the surviving merits of this distinction, it is clear that for the materialization of

84 Ian Brownlie, Principles of Public International Law 90 (2008). On the complex relations between the recognition of states and the recognition of governments *see* Roth, *supra* note 4, at 130–132.

85 *See* Chapter 5, at sec. 4.1.

86 Arthur Mark Weisburd, Use of Force: the Practice of States Since World War II 184–185 (1997).

87 *See* Chapter 8, at sec. 4.2.

88 Lauterpacht, *supra* note 12, at 98; M.J. Peterson, Recognition of Governments 35–39 (1997).

89 Lauterpacht, *supra* note 12, at 279.

90 *Id.* at 106–108.

91 *Id.* at 115–136 (outlining the practice of Britain and the United States in this context); compare Roth, *supra* note 4, at 139–141.

92 Lauterpacht, *supra* note 12, at 279, 284–294.

consent power, recognition of the opposition must be full and complete; any act short of recognizing it as the sole entity that speaks for the *state*, accepting thereby all legal and political consequences that such recognition entails,[93] will render any forcible support given to it – whether through direct use of military force or by provision of arms – a violation of Article 2(4) of the UN Charter.[94]

In this context, the movement away from strict territorial effectiveness approaches to *state* recognition, as discussed in the previous section, must also inform the debate about the recognition of governments. It is unreasonable that this process does not also trickle to the recognition of new governments, emerging from internal strife.[95] This is true, although several states have adopted, in recent times, a formal – and quite unrealistic – policy of not positively recognizing governments at all, but only states.[96]

Indeed, the question of recognition of governments emerging from internal armed conflicts merits an entire study for itself. Notably, some scholars identify a recent tendency to shy away from robust ideological criteria, as these were presented, for instance, in the EC Guidelines. However, this trend does not connote a return to strict criteria of territorial effectiveness, but rather the predominance of narrow substantive criteria that correlate more or less with the principle of protection.[97]

Two general directions can be pointed out in this context. The first is the widespread recognition of ineffective transitional governments established pursuant to multilateral reconciliation or reconstruction processes – the continuing recognition of the TFG being the quintessential example.[98] Such governments receive credit due to their perceived potential to mend internal differences – in a multilateral way and through engagement with the international community – in order to bring stability and to end mass atrocities. The second direction spawns from the percep-

93 *See* Talmon, *supra* note 37.

94 *See* Chapter 3, sec. 2.2.

95 *See, e.g.,* Matthew Griffin, Accrediting Democracies: Does the Credential Committee of the U.N. Promote Democracy through its Accreditation Process, and Should It? 32 New York University Journal of International Law and Politics 725, 725 (2000) (noting that between 1991 and 1999 the UN accredited five governments despite their lack of territorial effective control).

96 *See* Dapo Akande, Which Entity is the Government of Libya and Why does it Matter? European Journal of International Law: Talk! (June 16, 2011), www.ejiltalk.org/which-entity-is-the-government-of-libya-and-why-does-it-matter (outlining this policy and its unrealistic nature). Indeed, this policy seems to have collapsed in the context of Libya. *See* Dapo Akande, Recognition of Libyan National Transitional Council as Government of Libya, European Journal of International Law: Talk! (July 23, 2011), www.ejiltalk.org/recognition-of-libyan-national-transitional-council-as-government-of-libya.

97 Compare, e.g., Jean d'Aspremont, The Rise and Fall of Democracy Governance in International Law: A Reply to Susan Marks, 22 European Journal of International Law 549, 559–563 (2011).

98 *See* Chapter 7, at sec. 2.4.

tion of effective protection as a key determinant of sovereignty. Whether it will ultimately result in a wide transformation of the international law of government recognition during internal strife remains to be seen; however, it is undoubtedly a logical corollary of the idea of RtoP. Namely, the concept of effective protection can challenge the traditional, effective-control-based perception, according to which the opposition cannot be recognized as long as the conflict endures.

Recent events in Libya demonstrate this notion. In contrast to Somalia, for instance, Libya was by no means a failed state when the uprising erupted there.[99] However, the regime's violations of the protection principle have resulted in the rather swift – albeit gradual – recognition of the Libyan opposition. Thus, the opposing NTC has been recognized by several states as the "legitimate representative" of Libya or the Libyan people, long before it even showed minimal prospects of defeating the regime in battle. France became the first state to recognize the NTC as the "legitimate representative of the Libyan people" on March 10, 2011, only weeks after the conflict erupted, and more than seven months before the conflict's conclusion.[100] Italy went further, in April 2011, by recognizing the NTC "as the country's only legitimate interlocutor on bilateral relations";[101] Qatar and Kuwait issued similar statements.[102] Whether these statements amounted to full *de jure* recognition is highly doubtful.[103] However, they clearly reflected a movement towards the assessment of the rights of opposition parties according to the concept of protection of civilians.

Soon enough, the intentions of key members of the international community became clearer. In June 7, 2011, France "upgraded" the status of the NTC by labeling it as "the only holder of governmental authority in the contacts between France and Libya and its related entities." The United Arab Emirates did the same.[104] On July 15, 32 Western and Arab States (the Libya Contact Group) granted the NTC full recognition as the government of Libya, thus allowing it, in principle, to access the frozen assets of the regime.[105] In its statement, the Contact Group asserted that "the Al-Qadhafi regime no longer has any legitimate authority in

99 *See* Alex J. Bellamy, Libya and the Responsibility to Protect: The Exception and the Norm, 25 Ethics and International Affairs 1, 1–2 (2011).

100 *See Libya: France Recognises Rebels as Government*, B.B.C. News, March 10, 2011, *available at* www.bbc.co.uk/news/world-africa-12699183; Chapter 1, sec. 4.1.

101 Talmon, *supra* note 37.

102 C.J. Chivers and David D. Kirkpatrick, *Libyan Rebels Complain of Deadly Delays Under NATO's Command* New York Times, April 4, 2011, *available at* www.nytimes.com/2011/03/12/world/africa/12policy.html?_r=3&hpw.

103 *See* Talmon, *supra* note 37.

104 *Id.*

105 William Wan and William Booth, *United States Recognizes Libyan Rebels as Legitimate Government*, Washington Post, July 15, 2011, *available at* www.washingtonpost.com/world/middle-east/western-arab-leaders-meet-in-turkey-on-libyas-future/2011/07/15/gIQAZL-bjFI_story.html.

Libya. ... Henceforth and until an interim authority is in place, participants agreed to deal with the National Transitional Council (NTC) as the legitimate governing authority in Libya."[106] Significantly, the recognition was granted over three months before the NTC would establish a reasonable measure of effective authority over the state's territory.[107]

The dynamics of recognition in the Libyan conflict, as reflected in the Contact Group's statement concerning the regime's loss of "legitimate authority" – and the subsequent recognition of the yet ineffective NTC – arguably represent an application of the principle of effective protection in the context of government recognition.[108] This can indeed be a significant development in the law of recognition; the coming years will tell whether it will solidify as a leading doctrine.

In any case, it should be emphasized that in the Libyan crisis forcible intervention was mandated by a UNSC resolution.[109] Notwithstanding our claim that in such cases opposition consent can play a role in the Council's considerations,[110] it remains to be seen whether the unilateral recognition of opposition groups as governments, on counts of considerations of civilian protection, will be accepted as legitimate justifications for consensual interventions on their behalf, *absent* Council authorization. Considering the potential of abuse inherent in such dynamics, as discussed above, it should at least be required that such recognition will be granted through credible multilateral mechanisms – such as regional organizations – and by a substantial number of states. In other cases, the recognition and subsequent intervention might be deemed unlawful, and will therefore be analyzed through the prism of unilateral humanitarian intervention – which we will now turn to consider.

4 Consensual intervention and unilateral humanitarian intervention

4.1 Unilateral humanitarian intervention and RtoP: the unresolved debate

The debate regarding forcible intervention in internal strife has been dominated, in the past two decades – and most notably before the events

106 Republic of Turkey, Ministry of Foreign Affairs, Fourth Meeting of the Libya Contact Group Chair's Statement, 15 July 2011, Istanbul, *available at* www.mfa.gov.tr/fourth-meeting-of-the-libya-contact-group-chair_s-statement_-15-july-2011_-istanbul.en.mfa.

107 *Recognition of Libyan National Transitional Council as Government of Libya*, *supra* note 96.

108 Compare, however, the positions of the states that opposed the acceptance of credentials of the NTC as Libya's representative in the UN (Venezuela, Cuba and others). *See* U.N. GAOR, 66th Sess., 28th plen. Mtg. at 7–3, U.N. Doc. A/66/PV.2 (September 16, 2011).

109 *See* Chapter 1, sec. 4.1.

110 *See id.*

of September 11, 2001 – by the dilemma of *unilateral humanitarian intervention.*[111] The term "humanitarian intervention," as suggested by Holzgrefe, connotes "the threat or use of force across state borders by a state (or group of states) aimed at preventing or ending widespread and grave violations of fundamental human rights of individuals" without the consent of the target-state.[112] When the term is used in this work, we refer specifically to situations in which the intervention has been conducted unilaterally, meaning, without UNSC authorization.[113] Our definition thus includes scenarios such as the famous 1999 Kosovo intervention, and excludes, for instance, the 2011 intervention in Libya. Other frequently cited cases of unilateral humanitarian interventions are India's 1971 intervention in East Pakistan (Bangladesh); Vietnam's actions against the Khmer Rouge regime in Cambodia (1978); Tanzania's ousting of Idi Amin in Uganda (1979); or the 1991 allied operations in Northern Iraq following the regime's repression of the Kurds.[114]

Since we have elaborated, in previous chapters, on the principle of protection and RtoP, some conceptual clarification is merited. Humanitarian intervention and RtoP, ideally, set out to defend the same values – namely, the protection of civilians facing mass atrocities. However, RtoP has developed against the backdrop of the massive controversy spawned by the NATO operation in Kosovo, which was justified by some as a case of humanitarian intervention.[115] The ICISS Report sought to diffuse this controversy both on the terminological and the substantive levels. On the former level, the Report candidly admitted that it deliberately avoided the term "humanitarian intervention," although some aspects of RtoP, as reflected in the Report, are not far removed from it.[116] Substantively, by extending RtoP also to the responsibility to prevent and rebuild,[117] ICISS attempted to dilute the idea's forcible component, thereby presenting a more holistic approach than commonly attributed to humanitarian

111 *See* Tom J. Farer, *Humanitarian Intervention Before and After 9/11, in* Humanitarian Intervention: Ethical, Legal and Political Dilemmas, *supra* note 70, at 53, 53–59.

112 J.L. Holzgrefe, *The Humanitarian Intervention Debate, in id.* at 15, 18.

113 Keohane and Holzgrefe refer to such intervention as "unauthorized" humanitarian intervention. *See* Robert O. Keohane, *Introduction, in id.* at 1, 1.

114 *See* Allen Buchanan, *Reforming the International Law of Humanitarian Intervention, in* Humanitarian Intervention: Ethical, Legal and Political Dilemmas, *supra* note 70, at 130; *see also* Thomas M. Franck, *Interpretation and Change in the Law of Humanitarian Intervention, in id.* at 204, 216–226 (discussing these cases and others); Jane Stromseth, *Rethinking Humanitarian Intervention: The Case for Incremental* Change, *in id.* at 232, 248–252.

115 Anne Orford, International Authority and the Responsibility to Protect 27–28 (2011).

116 ICISS Report, *supra* note 67, ¶¶1.39–1.41 (2001); Alex J. Bellamy, Responsibility to Protect 42 (2009).

117 Indeed, as emphasized in the ICISS Report, "prevention is the single most important dimension of the responsibility to protect." *See* ICISS Report, *supra* note 67, at XI.

intervention.[118] Furthermore, RtoP shifted the discussion from the "right" of humanitarian intervention to the more executive-leaning, principled concept of "responsibility," which better addresses, at least in theoretical terms, the concerns of small states that the concept will be exploited by great powers.[119]

These terminological and substantive developments made it easier for ICISS to issue an implied challenge to the UNSC's general monopoly over the use of force.[120] However, it soon became clear that RtoP will not be universally accepted if implying – even indirectly – that unilateral humanitarian intervention can be acceptable. This accounts for the transformation of RtoP from its initial form, as found in the ICISS report, to the narrower concept reflected in the 2005 WSOD. As opposed to the ICISS report, the WSOD unequivocally reaffirmed the UNSC's monopoly over the authorization of forcible interventions.[121] Thus, while significantly clarifying the longstanding question whether the UNSC mandate extends to strictly internal situations,[122] the WSOD did not address the consequences of its *failure* to act in such instances. Therefore, the old debate regarding unilateral humanitarian intervention still retains its relevancy. This compels us to revisit some of the well recognized dilemmas of unilateral humanitarian intervention, and – in our context – their relation to the question of consent.

4.2 Intra-charter justifications for humanitarian intervention and the question of consent

Humanitarian intervention cannot – *ipso facto* – be a consensual intervention in favor of governments;[123] theoretically, thus, it can be considered an intervention pursued with opposition consent. The nexus between humanitarian and consensual intervention is a rather uncharted area of international law. Our approach towards this question must be informed by our perception regarding unilateral humanitarian intervention at large. If we categorically reject – whether on legal or ethical terms – any unilateral forcible intervention conducted without government consent, then, of course, consent by opposition groups cannot play any legalizing or

118 Cristina G. Badescu, Humanitarian Intervention and the Responsibility to Protect 10 (2010); Thomas G. Weiss, *RtoP Alive and Well after Libya*, 25 Ethics and International Affairs 1, 1–2 (2011).

119 Chapter 8, sec. 2.2.

120 *See id.* sec. 2.1.

121 *Id.*; *see also* Jennifer Welsh, *Civilian Protection in Libya: Putting Coercion and Controversy Back into RtoP*, 25 Ethics and International Affairs 1, 2 (2011), at 2; 2005 World Summit Outcome, G.A. Res. 60/1, ¶¶138–139, U.N. Doc. A/60/L.1 (September 15, 2005).

122 *See id.* sec. 2.2; *see also* the discussion in Holzgrefe, *supra* note 114, at 40–43.

123 *See, e.g.*, The Independent International Commission on Kosovo, The Kosovo Report 193 (2000).

legitimizing role in assessing intervention. If, however, we accept that unilateral humanitarian intervention can be permissible or justifiable in extreme situations, then the role of opposition consent depends on the legal or ethical basis upon which the intervention is grounded. In particular, the answer depends on whether we base our justification on intra or extra-UN Charter sources.

In terms of ethics, humanitarian intervention can be justified or rejected on utilitarian grounds, as classically reflected in the works of Mill or Bernard.[124] It can be based on cosmopolitan claims – whether founded on natural law or on principles of social-contractarianism.[125] Legally, nonetheless, the concept challenges the plain language of Article 2(4) of the UN Charter. However, attempts have been made to counter this challenge in two ways. The first interprets the Charter as accommodating such actions (intra-Charter justifications).[126] The second concedes that the Charter prohibits unilateral humanitarian intervention, but seeks extra-Charter or extra-*legal* sources for justification.

Simply put, the intra-Charter approach posits that Article 2(4), by prohibiting the use of force against the "territorial integrity and political independence of states, or in any other manner inconsistent with the Purposes of the United Nations," is actually meant to *permit* other types of forcible actions, meaning – those *not* conducted against the territorial integrity or independence of states,[127] or supposedly *consistent* with the purposes of the organization – such as those aimed to halt atrocities and promote human rights.[128] Another intra-Charter justification presents a hybrid claim: even if Article 2(4) does not accommodate humanitarian intervention in itself, it argues, once the UNSC has recognized that a certain situation constitutes a threat to international peace – there is no need for another resolution specifically authorizing the use of force.[129]

124 Montague Bernard, On the Principle of Non-Intervention 9–10 (1860); John Stuart Mill, *A Few Words on Non-Intervention* (1859), *in* Dissertations and Discussions 238 (1882); for a discussion on humanitarian intervention and utilitarianism *see* Holzgrefe, *supra* note 114, at 20–25.

125 *Id.* at 25–33.

126 For a concise summary of these attempts *see* Farer, *supra* note 111, at 61–69.

127 Holzgrefe, *supra* note 114, at 37.

128 *Id.* at 39; *compare, e.g.*, The Kosovo Report, *supra* note 123, at 167–169. This type of reasoning is reminiscent of the narrow interpretations given in the 1930s to the Kellogg–Briand Pact, as prohibiting war only when used a tool of "national policy." *See* Chapter 5, sec. 2.

129 *See* The Kosovo Report, *supra* note 123, at 171–172 (labeling this contention as "the most convincing" legal ground for NATO's intervention). This justification was invoked regarding the 1991 allied action in Northern Iraq in protection of the Kurds. *See* Stromseth, *supra* note 114, at 251. All of these intra-Charter constructions, for instance, were advanced by Belgium in justification of the NATO intervention in Kosovo. *See* Argument of Belgium before the I.C.J., at 11–12, (May 10, 1999), *available at* www.icj-cij.org/docket/files/105/4513.pdf.

Nonetheless, attempts to base unilateral humanitarian intervention on intra-Charter constructions are not convincing, and indeed, most international lawyers – and indeed many states – reject them.[130] The UN Charter, as any treaty, is to be interpreted in light of its "object and purpose," supplemented, *inter alia*, by the circumstances of its conclusion.[131] Clearly, the stated purpose of the UN to "maintain international peace and security, *and to that end:* to take effective *collective* measures"[132] places a heavy onus on those who interpret the Charter as condoning unilateral forcible intervention. Moreover, the context of the drafting of the Charter, in particular in light of the failed earlier attempts to restrict the war power of states,[133] establishes a strong interpretive presumption against any unilateral use of force.[134] This must be true also with regards to the interpretation of UNSC resolutions. Therefore, a general recognition by the UNSC that a situation threatens the peace cannot be interpreted as authorizing force.[135] However, such previous determination by the Council might still assist the intervener if invoking a claim of *necessity* – as the concept will be discussed shortly.

The objections above notwithstanding, if one still accepts the intra-Charter justifications – opposition consent could augment the legality of an intervention in specific instances. Thus, consent by forces opposing atrocities – in particular in cases in which they have formed relatively credible transitional entities – could indicate that the intervention is in fact not aimed to violate the territorial integrity or independence of the target state, nor contrary to the purposes of the United Nations. In particular, consent from a credible internal entity – which reasonably seeks to fulfill the responsibility to protect – can fortify a claim that the intervention seeks to promote the UN's purposes to encourage respect for human rights and fundamental freedoms, rather than strictly to promote self-interest.[136]

130 *See* Holzgrefe, *supra* note 114, at 37–40; *see also* Oscar Schachter, *The Legality of Pro-democratic Invasion*, 78 American Journal of International Law 646, 649 (1984) (labeling intra-Charter justifications as requiring an "Orwellian construction"); Byers and Chesterman, *supra* note 70, at 177–187; for the position of the Group of 77 regarding the Kosovo intervention *see* Ministerial Declaration on the South Summit, Adopted at the 23rd Annual Meeting of the Ministers of Foreign Affairs of the Group of 77, held at U.N. Headquarters on 24 September 1999, annex 1, ¶69 U.N. Doc. A/54/432 (October 6, 1999); *compare* The Kosovo Report, *supra* note 123, at 170–172 (noting the "fluidity" of the law on humanitarian intervention.)

131 Vienna Convention on the Law of Treaties arts. 31(1), 32, May 23, 1969, 1155 U.N.T.S.. 331.

132 U.N. Charter art. 1(1) [emphasis added].

133 Recall the various loopholes of the Charter of the League of Nations and the Kellogg–Briand Pact, as discussed in Chapter 5.

134 U.N. Charter, prmbl; *see also* The Kosovo Report, *supra* note 123, at 167–168.

135 *See id.* at 173; *see also* Byers and Chesterman, *supra* note 70, at 181–182.

136 U.N. Charter, art. 1(3).

Similarly, as the discussion of humanitarian intervention has shifted from a "rights"-based discourse to notions of executive "responsibility," deliberation with groups representing the victimized population, prior to intervention, can carry some weight – perhaps comparable to a process of "fair hearing" – in placing the intervention within the (widely interpreted) Charter paradigm. As in any case of unilateral forcible intervention, these assumptions would be fortified when interventions are conducted within the framework of regional organizations – assuming that in most cases, their collective decision-making process, coupled with their deeper understanding of the conflict, inherently reduces the potential for abuse.[137]

4.3 Extra-charter justifications for humanitarian intervention: necessity, just-war theory and consent

Although the purposes of the UN Charter seem to preclude unilateral humanitarian interventions, the same purposes can hardly be reconciled with the capricious use of their veto power by permanent Council members, which can block any collective action envisioned in Article 1 of the Charter.[138] This problem still remains, although the deadlock days of the Cold War are long gone.[139] A recent example could be found in the failure of the UNSC, as of December 2012, to adopt a Chapter VII resolution in response to the atrocities committed in Syria.[140] Instead, the Council resorted to relatively non-committal presidential statements,[141] and dispatched unarmed observer teams (UNSMIS) that could do little to halt the violence.[142] The "capricious veto" problem thus leads to an unbearable tension between the Charter's stated purposes and the procedures set forth for their achievement. This tension underlines much of the discussion of humanitarian intervention and the UN Charter, and has accordingly given rise to the second set of justifications for humanitarian intervention – *extra*-Charter ones.

As suggested by Buchanan, extra-Charter justifications for unilateral humanitarian intervention can be classified under three categories: one relies on fundamental *legal* principles beyond the Charter's provisions (the "Lawfulness Justification"). A second approach views humanitarian

137 *See* ICISS Report, *supra* note 67, ¶¶6.31–6.35.

138 *Id.* ¶6.20; *see also* Farer, *supra* note 111, at 64.

139 *See* Anne Orford, Reading Humanitarian Intervention: Human Rights and the Use of Force in International Law 2 (2003); *compare* Farer, *supra* note 111, at 64–65.

140 Draft Resolution by France, Germany, Portugal and the U.K. (October 4, 2011), U.N. Doc. S/2011/612 (vetoed by China and Russia;) Draft Resolution by Bahrain and 18 Others (February 2, 2012), U.N. Doc. S/2012/77 (vetoed by China and Russia.)

141 *Supra* note 30.

142 S.C. Res. 2042, U.N. Doc. S/RES/2042 (April 14, 2012); S.C. Res. 2043, U.N. Doc. S/RES/2043 (April 21, 2012).

intervention as an *illegal* action that can, however, serve to *reform* positive international law (the "Illegal Legal Reform Justification"). This can be potentially done in two ways. One is by establishing alternative collective intervention mechanisms.[143] Proponents of this idea envision a benevolent "league of democracies," acting in parallel to the UN system in order to halt mass atrocities.[144] Arguably, the member states of the AU have done just that – albeit in a regional context, and not based on "democracy" per se – when adopting Article 4(h) of the Constitutive Act of the African Union.[145] Another way would be through contrary state practice designed to create new customary international law, more amenable to humanitarian intervention.[146]

Both the "Lawfulness" and the "Illegal Legal Reform" justifications are fraught with difficulties. In general, their focus on "general principles" or on state practice does not attribute sufficient weight to the *jus cogens* nature of the prohibition on the use of force.[147] Whether peremptory *jus cogens* norms are special cases of customary international law or manifestations of "natural" law,[148] it is clear that in contemporary law, such norms – and specifically those entrenched in the UN Charter – cannot be circumvented simply by reference to other basic principles. Nor can they be altered merely through the regular creation of new customary law.[149] This "normative pyramid" correlates with the process of "constitutionalization" of international law at large – and of the UN Charter, namely through Article 103[150] – and the related decline of the perception of international law as a product only of state consent.[151]

143 Buchanan, *supra* note 114, at 138–139.

144 *Id.* at 138; *see also* The Kosovo Report, *supra* note 123, at 173–174; for a critical view of the idea *see* Bruce Jones *et al.*, Power and Responsibility: Building International Order in an Era of Transnational Threats 307–311 (2009).

145 *See* Chapter 10, sec. 3.3.

146 Buchanan, *supra* note 114, at 132–133, 140–141; *see also* Saira Mohamed, *Restructuring the Debate on Unauthorized Humanitarian Intervention,* 88 North Carolina Law Review 1275, 1287–1288 (2010); Stromseth, *supra* note 114, at 246.

147 *See, e.g.,* Ulf Linderfalk, *The Effect of Jus Cogens Norms: Whoever Opened Pandora's Box, Did You Ever Think About the Consequences?* 18 European Journal of International Law 853, 859 (2008) (arguing, although generally critical about *jus cogens*, that the principle of non-use of force is the least controversial example for *jus cogens*). Remember, here we assume that humanitarian intervention *cannot* be reconciled with the prohibition on the use of force as expressed in the UN Charter.

148 *See* John Francis Murphy, The Evolving Dimensions of International Law: Hard Choices for the World Community 23 (2010).

149 *See* International Law Commission, Fragmentation of International Law: Difficulties Arising from the Diversification and Expansion of International Law (April 13, 2006) ¶¶345, 367, U.N. Doc. A/CN.4/L.682 (2006); Linderfalk, *supra* note 147, at 854; *but see* Stromseth, *supra* note 114, at 246–255.

150 *See, e.g.,* Jan Klabbers *et al.*, Constitutionalization of International Law (2009); Bardo Fassbender, The U.N. Charter as the Constitution of the International Community (2009).

151 Buchanan, *supra* note 114, at 148–154.

Regarding the possibility of legal reform through alternative collective mechanisms, we have already addressed, in Chapter 8, the potential challenge to the UN system manifested in regional (or other) forward-looking intervention treaties. We have suggested that in cases of mass atrocities, when a government ceases to exercise effective protection, it will lose the sovereign power to withdraw the state's previously given consent. In this sense, we have reconciled, to an extent, between such treaties and Charter law, since our construction mitigates the conflict between these arrangements and Article 103 of the Charter, as well as with peremptory norms of *jus cogens.*[152] However, our analysis of forward-looking intervention treaties relies on the existence of an *initial* expression of consent by the target state. As such, our attempt at reconciliation cannot serve to justify intervention – reminiscent, perhaps, of the NATO operation in Kosovo – conducted by a hypothetical "league of democracies" against a state which was *never* a member in the alternative arrangement to begin with.

The third set of justifications suggested by Buchanan is based on the concept of "necessity": accepting the *prima facie* illegality of unilateral humanitarian intervention, but asserting nevertheless that in extreme situations, basic ethical values can legitimize it. This notion correlates with the "illegal, yet legitimate" paradigm, as famously advanced by the International Commission on Kosovo.[153] Necessity claims can be either "soft" or "hard." "Soft" claims point to necessity exceptions found in positive law, and therefore do not challenge the rule from a meta-legal point of view.[154] At the risk of oversimplifying, such claims may reflect an internationalized version of the domestic law defense of "necessity" – commonly understood as justifying an otherwise unlawful act[155] – or allude to like norms from within the international law of state-responsibility. "Hard" necessity claims,

152 *See* Chapter 8, sec. 3.5.

153 The Kosovo Report, *supra* note 123, at 186; for a similar view *see* Oscar Schachter, International Law in Theory and in Practice 126 (1991).

154 *See, e.g.*, Franck, *supra* note 116, 212–214; *see also* Mohamed, *supra* note 146, at 1291–1293 (explaining this notion as suggested by Thomas Franck).

155 Not to be confused with "excuse." As articulated by Fletcher, the distinction between these terms is that a "justification negates an assertion of wrongful conduct. An excuse negates a charge that the particular defendant is personally to blame for the wrongful conduct." George P. Fletcher, *The Right and the Reasonable*, 98 Harvard Law Review 949, 958 (1985). It should be noted that when discussing circumstances precluding wrongfulness, the Commentaries on the Articles of State Responsibility use the terms "justification" and "excuse" interchangeably. *See, e.g.*, International Law Commission Draft Articles on Responsibility of States for Internationally Wrongful Acts, with Commentaries, in Report of the International Law Commission, U.N. GAOR, 53d Sess., Supp. No. 10, A/56/20 (2001) at 71, 80. In the context of humanitarian intervention *see* Richard V. Meyer and Mark David Maxwell, *The Natural Right to Intervene: The Evolution of the Concepts of Justification and Excuse for Both State and Individual*, 7 Journal of International Criminal Justice 555 (2009).

conversely, are based on ethical principles, independent from any legal instrument recognizing or excluding such exceptions.[156]

Considering the difficulties with other types of extra-Charter justifications, the "necessity" paradigm seems to be the most coherent manner to discuss extra-Charter humanitarian intervention. However, this by no means implies that it is without its own problems. For one, in positive international law, "soft" doctrines of necessity are an extremely shaky ground upon which to base unilateral non-defensive uses of force.[157] While DASR, in Article 25, recognizes situations of "necessity" as precluding wrongfulness, the doctrine it sets forth is manifestly narrow. For instance, it requires that the act be the "only way" to safeguard an "essential interest against a grave and imminent peril" and that it will not "seriously impair" an essential interest of the target state or the "international community as a whole."[158]

Last, Article 26 expressly provides that necessity cannot justify acts that are contrary to peremptory norms of *jus cogens*.[159] Since the prohibition on the unilateral use of force is widely accepted as such a norm, it seems that recourse to the necessity doctrine cannot *legally* justify unilateral humanitarian intervention. Indeed, the Commentaries on DASR concede that the problem of humanitarian intervention cannot find its solution under Article 25, and that while "necessity" considerations might indeed "have a role" regarding this problem in general, the required balance is already "taken into account" within the primary obligations of the law on the use of force.[160]

However, since the "illegal but legitimate" paradigm is situated on the seam between questions of law and morality,[161] it must also be evaluated through the prism of "hard" necessity. Indeed, the question of moral necessity is first and foremost a subject for the political philosopher – and thus, its detailed analysis is beyond the scope of this work. Nonetheless, the fundamental criteria of traditional just-war theory will surely dominate any ethical discussion of humanitarian intervention.[162] As widely accepted, these criteria include *just cause*, meaning, in the context of humanitarian intervention, halting large-scale atrocities of the type referred to, for instance, in the WSOD; *right authority*, meaning, authorization by a sovereign political entity; *right intention*, meaning, that the action conforms to

156 *Compare* George P. Fletcher and Jens David Ohlin, Defending Humanity: When Force is Justified and Why 133–135 (2008).

157 *Compare* Legal Consequences of the Construction of a Wall in the Occupied Palestinian Territory, Advisory Opinion, 2004 I.C.J. 136, ¶40 (July 9).

158 DASR with Commentaries, *supra* note 155, art. 25(1); *see also* Mohamed, *supra* note 146, at 1304–1305.

159 *Id.* art. 26.

160 *Id.* at 84; *see also* Mohamed, *supra* note 146, at 1304–1305.

161 *See* The Kosovo Report, *supra* note 123, at 164.

162 *See also* Chapter 1, sec. 4.1.

the just cause, and not based on mere self-interest; *proportionality*, meaning, that the overall good achieved by the use of force be greater than the harm done; *last resort*, meaning, that no other means will achieve the justified ends; and that the act has *reasonable prospects of success* in fulfilling the just cause that prompted it.[163]

If generally accepting the moral plausibility of unilateral humanitarian intervention, it could be said that opposition consent, in general, is redundant, since the humanitarian catastrophe itself is the legitimizing agent, and not consent. However, closer analysis reveals that opposition consent can still affect the application of the just-war tests. The following exercise – by no means an exhaustive one – can lay down some directions for further thinking.

In our exercise, we shall assume the existence of a government that commits grave atrocities, faced with an opposition that generally seeks to protect the civilian population, and has formed a reasonably representative transitional entity. In such cases, it is rather intuitive that genuine consent by the representative opposition group can serve as an *indication* that just-war criteria are fulfilled;[164] and, in the same vein, that lack of consent might increase the culpability of the intervener if the intervention proves, *ex post*, to have been unjustified.[165] Indeed, as suggested by McMahan, the ethical role of consent in the question of humanitarian intervention can be paralleled to the requirement of state-consent in the context of the right of collective self-defense: just as it seems morally right that states can refuse third-party assistance when confronting an aggression, it seems just that victims of atrocities – assuming they have a reasonably representative voice – can reject an external intervention and thus derogate from its legitimacy.[166]

Regarding *right authority*, opposition consent does not seem to be of acute importance, since we presuppose that the intervention is conducted by a sovereign or a regional organization. However, it could be argued that when the opposition identifies and requests assistance from a specific actor, that actor would be the most suitable one to act, since the mere request adds to the legitimacy of the intervener, and creates at least some moral proximity between the intervener and the internal party.

163 Some include also the *aim of peace*, meaning, that the ultimate end of the action is to establish international stability, security and peaceful interaction. *See* James Turner Johnson, Morality and Contemporary Warfare 28–29 (1999); *compare* ICISS Report, *supra* note 67, at XII–XIII.

164 For an in depth discussion, *inter alia* of whether an intervention must be "welcomed" by the victims *see* James Pattison, Humanitarian Intervention and the Responsibility to Protect: Who Should Intervene 17, 69–89 (2010); *see also* Jeff McMahan, *Humanitarian Intervention, Consent and Proportionality, in* Ethics and Humanity: Themes from the Philosophy of Jonathan Glover 44, 48 (N. Ann Davis *et al.* eds., 2010).

165 *See id.* at 54.

166 *See id.* at 54–55; on consent and collective self-defense *see* Chapter 7, sec. 3.

Just cause can also be augmented by opposition consent. It is a reasonable assumption – although a clearly contestable one – that in most cases, credible opposition groups would not be quick to request forcible intervention unless the condition of their "constituencies" is genuinely dire. This is because superfluous reliance on external forces can significantly harm the opposition's internal credibility. Imagine, conversely, that major opposition groups are *against* a proposed humanitarian intervention. Intuitively, the reluctance of the opposition seems to adversely affect the just cause aspect of the intervention. If this is so, we must also accept the inverse claim: that *consent* by the same forces produces some legitimizing effect. Therefore, if the intervening party can demonstrate that a credible opposition group that opposes atrocities consents to its intervention, it would be harder to challenge the operation on grounds of absence of just cause.[167]

The existence of *right intention* can also be bolstered by the consent of reasonably representative opposition groups. For instance, genuine opposition consent can greatly reduce concerns that the intervener is acting only for *selfish* reasons. Of course, this notion is fortified when the intervener is operating pursuant to a decision of a regional organization, in which such concerns are lesser to begin with. As noted in the ICISS Report, *right intention* is "better assured" in "multilateral operations, clearly supported by regional opinion and the *victims concerned*."[168]

The *reasonable prospects* of an operation can be affected by the existence of consent, for obvious reasons. Thus, as demonstrated in Chapter 1, the UNSC, in virtually all of its operations, seeks some degree of consent by at least one party to the conflict and, conversely, can be reluctant to act when consent is not acquired. This tendency, as we have shown, is partially based on the practical advantages of consent – meaning, its contribution to the *prospects* of the operation's success.[169]

A closely related effect of opposition consent can be on the principle of *proportionality*. Cooperation of the intervener with at least some internal parties would necessarily result in an operation of a smaller scale, duration and intensity: not least because the intervener will confront only *some* internal elements and not all of them. Furthermore, for reasons of internal credibility, it is reasonable that the request or consent by the opposition will not go beyond what is actually required to tip the scale against the perpetrating regime. For instance, in the Libyan context, the opposition – probably in order to bolster its legitimacy – firmly asserted

167 *Compare* McMahan, *supra* note 164, at 53: "To the greatest extent possible, the potential intervener must allow the people themselves to decide whether to accept the risks [that intervention entails]."

168 ICISS Report, *supra* note 67, at XII (emphasis added).

169 *See* Chapter 1, sec. 4.1.

that no foreign ground troops should be used, thereby delineating, even if unofficially, the scope of the intervention.[170]

Indeed, while our assumptions about the moral power of consent within the just-war paradigm are by no means unchallengeable, they can, hopefully, delineate a structure for a further discussion regarding this ever-important question.

170 *Id.*

Selected bibliography

1 Books and other unitary works

Abass, Ademola, Regional Organisations and the Development of Collective Security: Beyond Chapter VIII of the UN Charter (2004)
Adams, Charles Francis, The Trent Affair: An Historical Retrospect (1912)
Alexandrov, Stanimir A., Self-Defense against the Use of Force in International Law (1996)
Ambrosio, Thomas, Irredentism (2001)
Arend, Anthony C., and Beck, Robert J., International Law and the Use of Force: Beyond the U.N. Charter Paradigm (1993)
Aust, Anthony, Modern Treaty Law and Practice (2007)
African Interventionist States (Oliver Furley and Roy May eds., 2001)
Badescu, Cristina G., Humanitarian Intervention and the Responsibility to Protect (2010)
Barak, Aharon, Proportionality: Constitutional Rights and Their Limitations (2012)
Barnidge, Robert P., Non-State Actors and Terrorism: Applying the Law of State Responsibility and the Due Diligence Principle (2007)
Becker, Tal, Terrorism and the State: Rethinking the Rules of State Responsibility (2006)
Beitz, Charles R., Political Theory and International Relations (1979)
Bellamy, Alex J., Responsibility to Protect (2009)
Bellamy, Alex J. *et al.* Understanding Peacekeeping (2010)
Bellamy, Alex J., Global Politics and the Responsibility to Protect (2011)
Bernard, Montague, On the Principle of Non-Intervention (1860)
Bobbitt, Philip, Terror and Consent (2008)
Bowett, D.W., United Nations Forces: A Legal Study (1964)
Brownlie, Ian, International Law and the Use of Force by States (1963)
Buchanan, Allen E., Justice, Legitimacy and Self-Determination: Moral Foundations for International Law (2004)
Buccheit, Lee, Secession: The Legitimacy of Self-Determination (1978)
Cassese, Antonio, Self-Determination of Peoples: A Legal Reappraisal (1995)
Cassese, Antonio, International Law (2005)
Castellino, Joshua, International Law and Self-Determination (2000)
Chesterman, Simon, Just War or Just Peace? Humanitarian Intervention in International Law (2001)

Civilians In War (Simon Chesterman ed., 2001)
Claude, Inis L., Swords into Plowshares: The Problems and Progress of International Organization (1971)
Colombos, John C., International Law of the Sea (6th ed., 1967)
Cook, Adrian, The Alabama Claims: American Politics and Anglo-American Relations, 1865–1872 (1975)
Crawford, James, The Creation of States in International Law (2006)
Cullen, Anthony, The Concept of Non-International Armed Conflict in International Humanitarian Law (2010)
Davis, Jefferson, The Rise and Fall of the Confederate Government (1881)
Democratic Governance and International Law (Gregory H. Fox and Brad R. Roth eds., 2000)
Deng, Francis M. *et al.*, Sovereignty as Responsibility (1996)
DeRouen, Karl R. and Uk, Heo, Civil Wars of the World: Major Conflicts since World War II (2007)
Dinstein, Yoram, War, Aggression and Self-Defense (5th ed., 2011)
Doyle, Michael W. and Sambanis, Nicholas, Making War and Building Peace: U.N. Peace Operations (2006)
Doyle, Michael W., Ways of War and Peace (1997)
Doyle, Michael W., Liberal Peace: Selected Essays (2011)
Enforcing Restraint: Collective Intervention in Internal Conflicts (Lori Fisler Damrosch, ed., 1989)
Evans, Gareth, The Responsibility to Protect: Ending Mass Atrocity Crimes Once and For All (2008)
Fassbender, Bardo, The U.N. Charter as the Constitution of the International Community (2009)
Ferraro, Tristan, International Committee of the Red Cross, Expert Meeting: Occupation and Other Forms of Administration of Foreign Territory (2012)
Ferrero, Guglielmo, Problems of Peace: From the Holy Alliance to the League of Nations (1919)
Fletcher, George P. and Ohlin, Jens David, Defending Humanity: When Force is Justified and Why (2008)
Franck, Thomas, The Power of Legitimacy among Nations (1990)
Garthoff, Raymond L., Détente and Confrontation: American-Soviet Relations from Nixon to Reagan (1994)
Goldsmith, Jack L. and Posner, Eric A., The Limits of International Law (2005)
Grant, Thomas D., The Recognition of States: Law and Practice in Debate and Evolution (1999)
Grotius, Hugo The Rights of War and Peace (William Whewell trans., 1853)
Gray, Christine, International Law and the Use of Force (2008)
Gurr, Ted Robert, Why Men Rebel (1970)
Hall, W.E., A Treatise on International Law (8th ed. 1924)
Henckaerts, Jean-Marie and Doswald-Beck, Louise, International Committee of the Red Cross, Customary International Humanitarian Law (2007)
Henkin, Louis, How Nations Behave: Law and Foreign Policy (1979)
Henkin, Louis, International Law: Politics and Values (1995)
Higgins, Rosalyn, Problems and Process: International Law and How We Use It (1995)
Hironaka, Ann, Neverending Wars: The International Community, Weak States and the Perpetuation of Civil War (2005)

Hohfeld, Wesley, Fundamental Legal Conceptions (Arthur Corbin ed., 1978)
Hufbauer, Gary Clyde *et al.*, Economic Sanctions Reconsidered (3rd ed. 2007)
Humanitarian Intervention: Ethical, Legal and Political Dilemmas (J.L. Holzgrefe and Robert O. Keohane eds., 2003)
International Economic Law and Armed Conflict (Harry H.G. Post ed., 1994)
International Humanitarian Law and Human Rights Law: Towards a New Merger in International Law (Roberta Arnold and Noëlle Quénivet eds., 2008)
Jones, Bruce *et al.*, Power and Responsibility: Building International Order in an Era of Transnational Threats (2009)
Johnson, James Turner, Morality and Contemporary Warfare (1999)
Jus Post Bellum: Towards a Law of Transition from Conflict to Peace (Carsten Stahn and Jann K. Kleffner eds., 2008)
Kant, Immanuel, Perpetual Peace: a Philosophical Essay (1759)
Kant, Immanuel, Fundamental Principles of the Metaphysic of Morals (1875)
Kelsen, Hans, General Theory of Law and State (1961)
Kelsen, Hans, Pure Theory of Law (5th ed. 2008)
Keohane, Robert O. and Nye, Joseph S., Power and Interdependence: World Politics in Transition (1977)
Klabbers, Jan *et al.*, Constitutionalization of International Law (2009)
Knop, Karen, Diversity and Self-Determination in International Law (2002)
Koskenniemi, Martti, The Politics of International Law (2011)
Lalonde, Suzanne, Determining Boundaries in a Conflicted World: The Role of *Uti Possidetis* (2002)
Law and Force in the New International Order (Lori Fisler Damrosch and David J. Scheffer eds., 1991)
Lauterpacht, Hersch, The Function of Law in the International Community (1933)
Lauterpacht, Hersch, Recognition in International Law (1948)
Leurdijk, J.H., Armed Intervention in International Politics: A Historical and Comparative Analysis (2006)
Luard, Evan, Conflict and Peace in the Modern International System (1968)
Lubell, Noam, Extraterritorial Use of Force against Non-State Actors (2010)
Melzer, Nils, International Committee of the Red Cross, Interpretive Guidance on the Notion of Direct Participation in Hostilities under International Humanitarian Law (2009)
Moir, Lindsay, The Law of Internal Armed Conflict (2003)
Murphy, John Francis, The Evolving Dimensions of International Law: Hard Choices for the World Community (2010)
Negotiating Culture and Human Rights (Lynda S. Bell *et al.* eds., 2001)
Neff, Stephen C., War and the Law of Nations: A General History (2005)
Ninčić, Djura, The Problem of Sovereignty in the Charter and in the Practice of the United Nations (1970)
Nolte, Georg, Eingreifen auf Einladung (1999)
O'Ballance, Edgar, Civil War in Lebanon, 1975–1992 (1998)
Oglesby, Roscoe R., Internal War and the Search for Normative Order (1971)
Oppenheim, Lassa, International Law: A Treatise (2nd ed., 1912)
Orford, Anne, Reading Humanitarian Intervention: Human Rights and the Use of Force in International Law (2003)
Orford, Anne, International Authority and the Responsibility to Protect (2011)

Ouimet, Matthew J., The Rise and Fall of the Brezhnev Doctrine in Soviet Foreign Policy (2003)
Pattison, James, Humanitarian Intervention and the Responsibility to Protect: Who Should Intervene (2010)
Peacemaking and Peacekeeping for the New Century (Olara A. Otunu and Michael W. Doyle eds., 1998)
Peterson, M.J., Recognition of Governments (1997)
Pollock, Frederick, The League of Nations (1920)
Raič, David Statehood and the Law of Self-determination (2002)
Rawls, John, The Law of Peoples (2001)
Regan, Patrick M., Civil Wars and Foreign Powers: Outside Intervention in Intrastate Conflict (2002)
Right v. Might: International Law and the Use of Force (Louis Henkin *et al.* eds., 1991)
Roth, Brad R., Governmental Illegitimacy in International Law (2001)
Ruys, Tom, 'Armed Attack' and Article 51 of the U.N. Charter: Evolutions in Customary Law and Practice (2010)
Schabas, William A., An Introduction to the International Criminal Court (2011)
Schachter, Oscar, International Law in Theory and Practice (1991)
Scott, James M., Deciding to Intervene: The Reagan Doctrine and American Foreign Policy (1996)
Secession: International Law Perspectives 23 (Marcelo G. Kohen ed., 2006)
Slaughter, Anne-Marie, A New World Order (2004)
Stacy, Helen, Human Rights for the 21st Century: Sovereignty, Civil Society, Culture (2009)
Stapleton, Augustus Granville, Intervention and Non-Intervention; or, The Foreign Policy of Great Britain from 1790 to 1865 (1866)
Stürchler, Nicholas, The Threat of Force in International Law (2009)
Tanca, Antonio, Foreign Armed Intervention in Internal Conflict (1993)
Teitel, Ruti G., Humanity's Law (2011)
Thakur, Ramesh, The Responsibility to Protect: Norms, Laws and the Use of Force in International Politics (2010)
The International Status of Taiwan in the New World Order: Legal and Political Considerations (Jean-Marie Henckaerts ed., 1996)
The Philosophy of International Law (Samantha Besson and John Tasioulas eds., 2010)
The Responsibility to Protect and International Law (Alex J. Bellamy *et al.* eds., 2010)
The Responsibility to Protect: From Principle to Practice 27 (Andre Nollkaemper and Julia Hoffman eds., 2012)
Thomas, Ann Van Wynen and Thomas, Aaron Joshua, Non-Intervention: The Law and its Import in the Americas (1956)
Tzanakópoulos, Antōnios, Disobeying the Security Council: Countermeasures against Wrongful Sanctions (2011)
U.S. Army, Counterinsurgency (2006)
Waltz, Kenneth, Theory of International Politics (1979)
Walzer, Michael, Just and Unjust Wars (4th ed. 2006)
Weinberger, Naomi Joy, Syrian Intervention in Lebanon: The 1975–1976 Civil War (1986)

Weisburd, Arthur Mark, Use of Force: The Practice of States since World War II (1997)
Wheatley, Steven, Democracy, Minorities and International Law (2005)
Wheaton's Elements of International Law (Richard Henry Dana ed., 1866)
Wilson, George Grafton, International Law (8th ed. 1922)
Wright, Quincy, The Role of International Law in the Elimination of War (1961)
Xanthaki, Alexandra, Indigenous Rights and United Nations Standards 141–142 (2007)
Vatell, Emmerich De, The Law of Nations (1797)

2 Articles and chapters in books

Abass, Ademola, *Consent Precluding State Responsibility: A Critical Analysis*, 53 International and Comparative Law Quarterly 211 (2004)
Abass, Ademola, *The African Union and the Responsibility to Protect: Principles and Limitations, in* The Responsibility to Protect: From Principle to Practice 132 (Andre Nollkaemper and Julia Hoffman eds., 2012)
Akande, Dapo, *Which Entity is the Government of Libya and Why does it Matter?* European Journal of International Law: Talk! (June 16, 2011)
Akande, Dapo, *The Newly Independent State of South Sudan – Should We Rethink the Right to Secession* European Journal of International Law: Talk! (July 15, 2011)
Akande, Dapo, *Recognition of Libyan National Transitional Council as Government of Libya*, European Journal of International Law: Talk! (July 23, 2011)
Allain, Jean, *The True Challenge to the U.N. System of the Use of Force: The Failures of Kosovo and Iraq and the Emergence of the African Union, in* 8 Max Planck Yearbook of United Nations Law 237 (Armin von Bogdandy and Rüdiger Wolfrum eds., 2004)
Alvarez, Jose E., *Judging the Security Council*, 90 American Journal of International Law 1 (1996)
Anderson, David G., *The International Arms Trade: Regulating Conventional Arms Transfers in the Aftermath of the Gulf War*, 7 American University International Law Review 749 (1992)
Barber, Rebecca J., *The Proportionality Equation: Balancing Military Objectives with Civilian Lives in the Armed Conflict in Afghanistan*, 15 Journal of Conflict and Security Law 467 (2010)
Bassett Moore, John, *International Law: Its Present and Future*, 1 American Journal of International Law 11 (1907)
Bassiouni, M. Cherif, *Legal Status of U.S. Forces in Iraq from 2003–2008*, 11 Chinese Journal of International Law 1 (2010–2011)
Baty, Thomas, *So-Called "De facto" Recognition*, 31 Yale Law Journal 469 (1922)
Beale, Joseph H. Jr., *The Recognition of Cuban Belligerency*, 9 Harvard Law Review 406 (1896)
Beck, Robert J., *International Law and the Decision to Invade Grenada: A Ten-Year Retrospective*, 33 Virginia Journal of International Law 765 (1993)
Bellamy, Alex J., *Libya and the Responsibility to Protect: The Exception and the Norm*, Ethics and International Affairs (2011)
Benvenisti, Eyal, *The Interplay Between Actors as a Determinant of the Evolution of Administrative Law in International Institutions*, 68 Law and Contemporary Problems 319 (2005)

Benvenisti, Eyal, *The Legal Battle to Define the Law on Transnational Asymmetric Warfare,* 20 Duke Journal of Comparative and International Law 339 (2010)

Benvenisti, Eyal, *Sovereigns as Trustees of Humanity: The Minimal Other-Regarding Obligations,* SSRN Working Paper (June 11, 2011)

Berkeley, Reginald, *The Work of the League of Nations,* 2 British Year Book of International Law 150 (1921–1922)

Berti, Benedetta, *Armed Groups as Political Parties and Their Role in Electoral Politics: The Case of Hizballah,* 34 Studies In Conflict and Terrorism 942 (2011)

Blank, Laurie R. and Farley, Benjamin R., *Characterizing U.S. Operations in Pakistan: Is the United States Engaged in an Armed Conflict?* 34 Fordham International Law Journal 151 (2010)

Blum, Gabriella, *On a Differential Law of War,* 52 Harvard International Law Journal 164 (2011)

Borchard, Edwin, *War, Neutrality and Non-Belligerency,* 35 American Journal of International Law 618 (1941)

Bowett, Derek, *The Interrelation of Theories of Intervention and Self-Defense, in* Law and Civil War in the Modern World 38 (John Norton Moore ed., 1974)

Brehm, Maya, *The Arms Trade and States' Duty to Ensure Respect for Humanitarian and Human Rights Law,* 12 Journal of Conflict and Security Law 21 (2008)

Briggs, Herbert W., *Relations Officeuses and Intent to Recognize: British Recognition of Franco,* 34 American Journal of International Law 47 (1940)

Brollowski, Hanna, *The Responsibility to Protect and Common Article 1 of the Geneva Conventions and Obligations of Third States, in* The Responsibility to Protect: From Principle to Practice 93 (Andre Nollkaemper and Julia Hoffman eds., 2012)

Brown, Philip M., *Editorial Comment: Undeclared Wars,* 33 American Journal of International Law 538 (1939)

Buchanan, Allen, *Reforming the International Law of Humanitarian Intervention, in* Humanitarian Intervention: Ethical, Legal and Political Dilemmas 130 (J.L. Holzgrefe and Robert O. Keohane eds., 2003)

Buchanan, Allen *Uncoupling Secession from Nationalism and Intrastate Autonomy from Secession, in* Negotiating Self-Determination 81 (Hurst Hannum and Eileen Babbitt eds., 2006)

Buchanan, Allen, *The Legitimacy of International Law, in* The Philosophy of International Law 79 (Samantha Besson and John Tasioulas eds., 2010)

Bugnion, Franccois, *Jus ad Bellum, Jus in Bello and Non-International Armed Conflicts,* 6 Yearbook of International Humanitarian Law 167 (2003)

Byers, Michael and Chesterman, Simon, *"You, the People": Pro-Democratic Intervention in International Law, in* Democratic Governance and International Law 259 (Gregory H. Fox and Brad R. Roth eds., 2000)

Cárdenas, Emilio J., and Canás, Maria Fernand, *The Limits of Self-Determination, in* The Self-determination of Peoples: Community, Nation, and State in an Interdependent World 101 (Wolfgang Danspeckgruber ed., 2002)

Cassese, Antonio, *The Nicaragua and the Tadic Tests Revisited in Light of the I.C.J. Judgment on Genocide in Bosnia,* 18 European Journal of International Law 649 (2007)

Cerna, Christina M., *Universal Democracy: An International Legal Right or the Pipe Dream of the West?* 27 New York University Journal of International Law and Politics 289 (1995)

Chesterman, Simon, *Introduction: Global Norms, Local Contexts, in* Civilians in War 1 (Simon Chesterman ed., 2001)

Chesterman, Simon, *"Leading from Behind": The Responsibility to Protect, the Obama Doctrine and Humanitarian Intervention after Libya*, Ethics and International Affairs (2011)

Cismas, Ioana, *Secession in Theory and Practice: The Case of Kosovo and Beyond*, 2 Goettingen Journal of International Law 531 (2010)

Cleaver, Gary and Massey, Simon, *D.R.C.: Africa's Scramble for Africa*, *in* African Interventionist States 193 (Oliver Furley and Roy May eds., 2001)

Cleveland, Sarah H., *Norm Internalization and U.S. Economic Sanctions*, 26 Yale Journal of International Law 1 (2001)

Coomans, Fons, *Some Remarks on the Extraterritorial Application of the International Covenant on Economic, Social and Cultural Rights*, *in* Extraterritorial Application of Human Rights Treaties 183 (Fons Coomans and Menno T. Kamminga eds., 2004)

D'Amato, Anthony, *The Invasion of Panama was a Lawful Response to Tyranny*, 84 American Journal of International Law 520 (1990)

Damrosch, Lori Fisler, *Commentary on Collective Military Intervention to Enforce Human Rights*, *in* Law and Force in the New International Order 219 (Lori Fisler Damrosch and David Scheffer eds., 1991)

d'Aspremont, Jean, *Legitimacy of Governments in the Age of Democracy*, 38 New York University Journal of International Law and Politics 877 (2005)

d'Aspremont, Jean and De Brabandere, Eric, *The Complementary Faces of Legitimacy in International Law: The Legitimacy of Origin and the Legitimacy of Exercise*, 34 Fordham International Law Journal 190 (2010)

d'Aspremont, Jean, *Responsibility for Coups D'état in International Law*, 18 Tulane Journal of International and Comparative Law 451 (2010)

d'Aspremont, Jean, *The Rise and Fall of Democracy Governance in International Law: A Reply to Susan Marks*, 22 European Journal of International Law 549 (2011)

Dickinson, Edwin D., *The Closure of Ports in Control of Insurgents*, 24 American Journal of International Law 70 (1930)

Doswald-Beck, Louise, *The Legal Validity of Military Intervention by Invitation of the Government*, 56 British Year Book of International Law 189 (1985)

Doyle, Michael W., *Kant, Liberal Legacies and Foreign Affairs*, 12 Philosophy and Public Affairs 205 (1983)

Doyle, Michael W., *A Few Words on Mill, Walzer, and Non-intervention*, 23 Ethics and International Affairs 349 (2009)

Doyle, Michael W., *The Folly of Protection*, Foreign Affairs (March 20, 2011)

Dumbauld, Edward, *Neutrality Laws of the United States*, 31 American Journal of International Law 258 (1937)

Dupuis. Martin D. *et al.*, *A Workshop on Customary International Law and the 1977 Protocols Additional to the 1949 Geneva Conventions*, 2 American University Journal of International Law and Policy 415 (1987)

Ehrenreich Brooks, Rosa, *War Everywhere: Human Rights, National Security and the Law of Armed Conflict in the Age of Terrorism*, 153 University of Pennsylvania Law Review 675 (2004)

Evangelista, Mathew, *Historical Legacies and the Politics of Intervention in the Former Soviet Union*, *in* The International Dimensions of Internal Conflict 108 (Michael E. Brown, ed., 2001)

Farer, Tom J., *Harnessing Rogue Elephants: A Short Discourse on Foreign Intervention in Civil Strife*, 82 Harvard Law Review 511 (1969)

Farer, Tom J., *Political and Economic Coercion in Contemporary International Law*, 79 American Journal of International Law 405 (1985)

Farer, Tom J., *Humanitarian Intervention Before and After 9/11, in* Humanitarian Intervention: Ethical, Legal and Political Dilemmas 53 (J.L. Holzgrefe and Robert O. Keohane eds., 2003)

Farley, Benjamin, *Calling a State a State: Somaliland and International Recognition*, 24 Emory International Law Review 777 (2011)

Fletcher, George P., *The Right and the Reasonable*, 98 Harvard Law Review 949 (1985)

Focarelli, Carlo, *The Responsibility to Protect Doctrine and Humanitarian Intervention: Too Many Ambiguities for a Working Doctrine*, 13 Journal of Conflict and Security Law 191 (2008)

Fox, Gregory H., *The Right to Political Participation in International Law*, 17 Yale Journal of International Law 539 (1992)

Fox, Gregory H. and Roth, Brad R., *Introduction: The Spread of Liberal Democracy and its Implications for International Law, in* Democratic Governance and International Law 1 (Gregory H. Fox and Brad R. Roth eds., 2000)

Fox, Gregory H. and Nolte, Georg, *Intolerant Democracies, in* Democratic Governance and International Law 389 (Gregory H. Fox and Brad R. Roth eds., 2000)

Franck, Thomas M., *The Emerging Right to Democratic Governance*, 86 American Journal of International Law 46 (1992)

Franck, Thomas M., *Legitimacy and Democratic Entitlement, in* Democratic Governance and International Law 25 (Gregory H. Fox and Brad R. Roth, eds. 2000)

Franck, Thomas M., *Interpretation and Change in the Law of Humanitarian Intervention, in* Humanitarian Intervention: Ethical, Legal, and Political Dilemmas 46 (J.L. Holzgrefe and Robert O. Keohane eds., 2003)

Garner, James W., *Editorial Comment: Questions of International Law in the Spanish Civil War*, 31 American Journal of International Law 66 (1937)

Garner, James W., *The United States Neutrality Act of 1937*, 31 American Journal of International Law 385 (1937)

Gill, Terry D., *Military Intervention at the Invitation of a Government, in* The Handbook of the International Law of Military Operations 229, 229 (Terry D. Gill and Dieter Fleck eds., 2010)

Gill, Terry D. and Fleck, D., *Concept and Sources of the International Law of Military Operations, in* The Handbook of the International Law of Military Operations (Terry D. Gill and Dieter Fleck eds., 2010)

Goldstone, Jack A., *Toward a Fourth Generation of Revolutionary Theory*, 4 Annual Review of Political Science 139 (2001)

Griffin, Matthew, *Accrediting Democracies: Does the Credential Committee of the U.N. Promote Democracy through its Accreditation Process, and Should It?* 32 New York University Journal of International Law and Politics 725 (2000)

Gross, Leo, *States as Organs of International Law and the Problem of Autointerpretation, in* Leo Gross: Essays on International Law and Organization 367 (1984)

Hargrove, John Lawrence, *Intervention by Invitation and the Politics of the New World Order, in* Law and Force in the New International Order 113 (Lori Fisler Damrosch and David. J. Scheffer eds., 1991)

Harling, Peter and Birke, Sarah, *Beyond the Fall of the Syrian Regime*, Middle East Research and Information (February 24, 2012)

Hathaway, Oona and Shapiro, Scott J., *Outcasting: Enforcement in Domestic and International Law,* 121 Yale Law Journal 252 (2011)

Heinigg, Wolff Heintschel von, *Benevolent Third States in International Armed Conflicts: The Myth of the Irrelevance of the Law of Neutrality, in* International Law and Armed Conflict: Exploring the Faultlines 543 (Michael N. Schmitt *et al.* eds., 2007)

Henkin, Louis, *The Invasion of Panama under International Law: A Gross Violation,* 29 Columbia Journal of Transnational Law 293 (1991)

Holzgrefe, J.L., *The Humanitarian Intervention Debate, in* Humanitarian Intervention: Ethical, Legal and Political Dilemmas 15 (J.L. Holzgrefe and Robert O. Keohane eds., 2003)

Hudson, Manley O., *The Permanent Court of International Justice,* 35 Harvard Law Review 245 (1922)

Hudson, Manley O., *Amendment of the Covenant of the League of Nations,* 28 Harvard Law Review 903 (1925)

Kapur, Amrita, *Humanity as the A and Ω of Sovereignty: Four Replies to Anne Peters,* 20 European Journal of International Law 560 (2009)

Kingsbury, Benedict *et al., The Emergence of Global Administrative Law,* 68 Law and Contemporary Problems 15 (2005)

Keohane, Robert O., *Realism, Neoralism and the Study of World Politics, in* Neorealism and its Critics 1 (Robert O. Keohane ed., 1986)

Keohane, Robert O., *Introduction, in* Humanitarian Intervention: Ethical, Legal and Political Dilemmas 1 (J.L. Holzgrefe and Robert O. Keohane eds., 2003)

Kerr, Malcolm, *The Lebanese Civil War, in* International Regulation of Civil Wars 65 (Evan Luard ed., 1972)

Kirkpatrick, Jeane J. and Gerson, Allan *The Reagan Doctrine, Human Rights and International Law, in* Right v. Might: International Law and the Use of Force 19, 20 (Louis Henkin *et al.* eds., 1991)

Kopelmanas, L., *The Problem of Aggression and the Prevention of War,* 31 American Journal of International Law 244 (1937)

Koskenniemi, Martti, *Intolerant Democracies: A Reaction,* 37 Harvard International Law Journal 231 (1996)

Kritsiotis, Dino, *Reappraising Policy Objections to Humanitarian Intervention,* 19 Michigan Journal of International Law 1005 (1998)

Kritsiotis, Dino, *Topographies of Force, in* International Law and Armed Conflict: Exploring the Faultlines. Essays in Honour of Yoram Dinstein 29 (Michael N. Schmitt and Jelena Pejic eds., 2007)

Kunz, Josef L., *The Meaning and the Range of the Norm Pacta sunt Servanda* 39 American Journal of International Law 180 (1945)

Laitin, David D., *Somalia: Civil War, and International Intervention, in* Civil Wars, Insecurity and Intervention 146 (Barbara F. Walter *et al.* eds., 1999)

Levitt, Jeremy, *African Interventionist States and International Law, in* African Interventionist States 15 (Oliver Furley and Roy May eds., 2001)

Le Mon, Christopher J., *Unilateral Intervention by Invitation in Civil Wars: The Effective Control Test Tested,* 35 New York University Journal of International Law and Politics 741 (2003)

Lieblich, Eliav, *Intervention and Consent: Consensual Forcible Interventions in Internal Armed Conflicts as International Agreements,* 29 Boston University International Law Journal 338 (2011)

Lieblich, Eliav *Consensual Intervention and the Responsibility to Protect, in* The Responsibility to Protect: From Theory to Practice 141 (Andre Nollkaemper and Julia Hoffman eds., 2012)

Linderfalk, Ulf, *The Effect of Jus Cogens Norms: Whoever Opened Pandora's Box, Did You Ever Think About the Consequences?* 18 European Journal of International Law 853 (2008)

Main, John, *The Civil War in Laos, in* International Regulation of Civil Wars 91 (Evan Luard ed., 1972)

Marks, Susan, *Human Rights and Root Causes,* 57 Modern Law Review 57 (2011)

Marks, Susan, *What Has Become of the Emerging Right to Democratic Governance?* 22 European Journal of International Law 507 (2011)

Martenczuk, Bernd, *Book Review: Eingreifen auf Einladung,* 11 European Journal of International Law 941 (2000)

McMahan, Jeff, *Humanitarian Intervention, Consent and Proportionality, in* Ethics and Humanity: Themes from the Philosophy of Jonathan Glover 44 (N. Ann Davis *et al.* eds., 2010)

McNair, Arnold D., *Collective Security,* 17 British Year Book of International Law 150 (1936)

McNulty, Mel, *From Intervened to Intervener: Rwanda and Military Intervention in Zaire/ DRC, in* African Interventionist States 173 (Oliver Furley and Roy May eds., 2001)

McQueen, Norrie, *Angola, in* African Interventionist States 93 (Oliver Furley and Roy May eds., 2001)

Meron, Theodor, *The Humanization of Humanitarian Law,* 94 American Journal of International Law 239 (2000)

Meyer, Richard V. and Maxwell, Mark David, *The Natural Right to Intervene: The Evolution of the Concepts of Justification and Excuse for Both State and Individual,* 7 Journal of International Criminal Justice 555 (2009)

Mill, John Stuart, *The Contest in America, in* Dissertations and Discussions 179 (1867)

Mill, John Stuart, *A Few Words on Non-Intervention* (1859), *in* Dissertations and Discussions 238 (1882)

Milner, Helen V., *Power, Interdependence and Nonstate Actors in World Politics: Research Frontiers, in* Power, Interdependence and Nonstate Actors in World Politics 3–30 (Helen V. Milner and Andrew Moravcsik eds., 2009)

Mohamed, Saira, *Restructuring the Debate on Unauthorized Humanitarian Intervention,* 88 North Carolina Law Review 1275 (2010)

Moore, John Norton *The Secret War in Central America and the Future of World Order,* 80 American Journal of International Law 43 (1986)

Müllerson, Rein, *Precedents in the Mountains: On the Parallels and Uniqueness of the Cases of Kosovo, South Ossetia and Abkhazia,* 8 Chinese Journal of International Law 2 (2009)

Murphy, Sean D., *Democratic Legitimacy and Recognition, in* Democratic Governance and International Law 123 (Gregory H. Fox and Brad R. Roth eds., 2000)

Murray, Gilbert, *A League of Nations: The First Experiment, in* The Background and Issues of the War 49 (H.A.L. Fisher *et al.* eds., 1940)

Nabulsi, Karma, *Evolving Conceptions of Civilians and Belligerents: One Hundred Years after the Hague Peace Conferences, in* Civilians In War 9 (Simon Chesterman ed., 2001)

Nolte, Georg, *Secession and External Intervention, in* Secession: International Law Perspectives 65 (Marcelo G. Kohen ed., 2006)

O'Connell, Mary Ellen, *Regulating the Use of Force in the 21st Century: The Continuing Importance of State Autonomy,* 36 Columbia Journal of Transnational Law 473 (1997)

O'Connell, Mary Ellen, *When is War Not a War? The Myth of the Global War on Terror,* 12 ILSA Journal of International and Comparative Law 5 (2006)

O'Rourke, Vernon A., *Recognition of Belligerency and the Spanish War,* 31 American Journal of International Law 398 (1937)

Pattison, James, *The Ethics of Humanitarian Intervention in Libya,* Ethics and International Affairs (2011)

Payandeh, Mehrdad, *The U.N., Military Intervention and Regime Change in Libya,* 52 Virginia Journal of International Law 355 (2012)

Perkins, John A., *The Right of Counterintervention,* 17 Georgia Journal of International and Comparative Law 171 (1987)

Poole, Thomas, *Sovereign Indignities: International Law as Public Law,* 22 European Journal of International Law 351 (2011)

Potter, Pitman B., *Editorial Comment: Legal Aspects of the Beirut Landing,* 52 American Journal of International Law 727 (1958)

Quénivet, Noëlle, *The History of the Relationship Between International Humanitarian Law and Human Rights Law, in* International Humanitarian Law and Human Rights Law: Towards a New Merger in International Law 1 (Roberta Arnold and Noëlle Quénivet eds., 2008)

Ravenal, Earl C., *The Requisites of Containment, in* Collective Defense or Strategic Independence? Alternative Strategies for the Future 273 (Ted Galen Carpenter ed., 1989)

Reinold, Theresa, *State Weakness, Irregular Warfare, and the Right to Self-Defense Post-9/11,* 105 American Journal of International Law 244 (2011)

Reisman, Michael W., *Allocating Competences to Use Coercion in the Post-Cold War World: Practices, Conditions, and Prospects, in* Law and Force in the New International Order 26 (Lori Fisler Damrosch and David J. Scheffer eds., 1991)

Reisman, Michael W., *Coercion and Self-Determination: Construing Article 2(4),* 78 American Journal of International Law 642 (1984)

Rich, Roland, *Recognition of States: The Collapse of Yugoslavia and the Soviet Union,* 4 European Journal of International Law 36 (1993)

Rogers, William D. *et al., The Brezhnev Doctrine and the Reagan Doctrine: Apples and Oranges?* 81 Amerian Society of International Law Proceedings 561 (1987)

Rosenau, James N., *Intervention as a Scientific Concept,* 13 Journal of Conflict Resolution 149 (1969)

Schachter, Oscar, *The Legality of Pro-democratic Invasion,* 78 American Journal of International Law 646, 649 (1984)

Schachter, Oscar, *The Right of States to Use Armed Force,* 82 Michigan Law Review 1620 (1984)

Scheffer, David J., *Introduction, in* Right v. Might: International Law and the Use of Force 1 (Louis Henkin *et al.* eds., 1991)

Schiffer, Walter, *The Idea of Collective Security, in* From Collective Security to Preventive Diplomacy 187 (Joel L. Larus ed. 1965)

Schmitt, Michael N., *Computer Network Attack and the Use of Force in International Law: Thoughts on a Normative Framework,* 37 Columbia Journal of Transnational Law 885 (1999)

Schmitt, Michael N., *Targeting and International Humanitarian Law in Afghanistan,* 85 International Legal Studies Series U.S. Naval War College 307 (2009)

Schmitt, Michael N., *Drone Attacks under the Jus ad Bellum and Jus in Bello: Clearing the "Fog of Law,"* 13 Yearbook of International Humanitarian Law 311 (2010)

Sharma, Serena K., *The 2007–08 Post-Election Crisis in Kenya: A Success Story for the Responsibility to Protect, in* The Responsibility to Protect: From Principle to Practice 27 (Andre Nollkaemper and Julia Hoffman eds., 2012)

Sloane, Robert D., *The Cost of Conflation: Preserving the Dualism of Jus ad Bellum and Jus in Bello in the Contemporary Law of War,* 34 Yale Journal of International Law 48 (2009)

Smith, H.A., *Some Problems of the Spanish Civil War,* 18 British Year Book of International Law 17 (1937)

Stahn, Carsten. Terrorist Acts as "Armed Attack": *The Right to Self-Defense, Article 51(1/2) of the U.N. Charter, and International Terrorism,* 27 Fletcher Forum of World Affairs 35 (2003)

Stahn, Carsten, *Responsibility to Protect: Political Rhetoric or Emerging Legal Norm?* 101 American Journal of International Law 99 (2007)

Stone, Juliud, *Hopes and Loopholes in the 1974 Definition of Aggression,* 71 American Journal of International Law 224 (1977)

Stromseth, Jane, *Rethinking Humanitarian Intervention: The Case for Incremental Change, in* Humanitarian Intervention: Ethical, Legal and Political Dilemmas 232, 245 (J.L. Holzgrefe and Robert O. Keohane 2003)

Talmon, Stefan, *Recognition of the Libyan Transitional Council,* 15 Amerian Society of International Law Insights (June 16, 2011)

Thom, William, G. *Congo-Zaire's 1996–1997 Civil War in the Context of Evolving Patterns of Military Conflict in Africa in the Era of Independence,* 19 Journal of Conflict Studies (1999)

Thomas, Ann Van Wynen and Thomas, A.J. Jr., *International Legal Aspects of the Civil War in Spain, 1936–1939, in* The International Law of Civil War 111 (Richard A. Falk ed., 1972)

Thürer, Daniel, *The "Failed State" and International Law* International Review of the Red Cross 731 (1999)

Tomuschat, Christian, *Secession and Self-Determination, in* Secession: International Law Perspectives 23 (Marcelo G. Kohen, ed., 2006)

Tsagourias, Nicholas *Consent, Neutrality/Impartiality and the Use of Force in Peacekeeping: Their Constitutional Dimension,* 11 Journal of Conflict and Security Law 465 (2009)

Waldron, Jeremy, *The Rule of International Law,* 30 Harvard Journal of Law and Public Policy 15 (2006)

Walzer, Michael, *The Argument about Humanitarian Intervention* 49(1) Dissent (2002)

Watkin, Kenneth, *Opportunity Lost: Organized Armed Groups and the ICRC "Direct Participation in Hostilities Interpretive Guidance,"* 42 New York University Journal of International Law and Politics 641 (2010)

Watson, K. William, *When in the Course of Human Events: Kosovo's Independence and the Law of Secession,* 17 Tulane Journal of International and Comparative Law 267 (2008)

Waxman, Mathew C., *Cyber-Attacks and the Use of Force: Back to the Future of Article 2(4),* 36 Yale Journal of International Law 421 (2011)

Weiss, Thomas G., *RtoP Alive and Well after Libya*, Ethics and International Affairs (2011)

Welsh, Jennifer *Civilian Protection in Libya: Putting Coercion and Controversy Back into RtoP*, Ethics and International Affairs (2011)

Wheatley, Steven, *Democracy in International Law: a European Perspective*, 51 International and Comparative Law Quarterly 225 (2002)

Williams, John Fischer, *Sanctions under the Covenant*, 17 British Year Book of International Law 130 (1936)

Williams, Paul D., *From Non-Intervention to Non-Indifference: The Origins and Development of the African Union's Security Culture*, 106 African Affairs 253 (2007)

Wilson, George Grafton, *Insurgency and International Maritime Law*, 1 American Journal of International Law 46 (1907)

Winer, Anthony S., *The Reagan Doctrine, the 2003 Invasion of Iraq, and the Role of a Sole Superpower*, 22 Law and Inequality 169 (2004)

Wippman, David, *Enforcing the Peace: ECOWAS and the Liberian Civil War*, *in* Enforcing Restraint: Collective Intervention in Internal Conflicts 157 (Lori Fisler Damrosch ed., 1993)

Wippman, David, *Treaty-Based Intervention: Who Can Say No?* 62 University of Chicago Law Review 607 (1995)

Wippman, David, *Change and Continuity in Legal Justifications for Military Intervention in Internal Conflict*, 27 Columbia Human Rights Law Review 435 (1996)

Wippman, David, *Military Intervention, Regional Organizations, and Host-State Consent*, 7 Duke Journal of Comparative and International Law 209 (1996)

Wippman, David *Pro-democratic Intervention by Invitation*, *in* Democratic Governance and International Law 293 (Gregory H. Fox and Brad R. Roth eds., 2000)

Woolsey, L.H., Editorial Comment: Closure of Ports by the Chinese Nationalist Government, 44 American Journal of International Law 350 (1950)

Woolsey, Theodore S., *The United States and the Declaration of Paris*, 3 Yale Law Journal 77 (1894)

Woolsey, Theodore S., *The Consequences of Cuban Belligerency*, 5 Yale Law Journal 182 (1896)

Woolsey, Theodore S., *Our Duty to Spain*, 7 Yale Law Journal 101 (1897)

Woolsey, Theodore S., *Lecture on International Law*, 8 Yale Law Journal 387(1899)

Wright, Quincy, *Editorial Comment: United States Intervention in the Lebanon*, 53 American Journal of International Law 112 (1959)

Wright, Quincy, *The American Civil War*, *in* The International Law of Civil War 30 (Richard A. Falk ed., 1972)

3 Reports and other international documents

Ago, Roberto *Eighth Report on State Responsibility*, 2 Yearbook of the International Law Commission, 3 (1979)

Agreement on Provisional Arrangements in Afghanistan Pending the Reestablishment of Permanent Government Institutions, annex I, U.N. Doc S/2001/1154 (December 5, 2001)

Human Rights Watch, *Hostages to Peace: Threats to Human Rights and Democracy in Somaliland* (July 13, 2009)

Independent International Commission on Kosovo, The Kosovo Report (2000)

Institut de Droit International, Annuaire 18, 229 (1900)

Institut de Droit International, The Principle of Non-Intervention in Civil Wars (August 14, 1975)

Institut de Droit International, Military Assistance on Request (September 8, 2011)

International Commission on Intervention and State Sovereignty, The Responsibility to Protect 29 (2001)

International Committee for the Application of the Agreement Regarding Non-Intervention in Spain, Resolution Relating to the Scheme of Observation of the Spanish Frontiers by Land and Sea (March 8, 1937) 31 American Journal of International Law Supp. 163 (1937)

International Crisis Group, *Congo at War: A Briefing of the Internal and External Players in the Central African Conflict,* ICG Congo Report No. 2 (November 17, 1998)

International Crisis Group, *How Kabila Lost His Way: The Performance of Laurent Désiré Kabila's Government,* ICG Congo Report No. 3 (May 21, 1999)

International Crisis Group, *From Kabila to Kabila, Prospects for Peace in the Congo,* ICG Africa Report No. 27 (March 16, 2001)

International Crisis Group, *The Kivus: The Forgotten Crucible of the Congo Conflict,* ICG Africa Report No. 56 (January 24, 2003)

International Crisis Group, *Somalia: Continuation of War by Other Means?* ICG Africa Report No. 88 (December 21, 2004)

International Crisis Group, *The Congo's Transition Is Failing: Crisis in the Kivus,* ICG Africa Report No. 91 (March 30, 2005)

International Crisis Group, *Can The Somali Crisis Be Contained,* ICG Africa Report No. 116 (August 10, 2006)

International Crisis Group, *Somalia: To Move Beyond the Failed State,* ICG Africa Report No. 147 (December 23, 2008)

International Crisis Group, *Somalia: The Tough Part is Ahead,* ICG Africa Briefing No. 45 (January 26, 2009)

International Crisis Group, *Yemen: Defusing the Saada Time Bomb,* ICG Middle East Report No. 86 (May 27, 2009)

International Crisis Group, *Congo: A Comprehensive Strategy to Disarm the FDLR,* ICG Africa Report No. 151 (July 9, 2009)

International Crisis Group, *Côte d'Ivoire: Is War the Only Option?* ICG Africa Report No. 171 (March 3, 2011)

International Crisis Group, *A Critical Period for Ensuring Stability in Côte D'Ivoire,* ICG Africa Report No. 176 (August 1, 2011)

International Crisis Group, *Popular Protest in North Africa and the Middle East (V): Making Sense of Libya,* ICG Middle East/North Africa Report No. 107 (June 6, 2011)

International Crisis Group, *Syria's Phase of Radicalisation,* ICG Middle East Briefing No. 33 (April 10, 2012)

International Law Commission, Draft Articles on Responsibility of States for Internationally Wrongful Acts, with Commentaries, Report of the International Law Commission, U.N. GAOR, 53d Sess., Supp. No. 10, A/56/20 (2001)

International Law Commission, Fragmentation of International Law: Difficulties Arising From the Diversification and Expansion of International Law (April 13, 2006) U.N. Doc. A/CN.4/L.682 (2006)

International Law Commission, Draft Articles on the Responsibility of International Organizations, Yearbook of the International Law Commission (2011)

Joint Communiqué Issued at the Conclusion of a Meeting between the

Government of Kenya and the Transitional Federal Government of Somalia, October 18, 2011

Letter Dated 25 October 1983 from the Permanent Representative of the U.S. to the U.N. Addressed to the President of the Security Council, U.N. Doc. S/16076 (October 25, 1983)

Letter Dated 29 July 1994 from the President of the Republic of Haiti addressed to the Secretary-General, U.N. Doc. S/1994/905 (July 29, 1994)

Letter Dated 19 December 2001 from the Permanent Representative of Afghanistan, U.N. Doc. S/2001/1223 (December 19, 2001)

Letter Dated 7 December 2008 From the Prime Minister of Iraq addressed to the President of the Security Council, S.C. Res 1859, U.N. Doc. S/RES/1859 (December 22, 2008)

Letter Dated 21 February 2011 from the Chargé d'affaires a.i. of the Permanent Mission of the Libyan Arab Jamahiriya to the United Nations addressed to the President of the Security Council, U.N. Doc. S/2011/102 (February 22, 2011), U.N. Doc. S/2011/102 (February 22, 2011)

Letter Dated 17 October 2011 from the Permanent Representative of Kenya to the United Nations addressed to the President of the Security Council, U.N. Doc. S/2011/646 (October 18, 2011)

Ministerial Declaration on the South Summit, Adopted at the 23rd Annual Meeting of the Ministers of Foreign Affairs of the Group of 77, held at U.N. Headquarters on 24 September 1999, annex 1, U.N. Doc. A/54/432 (October 6, 1999)

Report of the Group of Governmental Experts to Examine the Feasibility, Scope and Draft Parameters for a Comprehensive, Legally Binding Instrument Establishing Common International Standards for the Import, Export and Transfer of Conventional Arms, U.N. Doc. A/63/334 (August 26, 2008)

Report of the Independent International Fact-Finding Mission on the Conflict in Georgia (September 30, 2009)

Report of the Independent Inquiry into the Actions of the U.N. during the 1994 Genocide in Rwanda, U.N. Doc. S/1999/1257 (December 15, 1999)

Report of the Special Envoy of the Secretary-General on Kosovo's Future Status, U.N. Doc. S/2007/168 (March 26, 2007)

Rise of the Drones II: Examining the Legality of Unmanned Targeting: Hearings Before the Subcommittee on National Security and Foreign Affairs, 111th Congress (2010)

Special Rapporteur on Extrajudicial, Summary or Arbitrary Executions, *Study on Targeted Killings*, Human Rights Council, U.N. Doc. A/HRC/14/24/Add.6 (May 28, 2010) (by Philip Alston)

U.N. Commission on Human Rights, *Definition of Gross and Large-Scale Violations of Human Rights as an International Crime*, ¶¶12–22, U.N. Doc. E/CN.4/Sub.2/1993/10 (June 8, 1999)

U.N. GAOR, 66th Sess., 28th plen. Mtg., U.N. Doc. A/66/PV.2 (September 16, 2011) (Libya Credentials)

U.N. Human Rights Council, *Report of the Independent International Commission of Inquiry on the Syrian Arab Republic*, U.N. Doc. A/HRC/19/69 (February 22, 2012)

U.N. SCOR, 38th Sess., 2487th mtg., U.N. Doc. S/PV. 2487 (October 25, 1983) (Grenada)

U.N. SCOR, 38th Sess., 2489th mtg., U.N. Doc. S/PV.2489 (October 26, 1983) (Grenada)

U.N. SCOR, 38th Sess., 2491st mtg., U.N. Doc. S/2491 (October 27, 1983) (Grenada)

U.N. SCOR, 54th Sess., 3977th mtg., U.N. Doc. S/PV.3977, 14–15, 29–30 (February 2, 1999) (Protection of Civilians)

U.N. SCOR, 59th Sess., 5028th mtg., U.N. Doc. S/PV.5028 (September 2, 2004) (Syria-Lebanon)

U.N. SCOR, 63rd Sess., 5839th mtg., U.N. Doc. S/PV.5839 (February 18, 2008) (Kosovo)

U.N. SCOR, 63rd Sess., 6055th mtg., U.N. Doc. S/PV.6055 (December 22, 2008) (D.R.C.)

U.N. SCOR, 64th Sess., 6083rd mtg., U.N. Doc. S/PV.6083 (February 17, 2009) (D.R.C.)

U.N. SCOR, 64th Sess., 6104th mtg., U.N. Doc. S/PV.6104 (April 9, 2009) (D.R.C.)

U.N. SCOR 65th Sess., 6407th mtg. at 7, U.N. Doc. S/PV/6407 (October 21, 2010) (Somalia)

U.N. SCOR, 66th Sess., 6490th mtg. at 5, U.N. Doc. S/PV/6490 (February 25, 2011) (Libya)

U.N. SCOR, 66th Sess., 6491st mtg. at 7, U.N. Doc. S/PV/6491 (February 26, 2011) (Libya)

U.N. SCOR, 66th Sess., 6627th mtg., U.N. Doc. S/PV.6627 (October 4, 2011) (Syria)

U.N. Secretary General, *Report of the Secretary General to the Security Council on the Protection of Civilians in Armed Conflict*, U.N. Doc. S/1999/957 (September 8, 1999)

U.N. Secretary General, *Report of the Secretary General Pursuant to General Assembly Resolution 53/35: The Fall of Srebrenica*, U.N. Doc. A/54/549 (November 15, 1999)

U.N. Secretary General, *Report of the Secretary General to the Security Council on the Protection of Civilians in Armed Conflict*, U.N. Doc. S/2001/331 (March 30, 2001)

U.N. Secretary General, *Report of the Secretary General to the Security Council on the Protection of Civilians in Armed Conflict*, U.N. Doc. S/2002/1330 (November 26, 2002)

U.N. Secretary General, *Report of the Secretary General to the Security Council on the Protection of Civilians in Armed Conflict*, U.N. Doc. S/2004/431 (May 28, 2004)

U.N. Secretary General, *In Larger Freedom: Towards Development, Security and Human Rights for All*, U.N. Doc. A/59/2005 (March 21, 2005)

U.N. Secretary General, *Report of the Secretary General to the Security Council on the Protection of Civilians in Armed Conflict*, U.N. Doc. S/2005/740 (November 28, 2005)

U.N. Secretary General, *Implementing the Responsibility to Protect: Report of the Secretary General*, U.N. Doc. A/63/677 (January 12, 2009)

U.N. Secretary General, *Report of the Secretary General to the Security Council on the Protection of Civilians in Armed Conflict*, U.N. Doc. S/2009/277 (May 29, 2009)

U.N. Secretary General, *Report of the Secretary General to the Security Council on the Protection of Civilians in Armed Conflict*, U.N. Doc. S/2010/579 (November 11, 2010)

U.N. Secretary General, *The Role of Regional and Subregional Arrangements in Implementing the Responsibility to Protect*, U.N. Doc. A/65/877 (June 28, 2011)

U.N. Secretary General, *Responsibility to Protect: Timely and Decisive Response*, U.N. Doc. A/66/874 (July 25, 2012)

4 Selected media reports

Arrest Warrant Shows Gaddafi Lost Legitimacy, Reuters, June 27, 2011

Arsu, Sebnem and Erlanger, Steven, *Libya Rebels Get Formal Backing, and $30 Billion* New York Times, July 15, 2011

Arab League Deadline for Syria Action Passes, B.B.C. News, November 19, 2011

Bahrain Unrest: U.N. Rights Chief Criticises Crackdown, B.B.C. News, March 17, 2011

Bar'el, Zvi and Reuters, *Turkey FM Issues "Final Words" Calling on Syria to Halt Violent Crackdowns*, Haaretz, August 15, 2011

Batty, David, *Syrian Opposition Groups Unite to Chart Roadmap to Democracy*, The Guardian, December 31, 2011

Bronner, Ethan and Sanger, David E., *Arab League Endorses No-Flight Zone Over Libya*, New York Times, March 12, 2011

Chivers, C.J. and Kirkpatrick, David D., *Libyan Rebels Complain of Deadly Delays Under NATO's Command*, New York Times, April 4, 2011

Chulov, Martin, and Weaver, Matthew, *Saudi Arabia Backs Arming Syrian Opposition*, The Guardian, February 24, 2012

Cooper, Helene, *U.S. to Name a Liaison to Libyan Rebels*, New York Times, March 11, 2011

Dombey, Daniel and Daragahi, Borzou *U.S. Signals Support for Arming Syria Rebels*, Financial Times, April 1, 2012

Fahim, Kareem and Kirkpatrick, David D., *Libyan Rebels Said to Debate Seeking U.N. Airstrikes*, New York Times, March 1, 2011

Gettleman, Jeffery, *Ethiopian Troops Said to Enter Somalia, Opening New Front Against Militants*, New York Times, November 20, 2011

Kenya Invades Somalia: A Big Gamble, Economist, October 29, 2011

Kron, Josh, *Kenyan Offensive is not Welcome, Somalia's President Says*, New York Times, October 24, 2011

Libya: France Recognises Rebels as Government, B.B.C. News, March 10, 2011

Libyan U.N. Diplomats: Al-Qadhafi Should Resign, C.B.S. News, February 21, 2011

Libyan Delegation to U.N. Rights Council Resigns, Haaretz, February 25, 2011

Mali Leader Resigns Ahead of Power Transfer, Al-Jazeera, April 8, 2012

McGreal, Chris and Chulov, Martin, *Syria: Assad Must Resign, Says Obama*, The Guardian, August 18, 2011

Meter, Henry, *Russia Says Qaddafi Has Lost Legitimacy to Govern, Joining Support of NATO*, Bloomberg, May 27, 2011

Myers, Lee, and Goodman, J. David, *Clinton Says Russian Inaction May Lead to Syrian Civil War*, New York Times, May 31, 2012

Opposition Urges Arab League to Refer Syria to U.N., Reuters, January 21, 2012

Oweis, Khaled Yacoub, *Russia Stands by Assad as Pressure Mounts on Syria*, Reuters, November 17, 2011

Rice, Xan and Watt, Nicholas, *Ivory Coast's Laurent Gbagbo Arrested*, The Guardian, April 11, 2011

Shiil, Mohamed, *Kenya's Invasion of Somalia Raises Controversy*, All Headline News, November 8, 2011

Saudi Soldiers Sent into Bahrain, Aljazeera English, March 15, 2011

Somali Islamists Maintain Aid Ban and Deny Famine, B.B.C. News, July 22, 2011

Stack, Liam, *In Slap at Syria, Turkey Shelters Anti-Assad Fighters*, New York Times, October 27, 2011

Syria Defectors "Attack Military Base in Harasta," B.B.C. News, November 16, 2011
The United Nations and Congo: Unloved for Trying to Keep the Peace, The Economist, April 17, 2010
Turkey Urges "Immediate" Opening of Syria Aid Corridor after Bombing of Refugee Bridge, Al-Arabiya News, March 6, 2012
Yemenite Troops Target Al-Qaeda, Al-Jazeera, January 5, 2010
U.N. Declares Somalia Famine in Bakool and Lower Shabelle, B.B.C. News, July 20, 2011
U.N. Joins Battle with Congo Rebels, B.B.C. News, October 27, 2008, http://news.bbc.co.uk/2/hi/africa/7692932.stm
U.N. Ends Criticized Congo Campaign, B.B.C. News, December 16, 2009, http://news.bbc.co.uk/2/hi/africa/8417450.stm
Wan, William and Booth, William, *United States Recognizes Libyan Rebels as Legitimate Government,* The Washington Post, July 15, 2011

5 Others

African Union, *The Common African Position on the Proposed Reform of the U.N.: The Ezulwini Consensus* (March 7–8, 2005)
African Union Peace and Sec. Coun. Communique, PSC/PR/COMM.(CCCXVI) (April 3, 2012)
Annual Message of President Grant (December 6, 1869)
Annual Message of President Grant (December 7, 1875)
Annual Message of President Cleveland (December, 1895)
Annual Message of President McKinley (December 6, 1897)
Argument of Belgium before the I.C.J. (May 10, 1999)
Brennan, John O., The Ethics and Efficacy of the President's Counterterrorism Strategy, speech delivered at the Woodrow Wilson International Center for Scholars (April 30, 2012)
Decision of the African Union Peace and Security Council (December 9, 2010) (Côte d'Ivoire)
Draft Resolution by France, Germany, Portugal and the U.K., U.N. Doc. S/2011/612 (October 4, 2011) (Syria)
Full Text of the Chairman's Conclusions of the International Conference of the Group of Friends of the Syrian People (April 1, 2012)
Holder, Eric, Speech at Northwestern University School of Law (March 5, 2012)
Koh, Harold Hongju, Keynote Address at the Annual Meeting of the American Society of International Law: The Obama Administration and International Law (March 25, 2010)
Obama, Barack, Remarks at National Defense University, Washington, D.C. (March 28, 2011)
President's Address before a Joint Session of Congress on the State of the Union, 1985 Pub. Papers 135 (February 6, 1985)
Press Release, EU Naval Force Delivers Blow against Somali Pirates on Shoreline (May 15, 2012)
Republic of Turkey, Ministry of Foreign Affairs, Fourth Meeting of the Libya Contact Group Chair's Statement, 15 July 2011, Istanbul
Request for an Advisory Opinion of the ICJ on the Question "Is the Unilateral Declaration of Independence by the Provisional Institutions of Self-Government of Kosovo in Accordance with International Law?" Written Statement of the United Kingdom (April 17, 2009)

Rogin, Josh, *State Dept.: Russia and Iran Still Arming Bashar Al-Assad,* Foreign Policy, February 15, 2012

Royal Proclamation of May 13, 1861 (Britain)

S.C. Prst. 2012/6, U.N. Doc. S/PRST/2012/6 (Syria)

S.C. Prst. 2012/10, U.N. Doc. S/PRST/2012/10 (April 5, 2012) (Syria)

Special Message to the Congress on Greece and Turkey: The Truman Doctrine (March 12, 1947)

U.K. Materials on International Law, 57 British Year Book of International Law 614 (1986)

United States Attorney General, *Neutrality Act,* 13 U.S. Op. Atty. Gen. 177, 180 (December 16, 1869)

Index